PARK IT!®

NYC
COMPLETE GUIDE TO PARKING GARAGES

Third Edition

By Margot Tohn

PARK IT! GUIDES®

www.parkitguides.com
New York, NY

CREDITS

Book and Cover Design,
Production, Cartography
Todd Cooper
Chris Bartick, Emi Mimura, Paul Sternberg
Design Lab NYC, Inc.

Original Book and Cover Design
Julia Reich Design

Database
Steve Franzken

Neighborhood Map
John Tauranac, *Manhattan Block By Block*

Park It! NYC: Complete Guide to Parking Garages, Third Edition.
Copyright © 2009 Park It! Guides®.
Printed and bound in China.
All rights reserved.

Although Park It! Guides has made every effort to ensure the accuracy and completeness of information contained in this book, it assumes no responsibility for errors, inaccuracies, omissions, or any inconsistency herein. Any slights of people, places, or organizations are unintentional.
First printing 2007.

Park It! Guides did not solicit or accept any payment from any individuals, organizations, or businesses to be included in this book.

ISBN-13: 978-0-9790281-3-7;
ISBN-10: 0-9790281-3-2
Library of Congress Control Number: 2008907028

**ATTENTION CORPORATIONS AND
PROFESSIONAL ORGANIZATIONS:**
Special discounts are available for bulk purchases of this book for gift or promotional purposes. Custom mini-editions can also be created to fit specific needs.
Please contact:
Park It! Guides, 400 E 56th St, Suite 29F, NY, NY 10022
www.parkitguides.com

ACKNOWLEDGEMENTS

We are proud to bring you this third edition of *Park It!*®
NYC, which has been fully updated with the help of
several key people. Joe Unay spent 100 hours driving
so that we could personally research every one of the
1,093 garages and lots. Todd Cooper and his team at
Design Lab NYC, Inc., who have been with us since the
first edition, continued to apply their design expertise
so that you can find parking quickly, easily, and without
overpaying.

Park It! NYC continues to be recognized by national and
regional media including *The New York Times, AAA Car
& Travel*, network television and radio, and online media.
We are now noted as the authoritative resource for
parking garage information.

Once again, I send my most valued appreciation to
the core group who continue to listen to my ideas and
provide ongoing support of my various Park It! and other
entrepreneurial ventures: Risa, my family — Mum & Dad,
Ellen & John, Susan & Jordan, Daniel, Seth, Jeremy,
Lainie, and Elise. Special thanks to Deedy for her tireless
editing and proofing of seemingly endless data.

TABLE OF CONTENTS

INTRODUCTION

Welcome to the 3rd Edition of *Park It! NYC*. By now, most people appreciate why we created an entire book devoted solely to parking. Because every New Yorker has his or her horror story about overpaying or endlessly circling the block, or boasts of finding that "secret free space". In this city, finding parking is just as competitive as finding an apartment, a baby sitter, or a spouse.

Despite having a choice of 103,000 spaces and nearly 1,100 garages and lots, it just isn't that easy to find the garage that is either half a block from your destination or has the cheapest three-hour rate in the neighborhood. And once you do find it, you may not remember where it was for the next time.

This 3rd Edition continues to provide the most comprehensive and current information about Manhattan's parking garages and outdoor lots. We have added even more hints and tips to help you park faster and easier and never overpay. Be sure to check out the new sections Monthly Parking, Parking in the Theater District, and our lists of Self-Parking garages and Gas Stations. We've also added all the entrances and exits for the East Side and West Side Highways, along with a Zip Code map and an entire section to help you find parking near major tourist sites and landmarks.

Park It! NYC is designed for all those people who just need a little help finding great parking. Whether you're looking for convenience or the lowest rates, all the information you need is right here.

After all, shouldn't we spend our time and money on better things than parking?

Margot Tohn
Publisher

METHODOLOGY

Park It! Guides collected the information contained in this book by personally surveying every garage in Manhattan over a 10-day period in May and June 2008. For our earlier editions, we conducted the same research in May 2007, August 2006, and December 2005. We also worked with several garage operators to help us understand current trends in the industry. Park It! Guides did not solicit or accept payment from any individuals, organizations, or businesses to be included in this book.

THE NOT-SO-FINE-PRINT

Park It! Guides goes to great length to ensure the accuracy of the information in this book at the time of printing. However, information does change and we cannot be held responsible for any differences in rates or other information. Whenever possible, confirm the rate with the garage before leaving your car. Some companies, such as GMC, GGMC, Champion, and Imperial seem to have easier rates to understand.

Garages do close, but not at the rate that you might think. If your favorite place does close, just use your Park It! NYC book to find the nearest garage.

Rates do change, as well. Many operators change their rates annually and then make minor adjustments based on demand, competition and even seasonality. As with any business, many garages have increased their rates in the last twelve months. However, this year we saw a greater increase than the typical increase of $1–2 during the same period in 2006-2007, with the increases varying by neighborhood. The good news is that we did also find some garages that had actually reduced their rates.

Central Parking Rates
Central Parking has started post pre-tax rates that end in $.99. Once the NYC 18.375% tax is added, the final rate is not an even number, so we have rounded up or down the rate for you.

What you can do to help
If you find any inaccuracies or want to offer your opinion on a parking facility, please let us know with an email to garagefeedback@parkitguides.com.

HOW TO READ THE GARAGE LISTINGS

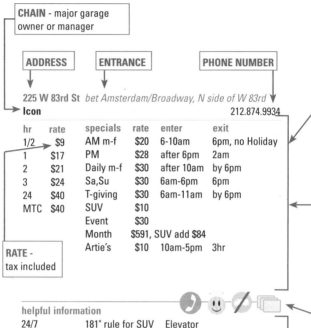

CHAIN - major garage owner or manager

ADDRESS

ENTRANCE

PHONE NUMBER

225 W 83rd St *bet Amsterdam/Broadway, N side of W 83rd*
Icon
212.874.9934

hr	rate	specials	rate	enter	exit
1/2	$9	AM m-f	$20	6-10am	6pm, no Holiday
1	$17	PM	$28	after 6pm	2am
2	$21	Daily m-f	$30	after 10am	by 6pm
3	$24	Sa,Su	$30	6am-6pm	6pm
24	$40	T-giving	$30	6am-11am	by 6pm
MTC	$40	SUV	$10		
		Event	$30		
		Month	$591, SUV add $84		
		Artie's	$10	10am-5pm	3hr

RATE - tax included

helpful information

24/7	181" rule for SUV	Elevator
107 spaces	Max bill $50	Damage, security inspection
AE, MC, V	No full size vans	
Eff. 4/08	8' clearance	

ABBREVIATIONS

M - Monday
T - Tuesday
W - Wednesday
Th - Thursday
F - Friday
Sa - Saturday
Su - Sunday
N - North
S - South
E - East
W - West
O/S - Oversize vehicle
M-F - Monday through Friday
M,F - Monday and Friday
12am - Midnight
12pm - Noon
bet - Between
MTC - Max to Close, the highest rate garage will charge to park until garage closes

SPECIAL RATES

This section lists all the rates that are not hourly rates.
Specials column - name of special rate
Rate column - dollar rate amount, tax included except for monthly parking
Enter column - when you must enter the garage
Exit column - when you must exit the garage

NOTES

If no enter time is listed, you may assume 'anytime' but check with the garage
If an enter or exit time is listed simply as a time, i.e. '7pm', we advise you to confirm if that means 'by' or 'after' 7pm
Days of the week may be added (in lowercase) after a particular special rate

AM - Early Bird special: typically park by a certain time in the am and leave by a certain time or number of hours
PM - Evening special: typically park after a certain time in the late afternoon or early evening and leave by a certain time or number of hours
SUV - Surcharge applied to SUVs and oversize vehicles, refer to p. 18 for more information
Event - May apply to holiday, parade, sporting event, music event, theater, etc.
Month - Rate for parking on a monthly basis, before tax. Shows any surcharges for SUV or Oversize vehicles
T-giving - Thanksgiving

	Takes reservations via website, only for Icon Parking
	Very friendly garage or received customer recommendation
	Accepts vans, red line will indicate no vans
	Accepts credit cards, red line will indicate cash only

HELPFUL INFORMATION

Hours of operation is always shown first
24/7 - Garage opens 7 days a week, 24 hours per day
M-F 7am-12am - Garage opens Monday through Friday, 7am - midnight
AE, MC, V, Disc, DC, CB - Garage accepts credit cards: American Express, MasterCard, Visa, Discover, Diners Club, Carte Blanche
Damage, Security inspection - Garage inspects for car damage and/or does a security check prior to parking
Eff. 4/06 - Dates rates went into effect
Hotel - Garage is located at or near a hotel
In and Out Service - Allows parkers a certain number of times to leave and re-enter the garage without paying extra
Max bill - Largest paper bill a garage will accept
Elevator - Garage uses elevator to transport cars
Lift - Outdoor lot uses hydraulic lift to store cars
181" rule for SUV - Specific guidelines determine if vehicle will incur a surcharge, refer to p. 18
Self-Parking - You can park your own car

HOW TO READ THE MAPS

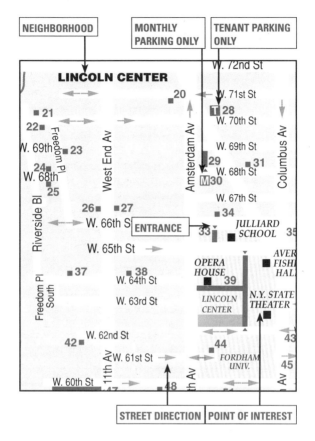

NEIGHBORHOOD

MONTHLY PARKING ONLY

TENANT PARKING ONLY

ENTRANCE

STREET DIRECTION

POINT OF INTEREST

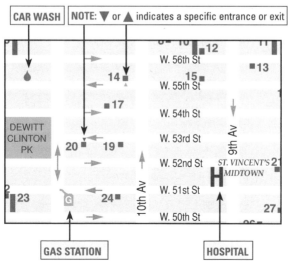

CAR WASH

NOTE: ▼ or ▲ indicates a specific entrance or exit

GAS STATION

HOSPITAL

TRENDS IN PARKING

Park It! NYC has been tracking the Manhattan parking garage industry since 2005. The two largest operators, Icon Parking and Central Parking, that collectively operate approximately 50% of all the garages and lots, sold their operations to outside investors for a combined price of $1.5 billion in 2007. Soon after, the investors sold some free-standing locations to developers. Experts thought that this trend would mean fewer garages, but that doesn't seem to have happened on a broad scale.

The good news is our analysis shows that **while more garages and lots closed than opened in 2007/2008, the number of actual parking spaces increased.**

Last year we also noticed that **Central Parking has started installing check out machines**. Garage valets seem pleased with the machines, saying that the check out process is faster.

Some Central Parking garages use the retail pricing strategy of rates ending in $.99. Traditionally, garages post a seemingly random rate that rounds to a simple dollar amount once the 18.375% NYC tax is applied. For example, $17.74 becomes $21, which is easy for you understand and Valets to calculate. We've done all the calculations for you on p. 380. A Central Parking rate of $17.99, however, comes to $21.30, making it just a bit harder for the Valets to calculate and give change. In this book, Central rates are rounded to the nearest dollar.

If you drive an Oversize vehicle or SUV, you have probably been charged a $5 – 10 surcharge by at least 90% of garages. This year, you can expect to pay more **— the average Oversize surcharge jumped to $10 and a number of garages charge $11.** We even found some locations charging $20! Where's the silver lining? There are about 130 garages that don't have this surcharge, mostly above 110th Street and the on the East Side below 23rd Street. Go to page 19 to find out more.

There are plenty of places to park and many deals to be found. Just use Park It! NYC to plan ahead and you'll never waste time or overpay for parking again.

CONGESTION PRICING

In March 2007, everyone was talking about Mayor Bloomberg's proposed Congestion Pricing plan, which would have been an $8 charge for cars entering the central business district of Manhattan below 86th Street, from 6am to 6pm.

What happened? The plan died in the State Legislature. NYC lost $354 million in federal funding to improve transportation in the five boroughs and non-Manhattan commuters rejoiced. At the time of printing, there is still talk of some form of Congestion Pricing and testing Demand Pricing for on-street meters.

HOW AND WHEN TO TIP

Every New Yorker has his own view on tipping — when, why, and how much.

Why tip
The average parking attendant earns $19,650*, which is less than half of the average salary in New York City. Additionally, attendants surveyed by Park It! Guides generally indicated that they would be inclined to 'go the extra mile' for a consistent and good 'tipper.'

When to tip
The majority of people tip, using that practiced sleight of hand, when the valet retrieves their car. Some garage companies suggested to us that customers tip when they *drop off* their cars as a way to ensure that the valet will take particular care when parking their vehicles. Another good reason to tip when dropping off is that valets who work during the day may not benefit from the tips customers give when they pick up their cars. However, most of the larger garages with multiple valets will pool their tips either by shift or for the entire day.

How much to tip
Most people tip $1-2 each time they park. Some monthly parkers give a larger amount during the holiday season.

*Bureau of Labor Statistics, May 2007

ARE GARAGES CLOSING ALL THE TIME?

Yes, garages do close. And new ones open as well.

From June 2007 to May 2008, we were surprised to find that only 30 of the nearly 1,100 garages and lots had closed, and that 17 news ones had opened. Despite a net loss of 13 garages – a mere 1% of the total garages, 106 new spaces were added!

We expected that garages would close in the area from 8th Avenue and 12th Avenue from W 23rd to W 59th Streets, and in fact, 7 garages did close in this area. But 4 locations also opened, and the number of spaces remains the same.

WHERE ARE THE NEW GARAGES?

4055 10th Ave	bet W 216th/W 218th
10th Ave/W 205th	NE corner
6 W 137 St	bet Lenox/5th Aves
418 W 127th St	bet Morningside/Amsterdam on 126th
E 116th St @ FDR	(opening July - October 2009)
520 W 53rd St	bet 10th/11th Aves
627 W 42nd St	bet 11th/12th Aves
248 E 53rd St	bet 2nd/3rd Aves
350 W 42nd St	bet 9th/8th Aves
346 W 40th St	bet 9th/8th Aves
102 W 39th St	bet 6th/Broadway
159 W 21st St	bet 6th/7th Aves
445 Lafayette St	bet Astor Pl/4th St
22 E 1st St	bet 2nd Ave/Bowery
1 E 1st St	bet 2nd Ave/Bowery
489 Canal St	NW corner of Canal/Hudson
123 Baxter St	bet Grand/Hester

MONTHLY PARKING

It's no surprise that monthly parking in Manhattan is one of the highest in the world.

As of June 2008, the price for monthly parking in Manhattan ranged from $106 to $1,014 ($121 to $1,153 with tax for Manhattan residents), with an average rate of $431. You can expect to pay more for an Oversize or luxury vehicle, or for parking on the main floor.

How and where can you find cheap monthly parking?

Negotiate - You may be able to negotiate a rate lower than the posted rate, and some garages will offer a discount if you commit to a six-to-twelve month contract.

Summer Rates - many residents take their cars out for the summers so garages will offer a ridiculously low monthly rate for June, July, and August.

Outdoor Lots - Generally, you will pay less for an outdoor lot.

Walk a Little - Park near the East and West edges of the city, or near the top above 110th Street.

So, what will it cost you to find a happy home for your vehicle each month?

Want to save money?
$208 above 125th Street
$311 in the Lower East Side
$346 in Chelsea/Clinton/Javits area West of 8th Ave from W23rd to W59th St

Want to pay a little more?
$440 from 14th St to Canal St
$444 in Midtown from 8th to the FDR and 23rd to 59th St
$473 in the Financial District
$476 on the Upper West Side from W59th to W110th St
$503 in Tribeca and Civic Center
$523 on the Upper East Side from E59th to E86th Street

Manhattan Resident Parking Tax Exemption
Manhattan residents who own and have registered their motor vehicles to a Manhattan address, park in long-term rented space and use their vehicles exclusively for personal use may be eligible for exemption from the additional New York City surtax levied on Manhattan parking space rentals. If you qualify, you will pay 10.375% instead of 18.375% tax.

For more information, contact:
NYC Dept of Finance: Parking Tax Exemption Section
59 Maiden Lane - 19th Floor, New York, NY 10038
212.232.1585

AVOIDING EXTRA CHARGES

The best way to avoid unexpected charges is to read the posted rate signs and to confirm the rate before you park and leave your car. Other ways are:

Read the claim check - Confirm that the time stamped on your claim check is the actual time you parked.

Overnight - Some garages charge the overnight rate only after 5-6am.

Leave your key - Forget to leave your key and the garage may charge you from $25 to the full towing fee.

Large vehicle surcharge - Know if the dimensions of your vehicle typically incur this surcharge.

Event rate - Garages have a range of rates for conventions, sports, and other events. Confirm the rate before you park your car. On major holidays or festivals (Thanksgiving, July 4th), consider parking just a little farther away and taking public transportation or walking to your destination.

Know the times - Most of the rates have a clearly posted entry time (e.g. by 7pm, 6-9am, after 3pm), but sometimes the exit time will simply read *9pm*. Be sure you know if these times are 'before' or 'after' the posted time.

WHY RATES CHANGE

Rates are competitive and a popular thing to complain about. The Department of Consumer Affairs (DCA) licenses and regulates all parking facilities. Garages must submit a rate change to the DCA at least 60 days prior to posting and charging the new rate. Garages will typically submit a relatively high rate increase and after the 60 days they can charge any rate that is *lower* without giving any notice. For example, ABC garage submits a rate increase from $10 to $50 for 1 hour. After the 60 days, it can charge anywhere up to $50 at any time. Garages are not required to post the new rates prior to implementing the increase. Here are some key events that may trigger a rate change.

Garage closes - when one garage or lot closes, other neighborhood garages will raise their rates.

Seasonality & events - some garages adjust their rates in areas where the demand for off-street parking increases or decreases during part of the year. Most garages will create an 'event' rate for major holidays and festivals.

PICKING A GARAGE

With 100,000 spaces available, there is a lot of choice. Some people look for convenience and the closest location, while others look for the cheapest rates. Here are some other factors you may not have considered.

Security - You may feel more comfortable parking in or walking late at night to a garage that is well-lit from the outside and inside, and where the valet booth is located near the entrance.

Reliability - The larger companies most likely have employee standards that provide for a more enjoyable parking experience and some recourse if you have a complaint. Of course, this is not to say that an independent garage owner would not strive to deliver superior service.

Discounts - From time to time, some of the larger garage companies offer discounted rates for frequent customers. Edison ParkFast's PayFast card allows you to pay in advance and receive a discount at the Hippodrome garage. Icon Parking offers discount coupons on its website.

Oversize vehicles - If your car, van, or truck exceeds certain height and/or length measurements, you will typically pay an extra five to ten dollars to park your car. Most garages use these guidelines:

SUVs and other Oversize vehicles 181" or longer or 70" or higher (or 75" regardless of length)

SAFETY TIPS

Take your valuables - Always try to take with you or conceal all your personal and valuable items when you park, such as house keys, loose change, EZ Pass, phone charger, and documents. Garages do typically have a strict no-tolerance policy when it comes to employee theft, but nearly every garage's claim check clearly states that 'garages are not responsible for items left in cars'.

Inspect your car - Walk around your car with the valet to confirm any existing damage that you may have. This documentation gives you recourse if you find any damage when you retrieve your car. Garages that inspect cars for damage are noted in this book by 'Damage Inspection'.

Know your numbers - Make sure you write down the exact address and phone number of the garage on your claim check. Then put the claim check where you won't forget it.

Bumper guards - Some garages provide these guards for a small fee, or you can purchase your own.

NYC PARKING CARD

The three Municipal Lots included in Park It! NYC all accept the NYC Parking Card. You can purchase a card at www.nyc.gov/dot, or at:

City Store, official store of The City of New York, located at the Manhattan Municipal Building, One Centre Street, North Plaza, in lower Manhattan (open Monday through Friday, 9:00am to 4:30pm).

NYC Department of Finance, Adjudication and Payment Center, located at 66 John Street, 2nd Floor, Manhattan, 8:30am to 4:30pm Monday through Friday.

To order by telephone, call the City Store at 311 (212-NEW-YORK outside New York City).

Currently, NYC Parking Cards are accepted at:

On-street Muni-Meters:
Kips Bay: 2nd Avenue from 30th to 33rd Street
Midtown: 30th Street between 1st and 2nd Avenue
27th to 59th Street from 2nd to 9th Avenue
72nd Street
14th Street: Union Square
8th Street: NYU area
Orchard Street
Canal Street West Broadway to Bowery

Single-space Meters:
Upper West Side: Broadway, Columbus and Amsterdam Avenues from 72nd Street to 86th Street
W 125th Street between Fifth and St. Nicholas Avenues

OVERSIZED VEHICLE SURCHARGE

These vehicles are most likely to incur the surcharge.

SUVs

Audi	Q7
BMW	X5
Buick	Enclave, Rainier, Rendezvous
Cadillac	Escalade, SRX
Chevrolet	Suburban, Tahoe, TrailBlazer SUV LT & SUV EXT
Chrysler	Aspen
Dodge	Durango
Ford	Excursion, Expedition, Explorer XLT V6 & Eddie Bauer V8
GMC	Acadia, Envoy SUV LT & EXT LT, Yukon
Hummer	H1, H2, H3
Infiniti	QX
Isuzu	Ascender
Jeep	Commander
Land Rover	LR3, Range Rover, Range Rover Sport
Lexus	GX, LX
Lincoln	Aviator, MKX, Navigator
Mazda	CX-9
Mercedes-Benz	G-Class, GL-Class, R-Class
Mercury	Mountaineer
Mitsubishi	Endeavor, Montero, Outlander
Nissan	Armada, Pathfinder
Pontiac	Aztek, Torrent
Porsche	Cayenne
Saab	9-7X
Saturn	Outlook
Subaru	B9 Tribeca
Toyota	4Runner, FJ Cruiser, Highlander SUV, Land Cruiser, Sequoia
Volkswagen	Touareg
Volvo	V70/XC70, XC90

MINI VANS

Buick	Terraza
Chevrolet	Astro, Express, Uplander, Venture
Chrysler	Town & Country
Dodge	Caravan/Grand Caravan, Sprinter
Ford	Econoline, Freestar,
GMC	Savana
Honda	Odyssey
Hyundai	Entourage
Kia	Sedona
Mercury	Monterey
Nissan	Quest
Saturn	Relay
Toyota	Sienna

SEDANS

Buick	LaCrosse, LeSabre, Lucerne, Park Avenue
Cadillac	DTS, STS
Chevrolet	Impala
Chrysler	300
Dodge	Charger
Ford	Crown Victoria, Five Hundred
Jaguar	XJ-Series
Lexus	LS 460
Lincoln	Town Car
Maserati	Quarttroporte
Mercury	Grand Marquis

SUV and Oversized Vehicle Surcharges

Let's face it, no one really enjoys paying for parking. And once you pay for your gas and bridge or tunnel tolls, actually find a parking garage, and come to grips with the price of parking, the last thing you want to get hit with is an additional $10 because you drive an SUV or Oversize vehicle.

What is considered an Oversize vehicle? The standard definition is:

SUVs and other Oversize vehicles 181" or longer or 70" or higher (or 75" regardless of length)

The opposite page lists the vehicles that typically incur the surcharge.

From 2006 – 2008, about 90% of all garages and lots charged between $5 – 10 extra, but rarely went over $10. When Park It! NYC surveyed all 1,093 garages in May 2008, we found that 88% of facilities continue to have an SUV/Oversize surcharge, but now the rate has increased to an average of $10. For the first time, we are seeing a number of garages charging $11 and a few locations are charging up to $20!

How to avoid the SUV/Oversize surcharge

Find the 130 garages that don't have this surcharge: Above 110th Street – of the nearly 100 garages above 110th St, only half charge an average surcharge of $7. That means that 50 garages don't charge at all!

E 86th to E 110th St – 15%, or 10 garages, don't have a surcharge

23rd St to Chambers between Park Ave S and Bowery – 27%, or 15 garages, don't have a surcharge

Avoid 42nd to 23rd St – 40 garages tack on $11-$20 extra

Gas Stations

There's never a gas station when you need one, right? Here's where you can find the 45 gas stations in Manhattan.

Inwood, p 24
Broadway & W 216th
10th Ave bet Isham/W211th
NW corner of W207th St/9th Ave
NE corner of W204th/Broadway
Corner of 10th Ave/W204th
Corner of Riverside Dr/Seaman Ave
Broadway bet W187th/W186th
Broadway bet W182nd/W183rd

Washington Heights, p 33
Amsterdam bet W181st/W180th
Broadway bet W174th/W173rd
SE corner of W167th/Amsterdam
NE corner of W155th/Broadway
SW corner of W155th/St. Nicholas
St. Nicholas/W150th
W145th bet Fred Douglass Bl/Adam Clayton Powell Jr. Blvd (7th Ave)

Hamilton Heights/Harlem, p 40
W145th bet Adam Clayton Powell Jr. Blvd (7th Ave)/Malcolm X Bl (Lenox), N and S side
NW corner of Broadway/W126th
Corner of W125th/W126
SW corner of E129th/Park
NW corner of 125th/3rd Ave

Morningside Heights/Harlem, p 48
SE corner of W125th/Riverside Dr E
Morningside Ave bet W124th/W125th
SW corner of W122nd/Frederick Douglass Bl
NE corner of E125th/2nd Ave
NE corner of 110th/Frederick Douglass Bl

Manhattan Valley/W110th-W86th, p 53
W96th bet West End Ave/Riverside Dr

East Harlem/Carnegie/Harlem/E110th – E86th, p 64
1st Ave bet E106th/E105th
Lexington bet E102nd/E101st
SE corner of E96th/1st Ave

Lenox Hill/Uptown East/E65th–E 59th, p 144
NE corner of E61st/York Ave

Clinton, W59th – W42nd/ 8th–12th Ave, p 156
SE corner of W51st/11th Ave
SW corner of W47th/11th Ave
10th bet E45th/W44th

Javits/Chelsea/W42nd–W23rd/8th–12th Ave, p 222
NE corner of W36th/10th Ave
11th Ave bet W30th/W29th
10th bet W28th/W27th
NW corner of W24th/10th Ave

Parking In the Theater District

Once you have paid $100 or more for a theater ticket, wouldn't it be great to find a garage or lot easily, not overpay for parking, and then retrieve your car quickly when you return?

Here are some ways to make your theater experience more enjoyable.

Pick Your Garage
Pre-plan your 1st and 2nd choices for parking. You'll save more than a few minutes when you don't have to circle the block.

Don't Overpay
Most theater district garages and lots post a higher rate for matinees and evening performances.

Make a Day of It – For matinees, find a great $10 Early Bird Special rate a little farther away. You'll feel great that you got a bit of exercise walking to the theater, and you can use your $20 plus in savings for shopping or a meal with a friend. For evening performances, park after 6 or 7pm and you'll get a great Evening Special rate.

Scout the Rates – Spend a little time researching the rates in Park It! NYC. There are some great deals; you just have to find them.

Get Your Car Quickly
Pay in Advance – if the garage has a flat rate, try to pay in advance so you can just pick your car up when you're done. Call Ahead – when you drop off your car, arrange that you'll telephone when you're 10 minutes away so they have your car ready.

Tip Beforehand – $1 to $2 can go a long way when you drop off your car.

PARKING YOUR OWN CAR

Garage Attendants are parking your car in 97% of Manhattan's garages. What do you do if you like to park your own car, rather than trusting the Valet?

Just park in these 21 garages and outdoor lots:

Note: We haven't included the Monthly or Tenant Only garages where you park your own car, just those for casual parking.

- Ch 1, #15: 3875 9th Ave
- Ch 2, #12: 115 Fort Washington Ave, Washington Heights
- Ch 3, #6: 3333 Broadway, Hamilton Heights
- Ch 3, #19: 121 W 125th St, Harlem
- Ch 6,#12: Mount Sinai Medical Center, 1 Gustave Levy Place, East Harlem
- Ch 7, #8: Museum of Natural History, 20 W 81st, Upper West Side
- Ch 7, # 39: 103 W 62nd St, Lincoln Center
- Ch 12, #43: Circle Line, Pier 83/12th Ave @ W 43rd St, Clinton
- Ch 12, #50: Circle Line , Pier 81/12th Ave @ W 41st, Clinton
- Ch 12, #51: 401 W 42nd St, Clinton
- Ch 16, #14: 1 Penn Plaza, Chelsea (Valet for special events)
- Ch 16, #18: 218 W 31st St, Chelsea
- Ch 17, #73: 2500 FDR bet 25th/26th, Kips Bay
- Ch 17, #83: New York Skyports Inc, E 23rd St & East River, Kips Bay
- Ch 18, #4: Chelsea Piers at W18th-W21st, Chelsea
- Ch 21, #1: Pier 40 West St/West Houston, Hudson Sq
- Ch 21, #26: 23 Baxter St – Automated Garage
- Ch 22, #2: Muni 2, Delancey & Essex Garage, 107 Essex St, Lower East Side
- Ch 22, #3: Muni 1, Broome & Ludlow Garage, Lower East Side
- Ch 24, #42: 55 Water St, Financial District
- Ch 24, #54: 56 Greenwich St, Financial District

DID YOU KNOW?

Manhattan has 100,000 licensed off-street parking spaces

- 66% of garages are open 24 hours
- 97% of garages have valet parking
- 80% of garages are indoor
- 88% of garages charge an average surcharge of $10 for SUVs and oversize vehicles
- 27% of garages do not take credit cards
- 17% of garages transport cars via an elevator. Of these garages, 61% have just one elevator while 37% have two elevators and only 2% have three elevators
- 2.8% of garages take only monthly parking
- 277 Park Ave is the most expensive garage for monthly parking

The streets with the most garages are:

16 garages	E 80th St
14 garages	W 56th St
14 garages	W 43rd St
12 garages	E 63rd St
12 garages	E 54th St
11 garages	W 58th St
10 garages	W 36th St

The steepest driveways are (we believe):
215 E 95th St   196 E 75th St

The longest driveway seems to be:
200 E 65th Street

The smallest garage is:
324 E 11th St, with 7 spaces

The largest garages are:

3500 spaces	Pier 40/West St
1850 spaces	1 West End Ave
1500 spaces	218 W 31st St
1365 spaces	115 Ft. Washington Ave
1248 spaces	E 116th @ FDR (opens 2009)
1000 spaces	622 W 57th St
998 spaces	401 W 42nd St (self park)
988 spaces	56 Greenwich St

13 hotels have their own garage:

Crowne Plaza	Hampton Inn	Hilton
Holiday Inn	Hyatt	Marriott
Millenium Hilton	NY Palace Hotel	Park Lane
Parker-Meridian	Skyline Hotel	Trump Parc
Waldorf-Astoria		

GGMC has the prettiest garages, with themed interiors

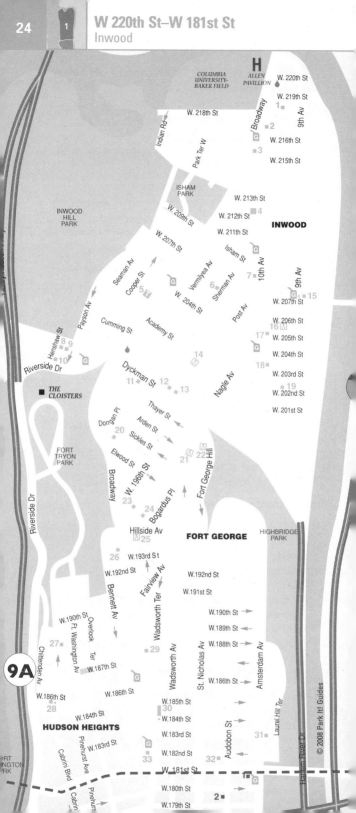

1. **443 W 218th St** *bet Broadway/9th, N side of W 218th*
   Seaman Parking Corp 212.569.9090

hr	rate	specials	rate	enter	exit
1	$8	SUV	$5		
12	$12	Event	$20		
24	$16	Month	$190		

helpful information
24/7	50 spaces	Cash

2. **4055 10th Ave** *bet W 216th/W 218th, E side of 10th*
   212.304.0315

hr	rate	specials	rate	enter	exit
1	$3	PM	$4	6pm-6am	1hr
2	$4	PM	$5	6pm-6am	2hr
3	$5	PM	$6	6pm-6am	4hr
4	$6	PM	$8	6pm-6am	8hr
8	$8	PM	$10	6pm-6am	10hr
24	$10	Month	$225, SUV add $25		
		Month	$125	day	

helpful information
24/7	Opened 2008	Outdoor, part covered
Cash	*enter 6am-6pm	

3. **4036 10th Ave** *bet W 215th/W 216th, W side of 10th*
   5060 Auto Service Inc 212.567.9504

hr	rate	specials	rate	enter	exit
1	$4	Daily	$9		
3	$7	Event	$15		
12	$10	SUV	1-5 add'l		
24	$15	Month	$203		
		Month	$118	m'cycle	
		Month	$118	day	
		Month	$63	week	

helpful information
24/7	100 spaces	Cash	Eff. 12/05

4. **3976 10th Ave** *W 212th/W 213th, W side of 10th*
   Edison/Park Fast 212.567.5186

hr	rate*	specials	rate	enter	exit
3	$5	PM	$6	4pm-4am	3hr
12	$8	PM	$11	4pm-4am	12hr
24	$15	PM	$15	4pm-4am	24hr
		Month	$200		
		Event	$20		

helpful information
24/7	AE, MC, V	Outdoor
88 spaces	*enter 4am - 4pm	

5. **4857 Broadway** *bet Academy/W 204th, W side of Broadway*

Fayne Parking Company

hr	rate	specials	rate	enter	exit

TENANT ONLY

helpful information
24/7 — Eff. 1/05
55 spaces — Outdoor
Cash — Self parking

---

6. **210 Sherman Ave** *W 204th/W 207th, W side of Sherman, near W 207th*

Sherman Parking, Inc 212.567.3629

hr	rate	specials	rate	enter	exit
1	$5	SUV	$2		
3	$7	Month	$190		
12	$10				
24	$15				

helpful information
24/7
65 spaces
Cash

---

7. **3896 10th Ave** *bet Post/Isham, W side of 10th*

Isham Parking 212.567.9818

hr	rate*	specials	rate	enter	exit
1	$6	PM	$10	8pm-8am	12hr
12	$10	PM	$12	8pm-8am	24hr
24	$12	Event	$15		
		Month	$190		

helpful information
24/7 — *8am-8pm
195 spaces
Cash

---

8. **284 Dyckman St** *bet Payson/Henshaw, S side of Dyckman*

Diamond Garage Inc 212.304.1568

hr	rate	specials	rate	enter	exit
4	$5	Month	$199		
24	$15				

helpful information
24/7 — Cash
100 spaces

9. 270 Dyckman St *bet Payson/Henshaw, S side of Dyckman*
MPG   212.304.0984

hr	rate	specials	rate	enter	exit
1	$7	Event	$20		
12	$10	SUV	$10		
24	$20	Month	$190-212		
		Month	$148	day	

helpful information
24/7   Cash
250 spaces

---

10. 284 Dyckman St *Riverside/Dyckman, E side of Henshaw*
Brilliant Parking Corp   212.569.6249

hr	rate	specials	rate	enter	exit
1	$10	Event	$20		
12	$14	SUV	$5		
24	$18	Month	$186, SUV add $68		

helpful information
24/7   Cash
75 spaces

---

11. 164 Dyckman St *bet Sherman/Vermilyea, S side of Dyckman*
Indoor Parking Corp   212.942.9804

hr	rate*	specials	rate	enter	exit
1	$5	PM	$10	7pm-6am	12hr
12	$10	PM	$14	7pm-6am	24hr
20	$12.50	Event	$25		
24	$14	SUV	$5		
		Month	$190, SUV add $21		
		Month	$127	m'cycle	

helpful information
24/7   Cash   Friendly
150 spaces   Steep driveway Clean, organized
*6am-7pm   Eff. 10/06

---

12. 133 Dyckman St *bet Sherman/Post, N side of Dyckman*
MPG   212.567.4919

hr	rate	specials	rate	enter	exit
2	$5	Event	$20		
12	$8	SUV	$3		
24	$12	Month	$169		

helpful information
24/7   AE, MC, V
63 spaces   Outdoor

13. **139 Dyckman St** *bet Sherman/Post, N side of Dyckman*
Dyckman Lot Inc

hr	rate*	specials	rate	enter	exit
2	$5	PM	$9	7pm-6am	12hr
12	$9	PM	$10	7pm-6am	20hr
20	$10	PM	$12	7pm-6am	24hr
24	$12	Event	$20		
		SUV	$5		
		Month	$161, SUV add $17		

helpful information
24/7	Outdoor
62 spaces	*6am-7pm
AE, MC, V	

14. **584 Academy St** *bet Sherman/Post, S side of Academy*
Valdes 212.567.0706

hr	rate	specials	rate	enter	exit
		Month	$160		

MONTHLY ONLY

helpful information
24/7	Outdoor
50 spaces	Self parking
Cash	

15. **3875 9th Ave** *bet W 207th/W 208th, E side of 9th*
207 Garage LLC 212.569.8229

hr	rate	specials	rate	enter	exit
24	$10	Truck	$25-35		24hr
		Month	$169		
		Van	$15		

helpful information
24/7	Outdoor
300 spaces	Self parking
Cash	

16. **414 W 206th St** *bet 9th/10th, S side of W 206th*
Marjo Parking Inc. 212.561.3195

hr	rate	specials	rate	enter	exit

MONTHLY ONLY

helpful information
24/7	Cash	Self parking
44 spaces	Outdoor	

17. *NE corner of 10th Ave/W 205th, W side of W 205th*

Martin Parking Lot

hr	rate	specials	rate	enter	exit
2	$7	Month	$180		
12	$10				
24	$15				

helpful information
24/7	30 spaces
Outdoor	

---

18. 3795 10th Ave *bet W 203rd/W 204th, E side of 10th*

FAJ Parking Corp   212.544.2411

hr	rate	specials	rate	enter	exit
1	$5	Event	$20		24hr
2	$6	SUV	$2		
12	$10	Month	$175		
24	$14				

helpful information
24/7	AE, MC, V
100 spaces	Car wash

---

19. 431 W 202nd St *bet 9th/10th, N side of W 202nd*

Rear End Parking Corp

hr	rate*	specials	rate	enter	exit
1	$4	SUV	$4		
2	$5	Event	$10		
12	$8	Month	$152, summer special $118		
24	$12				

helpful information
24/7	Outdoor
100 spaces	Car wash
Cash	*enter 6am-6pm

---

20. 2 Sherman Ave *bet Sickles/Ellwood, W side of Sherman*

Ellwood Parking Corp

hr	rate*	specials	rate	enter	exit
1	$4	PM	$6		1hr
3	$6	PM	$8		2hr
10	$8	PM	$12		12hr
12	$12	PM	$14		24hr
24	$14	Month	$225, SUV add $15		
		Month	$120	day 7am-7pm	

helpful information
24/7	Max bill $20
400 spaces	*6am-6pm
Cash	

21. 145 Nagle Ave *bet Ellwood/Dyckman, W (left) side of Hillside*
145 Nagle Ave Corp 347.297.0816

hr	rate	specials	$	enter	exit

NO RATE INFO AVAILABLE

helpful information
24/7   22 spaces   Cash   Outdoor

22. Fort George Hill *Fort George Hill, Right side of Fort George Hill*

hr	rate	specials	rate	enter	exit
		Month	$135		

CHURCH MEMBERS & PATRONS ONLY

helpful information
Cash   Outdoor

23. 4566 Broadway *bet Broadway/Ellwood, W side of Nagle*
Peak Time Parking Inc 212.942.4295

hr	rate	specials	rate	enter	exit
12	$10	SUV	$2		
24	$12	Month	$190, Van add $10		

helpful information
24/7   Cash   Outdoor
80 spaces

24. 31 Nagle Ave *bet Broadway/Ellwood, E side of Nagle*
Rapid Park 212.567.9266

hr	rate	specials	rate	enter	exit
1	$8	AM	$9	7-10am	4pm
3	$11	O/N	$13		
24	$13	SUV	$5		
		Month	$250, SUV add $50		

helpful information
24/7   100 spaces   AE, MC, V

25. 21 Hillside Ave *bet Broadway/Bogardus, Right side of Hillside*
Mory's Parking

hr	rate	specials	rate	enter	exit

MONTHLY ONLY

helpful information
26-50 spaces   Cash   Outdoor   Self parking

26. 4501 Broadway *bet Hillside/W 193rd, W side of Broadway*
EX Parking System Corp 646.796.9466

hr	rate*	specials	rate	enter	exit
1	$6	PM	$8	7pm-6am	1hr
2	$7	PM	$10	7pm-6am	12hr
12	$10	PM	$17	7pm-6am	24hr
24	$17	Event	$20		
		SUV	$5		
		Month	$225, SUV add $29		

helpful information
24/7	Cash	*6am-7pm
117 spaces		

27. 900 W 190th St *bet W 187th/W 190th, E side of Cabrini*
Fort Tryon Parking Corp 212.927.0500

hr	rate	specials	rate	enter	exit
		7D	$10	after 6am	6pm
		7D	$15	after 6am	12am
		7D	$25	after 6am	7am
		Month	$403		
		Month	$196	day	

helpful information
24/7	100 spaces	Cash

28. 200 Cabrini Blvd *at W 186th, W side of Cabrini*
GMC 212.795.9070

hr	rate	specials	rate	enter	exit
1	$10	O/N	$23		after 5am
2	$14	SUV	$10		
8	$17	Month	$375, SUV add $200		
24	$23				

helpful information
24/7	AE, MC, V	5 min grace period
525 spaces	Max bill $20	Castle Village Garage

29. 4388 Broadway *bet W 187th/W 189th, E side of Broadway*
Amamca Parking Corp.

hr	rate*	specials	rate	enter	exit
1	$5	AM	$5	by 7am	7pm
5	$9	PM	$5	6pm-6am	1hr
12	$10	PM	$9	6pm-6am	5hr
24	$15	PM	$10	6pm-6am	12hr
add'l hr	$2	PM	$15	6pm-6am	24hr
		O/N	$10	by 7pm	12hr
		SUV	$2		
		Month	$190, SUV add $10		
		Month	$85	day	

helpful information
24/7	Cash	*enter 6am-6pm
24 spaces	Outdoor	

30. **4320 Broadway** *bet Broadway/Wadsworth, N side of W 184th or S side of W 185th*

4320 Broadway Parking LLC   212.928.7251

hr	rate	specials	rate	enter	exit
1	$6	PM	$12	5pm-5:59am	12pm
2	$8	Daily	$7	6am-4:59pm	12am
3	$10	Month	$224, Van add $8		
24	$16	Month	$118	day	

helpful information

24/7	Cash	At Staples store
375 spaces	Max bill $20	

---

31. **2479 Amsterdam Ave** *at W 183rd, E side of Amsterdam*

Icon   212.923.9102

hr	rate	specials	rate	enter	exit
1	$6	Month	$296, SUV add $85		
2	$7				
3	$8				
10	$12				
24	$17				

helpful information

Su-Th 6am-2am	140 spaces
F 6am-4pm	AE, MC, V
Sa 5pm onwards	Closed Sat, all Jewish holidays

---

32. **562 W 182nd St** *bet Audobon/St. Nicholas, S side of W 182nd*

Zitro Parking   212.740.8039

hr	rate	specials	rate	enter	exit
1	$6	SUV	$2-7		
2	$8.50				
4	$11				
12	$17				
24	$21				

helpful information

35 spaces	Outdoor
Cash	Very friendly

---

33. **4275 Broadway** *at W 182nd, W side of Broadway*

Sami's Service Station Inc   212.928.3112

hr	rate	specials	rate	enter	exit
1	$5	O/N	$10	after 10pm	7am
2	$8	Month	$200	< 12', Van add $25	
5	$10	Month	$215	> 14'	
10pm	$16				

helpful information

24/7	Cash	Eff. 4/08
50 spaces	Outdoor	Gas station

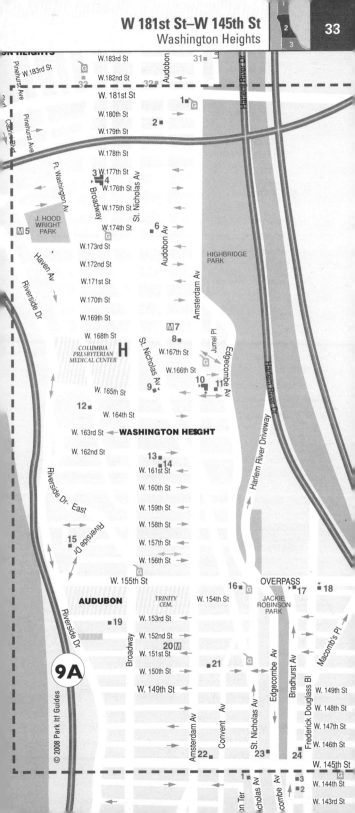

ON HEIGHTS

W.183rd St

Pinehurst Ave

W.183rd St

W.182nd St

W. 181st St

W.180th St

W.179th St

W.178th St

W.177th St

W.176th St

W.175th St

W.174th St

W.173rd St

W.172nd St

W.171st St

W.170th St

W.169th St

W. 168th St

W.167th St

W.166th St

W. 165th St

W. 164th St

W. 163rd St

W. 162nd St

W. 161st St

W. 160th St

W. 159th St

W. 158th St

W. 157th St

W. 156th St

W. 155th St

W. 154th St

W. 153rd St

W. 152nd St

W. 151st St

W. 150th St

W. 149th St

W. 148th St

W. 147th St

W. 146th St

W. 145th St

W. 144th St

W. 143rd St

W. 149th St

Audubon

Harlem River Dr

Pinehurst Ave

Cabrini Blvd

Ft. Washington Av

Broadway

St. Nicholas Av

Audubon Av

Amsterdam Av

Jumel Pl

Edgecombe Av

Harlem River Dr

Harlem River Driveway

Riverside Dr

Haven Av

Riverside Dr. East

Riverside Dr

Broadway

Amsterdam Av

Convent Av

St. Nicholas Av

Edgecombe Av

Bradhurst Av

Frederick Douglass Bl

Macomb's Pl

J. HOOD WRIGHT PARK

M 5

HIGHBRIDGE PARK

COLUMBIA PRESBYTERIAN MEDICAL CENTER H

M 7

◄ **WASHINGTON HEIGHT**

AUDUBON

TRINITY CEM.

JACKIE ROBINSON PARK

OVERPASS

9A

9A

2008 Park It! Guides

31

32

1

2

3

4

6

7

8

9

10

11

12

13

14

15

16

17

18

19

20 M

21

22

23

24

1

2

3

G

1. **506 W 181st St** *bet Audubon/Amsterdam, S side of W 181st, just before bridge*

   Parking Guys   212.781.7351

hr	rate*	specials	rate	enter	exit
1	$6	Daily	$8	7am-8pm	8pm
2	$8	Event	$25		
3	$10	Month	$211		
24	$18	Monthly special rates for new customers			

   helpful information

24/7	AE, MC, V	*apply 7am-7pm,
197 spaces	Elevator	apply again after 7pm

2. **284 Audubon Ave** *bet W 179th/W 180th, W side of Audubon*

   Parking Guys   212.781.5419

hr	rate*	specials	rate	enter	exit
1	$7	AM	$8	6-10am	7pm
3	$10	Month	$211, SUV add $13		
12	$12	Monthly special rates for new customers			
24	$18				

   helpful information

24/7	AE, MC, V	*apply 7am-7pm,
138 spaces	Elevator	apply again after 7pm

3. **4172 Broadway** *bet W 177th/W 176th, E side of Broadway or S side of W 177th*

   MPG   212.543.2700

hr	rate*	specials	rate	enter	exit
1	$8	AM	$12	6-10am	7pm
2	$12	SUV	$5		
12	$16	Month	$203		
24	$22	Event	$30		
Taxi	$12				

   helpful information

24/7	3 elevators
398 spaces	*M-Su enter 10-6am
Cash	

4. **4162 Broadway** *bet W 176th/W 177th, E side of Broadway*

   Parking Guys   212.781.6488

hr	rate	specials	rate	enter	exit
1	$7	AM	$9	7-10am	7pm
3	$10	Month	$190		
12	$12	Special monthly rates for new customers			
24	$18				

   helpful information

24/7	AE, MC, V	No exit or entrance on W 176th
107 spaces	Elevator	

5. 200 Haven Ave *bet W 176th/W 173rd, W side of Haven*
200 Garage Corp 212.543.2900

hr	rate	specials	rate	enter	exit
		Month	$266		
		Month	$175	day	

MONTHLY ONLY

helpful information
24/7
Cash

6. 554 W 174th St *bet St. Nicholas/Audubon, S side of W 174th*
MN Parking Corp 212.795.6905

hr	rate*	specials	rate	enter	exit
1	$7	AM	$10	by 6am	6pm
3	$10	Month	$190, SUV add $21		
12	$12				
24	$18				

helpful information
24/7   Elevator
75 spaces   *Enter 7am-7pm
Cash

7. 65 Audubon Ave *bet W 168th/W 169th, E side of Audubon*
201.986.9816

hr	rate	specials	rate	enter	exit
		Month	$199		

MONTHLY ONLY

helpful information
22 spaces   24/7 Key access for monthly tenants
Self parking
Outdoor

8. 514 W 168th St *bet Audubon/Amsterdam, S side of W 168th*
Parking Guys 212.928.9613

hr	rate	specials	rate	enter	exit
1	$7	Month	$165		
2	$9				
24	$15				
MTC	$11				

helpful information
M-F 6:30am-6:30pm   Outdoor
35 spaces
Cash

9. 3960 Broadway bet W 165th/W 166th, W side of St. Nicholas
Kinney 212.543.3629

hr	rate	specials	rate	enter	exit
1	$10	O/N	$11	by 7pm	7am
2	$15	SUV	$10		
3	$19	Month	$296, SUV add $42		
10	$23				
24	$30				

helpful information
24/7 — AE, MC, V
99 spaces — Outdoor

---

10. 477 W 165th St bet Edgecombe/Amsterdam, N side of W 165th
or E side of Amsterdam

J B Parking Garage 212.543.3328

hr	rate*	specials	rate	enter	exit
1	$6	PM	$12	11pm-7am	12hr
12	$9	SUV	$1-5		
		Month	$170, Van add $20-80		

helpful information
24/7 — 7pm gate closes — *enter 7am-11pm
Cash — Outdoor

---

11. 467 W 165th St bet Edgecombe/Amsterdam, N side of W 165th
The Barrington Travel Group, Inc. 212.923.7239

hr	rate	specials	rate	enter	exit
12	$9	Day	$8	7am-7pm	
24	$13	SUV	$10		12hr
		SUV	$13		24hr
		SUV large	$15		24hr
		Month	$160		

helpful information
24/7 — Cash
71 spaces — Outdoor

---

12. 115 Fort Washington Ave bet W 164th/W 165th, W side of
Fort Washington

Central 212.305.2718

hr	rate	specials	rate	enter	exit
1/2	$12	Month	$211	M-F 6pm-8am, Sa-Su 24/7	
1	$16				
2	$23				
4	$26				
8	$28				
24	$32				

helpful information
24/7 — AE, MC, V — Self parking
1365 spaces — — Pay at cashier before exiting

13. **528 W 162nd St** *bet Broadway/St. Nicholas, S side of W 162nd*
Westbury Realty LLC 212.568.4156

hr	rate	specials	rate	enter	exit
1	$8	AM	$10	7am	7pm
3	$12	Month	$190, SUV add $21		
12	$15				
24	$20				

helpful information
24/7   Cash
171 spaces

---

14. **519 W 161st St** *bet Amsterdam/Broadway, N side of W 161st*
Jerome Parking Corp 212.781.3470

hr	rate	specials	rate	enter	exit
1	$5	AM	$10	7am	7pm
2	$7	Month	$190, SUV add $21		
12	$12				
24	$18				

helpful information
24/7   Cash
100 spaces   Elevator

---

15. **779 Riverside Dr** *Un-named street off Riverside, S side of W 158th*

hr	rate	specials	rate	enter	exit

MAY BE CLOSED

helpful information
24/7
90 spaces

---

16. **404 W 155th St** *bet Edgecombe/St. Nicholas, S side of W 155th*
QuikPark 347.226.4290

hr	rate	specials	rate	enter	exit
1/2	$4	Event	$35		
2	$8	SUV	$5		
12	$12	Month	$300, SUV add $42		
24	$20	Yankee Game	$25		

helpful information
24/7   AE, MC, V   Eff. 4/08
300 spaces

---

17. 250 Bradhurst Ave *bet W 154th/W 155th, E side of Bradhurst*
Westbury Realty LLC 212.281.4879

hr	rate	specials	rate	enter	exit
1	$5	Month	$175, Van add $75		
3	$10				
12	$12				
24	$20				

helpful information
24/7	9' clearance
145 spaces	No entrance from W 155th
Cash	

---

18. 280 W 155th St *bet Frederick Douglass/Macombs-HRD, S side of W 155th*

J & L Parking Inc 212.283.7778

hr	rate	specials	rate	enter	exit
1	$6	Monthly Rates:			
2	$7	Car	$145		
3	$8	Car	$75-125 weekly		
4	$9	Van	$155		
5	$10	Truck < 22'	$250		
12	$12	Truck > 22'	$300		
24	$20	Passenger Bus	$300		
		Yankee Game	$20		

helpful information
24/7	Outdoor
300 spaces	
Cash	

---

19. 614 W 153rd St *bet Broadway/Riverside, S side of W 153rd*
Stable Car Parking, Inc 212.491.5572

hr	rate	specials	rate	enter	exit
3	$8.50	Month	$224, O/S add $38		
12	$14	Month	$127	m'cycle	
24	$18				

helpful information
24/7	Max bill $50	Cash
135 spaces	Eff. 12/06	

---

20. 503 W 151st St *bet Amsterdam/Broadway, N side of W 151st*
Nicholson & Nicols

hr	rate	specials	rate	enter	exit
		Month	$175		

MONTHLY ONLY

helpful information
20 spaces	Outdoor
Cash	24/7 Key access

21. 457 W 150th St *bet Amsterdam/Convent, N side of W 150th*
LAZ 212.281.4064

hr	rate	specials	rate	enter	exit
1/2	$1.75	SUV	$10		
1	$7	Month	$190, SUV add $84		
2	$10				
12	$15				
24	$20				

helpful information
24/7 — AE, MC, V
125 spaces — Elevator

---

22. 1721 Amsterdam Ave *bet Amsterdam/Convent, N side of W 145th*
MPG No telephone

hr	rate	specials	rate	enter	exit
1/2	$5	Month	$106	non-employee, M-F 8am-6pm	
MTC	$9				

helpful information
M-F 8am-6pm — Cash — 53 spaces
Sa,Su,Hol Closed

---

23. 261 Edgecombe Ave *bet W 150th/W 145th, W side of Edgecombe, near W 145th*

MTP 212.234.9227

hr	rate	specials	rate	enter	exit
1	$4	SUV	$3		
12	$5	Month	$169		
		Month	$120-140	O/N only	
		Holiday	$12		

helpful information
7D 7am-12am — 42 spaces — Cash

---

24. 68 Bradhurst Ave *bet Bradhurst/Federick Douglass Blvd, S side of W 146th*

Imperial 212.281.2770

hr	rate	specials	rate	enter	exit
1/2	$4	Daily	$10	after 6am	8hr, by 12am
2	$6	O/N	$20		
8	$10	SUV	$10		
24	$20	Month	$250	tenant	
		Month	$300-400	non-tenant	

helpful information
24/7 — 63 spaces — AE, MC, V — Eff. 5/08

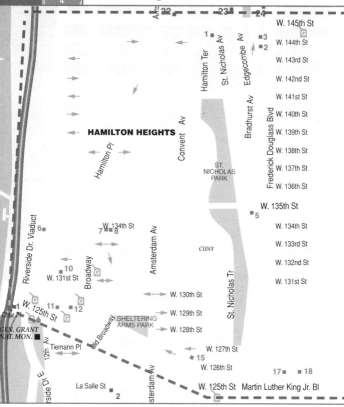

1. **673 St. Nicholas Ave** *just below W 145, W side of St. Nicholas*
Marvel Parking Ltd.

hr	rate	specials	rate	enter	exit
2	$6				
3	$8				
12	$10				
24	$17				

PERMIT ONLY CITY COLLEGE

helpful information
6am-10pm   For City College students,
180 spaces faculty, staff

---

2. **310 W 144th St** *bet Bradhurst/Frederick Douglass, S side of W 144th*
144 West Garage LLC   212.293.2816

hr	rate	specials	rate	enter	exit
1/2	$4	SUV	$3		
12	$6	Month	$190	tenant, SUV add $21	
24	$12	Month	$211	non-tenant, SUV add $21	

helpful information
24/7   AE, MC, V
130 spaces   Elevator

© 2008 Park It! Guides

---

3. **300 W 145th St** *bet Bradhurst/Frederick Douglass, N side of W 144th*

MPG 212.368.8441

hr	rate	specials	rate	enter	exit
1/2	$4	SUV	$3		
12	$6	Month	$190	tenant	
24	$12	Month	$211	non-tenant	
		PathMark	$1		2hr

helpful information

24/7	158 spaces	Cash

---

4. **6 W 137th St** *bet Lenox/5th Ave*

Uptown Parking Corp 212.939.8615

hr	rate*	specials	rate	enter	exit
1/2	$10	SUV	$10		
1	$15	Month	$76	employee, SUV add $42	
2	$18	Month	$211	non-employee, SUV add $42	
12	$22				
24	$30				

helpful information

24/7	Outdoor	Garage moved from
150 spaces	*Rates repeat after 12hr	Lenox Ave 6/07
AE, MC, V	Main office 212.490.3460	Harlem Hospital

5. **300 W 135th St** *bet Frederick Douglass/St. Nicholas, S side of W 135th*
Little Man Parking 212.368.1745

hr	rate	specials	rate	enter	exit
1	$8	Sa,Su	$10	all day	
2	$10	SUV	$10		
12	$14	Month	$240, O/S add $300		
24	$20				

helpful information
24/7	6'11" clearance
140 spaces	No signage on street
Cash	Striver's Garden Garage

---

6. **3333 Broadway** *on W 134th off Riverside, S side of W 134th, enter from Riverside Dr Viaduct*
MPG 212.281.0698

hr	rate	specials	rate	enter	exit
1	$7	Month	$211-253		
2	$7	Month	$127	m'cycle	
3	$8				
12	$12				
24	$20				

helpful information
24/7	6' clearance
360 spaces	Self parking
AF, MC, V, DIS, DC	

---

7. **536 W 134th St** *bet Broadway/Amsterdam, S side of W 134th, near Broadway*
MTP 212.926.9732

hr	rate	specials	rate	enter	exit
1/2	$7	AM	$12	by 7am	7pm
1	$10	Month	$275, SUV add $25		
12	$15	Month	$325	Van	
24	$20				

helpful information
24/7	Cash
125 spaces	

---

8. **526 W 134th St** *bet Broadway/Amsterdam, S side of W 134th, near Broadway*
Y & H Garage

hr	rate	specials	rate	enter	exit
24	$20	PM	$15	after 5pm	24hr, by 6am
		Day	$8	after 6am	5pm
		Month	$140, Van add $10		

helpful information
24/7	
175 spaces	
Cash	

9. **161 W 132nd St** *bet Lenox/7th, N side of W 132nd*
VFC Parking 212.926.0270

hr	rate	specials	rate	enter	exit
1	$8	M-F	$8	6-11am	8pm
2	$10	O/N	$19		after 5am
10	$14	SUV	$10		
24	$19	Month	$250, Van add $30		
		Month	$85 m'cycle		

helpful information
24/7
135 spaces
AE, MC, V, Dis, DC

Elevator
New owner 3/08

---

10. **627 W 131st St** *bet Broadway/12th, N side of W 131st*
MTP 212.368.2579

hr	rate	specials	rate	enter	exit
1	$5	SUV	add 30%		
12	$15	Month	$199		
24	$18	Event	$25		

helpful information
6am-12am
100 spaces
Cash

---

11. **627 W 129th St** *bet Broadway/W 125th, N side of W 129th, near W 125th*
MTP 212.280.7487

hr	rate	specials	rate	enter	exit
1/2	$2	SUV	$5		
12	$10	Month	$250		
24	$15	Month	$160	Day only	
		Month	$99	m'cycle	

helpful information
24/7   Cash   Elevator
200 spaces   Takes full size van for monthly

12. **605 W 129th St** *bet Broadway/W 125th, N side of W 129th, near Broadway*

GMC 212.749.2548

hr	rate	specials	rate	enter	exit
1	$10	O/N	$21		after 5am
2	$13	SUV	$10		
8	$17	Month	$250, SUV or Van add $50		
24	$21	Month	$400	truck	

helpful information
24/7　　　　　AE, MC, V
134 spaces　　Outdoor

13. **380 Lenox Ave** *bet 5th/Lenox, N side of W 129th*
Car Park Systems 212.987.0429

hr	rate	specials	rate	enter	exit
1	$8	Daily	$10	6-11am	8pm
2	$11	SUV	$5		
3	$18	Month	$275, SUV or Van add $42		
12	$20	Month	$169	day	
24	$22				

helpful information
24/7　　　　　AE, MC, V　　　　61 W 129th St
77 spaces　　Elevator

14. *at Park Ave, N side of E 127th, under Metro-North tracks*
Aspire 718.736.4712

hr	rate	specials	rate	enter	exit
1	$9	AM	$10	6-10am	8pm
3	$13	O/N	$19		
10	$15	SUV	$10		
close	$19	Month	$148		

helpful information
M-F 7am-8pm　Cash
Sa 8am-4pm　　Outdoor
59 spaces　　　Under Metro-North tracks

15. **418 W 127th St** *bet Morningside/Amsterdam, N side of W 126th*
Flash Parking 212.866.2919

hr	rate	specials	rate	enter	exit
1	$6	Month	$190, SUV add $21		
2	$7.50	Month	$253	truck	
10	$10				
12	$12				
24	$20				

helpful information
24/7　　　　　AE,MC,V　　　　Opened 12/07
36 spaces　　Outdoor

16. 1845 Park Ave *East of Park, E end of E 127th*
EZ Park East 212.996.8449

hr	rate	specials	rate	enter	exit
1	$7	AM	$10	6-11am	8pm
2	$10	PM	$10	6-11pm	7am
3	$12	SUV	$5		
4	$15	Month	$176		
6	$19				

helpful information
24/7 — Cash
275 spaces — Outdoor

---

17. 270 W 126th St *bet 7th/Frederick Douglass, S side of W 126th, near Frederick Douglass*
270 W 126th St. Parking Inc

hr	rate	specials	rate	enter	exit
1	$10	AM	$10	6-10am	6pm
2	$12	AM	$20	6-10am	after 6pm
3	$14	PM	$12	after 6pm	7am
4	$16	Event	$20		
6	$19	Month	$200		
24	$30				

helpful information
24/7 — Cash
159 spaces — Outdoor

---

18. 215 W 125th St *bet 7th/Frederick Douglass, S side of W 126th*
Impark 125, LLC 212.665.9899

hr	rate	specials	rate	enter	exit
1	$10	AM	$10	6-9:30am	7pm
2	$14	SUV	$10		
10	$21	Month	$211, SUV add $42		
24	$26	Event	$21		
O/N	$26				

helpful information
M-F 6am-10pm — MC, V
60 spaces — Max bill $20

---

19. 121 W 125th St *bet Malcolm X/7th, S side of W 126th*
Impark 212.531.3418

hr	rate	specials	rate	enter	exit
1	$9	AM	$9	6-10am	7pm
2	$13	O/N	$10	after 6pm	9am
10	$18	Month	$211		
24	$26				

helpful information
24/7 — Cash — Self parking
304 spaces — Max bill $20

20. 55 W 125th St *bet 5th/Lenox, S side of W 126th*
Rapid Park

hr	rate	specials	rate	enter	exit
1	$9	AM	$9	7-9am	9pm
2	$13	SUV	$10		
24	$18	Month	$175, SUV add $100		
O/N	$18				
Close	$18				

TENANT ONLY

helpful information

M-F 7am-9pm	Payment unknown
47 spaces	Eff. 9/07

---

21. 1824 Park Ave *SW corner of E 126th/Park, S side of E 126th*
E-Z Parking Management Inc.   212.831.7282

hr	rate	specials	rate	enter	exit
1	$9	AM	$10	6-10am	6pm
2	$10	PM	$10	by 6pm	7am
3	$12	Event	$20		
4	$15	Month	$200, SUV or Van add $65		
6	$19	Month	$275	truck	

helpful information

24/7	Outdoor
135 spaces	
Cash	

---

22. 162 E 126th St *bet Lexington/3rd, S side of E 126th*
Champion   212.289.9319

hr	rate	specials	rate	enter	exit
2	$12	AM	$11	6-10am	8pm
4	$13	SUV	$5		
12	$14	Month	$211, SUV add $105		
24	$17				

helpful information

24/7	AE, MC, V	181" rule for SUV
204 spaces	Outdoor	

23. **227 E 125th St** *bet 3rd/2nd, N side of E 125th*
    East End Parking Corp   212.534.8090

hr	rate	specials	rate	enter	exit
12	$10	SUV	$12		12hr
24	$15	SUV	$18		24hr
		Truck	$18-20	10'-20'	
		Truck	$20-25	22'-36'	
		Truck	$25-$30	36'-40'	
		Truck	$30-$40	42'-53'	
		Truck	$40-$55	53'-60'	
		Month	$195, SUV add $20, Van add $65		

helpful information

24/7	Close to DMV
Cash	Outdoor

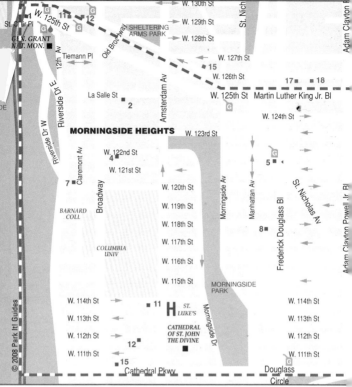

---

1. **69 St. Clair Pl** *left off W 125th, enter on left*
   MTP   212.665.4929

hr	rate	specials	rate	enter	exit
1/2	$2	SUV	30%		
12	$5	Month	$235		
24	$9	Month	$165	O/N	
		Month	$354	Truck	
		Month	$83	m'cycle	
		Event	$25		

helpful information
24/7   Cash   Located under West
70 spaces   Outdoor   Side Highway

---

2. **3100 Broadway** *bet Broadway/Amsterdam, S side of LaSalle*
   Morningside Heights Housing Corp   212.749.1170

hr	rate	specials	rate	enter	exit
1	$10	Month	$176	tenant	
2	$12	Month	$237	non-tenant	
6	$16				
24	$20				

helpful information
24/7   Cash
291 spaces   Gate closes 2-6 am

---

3. **160 W 124th St** *bet Adam Clayton Powell/Lenox, S side of W 124th*
   Parking Uptown Corp

hr	rate	specials	rate	enter	exit
1	$3	Month	$139		after 6am
2	$5	KISS	$0		2hr, $100 purchase
10	$6				
24	$9				

TEMPORARILY CLOSED

helpful information

24/7	Cash	Eff. 6/06
175 spaces	2 elevators	

---

4. **532 W 122nd St** *bet Broadway/Amsterdam, S side of W 122nd*
   GMC   212.961.1075

hr	rate	specials	rate	enter	exit
1	$16	O/N	$40		after 2am
2	$20	SUV	$10		
8	$30	Month	$350, SUV add $200+		
24	$40	Event	$45		8hr

helpful information

24/7	2 elevators
180 spaces	Takes passenger van
AE, MC, V	

5. **225 St. Nicholas Ave** *NW corner of W 121st/St. Nicholas,*
   enter via St. Nicholas

   Magic Parking LLC   212.222.2041

hr	rate*	specials	rate	enter	exit
1	$6	PM	$8	after 7pm	1hr
2	$8	PM	$10	after 7pm	2hr
7pm	$10	PM	$12	after 7pm	12am
		O/N	$18	after 7pm	
		Month $211-231, SUV add $42			

   helpful information

24/7	AE, MC, V	Elevator
160 spaces	Takes stretch limo	*enter 7am-7pm

6. **221 E 122nd St** *bet 3rd/2nd, N side of E 122nd*
   Taino Towers Garage Corp   212.410.9174

hr	rate	specials	rate	enter	exit
1	$7	SUV van	$18		12hr
6	$9	SUV van	$24		24hr
12	$12	Month	$175, van $200		
24	$14				

   helpful information

24/7	Cash
200 spaces	Miller Parking

7. **480 Riverside Dr** *bet Riverside/Claremont, N side of W 120th*
   RapidPark   212.870.6736

hr	rate	specials	rate	enter	exit
1	$14	PM	$10	after 4pm	1hr
2	$17	PM	$19	after 4pm	12am
4	$25	Sa	$20	after 7am	6pm
24	$35	Su	$4	by 7am	6pm
O/N	$35	SUV	$10		
6pm	$30	Month	$355		
		Month	$455	SUV	

   helpful information

M-Sa 7am-12am	Riverside Church
200 spaces	Long Driveway
AE, MC, V	

8. **316 W 118th St** *bet Manhattan/Frederick Douglass,*
   S side of W 118th

   VMC Parking   212.531.2924

hr	rate	specials	rate	enter	exit
24	$15	Van	$20		24hr
		Large Van	$22		24hr
		Month	$210, Van add $20		

   helpful information

24/7	130 spaces	Cash	Elevator

9. **130 Malcolm X Blvd** *bet 5th/Lenox, N side of W 116th, enter via St. Nicholas*

Imperial   212.860.7691

hr	rate	specials	rate	enter	exit
1	$10	AM m-f	$9	6-10am	8pm
2	$11	SUV	$10		
12	$14	Month	$250, SUV add $100		
24	$23	Month	$125	m'cycle	
O/N	$23				

helpful information

24/7	Cash	Eff. 5/08
273 spaces	Takes trucks 15'+	

---

10. **220 E 117th St** *bet 3rd/2nd, S side of E 117th*

117th Street Corp   212.987.6003

hr	rate	specials	rate	enter	exit
1	$10	Daily m-f	$10	after 6am	by 7pm
2	$12	SUV	$4		
3	$15	Month	$250, SUV/Van add $65		
24	$15				
O/N	$15				

helpful information

7D 7am-12am	AE, MC, V	Budget rental
100 spaces	12am gate closes	Takes trucks 15'+

---

11. **1090 Amsterdam Ave** *bet Broadway/Amsterdam, S side of W 114th, near Amsterdam*

Propark   212.523.1051

hr	rate	specials	rate	enter	exit
1	$14	SUV	$10		
2	$18	Month	$439		
10	$27				
24	$35				

helpful information

24/7	2 elevators
135 spaces	St. Luke's Hospital
Cash	6'6" clearance

---

12. **516 W 112th St** *bet Broadway/Amsterdam, S side of W 112th*

GGMC   212.865.1754

hr	rate	specials	rate	enter	exit
1	$15	AM	$20	6-9am	7pm
2	$21	Month	$400		
24	$32	O/N	$32	by 12am	after 4am
MTC	$23				

helpful information

M-Sa 6am-1am	77 spaces	6'4" clearance
Su 7am-1am	AE, MC, V, DC, CB	Steep driveway
		No large SUV

---

13. 1330 5th Ave *bet 5th/Lenox, N side of E 111th*
V & M Parking Corp   212.722.9661

hr	rate	specials	rate	enter	exit
1	$8	AM	$12	by 6am	5pm
12	$14	Month	$270, SUV add $59		
24	$20				

helpful information
24/7   Eff. 11/07
58 spaces   Exit only on E 112th
Cash

---

14. 1325 5th Ave *bet Madison/5th, N side of E 111th*
V & M Parking Corp.   212.722.9590

hr	rate	specials	rate	enter	exit
1	$10	Month	$270, SUV/Van add $59		
12	$14				
24	$20				

helpful information
24/7   Cash   Gate closes at 10pm
58 spaces   Exit only on E 112th

---

15. 543 W 110th St *bet Broadway/Amsterdam, N side of W 110th*
near Broadway

MPG   212.222.7813

hr	rate	specials	rate	enter	exit
1/2	$10	AM, 7D	$15	6-8am	12hr
1	$14	SUV	$10		
2	$19	Month	$380, SUV add $84		
10	$24	Month	$169	m'cycle	
24	$30				

helpful information
24/7   Takes vans
190 spaces
AE, MC, V

---

16. E 116th St at the FDR *bet 1st/Pleasant, N side of E 116th*
East River Plaza

hr	rate	specials	rate	enter	exit

NEW GARAGE

helpful information
1248 spaces
Opening July - October 2009

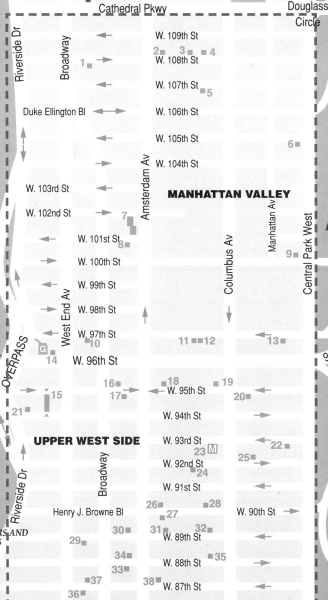

W. 111th St

15

Cathedral Pkwy

W. Douglass Circle

Riverside Dr

Broadway

W. 109th St

2 3 4

1 W. 108th St

W. 107th St 5

Duke Ellington Bl

W. 106th St

W. 105th St

6

W. 104th St

Amsterdam Av

MANHATTAN VALLEY

W. 103rd St

W. 102nd St

7

W. 101st St

8

Columbus Av

Manhattan Av

Central Park West

9

W. 100th St

W. 99th St

West End Av

W. 98th St

W. 97th St

10

14

W. 96th St

OVERPASS

11 12

13

96th

16 18

17 W. 95th St 19

15

W. 94th St 20

21

UPPER WEST SIDE

W. 93rd St

23 M

22

25

Broadway

W. 92nd St

24

W. 91st St

26 28

Henry J. Browne Bl

27

30 31 32 W. 90th St

ERS AND RS

Riverside Dr

29 W. 89th St

34 35

33 W. 88th St

37 38 W. 87th St

36

86th

W. 86th St

W. 85th St

Edgar Allan Poe St

W. 84th St

End Av

1 2 4

3 W. 83rd St

M 5 W. 82nd St

us Av

Park West

6

dam Av

© 2008 Park It! Guides

1. **234 W 108th St** *bet Broadway/Amsterdam, S side of W 108th*
   W 108th St Parking Garage Corp — 212.222.8800

hr	rate*	specials	rate	enter	exit
1	$7	PM	$7	after 6pm	1hr
2	$10	PM	$10	after 6pm	2hr
3	$13	PM	$13	after 6pm	3hr
4	$16	PM	$16	after 6pm	4hr
24	$24	PM	$18	after 6pm	2am
+1hr after		SUV	$5		
6pm	$.85	Month	$330, 14' add $100		

helpful information
7D 7am-2am	AE, MC, V, Dis	Elevator
98 spaces	No vans, takes cars 16ft+	Eff. 9/04
*Enter 7am-6pm		

2. **151 W 108th St** *bet Amsterdam/Columbus, N side of W 108th*
   HRF Operating Corp — 212.865.2314

hr	rate*	specials	rate	enter	exit
2	$7	PM	$11	after 6pm	10am
24	$15	SUV	$5		
7pm	$9	Month	$280, SUV add $30		
12am	$11	Columbia Graduation Day $15			

helpful information
24/7	Cash	Eff. 9/99
250 spaces	Elevator	*6am-7pm

3. **143 W 108th St** *bet Amsterdam/Columbus, N side of W 108th*
   E & B Oper Corp — 212.865.8315

hr	rate*	specials	rate	enter	exit
2	$7	PM	$11	after 6pm	10am
24	$15	Month	$280, SUV add $30		
7pm	$9	Graduation Day $15			
12am	$11				

helpful information
24/7	Cash	*6am-6pm
300 spaces	2 elevators	Takes vans

4. **103 W 108th St** *bet Amsterdam/Columbus, N side of W 108th*
   A & S Parking — 212.864.0137

hr	rate*	specials	rate	enter	exit
9	$10	O/N	$17	after 6pm	24hr, by 6pm
add'l hr $1		PM	$12	4pm-1am	9hr
		PM	$1	4pm-1am	add'l hr after 9 hrs
		SUV†	$10		
		Month	$325, O/S add $50		

helpful information
24/7	Cash	†Surcharge 8am-4pm
125 spaces	Elevator	*7am-4pm

5. 102 W 107th St *bet Columbus/Amsterdam, S side of W 107th*
Oliantha Garage Corp 212.870.4970

hr	rate*	specials	rate	enter	exit
2	$7	PM	$11	after 6pm	10am
24	$15	SUV	$5		
7pm	$9	Month	$280, SUV add $30		
12am	$11				

helpful information

Su-Th 6am-12am	Cash	NY Rent-A-Car
F-Sa 6am-1am	Elevator	Car wash
188 spaces	Eff. 2/96	*Enter 6am-7pm

---

6. 455 Central Park West *bet CPW/Columbus, S side of W 105th*
Central 212.666.7246

hr	rate	specials	rate	enter	exit
1	$12	AM	$8	by 11am	10hr
2	$16	SUV	$10		
12	$20	Month	$422, O/S add $84		
24	$30	Month	$169	m'cycle	

helpful information

24/7	Cash	Max bill $50
70 spaces	Elevator	

---

7. 205 W 101st St *bet Amsterdam/Broadway, N side of W 101st
or S side of W 102nd*

Rapid Park 212.864.8605

hr	rate	specials	rate	enter	exit
1	$15	O/N	$35		after 5am
2	$19	Event	$40		
4	$25	SUV	$10		
10	$31	Month	$450, O/S add $100		
24	$35				

helpful information

M-F 6am-12am	AE, MC, V	204 W 102nd
Sa,Su 7am-12am	2 elevators	
300 spaces	Max bill $20	

---

8. 204 W 101st St *bet Amsterdam/Broadway, S side of W 101st*
Rapid Park

hr	rate	specials	rate	enter	exit
1	$15	O/N	$35		after 5am
2	$19	Event	$40		
4	$25	SUV	$10		
10	$31	Month	$450, O/S add $100		
24	$35				

helpful information

24/7	AE, MC, V	Max bill $20
300 spaces	2 elevators	

9. **9 W 100th St** *bet Columbus/Central Park West, N side of W 100th, near CPW*

Rapid Park 212.531.4828

hr	rate	specials	rate	enter	exit
1	$10	Day	$16	7-11am	by 7pm
2	$19	SUV	$10		
12	$26	Month	$400, O/S add $100		
24	$30				
O/N	$30				

helpful information

24/7	Cash
75 spaces	Max bill $20

---

10. **275 W 96th St** *bet Broadway/West End Ave, S side of W 97th*

QuikPark 212.864.9352

hr	rate	specials	rate	enter	exit
1	$15	AM m-f	$14	6-10am	7pm
2	$18	O/N	$35		after 1am
10	$23	SUV	$10		
24	$35	Month	$500, O/S add $42		

helpful information

24/7	Exact change after 8pm	2561 Broadway
200 spaces	Elevator	
AE, MC, V, DC	Max bill $20	

---

11. **120 W 97th St** *bet Columbus/Amsterdam, S side of W 97th*

MPG 212.961.1542

hr	rate	specials	rate	enter	exit

MONTHLY ONLY

helpful information

24/7	Cash
250 spaces	

---

12. **750 Columbus Ave** *bet Columbus/Amsterdam, S side of W 97th*

Imperial 212.678.5456

hr	rate	specials	rate	enter	exit
1/2	$8	SUV	$10		
1	$8-12	Month	$385, O/S add $100		
2	$15	Month	$200	m'cycle	
10	$19				
24	$33				
O/N	$33				

helpful information

24/7	AE, MC, V
80 spaces	Max bill $20

13. 50 W 97th St *bet Central Park West/Columbus, S side of W 97th*

Icon   212.864.9557

hr	rate	specials	rate	enter	exit
1/2	$8	AM	$13	7-10am	6pm
1	$12	T-giving	$25	6-11am	by 6pm
2	$15	SUV	$10		
12	$21	Month	$422, SUV add $84		
24	$32				

helpful information

24/7	181" rule for SUV
114 spaces	
Cash	

---

14. 303 W 96th St *bet West End Ave/Riverside, N side of W 96th*

Empire Parking Corp   212.222.8333

hr	rate	specials	rate	enter	exit
1/2	$7	AM	$11	5-10am	6pm
1	$13	Day	$18		by 12am or 10hr
2	$17	Sa,Su	$11	after 6am	12hr
10	$24	SUV	$8		
24	$32	Month	$570, SUV add $21		

helpful information

24/7	AE, MC, V	Exxon Station
95 spaces	Lift	Car wash

---

15. 711 West End Ave *bet Riverside/West End Ave, N side of W 94th or S side of W 95th, near WEA*

Kinney   212.866.5651

hr	rate	specials	rate	enter	exit
1	$15	AM m-sa	$13	7-10am	6pm
2	$21	SUV	$11		
10	$28	Month	$510, SUV add $85		
24	$37				

helpful information

24/7	AE, MC, V
125 spaces	7' clearance

---

16. 215 W 95th St *bet Broadway/Amsterdam, N side of W 95th*

Icon   212.864.8901

hr	rate	specials	rate	enter	exit
1	$12	AM m-f	$13	7-10am	6pm
2	$14	T-giving	$30	5-11am	by 6pm
10	$20	SUV	$15		
24	$30	Month	$550		

helpful information

24/7	AE, MC, V	No vans
77 spaces	181" rule for SUV	Very steep driveway

17. 214 W 95th St *bet Broadway/Amsterdam, S side of W 95th*

Hertz 212.486.5914

hr	rate	specials	rate	enter	exit
1	$11	AM	$13	6:30-10am	7pm
2	$12	PM	$18	after 7pm	close, no O/N
10	$18	Sa,Su	$18		10hr, no O/N
24	$30	Parade	$30		
		T-giving	$30		
		SUV	$10-15		
		Month	$400	day only $225	

helpful information

7D 6:30am-11pm	AE, MC, V	Hertz rental
250 spaces	2 elevators	

---

18. 721 Amsterdam Ave *bet Columbus/Amsterdam, N side of W 95th, near Amsterdam*

Icon 212.749.6218

hr	rate	specials	rate	enter	exit
1	$12	AM m-f	$13	7-10am	7pm
2	$14	T-giving	$30	5-11am	6pm
10	$20	SUV	$10		
24	$33	Month	$591, O/S add $84		

helpful information

24/7	AE, MC, V	167 W 95th
185 spaces	181" rule for SUV	No full size vans

---

19. 730 Columbus Ave *bet Columbus/Amsterdam, N side of W 95th*

Imperial 212.678.1554

hr	rate	specials	rate	enter	exit
1/2	$5	AM m-f	$11	7-10am	7pm
1	$12	SUV	$7		
2	$15	Month	$415, O/S add $100		
10pm	$18	Month	$150	m'cycle	
24	$33				
O/N	$33				

helpful information

Su-F 7am-2am	44 spaces	No vans
Sa 7am-3am	AE, MC, V	Low clearance

---

20. 70 W 95th St *bet Central Park West/Columbus, S side of W 95th*

North Carolina Leasing 212.864.4840

hr	rate	specials	rate	enter	exit
1	$12	AM	$15	6-11am	7pm
2	$15	PM	$20	after 5pm	12pm/noon
6	$20	SUV	$5		
12	$24	Month	$450, SUV add $25		
24	$34	Month	$246	day only	

helpful information

24/7	142 spaces	AE, MC, V	Eff. 6/08

21. **222 Riverside Dr.** *bet Riverside/West End Ave, N side of W 94th, at Riverside*

Alliance Parking
212.663.8683

hr	rate	specials	rate	enter	exit
1	$15	AM	$10	by 11am	7pm
2	$20	SUV	$10		
10	$27	Month	$550, SUV add $84		
24	$35	Monthly	$127	m'cycle	

helpful information

M-F 6am-2am	AE, MC, V	No vans
Sa,Su 7am-2am	6'2" clearance	
36 spaces	Max bill $50	

---

22. **50 W 93rd St** *bet Central Park West/Columbus, S side of W 93rd*

Kinney
212.663.7154

hr	rate	specials	rate	enter	exit
1	$12	AM	$12	6-10am	7pm
2	$15	SUV	$11		
10	$22	Month	$450	tenant, SUV add $85	
24	$31	Month	$150	m'cycle	

helpful information

24/7	AE, MC, V
62 spaces	

---

23. **100 W 93rd St** *bet Columbus/Amsterdam, S side of W 93rd*

Central
212.579.6444, 212.866.8978

hr	rate	specials	rate	enter	exit

MONTHLY ONLY

helpful information

24/7	Max bill $20
106 spaces	
AE, MC, V	

---

24. **100 W 92nd St** *bet Amsterdam/Columbus, S side of W 92nd*

Impark
212.874.3001

hr	rate	specials	rate	enter	exit
1	$16	AM	$13	6-10am	7pm
2	$23	SUV	$10		
10	$28	Month	$444, O/S add $84		
24	$37				

helpful information

24/7	Max bill $20
106 spaces	
AE, MC, V	

25. 70 W 93rd St *bet Columbus/Central Park West, N side of W 92nd, near Columbus*

Kinney   212.866.8978

hr	rate	specials	rate	enter	exit
1	$12	AM	$13	6-10am	7pm
2	$15	SUV	$11		
10	$22	Month	$430, SUV add $85		
24	$31	Month	$150	m'cycle	

helpful information
24/7   AE, MC, V
88 spaces

26. 175 W 90th St *bet Amsterdam/Columbus, N side of W 90th, near Amsterdam*

Icon   212.874.8983

hr	rate	specials	rate	enter	exit
1	$8	AM	$13	6-11am	7pm
2	$15	SUV	$10		
3	$17	Month	$591, SUV add $84		
12	$24	Month	$211	m'cycle	
24	$31				

helpful information
24/7   181" rule for SUV
90 spaces
AE, MC, V

27. 601 Amsterdam Ave *bet Amsterdam/Columbus, S side of W 90th, near Amsterdam*

MPG   212.724.2818

hr	rate*	specials	rate	enter	exit
1/2	$5	AM	$5	6-10am	1/2hr
1	$7	AM	$7	6-10am	1hr
2	$14	AM	$13	6-10am	7pm
12	$25	AM	$30	6-10am	24hr
24	$30	Sa	$5	4pm-12am	1/2hr
		Sa	$10	4pm-12am	1hr
		Sa	$15	4pm-12am	2hr
		Sa	$25	4pm-12am	12hr
		Sa	$30	4pm-12am	24hr
		Event, Hol	$25		12hr
		SUV	$10		
		Month	$591		
		Carmine's	$4 discount		
		Dock's	$4 discount		

helpful information
24/7   AE, MC, V   Eff. 6/08
85 spaces   *Enter 10am-6am

28. **101 W 90th St** *bet Amsterdam/Columbus, N side of W 90th, near Columbus*

Imperial
212.721.5265

hr	rate*	specials	rate	enter	exit
1/2	$5	AM 7D	$12	7-11am	7pm
1	$7	Sa, Su	$13		12hr, no O/N
2	$14	SUV	$10		
3	$18	Month	$465, SUV add $100		
12	$23	Month	$150	m'cycle	
24	$30				
O/N	$30				

helpful information

M-Th 6am-1am	Su 7am-1am	6'8" clearance
F 6am-2am	95 spaces	*11am-7am
Sa 7am-2am	AE, MC, V	

---

29. **250 W 89th St** *bet Broadway/West End Ave, S side of W 89th*

GMC
212.874.2486

hr	rate	specials	rate	enter	exit
1	$20	O/N	$45		after 5am
2	$31	SUV	$10		
24	$45	Month	$595, O/S add $200, 16'+ add $200		

helpful information

7D 6am-2am	52 spaces	MC, V

---

30. **205 W 89th St** *bet Amsterdam/Broadway, N side of W 89th*

Icon
212.874.9867

hr	rate	specials	rate	enter	exit
1	$15	AM	$12	7-11am	6pm
2	$19	Daily	$20	after 11am	6pm
10	$24	SUV	$10		
24	$31	Month	$591, O/S add $84		
		Month	$211	m'cycle	

helpful information

24/7	Lifts	No vans/SUVs
51 spaces	181" rule for SUV	208 W 90th
AE, MC, V	Steep driveway	2420 Broadway

---

31. **137 W 89th St** *bet Columbus/Amsterdam, N side of W 89th*

Monterey Garage Corp
212.724.4600

hr	rate*	specials	rate	enter	exit
1	$7	PM	$15	after 6pm	1am
24	$27	SUV	$5		
O/N	$27	Month	$400		
6pm	$16				
after 6pm $4 add'l					

helpful information

7D 7am-1am	Elevator
100 spaces	Eff. 10/06
Cash	*Enter 7am-5pm

32. 690 Columbus Ave *bet Columbus/Amsterdam, N side of W 89th*

Rapid Park   212.874.7086

hr	rate*	specials	rate	enter	exit
1/2	$6	AM m-f	$15	4-11am	7pm
1	$15	SUV	$10		
2	$18	Month	$500, SUV add $100		
10	$30	Month	$150	m'cycle	
24	$40				
O/N	$40				

helpful information

24/7	AE, MC, V	6'11" clearance
101 spaces	Lift	

---

33. 214 W 88th St *bet Broadway/Amsterdam, S side of W 88th*

Kinney   212.877.6833

hr	rate	specials	rate	enter	exit
1	$14	AM	$12	6-10am	6pm
2	$20	SUV	$11		
10	$26	Month	$550, SUV add $84		
24	$38	Month	$150	m'cycle	

helpful information

24/7	AE, MC, V	Montana Garage
131 spaces	Max bill $50	Vans OK

---

34. 207 W 88th St *bet Broadway/Amsterdam, N side of W 88th*

Quik Park   212.496.2437

hr	rate	specials	rate	enter	exit
1/2	$11	AM	$11	6-10am	6pm
1	$15	Sa, Su	$11	all day	
2	$23	SUV	$10		
10	$27	Month	$465, O/S add $84		
24	$40				

helpful information

24/7	MC, V	Max bill $20
36 spaces	Eff. 5/06	No full size vans, reg. vans OK

---

35. 100 W 89th St *bet Amsterdam/Columbus, N side of W 88th, near Columbus*

Imperial   917.441.8056

hr	rate	specials	rate	enter	exit
1/2	$7	SUV	$10		
1	$13	Month	$515, O/S add $84		
2	$16				
10	$24				
24	$35				
O/N	$35				

helpful information

24/7	AE, MC, V	
204 spaces	Max bill $20	

---

36. 2361 Broadway *bet Broadway/West End Ave, S side of W 87th*
Icon   212.874.9899

hr	rate*	specials	rate	enter	exit
1/2	$9	AM m-f	$16	6-10am	6pm
1	$14	T-giving	$30	5-11am	6pm
2	$22	SUV	$10		
10	$29	Month	$676, SUV add $84		
24	$41				

---

helpful information

24/7	181" rule for SUV *Enter 6am-6pm
124 spaces	Max bill $20
AE, MC, V	No full size vans

---

37. 267 W 87th St *bet Broadway/West End Ave, N side of W 87th*
GMC   212.724.6833

hr	rate	specials	rate	enter	exit
1	$15	AM	$16	6-10am	6pm
2	$25	O/N	$40		after 5am
10	$30	SUV	$10		
24	$45	Month	$575, O/S add $200		
		Car 16' add'l $25			

---

helpful information

24/7	3 elevators
201 spaces	
AE, MC, V	

---

38. 175 W 87th St *bet Columbus/Amsterdam, N side of W 87th*
Garsch Garage Corp   212.724.6927

hr	rate	specials	rate	enter	exit
1	$11	O/N	$30		after 12am
2	$14	SUV	$5		
3	$18	Month	$450, SUV add $20		
24	$30	Month	$145	m'cycle	
7pm	$21				
11pm	$23				
12am	$25				

---

helpful information

24/7	Hard to see from street
150 spaces	
Cash	

1. **179 E 108th St** *bet Lexington/3rd, N side of E 108th*
   La Palma Del Barrio Corp 212.369.7545

hr	rate	specials	rate	enter	exit
1	$6	SUV	$5		
2	$9	Month	$175, Van add $50		
4	$13				
12	$19				

helpful information
24/7	Cash
30 spaces	Outdoor

2. **127 E 107th St** *bet Park/Lexington, S side of E 108th*
   E-Z Going South Inc 212.369.6369

hr	rate	specials	rate	enter	exit
1	$10	AM	$10	6-10am	6pm
2	$12	PM	$10	after 6pm	7am
3	$14	Event	$20		
4	$16	Month	$250, SUV add $25		
6	$19	Month	$350	van	
24	$30	Month	$400	truck	

helpful information
24/7	Cash	Takes trucks
228 spaces	Outdoor	

3. **158 E 108th St** *bet Lexington/3rd, S side of E 108th*
   Lease Parking Lot 212.860.6718

hr	rate	specials	rate	enter	exit
1	$6	O/N	$22		
4	$8	Month	$182		
6	$9				
8	$10				
10	$11				
12	$13				
add'l hr $4					

helpful information
7D 7am-12am	Cash
40 spaces	Outdoor

4. **12 E 107th St** *bet Madison/5th, S side of E 107th*
   Icon 212.722.9498

hr	rate	specials	rate	enter	exit
1	$11	SUV	$10		
2	$15	Month	$338, LUX add $84		
12	$20				
24	$25				

helpful information
24/7	AE, MC, V	Max bill $20
1000 spaces	181" rule for SUV	

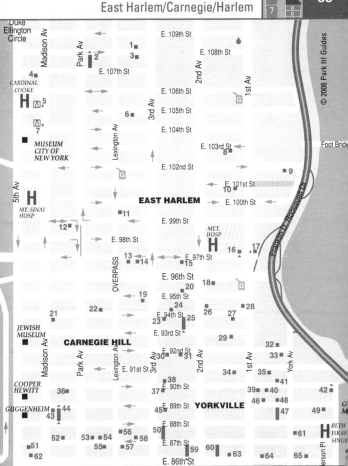

5. **1560 Madison Ave** *bet E 105th/E 106th, W side of Madison*
T Cardinal Cooke Health Care Center   212.360.1199

hr	rate	specials	rate	enter	exit

MONTHLY ONLY MT. SINAI & T CARDINAL COOK EMPLOYEES

helpful information
350 spaces   Some public parking available

---

6. **156 E 105th St** *bet 3rd/Lexington, S side of E 105th*
Icon   212.534.7619

hr	rate	specials	rate	enter	exit
1	$10	SUV	$10		
2	$12	Event	$30		
10	$15	Month	$338		
24	$23				

helpful information
24/7   AE, MC, V   181" rule for SUV
89 spaces   Elevator

---

7. **1532 Madison Ave** *NW corner of Madison/E 104th, W side of Madison*

Central/Madison Avenue Parking Corp

hr	rate	specials	rate	enter	exit

MONTHLY ONLY
MT. SINAI EMPLOYEES

helpful information
Mt. Sinai employees only   53 spaces   Outdoor

---

8. **333 E 102nd St** *bet 1st/2nd, S side of E 103rd*
East 102nd St Realty LLC   212.369.0764

hr	rate	specials	rate	enter	exit
1	$6	AM	$10	6-10am	8pm
3	$10	SUV	$7.50		12hr
9	$15	Month	$241	tenant	
24	$21	Month	$262	non-tenant	

helpful information
24/7   Max bill $20
155 spaces   Hampton Court Garage
MC, V

---

9. **440 E 102nd St** *bet 1st/FDR, S side of E 102nd*
MPG   212.860.7741

hr	rate	specials	rate	enter	exit
3	$6	Month	$200		
24	$12				

helpful information
24/7
721 spaces
AE, MC, V

10. 1955 1st Ave *bet 1st/2nd, S side of E 101st, near 1st*
Imperial 212.996.3074

hr	rate	specials	rate	enter	exit
1/2	$6	AM	$10	6-11am	8pm
1	$12	SUV	$5		
2	$15	Month	$275		
12	$20	Nurse/Doctor special: $8			12hr, No O/N
24	$23				
O/N	$23				

helpful information
24/7   109 spaces   AE, MC, V, Dis

11. 1559 Lexington Ave *bet E 99th/E 100th, E side of Lexington*
Parking Guys 212.828.5282

hr	rate	specials	rate	enter	exit
1	$10	AM	$10	6-10am	6pm
2	$15	SUV	$10		
3	$18	Month	$338, O/S add $84		
24	$24				

helpful information
7D 6am-12am   80 spaces   AE, MC, V   Outdoor

12. 1 Gustave Levy Pl *bet Park/Madison, S side of E 99th*
Mount Sinai Medical Center 212.241.5125

hr	rate	specials	rate	enter	exit
1	$7.75	Hospital employee discount			
2	$12.30				
3	$14.60				
12	$17.55				
13	$25.40				
14	$29.50				
15	$32.20				
24	$35.20				

helpful information
7D 5am-12:30am   6'4" clearance   6-12:30am pay at cashier
400 spaces   Self parking   12:30am-6am pay at security
AE, MC, V   Eff. 1/07

13. 1501 Lexington Ave *bet 3rd/Lexington, S side of E 97th*
Imperial 212.831.4265

hr	rate	specials	rate	enter	exit
1	$9	AM	$12	4-11am	7pm
2	$10	PM	$7	after 5pm	12am
3	$12	SUV	$7		
12	$17	Month	$425		
24	$26				
O/N	$26				

helpful information
24/7   Eff. 11/07   AE, MC, V
150 spaces

---

14. 175 E 96th St *bet 3rd/Lexington, S side of E 97th, near 3rd*
Imperial   212.426.2536

hr	rate	specials	rate	enter	exit
1	$9	AM	$12	5-10am	7pm
2	$10	SUV	$7		
3	$12	Month	$425, SUV add $100		
12	$17	Month	$150	m'cycle	
24	$26				
O/N	$26				

helpful information
24/7   AE, MC, V   Max bill $20
209 spaces

---

15. 217 E 96th St *bet 2nd/3rd, S side of E 97th*
MPG   212.410.5270

hr	rate*	specials	rate	enter	exit
1	$7	AM 7D	$7	12am-10am	1hr
2	$12	AM 7D	$11	12am-10am	12hr
3	$15	AM 7D	$28	12am-10am	24hr
12	$18	PM 7D	$7	3pm-12am	1hr
		PM 7D	$10	3pm-12am	12hr
		SUV	$10		
		Month	$422, SUV add $63, Day $274		
		Month	$211	m'cycle	

helpful information
24/7   AE, MC, V   *10am-3pm
416 spaces   Takes vans

---

16. 1901 1st Ave *bet 1st/2nd, N side of E 97th, near 1st*
MPG   no telephone

hr	rate	specials	rate	enter	exit
1	$13	SUV	$10		
2	$15	Month	$296, O/S add $42		
12	$20				
24	$30				

helpful information
M-F 7am-6pm   95 spaces   Outdoor
Closed holidays   Cash   Exit also on 1st

---

17. 1918 1st Ave *bet E 97th/E 99th, E side of 1st , near E 97th*
MPG   212.987.4980

hr	rate	specials	rate	enter	exit
1	$12	SUV	$10		
2	$14	Month	$300, O/S add $50		
12	$20				
24	$30				

helpful information
24/7   Max bill $50   Lifts
233 spaces   Outdoor   Eff. 7/08
Cash   Exit also on E 97th

18. 302 E 96th St *bet 2nd/1st, S side of E 96th*
Rapid Park   212.534.9640

hr	rate	specials	rate	enter	exit
1	$10	AM m-f	$12	6-10am	6pm
2	$15	Sa,Su	$10	6am-6pm	10hr
3	$16	SUV	$10		
10	$21	Month	$325, SUV add $100		
24	$27	Month	$150	m'cycle	
O/N	$27				

helpful information

7D 6am-1am	AE, MC, V	Elevator
90 spaces	$150 max charge on MC	Max bill $20

---

19. 182 E 95th St *bet 3rd/Lexington, S side of E 95th*
Icon   212.289.9760

hr	rate	specials	rate	enter	exit
1	$11	AM 7D	$12	6-10am	6pm
2	$14	SUV	$10		
3	$18	Month	$422, SUV add $84		
10	$23				
24	$30				

helpful information

24/7	AE, MC, V
112 spaces	Max bill $20

---

20. 215 E 95th St *bet 2nd/3rd, N side of E 95th, closer to 2nd*
Icon   212.735.6767

hr	rate	specials	rate	enter	exit
1	$11	AM	$12	6-10am	7pm
2	$14	SUV	$10		
12	$23	Month	$422, SUV add $84		
24	$30	Month	$211	m'cycle	

helpful information

24/7	AE, MC, V	Max bill $50
320 spaces	181" rule for SUV	No full size vans

---

21. 60 E 94th St *bet Madison/Park, S side of E 94th, closer to Madison*
GGMC   212.722.9525

hr	rate	specials	rate	enter	exit
1	$15	AM	$15	6-10am	1hr
2	$25	AM	$25	6-10am	2hr
12	$35	AM	$27	6-10am	8pm
24	$42	O/N	$42	by 12am	after 4pm
		SUV	$10		
		Month	$700 , O/S add $275		

helpful information

M-Th 6am-1am	AE, MC, V, Dis	Max bill $50
F-Su 6am-2am	181" rule for SUV	No vans
110 spaces	6'4" clearance	

22. 1199 Park Ave *bet Park/Lexington, N side of E 94th*
Ulltra 212.534.9616

hr	rate*	specials	rate	enter	exit
1	$15	AM m-f	$25	6-10am	8pm
2	$23	PM m-f	$17	after 4pm	1am
12	$32	Sa,Su	$17	after 7am	12am
24	$38	SUV	$10		
O/N	$38	Month	$565, Van add $63		

helpful information
24/7 · AE, MC, V
74 spaces · *7am-7pm

23. 1675 3rd Ave *bet 3rd/2nd, S side of E 94th*
Imperial 212.860.1976

hr	rate	specials	rate	enter	exit
1/2	$5	AM m-f	$13	4-11am	7pm
1	$11	SUV	$5		
2	$17	Month	$450, SUV add $100		
10	$21	Month	$150	m'cycle	
24	$31				
O/N	$31				

helpful information
24/7 · AE, MC, V · Max bill $20
90 spaces · 7'6" clearance

24. 231 E 94th St *bet 3rd/2nd, N side of E 94th, closer to 2nd*
GMC 212.722.4600

hr	rate	specials	rate	enter	exit
1	$11	Sa	$13	after 6am	2am
2	$17	Su	$13	after 6am	7pm
10	$21	O/N	$31		after 5am
24	$31	SUV	$10		
		Month	$395, Van add $100		

helpful information
24/7 · AE, MC, V · Yorkville Garage
390 spaces · Elevator

25. 245 E 93rd St *bet 2nd/3rd, N side of E 93rd or S side of E 94th, closer to 2nd*
Central 212.722.0066

hr	rate	specials	rate	enter	exit
1	$10	AM 7D	$10	6-11am	7pm
2	$16	SUV	$10		
10	$21	Month	$507, SUV add $84		
24	$37	Month	$169	m'cycle	

helpful information
24/7 · AE, MC, V
112 spaces · Astor Terrace Garage

26. 1832 2nd Ave *bet E 94th/E 95th, E side of 2nd*
9495 Parking Corp   212.289.3800

hr	rate	specials	rate	enter	exit

TEMPORARILY CLOSED DUE TO CONSTRUCTION

helpful information
24/7   AE, MC, V, Dis, DC
180 spaces   Eff. 9/04

---

27. 340 E 94th St *bet 2nd/1st, S side of E 94th, closer to 1st*
Rapid Park   212.534.9043

hr	rate	specials	rate	enter	exit
1	$10	Day	$9	5am-12pm	by 7pm
2	$15	SUV	$10		
24	$30	Month	$360, SUV add $100		
O/N	$30	Month	$150	m'cycle	
2am	$22				

helpful information
24/7   Max bill $20
124 spaces   No vans
AE, MC, V

---

28. 345 E 94th St *bet E 94th/E 95th, W side of 1st*
Imperial   212.828.7559

hr	rate	specials	rate	enter	exit
1/2	$6	Sa,Su	$9	6am-12pm	12hr
1	$9	SUV	$10		
2	$13	Month	$320		
24	$30				
O/N	$30				
2am	$20				

helpful information
24/7   Lifts - 4 levels
36 spaces   Enterprise rental
AE, MC, V   Large SUV only

29. 1781 1st Ave *bet 1st/2nd, S side of E 93rd*
GMC 212.876.8388

hr	rate	specials	rate	enter	exit
1	$10	AM	$11	6-10am	8pm
2	$13	Sa,Su	$9	all day	8pm
24	$28	O/N	$28		after 5am
2am	$20	SUV	$10		
		Month	$360, SUV add $100		

helpful information
7D 6am-2am | AE, MC, V
146 spaces | 6' clearance

30. 1623 3rd Ave *bet 3rd/2nd, S side of E 92nd*
GGMC 212.410.2184

hr	rate	specials	rate	enter	exit
1	$10	AM	$13	6-11am	6pm
2	$12	AM	$3	6-11am	add'l hr after 6pm
4	$14	O/N	$30	by 12am	after 4am
10	$18	SUV	$8		
24	$30	Month	$355, SUV add $125		

helpful information
24/7 | AE, MC, V | Max bill $20 | Eff. 11/07
301 spaces | 6'6" clearance | May take 16' van

31. 1751 2nd Ave *bet 2nd/3rd, S side of E 92nd, near 2nd*
GGMC 212.860.1213

hr	rate	specials	rate	enter	exit
1	$10	AM	$13	6-11am	6pm
2	$12	AM	$3	6-11am	add'l hr after 6pm
4	$14	O/N	$30	by 12am	after 4am
10	$18	SUV	$8		
24	$30	Month	$355, SUV add $125		

helpful information
7D 7am-1am | 6'10" clearance | Eff. 11/07
104 spaces | Max bill $20
Cash | 240 E 92nd

32. 441 E 92nd St *bet York/1st, N side of E 92nd, near York*
Glenwood 212.860.9627

hr	rate	specials	rate	enter	exit
1/2	$8.50	AM	$11	6-10am	6:30pm
1	$11	SUV	$6		12hr
3	$16	Month	$351	tenant	
5	$19	Month	$366	non-tenant	
9	$21	Swim Meet	$10		2hr
24	$35				

helpful information
24/7 | MC, V
137 spaces | Brittany Garage

33. 1755 York Ave *bet 1st/York, S side of E 92nd, closer to York*
Glenwood   212.860.9888

hr	rate	specials	rate	enter	exit
1/2	$8.50	AM 7D	$11	6-10am	6:30pm
1	$11	SUV	$6		12hr
3	$16	Month	$351	tenant, SUV add $ 30	
5	$19	Month	$366	non-tenant, SUV add $30	
9	$21				
24	$35				

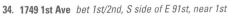

helpful information
24/7
150 spaces
MC, V

34. 1749 1st Ave *bet 1st/2nd, S side of E 91st, near 1st*
1749 First Ave Garage Corp.   212.369.0284

hr	rate	specials	rate	enter	exit
1	$12	AM m-f	$13	7-10am	7pm
2	$14	Sa,Su	$15	6am-12pm	10hr
8	$21	SUV	$10		
24	$31	Month	$385		
O/N	$31				

helpful information
24/7	MC, V	Steep driveway
21 spaces	7' clearance	

35. 422 E 91st St *bet York/1st, S side of E 91st*
Eli's Leasing Inc   212.534.9395

hr	rate	specials	rate	enter	exit
1	$11	AM	$11	7-9:30am	6pm
3	$15	Month	$350		
5	$18	Month	$150	m'cycle	
9	$21	The Vinegar Factory: 1hr free with $25			
MTC	$30	purchase. Can't use w/AM special.			

helpful information
Su-Th 6am-12am	Cash	David Garage
F-Sa 6am-1am	Elevator	
135 spaces	Eff. 6/05	

36. 60 E 90th St *bet Madison/Park, S side of E 90th*

Sylvan   212.987.3591

hr	rate	specials	rate	enter	exit
1	$25	O/N	$50		after 6am
2	$35	SUV	$15		
3	$42	Month	$650, SUV add $148		
12	$45				
24	$50				

helpful information
24/7
268 spaces
AE, MC, V

---

37. 200 E 90th St *bet 3rd/2nd, S side of E 90th, near 3rd*

GGMC   212.369.6003

hr	rate	specials	rate	enter	exit
1	$10	O/N	$30	by 12am	after 4am
2	$12	SUV	$8		
4	$14	Month	$355, SUV add $125		
10	$18				
24	$30				

helpful information
7D 7am-1am   Cash
109 spaces   Max bill $20

---

38. 1601 3rd Ave *bet 3rd/2nd, N side of E 90th*

GGMC   212.722.0188

hr	rate	specials	rate	enter	exit
1	$10	AM	$13	6-11am	6pm
2	$12	AM	$3	6-11am	add'l hr after 6pm
4	$14	SUV	$8		
10	$18	Month	$340		
24	$30				
O/N	$30				

helpful information
24/7   AE, MC, V
220 spaces

---

39. 400 E 90th St *bet 1st/York, S side of E 90th*

Impark   212.876.2712

hr	rate	specials	rate	enter	exit
1	$17	AM	$9	6-11am	7:30pm, 12hr
2	$22	Sa,Su	$18	anytime	10hr
10	$33	SUV	$10		
24	$40	Month	$465, SUV add $84		
O/N	$40				

helpful information
7D 6am-12am   AE, MC, V   Century Tower
31 spaces   Long, steep driveway   Hard to see from street

40. 412 E 90th St *bet 1st/York, S side of E 90th*
Hertz 212.486.5923

hr	rate	specials	rate	enter	exit
1	$10	Day	$10		12hr, no O/N
2	$12	SUV	$10		
24	$25	Month	$350 , SUV add $125		
O/N	$25				

helpful information
7D 6am-12am	AE, MC, V	Max bill $20
150 spaces	Hertz rental	Car wash

---

41. 1735 York Ave *bet 1st/York, N side of E 90th*
Glenwood 212.289.9673

hr	rate	specials	rate	enter	exit
1	$11	PM	$20	after 8pm	7:30am
3	$15	Day	$11	after 6am	7:30pm
5	$18	SUV	$6		12hr
9	$23	Month	$418	tenant	
24	$33	Month	$439	non-tenant, SUV add $30	

helpful information
24/7	MC, V	Good security
92 spaces	181" rule for SUV	

---

42. 200 East End Ave *SW corner of E 90th/East End, S side of E 90th, near East End*
Champion 212.876.4033

hr	rate	specials	rate	enter	exit
1/2	$17	AM	$8	6-11am	6pm
1	$23	Sa,Su	$8	after 6am	6pm
2	$25	SUV	$10		
3	$29	Month	$486, SUV & O/S add $316		
24	$41				
O/N	$41				

helpful information
24/7	AE, MC, V
41 spaces	No full size vans

---

43. 40 E 89th St *bet Park/Madison, S side of E 89th, near Madison*
Impark 212.987.0855

hr	rate	specials	rate	enter	exit
1	$21	AM	$16	6-9am	6pm
2	$29	SUV	$10		
10	$39	Month	$550, SUV add $84		
24	$44	Guggenheim Museum $19			8hr
O/N	$44	Jewish Museum $19			8hr

helpful information
7D 7am-12am	MC, V	1229 Madison
43 spaces	Max bill $20	

44. 50 E 89th St *bet Madison/Park, N side of E 88th*

GMC   212.831.8816

hr	rate	specials	rate	enter	exit
1	$25	O/N	$45		after 5am
2	$30	SUV	$10		
3	$35	Month	$675, Van add $200		
24	$45				

helpful information

24/7	5 min grace period	Low clearance
153 spaces	Park Regis	Max bill $50
AE, MC, V		E 89th–no sign, exit only

---

45. 200 E 89th St *bet 2nd/3rd, S side of E 89th, near 3rd*

Icon   646.672.0080

hr	rate	specials	rate	enter	exit
1	$16	AM	$14	7-11am	7pm
2	$22	SUV	$10		
10	$27	Month	$422, SUV add $84		
24	$37	Month	$211	m'cycle	

helpful information

24/7	181" rule for SUV	2 elevators
70 spaces	6'6" clearance	
AE, MC, V	Max bill $50	

---

46. 401 E 89th St *bet York/1st, N side of E 89th, near 1st*

Imperial   212.360.6186

hr	rate	specials	rate	enter	exit
1/2	$5	AM 7D	$11	11am	6pm
1	$12	Sa	$2	anytime	1/2hr
2	$14	SUV	$7		
12	$22				
24	$32				
O/N	$32				

helpful information

Su-F 7am-2am	AE, MC, V	No full size vans
Sa 7am-3am	Elevator	
141 spaces	Max bill $20	

47. 1675 York Ave *bet York/1st, N side of E 88th or S side of E 89th*
Glenwood 212.534.9465

hr	rate	specials	rate	enter	exit
1/2	$7	M-F	$10	6:30am-7pm	7pm
1	$10	Sa,Su	$11	after 6am	7:30pm
3	$18	SUV	$8		12hr
5	$20	Month	$365	tenant	
10	$24	Month	$414	non-tenant, SUV add $42	
24	$34				

helpful information

24/7	181" rule for SUV	E 88th gate closes at 12am
136 spaces	6'7" clearance	
MC, V	Damage inspection	

48. 1725 York Ave *bet York/1st, N side of E 89th*
Icon 212.722.9375

hr	rate	specials	rate	enter	exit
1	$15	AM 7D	$10	7-10am	6pm
2	$17	7D	$5	7am-6pm	1/2 hr
3	$19	Day	$13	10am-6pm	by 6pm
12	$25	SUV	$10		
24	$36	Month	$444	tenant	
		Month	$507	non-tenant	

helpful information

24/7	Max bill $50	12am gate closes
104 spaces	Damage inspection	
AE, MC, V	No full size vans	

49. 180 East End Ave *bet East End/York, S side of E 89th*
Waterview Parking, Inc 212.650.9320

hr	rate	specials	rate	enter	exit
1	$13	AM 7D	$11	8-10am	6pm
3	$17	Month	$250	tenant	
5	$20	Month	$450	non-tenant	
9	$26				
24	$38				

helpful information

24/7	8pm gate closes	No vans
115 spaces	Eff. 9/05	No vehicle over 68"
AE, MC, V, Dis	Damage inspection	

50. 200 E 88th St *bet 2nd/3rd, N side of E 87th or S side of E 88th*
Central/Kinney   212.987.3879

hr	rate	specials	rate	enter	exit
1/2	$11	AM 7D	$13	6-10am	7pm
1	$17.50	SUV	$11		
2	$20	Parade	$40		24hr
8	$26	Month	$423, SUV add $84		
24	$40	Month	$169	m'cycle	

helpful information

24/7	6'6" clearance E 87th
218 spaces	5' clearance E 88th
AE, MC, V, DC	May take handicapped van

---

51. 1056 5th Ave *bet Madison/5th, S side of E 87th, near 5th*
Icon   212.534.9437

hr	rate	specials	rate	enter	exit
1	$25	SUV	$10		
2	$30	Month	$844, SUV add $84		
10	$35				
24	$40				

helpful information

Su-Th 6am-1am	AE, MC, V
F-Sa 6am-2am	181" rule for SUV
55 spaces	

---

52. 55 E 87th St *bet Park/Madison, N side of E 87th*
Rapid Park   212.831.4818

hr	rate	specials	rate	enter	exit
1	$21	SUV	$10		
2	$26	Month	$550	tenant, SUV add $100	
3	$32	Month	$600	non-tenant, SUV add $100	
24	$42				
12am	$40				

helpful information

Su-Th 6am-1am	57 spaces
F-Sa 6am-2am	AE, MC, V

---

53. 1065 Park Ave *bet Lexington/Park, N side of E 87th, closer to Park*
GMC   212.860.3428

hr	rate	specials	rate	enter	exit
1	$25	SUV	$10		
2	$30	Month	$550		
3	$35				
24	$40				
O/N	$40				

helpful information

7D 6am-2am	AE, MC, V
30 spaces	Eff. 2/07

54. 115 E 87th St *bet Lexington/Park, N side of E 87th*
Central   212.289.5040

hr	rate	specials	rate	enter	exit
1	$17	AM 7D	$15	6-11am	7pm
2	$21	SUV	$11		
10	$30	Month	$528, SUV add $84		
24	$40				

helpful information

24/7	AE, MC, V	Max bill $50
198 spaces	Low clearance	No vans

---

55. 120 E 87th St *bet Lexington/Park, S side of E 87th, near Lexington*
P.A.C. Garage Corp   212.737.3279

hr	rate	specials	rate	enter	exit
1	$17	AM 7D	$11	7-11am	7pm
2	$21	SUV	$10		
10	$29	Month	$422, SUV add $84		
24	$36				
O/N	$36				

helpful information

24/7	Cash	Next to Staples
150 spaces	2 elevators	Eff. 2/08

---

56. 160 E 88th St *bet E 87th/E 88th, E side of Lexington*
Icon   212.534.9106

hr	rate	specials	rate	enter	exit
1	$22	SUV	$10		
2	$25	Month	$465, O/S add $42		
12	$35				
24	$42				

helpful information

Su-Th 7am-1am	AE, MC, V	No full size vans
F-Sa 7am-2am	181" rule for SUV	
36 spaces	Low clearance	

---

57. 154 E 87th St *bet Lexington/3rd, S side of E 87th, near Lexington*
Meyers Parking System Inc   212.722.6500

hr	rate	specials	rate	enter	exit
1	$17	AM 7D	$12	3-11am	7pm
2	$21	Parade	$40		24hr
8	$30	SUV	$10		
12	$41	Month	$549, O/S add $127		
24	$41	Yankee game $10			10hr

helpful information

24/7	2 elevators	Tight for conversion van
515 spaces	Dollar rental	Budget rental
AE, MC, V, Dis	Max bill $50	Alan Garage

58. 169 E 87th St *bet 3rd/Lexington, N side of E 87th*
Champion — 212.369.2059

hr	rate	specials	rate	enter	exit
1	$18	AM 7D	$14	6-11am	8pm
2	$23	Parade	$35		
10	$29	SUV	$10		
24	$32	Month	$465		
O/N	$32				

helpful information

24/7	AE, MC, V	181" rule for SUV
175 spaces	2 elevators	No large vans

59. 249 E 86th St *bet 2nd/3rd, N side of E 86th*
Icon — 212.534.9303

hr	rate	specials	rate	enter	exit
1/2	$5	AM 7D	$12	8-10am	6pm
1	$19	Parade	$30		6pm
2	$22	SUV	$10		
12	$31	Month	$486, SUV add $84		
24	$40				

helpful information

24/7	AE, MC, V	Exit only from E 87th
146 spaces	181" rule for SUV	

60. 305 E 86th St *bet 1st/2nd, N side of E 86th or S side of E 87th*
Icon — 212.289.9905

hr	rate	specials	rate	enter	exit
1/2	$7	AM 7D	$11	7-11am	7pm
1	$13	Parade	$20		6pm
2	$17	SUV	$10		
12	$29	Month	$465, O/S add $84		
24	$40				

helpful information

24/7	AE, MC, V	No full size vans
168 spaces	181" rule for SUV	

61. 501 E 87th St *bet E 87th/E 88th, E side of York*
Central — 212.650.0533

hr	rate	specials	rate	enter	exit
1	$16	AM	$8	7-10am	6:30pm
2	$19	SUV	$11		
10	$32	Month	$435, O/S add $76		
24	$36				

helpful information

24/7	Cash
66 spaces	Rivers Bend Garage

62. 1050 5th Ave *bet Madison/5th, N side of E 86th, near 5th*

1050 Garage Corp 212.289.9761

hr	rate	specials	rate	enter	exit
2	$24	SUV	$5		
10	$30				
24	$40				
O/N	$40				

helpful information

7D 7am-1am   Cash
49 spaces   No signage

---

63. 345 E 86th St *bet 1st/2nd, N side of E 86th*

Safeway Parking Corp 212.410.9603

hr	rate	specials	rate	enter	exit
1/2	$4	AM m-f	$14	6-10am	10hr
1	$7	Parade	$20		
2	$9	SUV	$5		
3	$11	Month	$381, O/S add $84		
12	$18				
24	$25				
O/N	$25				

helpful information

24/7   6'5" clearance   Safeway Garage
56 spaces   Max bill $100
Cash   No vans

---

64. 401 E 86th St *bet York/1st, N side of E 86th*

GMC 212.876.7669

hr	rate	specials	rate	enter	exit
1	$15	O/N	$35		after 5am
2	$20	SUV	$10		
10	$25	Month	$495, SUV add $100		
24	$35				

helpful information

24/7   AE, MC, V   Max bill $50
46 spaces   5 min grace period   Steep driveway

---

65. 525 E 86th St *bet East End/York, N side of E 86th*

Imperial 212.249.2674

hr	rate	specials	rate	enter	exit
1	$12	O/N	$29		
2	$15	SUV	$5		
10	$20	Month	$581		
24	$29				

helpful information

Su-Th 7am-1:30am   40 spaces   Steep Driveway
F-Sa 7am-2am   AE, MC, V, DC

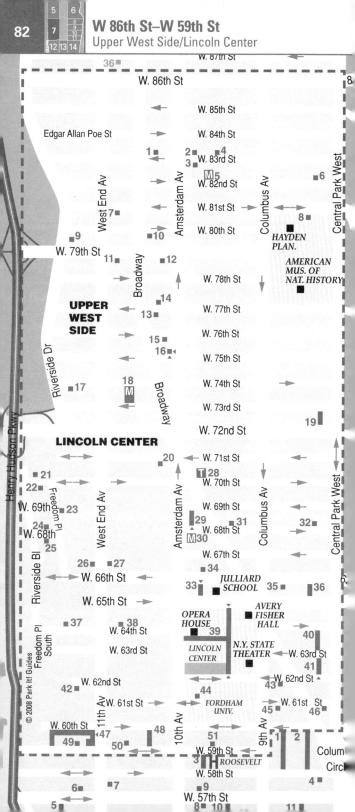

W. 87th St

W. 86th St

8

W. 85th St

Edgar Allan Poe St

W. 84th St

W. 83rd St

W. 82nd St

W. 81st St

W. 80th St

HAYDEN PLAN.

AMERICAN MUS. OF NAT. HISTORY

W. 79th St

W. 78th St

UPPER WEST SIDE

W. 77th St

W. 76th St

W. 75th St

W. 74th St

W. 73rd St

W. 72nd St

LINCOLN CENTER

W. 71st St

W. 70th St

W. 69th St

W. 68th St

W. 67th St

JULLIARD SCHOOL

W. 66th St

W. 65th St

OPERA HOUSE

AVERY FISHER HALL

N.Y. STATE THEATER

LINCOLN CENTER

W. 63rd St

W. 62nd St

W. 61st St

FORDHAM UNIV.

W. 60th St

W. 59th St

ROOSEVELT

W. 58th St

Colum Circ

W. 57th St

Central Park West

Columbus Av

Amsterdam Av

Broadway

West End Av

Riverside Dr

Henry Hudson Pkwy

Freedom Pl

Riverside Bl

Freedom Pl South

11th Av

10th Av

9th Av

© 2008 Park Itl Guides

1. 225 W 83rd St *bet Amsterdam/Broadway, N side of W 83rd*
Icon 212.874.9934

hr	rate	specials	rate	enter	exit
1/2	$9	AM m-f	$20	6-10am	6pm, no Holiday
1	$17	Daily m-f	$30	after 10am	by 6pm
2	$21	Sa,Su	$30	6am-6pm	6pm
3	$24	T-giving	$30	6am-11am	by 6pm
24	$40	SUV	$10		
		Month	$591, SUV add $84		

helpful information		
24/7	AE, MC, V	No full size vans
107 spaces	181" rule for SUV	Max bill $50

2. 157 W 83rd St *bet Columbus/Amsterdam, N side of W 83rd*
Central 212.362.3900

hr	rate*	specials	rate	enter	exit
1/2	$7	AM m-f	$18	6-10am	6pm
1	$16	Sa, Su	$16		1hr
2	$22	Sa, Su	$20		2 hr
3	$25	Sa, Su	$30		10hr
10	$30	Sa, Su	$45		24hr
24	$45	Event	$50		
		SUV	$10		
		Month	$510, SUV add $84.		
		Month	$170	m'cycle	
		Lucerne, Excelsior, On the Avenue Hotels			
			$25		24hr
		Children's Museum $15			5hr

helpful information		
24/7	AE, MC, V	Max bill $50
182 spaces	2 elevators	*M-F

3. 150 W 83rd St *bet Columbus/Amsterdam, S side of W 83rd*
Central 212.877.6300

hr	rate	specials	rate	enter	exit
1	$18	AM m-f	$15	6-10am	6pm
2	$24	Sa,Su	$16		1hr
10	$32	Sa, Su	$21		2hr
24	$46	Sa,Su	$31		10hr
		Sa,Su	$46		24hr
		Event	$50		
		SUV	$11		
		Month	$510, SUV add $84		
		Month	$170	m'cycle	
		Lucerne, Excelsior, On the Avenue Hotels			
			$25		24hr
		Children's Museum $15			5hr

helpful information		
24/7	Elevator	Max bill $50
156 spaces	Thrifty rental next door	
AE, MC, V	8' clearance	

4. **147 W 83rd St** *bet Columbus/Amsterdam, N side of W 83rd*
   Central   212.362.3900

hr	rate*	specials	rate	enter	exit
1	$18	AM m-f	$12	6-10am	6pm
2	$24	Sa, Su	$16		1hr
10	$32	Sa, Su	$21		2hr
24	$46	Sa, Su	$31		10hr
		Sa, Su	$46		24hr
		SUV	$11		
		Month	$510, SUV add $84		
		Month	$170	m'cycle	
		Lucerne, Excelsior, On the Avenue Hotels			
			$25		24hr
		Children's Museum $15			5hr

helpful information
24/7	Elevator	*M-F
182 spaces	Enterprise rental	
AE, MC, V	Max bill $50	

5. **161 W 82nd St** *bet Amsterdam/Columbus, N side of W 82nd*
   A R Walker & Company Inc   212.724.5803

hr	rate	specials	rate	enter	exit

MONTHLY ONLY

helpful information
24/7 with key	Eff. 9/05
15 spaces	Outdoor
Payment unknown	Self parking

6. **5 W 82nd St** *bet Columbus/Central Park West, N side of W 82nd St, near CPW*
   Champion   212.874.9114

hr	rate	specials	rate	enter	exit
1/2	$25	SUV	$10		
1	$31	Month	$866, SUV add $169		
2	$41				
3	$52				
24	$65				
O/N	$65				

helpful information
24/7	Near Museum of Nat. History	225 CPW
58 spaces	181" rule for SUV	
AE, MC, V	6'2" clearance	

7. 424 West End Ave *bet Broadway/West End Ave, S side of W 81st*
Icon 212.874.9633

hr	rate	specials	rate	enter	exit
1/2	$10	Daily m-f	$20	6am-6pm	6pm , no Holiday
1	$17	Sa,Su	$26	6am-6pm	12hr
2	$20	T-giving	$30	6-11am	by 6pm
3	$23	SUV	$10		
24	$38	Month	$591, O/S add $84		
		Month	$211	m'cycle	

helpful information

24/7	181" rule for SUV
83 spaces	Max bill $50
AE, MC, V	No full size vans

8. 20 W 81st *bet Columbus/Central Park West, S side of W 81st*
Standard 212.313.7275

hr	rate	specials	rate	enter	exit
1	$18	Museum of Natural History visitor rates:			
2	$21		$19		2hr
5	$31		$27		5hr
10	$43		$39		10hr
MTC	$46		$46		close

helpful information

7D 8am-11pm	AE, MC, V	Museum of Natural History
388 spaces	Self parking	

9. 70 Riverside Dr. *bet W 79th/W 80th, E side of Riverside Dr*
Rapid Park 212.873.1277

hr	rate	specials	rate	enter	exit
1	$20	O/N	$50		
2	$30	T'giving	$40	6am-12pm	3hr
3	$40	T'giving	$45	6am-12pm	10hr
10	$46	SUV	$10		
24	$50	Month	$600, O/S add $100		

helpful information

7D 7am-2am	Max bill $20
80 spaces	
AE, MC, V	

10. 214 W 80th St *bet Broadway/Amsterdam, S side of W 80th*
Central   212.580.7413

hr	rate	specials	rate	enter	exit
1	$17	Sa,Su	$18		1hr
2	$20	Sa,Su	$20		2hr
10	$28	Sa,Su	$28		10hr
24	$40	Sa,Su	$40		24hr
		SUV	$10		
		Month	$422, O/S add $84		
		Month	$169	m'cycle	
		Zabar's	$8		2hr, spend $25

helpful information
24/7   AE, MC, V
147 spaces   Elevator

---

11. 254 W 79th St *bet Broadway/West End Ave, S side of W 79th, near WEA*
Rapid Park   212.874.8532

hr	rate	specials	rate	enter	exit
1	$19	AM	$20	6-9am	6pm
2	$26	Event	$40		
3	$31	Parade	$40		
24	$46	SUV	$10		
O/N	$46	Month	$575		

helpful information
24/7   7'6" clearance
100 spaces   Max bill $20
AE, MC, V

---

12. 200 W 79th St *bet Amsterdam/Broadway, S side of W 79th*
W 79th Street Parking Corp   212.874.9149

hr	rate*	specials	rate	enter	exit
1	$18	AM m-f	$16	6-9am	6pm
2	$25	SUV	$10		
3	$30	Month	$528, O/S add $84		
10	$36				
24	$45				

helpful information
24/7   No vans
95 spaces   *M 6am-F 6pm
AE, MC, V

13. **210 W 77th St** *bet Amsterdam/Broadway, S side of W 77th*
The Hertz Corp 212.486.5919

hr	rate*	specials	rate	enter	exit
1	$13	PM m-f	$19	6pm-close	1hr
2	$16	PM m-f	$23	6pm-close	2hr
10	$24	PM m-f	$38	6pm-close	3hr
24	$38	Sa,Su	$19		1hr
		Sa,Su	$23		2hr
		Sa,Su	$38		24hr
		Event	$39		
		SUV	$15		
		Month	$450		

helpful information
7D 6:30am-12am   AE, MC, V   *M-F 6:30am-6pm
250 spaces   Hertz rental

---

14. **203 W 77th St** *bet Amsterdam/Broadway, N side of W 77th*
Barmax Garage 212.362.2308

hr	rate*	specials	rate	enter	exit
1	$16	AM	$16	5-10am	6pm
2	$19	PM	$28	5pm-7am	1hr
10	$28	PM	$32	5pm-7am	2hr
24	$43	PM	$43	5pm-7am	24hr
		Sa,Su,Hol,Event	$28		1hr
		Sa,Su,Hol,Event	$32		2hr
		Sa,Su,Hol,Event	$43		24hr
		SUV	$10		
		Month	$550, O/S add $150		

helpful information
24/7   Elevator   *M-F 7am-6pm
75 spaces   AE, MC, V

---

15. **210 W 76th St** *bet Broadway/Amsterdam, S side of W 76th*
Beacon 76 Garage Corp 212.769.2630

hr	rate*	specials	rate	enter	exit
1	$25	AM m-f	$18	5-9am	6pm
12	$33	PM m-f	$25	5pm-3am	1hr
24	$50	PM m-f	$33	5pm-3am	2hr
O/N	$50	PM m-f	$50	5pm-3am	24hr
		Sa,Su, Hol	$25		1hr
		Sa,Su, Hol	$33		2hr
		Sa,Su, Hol	$50		24hr
		Event	$50		
		SUV	$12		
		Month	$551		

helpful information
24/7   Cash   Near Avis rental
300 spaces   Elevator   *M-F enter after 3am, exit by 5pm

---

16. **201 W 75th St** *NW corner of W 75th/Amsterdam, W side of Amsterdam or N side of 75th*

Champion					212.874.0581
hr	rate*	specials	rate	enter	exit
1/2	$25	AM 7D	$20	4-9:30am	6pm
1	$33	PM 7D	$33	5pm-3am	1hr
10	$37	PM 7D	$39	5pm-3am	2hr
24	$55	PM 7D	$55	5pm-3am	24hr or O/N
O/N	$55	Sa,Su	$32	3am-5pm	1hr
		Sa,Su	$40	3am-5pm	2hr
		Sa,Su	$46	3am-5pm	3hr
		Sa,Su	$55	3am-5pm	24hr or O/N
		Marathon	$55		
		T-giving	$55		
		SUV	$15		
		Month	$612, SUV add $359		

helpful information

24/7	AE, MC, V	181" rule for SUV
278 spaces	Elevator	*M-F enter 3am-5pm

---

17. **11 Riverside Dr.** *bet Riverside/West End Ave, S side of W 74th*

Eleven Riverside Drive Garage Corp					212.724.5345
hr	rate*	specials	rate	enter	exit
1	$17	AM m-f	$18	by 9am	7pm
2	$21	PM	$21	after 6pm	1hr
3	$24	PM	$24	after 6pm	2hr
12	$28	PM	$35	after 6pm	24hr or O/N
24	$35	SUV	$10		
		Month	$475, O/S add $75		

helpful information

24/7	Eff. 6/07	Schwab House
200 spaces	*6am-6pm	Monthly only after 1am
Cash		

---

18. **2101 Broadway** *bet Broadway/West End Ave, N side of W 73rd or S side of W 74th*

2109 Broadway Parking LLC					212.874.9315
hr	rate	specials	rate	enter	exit
		Month	$398, SUV add $25		

TENANT ONLY

helpful information

24/7	Cash	Ansonia
110 spaces	Eff. 5/08	

19. **15 W 72nd St** *bet CPW/Columbus, N side of W 72nd or S side of W 73rd, near CPW*

RapidPark 212.874.9904

hr	rate	specials	rate	enter	exit
1	$27	O/N	$55		after 5am
2	$40	SUV	$10		
3	$45	Month	$700	tenant	
8	$48	Month	$770	non-tenant	
24	$55	Month	$300	m'cycle	

helpful information
24/7	AE, MC, V
176 spaces	Max bill $20

20. **200 W 71st St** *bet Amsterdam/West End Ave, S side of W 71st*

Icon 212.362.7622

hr	rate*	specials	rate	enter	exit
1/2	$13	AM m-f	$14	5-11am	6pm
1	$20	PM	$15	4pm-5am	1/2hr
2	$24	PM	$22	4pm-5am	1hr
12	$34	PM	$27	4pm-5am	2hr
24	$40	PM	$34	4pm-5am	12hr
7pm	$29	PM	$40	4pm-5am	24hr
		AM sa-su	$20	5-10am	4pm
		Sa,Su	$15	10am-4pm	1/2hr
		Sa,Su	$22	10am-4pm	1hr
		Sa,Su	$27	10am-4pm	2hr
		Sa,Su	$34	10am-4pm	12hr
		Sa,Su	$40	10am-4pm	24hr
		T-giving	$30	2-11am	by 4pm
		SUV	$10		
		Month	$549, SUV add $84		
		Month	$211	m'cycle	

helpful information
24/7	181" rule for SUV	*M-F 11am-4pm
262 spaces	7'2" clearance	
AE, MC, V	Steep driveway	

21. **220 Riverside Dr South** *bet Freedom Pl/Riverside Blvd, N side of W 70th*

212.501.0016

hr	rate	specials	rate	enter	exit
1	$14	AM	$11	6-10am	12hr
2	$20	T-giving	$30	5am-11am	6pm
12	$22	SUV	$10		
24	$33	Month	$380		

helpful information
24/7	181" rule for SUV	Takes vans
290 spaces	220 Riverside Blvd	
AE, V, MC		

22. **300 Riverside Dr South** *bet Riverside Blvd/Freedom Pl, S side of W 70th*

QuikPark   212.362.0161

hr	rate	specials	rate	enter	exit
1	$11	AM	$11	5-10am	12hr
2	$18	SUV	$5		
12	$25				
24	$36				

helpful information

24/7	181" rule for SUV
284 spaces	200 Riverside Blvd
AE, MC, V	Takes vans

23. **185 West End Ave** *Freedom Pl at W 69th, E side of Freedom Pl*

Icon   212.874.9995

hr	rate*	specials	rate	enter	exit
1	$11	AM	$11	6-10am	12hr
2	$17	PM m-f	$12	6pm-5am	1hr
3	$19	PM m-f	$18	6pm-5am	2hr
12	$20	PM m-f	$19	6pm-5am	3hr
24	$31	PM m-f	$21	6pm-5am	12hr
		PM m-f	$31	6pm-5am	24hr
		T-giving	$30	5-11am	by 6pm
		SUV	$10		
		Month	$422, O/S add $84		
		Month	$211	m'cycle	

helpful information

24/7	181" rule for SUV
411 spaces	Max bill $50
Cash	*enter 10am-6pm

24. **180 Riverside Blvd** *bet Riverside Blvd/Freedom Pl, N side of W 68th*

QuikPark   212.501.9040

hr	rate	specials	rate	enter	exit
1	$11	AM	$11	by 10am	12hr
2	$18	SUV	$10		
12	$25	Month	$401		
24	$36				

helpful information

24/7	AE, MC, V
210 spaces	181" rule for SUV

25. 160 Riverside Blvd *bet Riverside Blvd/Freedom Pl, S side of W 68th*

QuikPark   212.724.0869

hr	rate	specials	rate	enter	exit
1	$11	AM	$11	5-10am	12hr
2	$18	SUV	$10		
12	$25				
24	$36				

helpful information
24/7	181" rule for SUV
208 spaces	
AE, MC, V	

---

26. 165 West End Ave *bet W 66th/W 67th, W side of West End Ave*
Icon   212.874.8426

hr	rate*	specials	rate	enter	exit
1	$11	AM	$12	6-10am	12hr
2	$17	PM m-f	$12	6pm-5am	1hr
3	$19	PM m-f	$18	6pm-5am	2hr
12	$20	PM m-f	$19	6pm-5am	3hr
24	$31	PM m-f	$21	6pm-5am	12hr
		PM m-f	$31	6pm-5am	24hr
		T-giving	$30	5-11am	by 6pm
		SUV	$10		
		Month	$380		

helpful information
24/7	Max bill $50
445 spaces	No trucks
Cash	*M-F 10am-6pm

---

27. 150 West End Ave *bet W 66th/W 67th, E side of West End Ave*
Icon   212.874.8274

hr	rate*	specials	rate	enter	exit
1	$11	Daily m-f	$18	6am-6pm	12hr
2	$17	PM m-f	$12	6pm-6am	1hr
3	$19	PM m-f	$18	6pm-6am	2hr
12	$21	PM m-f	$19	6pm-6am	3hr
24	$31	PM m-f	$23	6pm-6am	12hr
		PM m-f	$31	6pm-6am	24hr
		T-giving	$30	5-11am	by 6pm
		Month	$422, O/S add $84		
		SUV	$10		

helpful information
24/7	181" rule for SUV	No full size vans
163 spaces	Max bill $50	
Cash	*enter 6am-6pm	

---

28. **155 W 70th St** *bet Broadway/Columbus, N side of W 70th*
Icon   212.874.8014

hr	rate	specials	rate	enter	exit
		Month	$549		

TENANT ONLY

helpful information

24/7	Cash	6'3" clearance
43 spaces	181" rule for SUV	

---

29. **143 W 68th St** *bet Amsterdam/Broadway, N side of W 68th or S side of W 69th*
Icon   212.874.9664

hr	rate*	specials	rate	enter	exit
1/2	$9	AM m-f	$14	5-11am	6pm
1	$16	Daily m-f	$25	11am-5pm	by 6pm, no Holiday
2	$22	F,Sa,Su	$9	5pm-5am	1/2hr
24	$36	F,Sa,Su	$19	5pm-5am	1hr
6pm	$29	F,Sa,Su	$24	5pm-5am	2hr
		F,Sa,Su	$36	5pm-5am	24hr
		PM m-th	$9	5pm-5am	1/2hr
		PM m-th	$16	5pm-5am	1hr
		PM m-th	$22	5pm-5am	2hr
		Sa,Su	$9	5am-5pm	1/2hr
		Sa,Su	$17	5am-5pm	1hr
		Sa,Su	$22	5am-5pm	2hr
		Sa,Su	$36	5am-5pm	24hr
		Sa,Su	$29	5am-5pm	6pm
		T-giving	$30	5-11am	by 6pm
		SUV	$10		
		Month	$507, SUV add $84		
		Month	$211	m'cycle	

helpful information

24/7	181" rule for SUV	166 W 69th
271 spaces	No full size vans	
AE, MC, V	*enter 5am-5pm	

---

30. **150 W 68th St** *bet Amsterdam/Broadway, S side of W 68th*
Icon   212.874.9707

hr	rate	specials	rate	enter	exit
		Month	$422		

MONTHLY ONLY

helpful information

24/7	Cash	Steep driveway
158 spaces	181" rule for SUV	

31. 2000 Broadway *bet Broadway/Columbus, N side of W 68...*

GMC 212.787.699u

hr	rate*	specials	rate	enter	exit
1	$20	PM	$20	5pm-5am	1hr
10	$25	PM	$30	5pm-5am	2hr
24	$35	PM	$40	5pm-5am	24hr or O/N
		SUV	$10		
		Month	$450, SUV add $200		

helpful information

Su-Th 6am-2am	AE, MC, V	*enter 5am-5pm
F-Sa 24hr	Elevator	
57 spaces		

---

32. 80 Central Park West *bet Columbus/CPW, N side of W 68th, near CPW*

Jo Meg Garage Corp 212.874.9425

hr	rate	specials	rate	enter	exit
2	$16	AM	$11	by 10am	6pm
10	$22	SUV	$10		
MTC	$30				

helpful information

Su-Th 6:30am-1am	83 spaces	Steep driveway
F,Sa 24hr	Cash	

---

33. 127 Amsterdam Ave *bet Columbus/Amsterdam, N side of W 65th or S side of W 66th*

Icon 212.769.0134

hr	rate	specials	rate	enter	exit
1/2	$9	AM su-f	$13	5-10am	6pm
1	$19	AM Sa	$20	6-10am	4pm
2	$22	Su-F	$26	10am-4pm	6pm
12	$34	Event/Mat	$30	7am-4pm	6pm
24	$37	T-giving	$30	5-11am	12hr
		SUV	$10		
		Month	$507, SUV add $84		

helpful information

24/7	Across from Lincoln Center	160 W 66th St
375 spaces	181" rule for SUV	No exit on W 65th
AE, MC, V	6'3" clearance	No vans

Broadway/Amsterdam, S side of W 66th

212.874.9508

		specials	rate	enter	exit
		AM su-f	$13	6-10am	6pm
1		T-giving	$30	7-11am	by 6pm
2	$21	SUV	$10		
12	$32	Month	$422, O/S add $84		
24	$35	Month	$211	m'cycle	

helpful information

7D 7am-2am	181" rule for SUV
77 spaces	Max bill $20
AE, MC, V	No full size vans

---

35. 2 Lincoln Plaza *bet CPW/Columbus, S side of W 66th, near Columbus*

Icon

212.874.8639

hr	rate	specials	rate	enter	exit
1/2	$10	AM	$17	6-10am	12hr
1	$17	T-giving	$30	5-11am	6pm
12	$30	SUV	$10		
24	$37	Month	$550, SUV add $84		

helpful information

24/7	AE, MC, V	Max bill $50
80 spaces	181" rule for SUV	

---

36. 10 W 66th St *bet CPW/Columbus, N side of W 65th or S side of W 66th*

GGMC

212.874.1100

hr	rate	specials	rate	enter	exit
1	$16	AM m-f	$13	5-10am	6pm
2	$22	AM m-f	$3	5-10am	add'l hr
4	$29	O/N	$35	by 12am	after 4am
24	$35	SUV	$10		

helpful information

24/7
195 spaces
AE, MC, V

37. 101 West End Ave *bet West End Ave/river, N side of ...*

Icon   212.874...

hr	rate	specials	rate	enter	exit
1	$12	AM m-sa	$12	5-10am	12hr
2	$17	T-giving	$30	5-11am	by 6pm
12	$22	SUV	$10		
24	$32	Month	$465, SUV add $84		
		Month	$211	m'cycle	

helpful information

24/7	AE, MC, V	
166 spaces	181" rule for SUV	

---

38. 110 West End Ave *bet West End Ave/Amsterdam, N side of W 64th*

Icon   212.874.9828

hr	rate	specials	rate	enter	exit
1	$12	AM m-f	$12	6-10am	6pm
2	$15	T-giving	$30	5-11am	by 6pm
12	$20	SUV	$10		
24	$33	Month	$338, SUV add $84		
		Month	$211	m'cycle	

helpful information

24/7	Cash	7' clearance
106 spaces	181" rule for SUV	No full size vans

---

39. 103 W 62nd St *bet Columbus/Amsterdam, N side of W 62nd or S side of W 65th*

QuikPark   212.874.9021

hr	rate*	specials	rate	enter	exit
1/2	$9	AM m-f	$15	by 8:30am	6pm
1	$17	M-F	$24	4am-4pm	6pm
2	$19	M-F	$38	4am-4pm	10am
		M-F	$6	4am-4pm	add'l hr
		M-F mat	$31	4am-4pm	6pm
		Sa,Hol	$32	4am-4pm	6pm
		Sa,Hol	$42	4am-4pm	10am
		Su	$31	4am-4pm	12am
		Su	$38	4am-4pm	10am
		M-F	$9	4pm-4am	1/2hr
		M-F	$19	4pm-4am	1hr
		M-F	$22	4pm-4am	2hr
		PM su-w	$35	4pm-4am	10am
		PM th-sa	$36	4pm-4am	10am
		SUV	$0		
		Month	$465		

helpful information

24/7	*enter 4am-4pm	6'2" clearance
721 spaces	Lincoln Center	Self parking
AE, MC, V		

'W/Broadway, N side of W 63rd or
e of W 64th

212.724.6282

		cials	rate	enter	exit
		m-f	$14	4-10am	12am
2		-F	$27	10am-4pm	10hr
10	$29	-giving	$30	5-11am	6pm
24	$35	SUV	$10		
		Month	$465, SUV add $84		

helpful information

24/7	181" rule for SUV	41 W 63rd
400 spaces	Max bill $50	18 W 64th
AE, MC, V		

---

41. 1886 Broadway *bet CPW/Broadway/Columbus, N side of W 62nd or S side of W 63rd*

Central   212.586.1660

hr	rate	specials	rate	enter	exit
1/2	$8	AM m-f	$13	6-10am	7pm
1	$14	SUV	$10		
2	$18	Month	$422	tenant, O/S add $84	
10	$29	Month	$507	non-tenant, O/S add $84	
24	$33				

helpful information

24/7	AE, MC, V	6'6" clearance
75 spaces		

---

42. 35 West End Ave *bet West End Ave/river, S side of W 62nd*

West End Towers Garage Corp   212.974.8036

hr	rate	specials	rate	enter	exit
12	$10	SUV	$5		
		Month	$300		
		Event	$15		12hr

helpful information

24/7	MC, V	181" rule for SUV
441 spaces	Max bill $20	

43. 44 W 62nd St *bet Broadway/Columbus, S side of W 62nd*

GMC 212.262.3800

hr	rate*	specials	rate	enter	exit
1	$20	PM	$25	5pm-5am	1hr
2	$25	PM	$35	5pm-5am	10hr
10	$30	PM	$45	5pm-5am	24hr or O/N
24	$40	SUV	$10		
O/N	$40	Month	$495, O/S add $200		

helpful information

24/7	AE, MC, V	Lincoln Tower Plaza Garage
143 spaces	*enter 5am-5pm	

---

44. 161 W 61st St *East of Amsterdam, N side of W 61st*

GGMC 212.397.8933
212.397.8949

hr	rate	specials	rate	enter	exit
1	$15	AM	$13	6-9am	10hr
2	$17	M-F	$20	after 9am	12hr
10	$26	O/N sa,su	$31	by 12am	after 6am
24	$31	O/N m-f	$25	by 12am	after 6am
		SUV	$10		
		Month	$425, SUV add $200		

helpful information

7D 6am-1am	6'8" clearance	Eff. 5/08
140 spaces	Max bill $20	
AE, MC, V, Dis, DC		

---

45. 40 W 61st St *bet Columbus/Broadway, S side of W 61st*

Icon 212.245.9594

hr	rate	specials	rate	enter	exit
1/2	$11	AM	$15	5-10:30am	6:30pm
1	$20	SUV	$10		
3	$23	T-giving	$30	5am-11am	12hr
12	$30	Fordham, NYIT	$16	7am-1am	12hr
24	$35				

helpful information

24/7	181" rule for SUV	21 Columbus Ave
205 spaces	Max bill $50	
AE, MC, V	39 W 60th	

46. **1 Central Park West** *bet Broadway/CPW, S side of W 61st, near CPW*

World Parking Garage LLC 212.265.4199

hr	rate	specials	rate	enter	exit
1/2	$10	AM	$15	6-10am	7pm
1	$16	SUV	$10		
2	$23	Month	$600, O/S add $150		
3	$25				
10	$37				
24	$49				

helpful information

24/7	MC, V
88 spaces	Elevator

47. **1 West End Ave** *bet W 59th/W 60th, W side of West End Ave*

Central 212.246.4256

hr	rate	specials	rate	enter	exit
12	$15	SUV	$8		
24	$26	Month	$255, Truck $423		

helpful information

24/7	Lifts	Free shuttle to 5th Ave
1850 spaces	Outdoor	
AE, V, MC	Takes trucks 40ft+	

48. **200 W 60th St** *bet Amsterdam/West End Ave, N side of W 59th or S side of W 60th*

Concerto Garage Corp 212.246.5769

hr	rate	specials	rate	enter	exit
1	$7.30	Sa,Su	$9		12hr
2	$16	SUV	$10		
10	$19	John Jay, Fordham student $13			10hr
24	$24	Month	$325, SUV add $96		

helpful information

24/7
265 spaces
Cash

49. 641 W 59th St *bet 11th/West Side Highway, N side of W 59th*
MTP   212.397.3773

hr	rate	specials	rate	enter	exit
12	$15	SUV	$5		
24	$25	Month	$254, SUV add $40		

helpful information
7D 6am-12am	Cash
537 spaces	Max bill $100

---

50. 515 W 59th St *bet 10th/11th, N side of W 59th*
Propark   212.957.3692

hr	rate	specials	rate	enter	exit
1	$14	AM	$14	5-10am	8pm
2	$17	SUV	$10		
10	$20	Month	$380		
24	$26				

helpful information
24/7	Cash	6'10" clearance
190 spaces	Near John Jay College	Max bill $50

---

51. 429 W 59th St *bet 9th/10th, N side of W 59th*
Allie Garage Corp   212.246.7220

hr	rate	specials	rate	enter	exit
4	$20	AM	$14	1-9am	12hr
12	$22	Sa,Su	$18	Sa 6am-M 6am	12hr
24	$26	Event	$15		
		SUV	$10		
		Student	$12		12hr

helpful information
24/7	Cash
125 spaces	181" rule for SUV

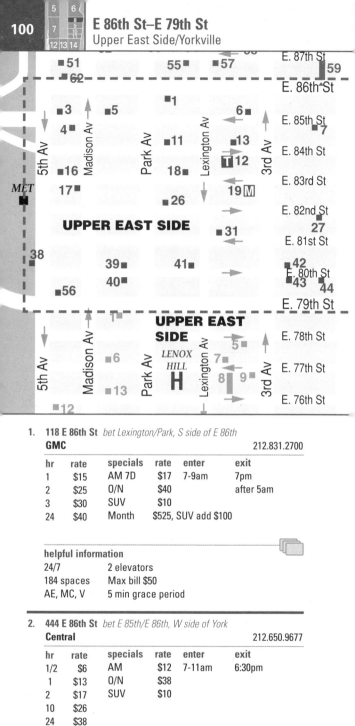

1. **118 E 86th St** *bet Lexington/Park, S side of E 86th*
   GMC   212.831.2700

hr	rate	specials	rate	enter	exit
1	$15	AM 7D	$17	7-9am	7pm
2	$25	O/N	$40		after 5am
3	$30	SUV	$10		
24	$40	Month	$525, SUV add $100		

helpful information
24/7	2 elevators
184 spaces	Max bill $50
AE, MC, V	5 min grace period

2. **444 E 86th St** *bet E 85th/E 86th, W side of York*
   Central   212.650.9677

hr	rate	specials	rate	enter	exit
1/2	$6	AM	$12	7-11am	6:30pm
1	$13	O/N	$38		
2	$17	SUV	$10		
10	$26				
24	$38				

helpful information
M-W 6am-12am	126 spaces
Th-F 6am-2am	AE, MC, V, Dis, DC
Sa,Su 7am-2am	Max bill $50

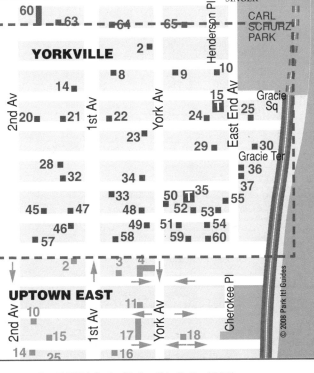

YORKVILLE

2nd Av
1st Av
York Av
Henderson Pl
East End Av
SINGER
CARL SCHURZ PARK
Gracie Sq
Gracie Ter

UPTOWN EAST

2nd Av
1st Av
York Av
Cherokee Pl

© 2008 Park It! Guides

---

3. **12 E 86th St** *bet Madison/5th, N side of E 85th*
Croyden Parking   212.650.1739

hr	rate	specials	rate	enter	exit
1	$11	AM m-f	$18	by 10am	8pm
2	$18	SUV	$10		
10	$30	Month	$500		
24	$36				

helpful information
M-Th 7am-1am   MC, V
F-Su 24hr   181" rule for SUV
72 spaces

---

4. **30 E 85th St** *bet Madison/5th, S side of E 85th*
Icon   212.249.5290

hr	rate	specials	rate	enter	exit
1	$21	SUV	$10		
2	$27	Month	$570, SUV add $84		
10	$31				
24	$43				

helpful information
S-Th 6am-1am   AE, MC, V
F-Sa 6am-2am   181" rule for SUV
43 spaces

5. **35 E 85th St** *bet Park/Madison, N side of E 85th*
Imperial 212.472.4713

hr	rate	specials	rate	enter	exit
1/2	$12	AM 7D	$24	7-10am	10hr
1	$24	Event	$50		
2	$27	SUV	$10		
10	$35	Month	$635		
24	$45				
O/N	$45				

helpful information

24/7	AE, MC, V
72 spaces	Eff. 5/08

6. **185 E 85th St** *bet 3rd/Lexington, N side of E 85th*
Central 212.722.5529

hr	rate	specials	rate	enter	exit
1	$15	AM 7D	$16	4-10am	10hr
2	$18	SUV	$10		
10	$25	Month	$431	tenant, O/S add $97	
24	$35	Month	$448	non-tenant, O/S add $97	
		Month	$144	m'cycle	

helpful information

24/7	AE, MC, V
320 spaces	Takes 16 passenger van

7. **234 E 85th St** *bet 2nd/3rd, S side of E 85th*
Champion 212.879.3737

hr	rate*	specials	rate	enter	exit
1/2	$12	AM 7D	$15	4-11am	12am
1	$15	PM	$17	5pm-4am	1/2hr
1 1/2	$17	PM	$20	5pm-4am	1hr
2	$23	PM	$28	5pm-4am	2hr
24	$29-35	PM	$35	5pm-4am	24hr
O/N	$35	PM	$35	5pm-4am	O/N
		Parade	$35		
		SUV	$10		
		Month	$401		
		Month	$194	m'cycle	

helpful information

24/7	2 elevators	12am gate closes
280 spaces	181" rule for SUV	Eff. 10/06
AE, MC, V	No full size vans	Thrifty *4am-5pm

8. **400 E 85th St** *bet York/1st, S side of E 85th, near 1st*
Imperial 212.650.1683

hr	rate	specials	rate	enter	exit
1	$12	AM 7D	$10	7-11am	7pm
2	$14	SUV	$10		
10	$22	Month	$450, SUV add $100		
24	$34	Month	$185	day, m-f, 7am-7pm	
O/N	$34	Month	$140	m'cycle	
MTC	$28				

helpful information
Su-Th 7am-2am   80 spaces
F-Sa 7am-3am   AE, MC, V

---

9. **500 E 85th St** *bet East End/York, S side of E 85th, near York*
Glenwood 212.650.9178

hr	rate	specials	rate	enter	exit
1/2	$6	AM 7D	$9	6:30-10am	7pm
1	$10	SUV	$9		12hr
2	$12	Month	$422	tenant, SUV add $65	
5	$17	Month	$456	non-tenant, SUV add $65	
10	$20				
24	$34				

helpful information
M-Th 6:30am-1am   Su 7am-1am   MC, V
F-Sa 6:30am-2am   77 spaces   Damage inspection

---

10. **110 East End Ave** *bet East End/York, S side of E 85th*
Imperial 212.734.4080

hr	rate	specials	rate	enter	exit
1/2	$5	SUV	$10		
1	$10	Month	$500, SUV add $150		
2	$12				
10	$19				
24	$34				
O/N	$34				
1am	$22				

helpful information
7D 6am-1am   AE, MC, V   Eff. 11/06
40 spaces   Max bill $20

---

11. **113 E 84th St** *bet Park/Lexington, N side of E 84th, near Park*
GMC 212.288.9170

hr	rate	specials	rate	enter	exit
1	$22	O/N	$40		after 5am
2	$32	SUV	$10		
3	$37	Month	$625, O/S add $100		
24	$42				

helpful information
7D 6am-2am   5 min grace period   Elevator
125 spaces   Belmont Garage   10pm gate closes
AE, MC, V   No vans

12. 160 E 84th St *bet 3rd/Lexington, S side of E 84th*
160 E 84th Street Associates   212.279.7600

hr	rate	specials	rate	enter	exit

TENANT ONLY

helpful information
Cash

---

13. 171 E 84th St *bet 3rd/Lexington, N side of E 84th*
GMC   212.628.4550

hr	rate	specials	rate	enter	exit
1	$18	O/N	$40		after 5am
2	$27	SUV	$10		
10	$37	Month	$540, SUV add $100		
24	$41				

helpful information
7D 6am-2am   11pm gate closes
75 spaces   Takes handicapped van
AE, MC, V   Evans Tower bldg

---

14. 351 E 84th St *bet 1st/2nd, N side of E 84th, near 1st*
GMC   212.628.1994

hr	rate	specials	rate	enter	exit
1	$13	SUV	$10		
2	$16	Month	$450, SUV add $100		
3	$22				
24	$31				
O/N	$31				

helpful information
7D 6am-2am   Eff. 1/07
92 spaces   Adam's Tower apt bldg
AE, MC, V   No full size vans

---

15. 90 East End Ave *bet York/East End, S side of E 84th, near East End*
Imperial

hr	rate	specials	rate	enter	exit

TENANT ONLY

helpful information
Cash

16. **1025 5th Ave** *bet Madison/5th, N side of E 83rd*
Imperial 212.861.0510

hr	rate	specials	rate	enter	exit
1/2	$12	Event	$50		by 10pm
1	$22	SUV	$12		
2	$30	Month	$700, SUV add $100		
8	$42				
24	$51				

helpful information
24/7   6'6" clearance
95 spaces   Steep driveway
AE, MC, V

---

17. **8 E 83rd St** *bet Madison/5th, S side of E 83rd*
GMC 212.535.2890

hr	rate	specials	rate	enter	exit
1	$22	O/N	$47		after 5am
2	$33	SUV	$12		
3	$42	Month	$690, SUV add $100		
24	$47				

helpful information
7D 6am-2am   Steep driveway
48 spaces   No vans
AE, MC, V

---

18. **127 E 83rd St** *bet Lexington/Park, N side of E 83rd*
GMC, Red Ball 212.439.9022

hr	rate	specials	rate	enter	exit
1	$22	AM m-f	$18	7-9am	6pm
2	$32	SUV	$10		
3	$37	Month	$595, SUV add $100		
24	$40	O/N	$40		after 5am

helpful information
7D 6am-2am   5 min grace period
200 spaces   Elevator
AE, MC, V   Max bill $50

---

19. **170 E 83rd St** *bet 3rd/Lexington, S side of E 83rd*
Kinney

hr	rate	specials	rate	enter	exit
		Month	$700		

MONTHLY ONLY

helpful information
7D 8am-6pm
28 spaces
Cash

20. 303 E 83rd St *bet 1st/2nd, N side of E 83rd*
Champion — 212.535.9419

hr	rate	specials	rate	enter	exit
1/2	$7-19	AM	$11	5-11am	7pm
1	$25	Parade	$35		
2	$31	SUV	$10		
24	$37	Month	$435, SUV add $42		
O/N	$37				

helpful information
24/7   AE, MC, V
115 spaces   181" rule for SUV

---

21. 351 E 83rd St *bet 1st/2nd, N side of E 83rd, near 1st*
GGMC — 212.650.0893

hr	rate	specials	rate	enter	exit
1/2	$5	7D	$10	5am-6pm	by 7pm
1	$11	PM m-f	$12	after 6pm	1am
2	$13	New Year	$30	after 9pm	7am
4	$17	SUV	$10		
10	$21	Month	$400		
24	$30				
O/N	$30				

helpful information
24/7   AE, MC, V, DC, CB   Max bill $20
138 spaces   6'8" clearance

---

22. 400 E 84th St *bet York/1st, N side of E 83rd, near 1st*
MPG — 212.535.5242

hr	rate*	specials	rate	enter	exit
1/2	$5	AM	$10	6-10am	7pm
1	$8	AM	$30	6-10am	24hr
2	$14	SUV	$10		
3	$19	Month	$507, O/S add $84		
24	$30	Month	$211	m'cycle	

helpful information
24/7   AE, MC, V
63 spaces   *7D, enter 10am-6pm

---

23. 450 E 83rd St *bet York/1st, S side of E 83rd, near York*
Central — 212.744.2312

hr	rate	specials	rate	enter	exit
1	$11	SUV	$10		
2	$13	Month	$676, SUV add $84		
10	$16	Month	$170	m'cycle	
24	$35				

helpful information
24/7   AE, MC, V   Takes vans
44 spaces   Elevator   Hard to see from street

24. 80 East End Ave *bet East End/York, N side of E 83rd*

GMC 212.517.5709

hr	rate	specials	rate	enter	exit
1	$12	SUV	$15		
2	$17	Month	$500		
8	$20				
24	$31				
O/N	$31				

helpful information

7D 6am-2am	AE, MC, V
35 spaces	No large vans

---

25. 611 E 83rd St *bet East End/river, N side of E 83rd*

Impark 212.249.5124

hr	rate	specials	rate	enter	exit
1	$15	AM	$9	8-10am	5pm
2	$20	SUV	$10		
8	$25	Month	$262	rent-stab. tenant, SUV add $84	
24	$30	Month	$465	other tenant, SUV add $84	
O/N	$30				

helpful information

7D 7am-1am	AE, V	Steep driveway
91 spaces		

---

26. 111 E 82nd St *bet Park/Lexington, N side of E 82nd*

GMC 212.288.9645

hr	rate	specials	rate	enter	exit
1	$22	O/N	$47		after 5am
2	$32	SUV	$10		
3	$42	Month	$690, SUV add $100		
24	$47				

helpful information

7D 6am-2am	5 min grace period	Max bill $50
143 spaces	Elevator	Hard to see from street
AE, MC, V		

---

27. 240 E 82nd St *bet 3rd/2nd, S side of E 82nd*

Elco 212.744.5503

hr	rate	specials	rate	enter	exit
1/2	$9	AM	$12	6-10am	6pm
1	$14	SUV	$10		
2	$16	Month	$485	less than 14'	
3	$19	Month	$503	longer than 14'	
10	$23				
24	$30				

helpful information

24/7	Cash	Eff. 1/08
48 spaces	Max bill $20	

28. 350 E 82nd St *bet 2nd/1st, S side of E 82nd*
QuikPark 212.988.9099

hr	rate	specials	rate	enter	exit
1	$7	AM m-f	$10	6-11am	7pm
2	$11	SUV	$5		
3	$13	Month	$495, O/S add $42		
8	$21				
24	$27				

helpful information
24/7   181" rule for SUV
53 spaces   Max bill $20
AE, MC, V

---

29. 60 East End Ave *bet York/East End, N side of E 82nd*
Central 212.650.9760

hr	rate	specials	rate	enter	exit
1	$10	AM 7D	$10	6-10am	7pm
3	$14	SUV	$1.50		4hr
5	$17	Month	$260	tenant	
7	$21	Month	$450	non-tenant	
24	$27	Month	$152	day, enter 8am, exit 7pm	

helpful information
Su-Th 6am-1am   AE, MC, V, Dis, DC
F-Sa 6am-2am   Max bill $50
120 spaces   Short driveway

---

30. 61 East End Ave *bet East End/river, N side of E 82nd*
GMC/Mutual Parking Inc 212.737.2568

hr	rate	specials	rate	enter	exit
1	$10	O/N	$34		after 5am
2	$13	SUV	$10		
8	$17	Month	$490, SUV add $150		
24	$34				

helpful information
24/7   Cash
132 spaces

---

31. 145 E 81st St *bet 3rd/Lexington, N side of E 81st*
Glenwood 212.650.9156

hr	rate	specials	rate	enter	exit
1/2	$10	AM	$15	6:30-10am	7pm
1	$19	SUV	$10		12hr
2	$22	Month	$514	tenant, SUV add $55	
5	$27	Month	$543	non-tenant, SUV add $55	
9	$33				
24	$40				

helpful information
Su-Th 6am-1am   Cash   Max bill $20
F-Sa 6:30am-2am   Elevator   No signage on street
22 spaces   181" rule for SUV   Marlowe garage

---

32. **345 E 81st St** *bet 1st/2nd, N side of E 81st*
81st Street Parking LLC
212.879.5968

hr	rate	specials	rate	enter	exit
1	$7	AM 7D	$10	6-11am	7pm
2	$10	SUV	$5		
3	$12				
10	$18				
24	$25				

helpful information

Su-Th 6am-1am	Cash	6'10" clearance
F-Sa 6am-2am	5 min grace period	
53 spaces	Eff. 1/05	

---

33. **400 E 81st St** *bet York/1st, S side of E 81st, near 1st*
QuikPark
212.650.1854

hr	rate	specials	rate	enter	exit
1	$7-8	AM 7D	$11	6-11am	7pm
2	$12	SUV	$10		
3	$14	Month	$465, SUV add $42		
8	$22				
24	$28				

helpful information

24/7	181" rule for SUV
129 spaces	Damage inspection
AE, MC, V	

---

34. **1533 York Ave** *bet York/1st, N side of E 81st*
Double Garage Corp
212.744.9669

hr	rate*	specials	rate	enter	exit
1	$9	AM 7D	$10	6-10am	6pm
3	$13	PM 7D	$10	after 6pm	1hr, by 6am
6	$15	PM 7D	$16	after 6pm	3hr, by 6am
24	$26	PM 7D	$26	after 6pm	24hr, by 6am
		F,Sa	$11		
		add'l 1/2hr	$4		
		SUV	$10		
		Month	$380, SUV add $60		

helpful information

24/7	Cash
114 spaces	*6am-6pm, add'l 1/2 hr $4

---

35. **520 E 81st St** *bet East End/York, S side of E 81st*
520 East 81 Street Garage Corp

hr	rate	specials	rate	enter	exit

TENANT ONLY

helpful information

Cash	Self parking

36. **55 East End Ave** *bet E 81st/E 82nd, E side of East End*
Imperial   212.650.1916

hr	rate	specials	rate	enter	exit
1/2	$5	AM 7D	$8	7-11am	6pm
1	$11	SUV	$10		
2	$12	Month	$480, SUV add $100		
10	$17	Month	$200	m'cycle	
24	$34				
O/N	$34				

helpful information
24/7   AE, MC, V
110 spaces

37. **45 East End Ave** *bet E 81st/E 82nd, E side of East End*
Central   212.744.7641

hr	rate	specials	rate	enter	exit
1	$12	AM m-f	$7	7-11am	7pm
2	$13	SUV	$10		
10	$17	Month	$527, SUV add $84		
24	$38				

helpful information
24/7   AE, MC, V
77 spaces   Max bill $50

38. **1000 5th Ave** *bet E 80th/E 81st, W side of 5th, near E 80th*
Central   212.879.5500

hr	UNVALIDATED		VALIDATED	
	12am-5pm	5pm-12am	12am-5pm	5pm-12am
1	$17	$14	$15	$12
2	$22	$17	$18	$14
3	$27		$23	
5	$30	$19	$26	$16
10	$35		$35	
10am		$22		$22
close	$40		$40	
	Month	$697	Month	$697

helpful information
24/7   6'6" clearance   No vans
460 spaces   Self parking   Metropolitan Museum of Art
AE, MC, V, Dis

39. 920 Park Ave *bet Madison/Park, N side of E 80th*

Rapid Park 212.794.7245

hr	rate	specials	rate	enter	exit
1	$21	SUV	$10		
2	$30	Month	$700, SUV add $200		
4	$35	Month	$150	m'cycle	
10	$45				
24	$50				
O/N	$50				

helpful information

7D 7am-1am	AE, MC, V	Steep driveway
27 spaces	Max bill $20	

---

40. 900 Park Ave *bet Madison/Park, S side of E 80th*

Icon 212.650.1612

hr	rate	specials	rate	enter	exit
1/2	$10	SUV	$10		
1	$20	Month	$760, SUV add $84		
2	$30	Whitney	$20		3hr
10	$35				
24	$47				

helpful information

7D 7am-1am	181" rule for SUV	Elevator
61 spaces	Max bill $20	
AE, MC, V	No full size vans	

---

41. 120 E 81st St *bet Park/Lexington, N side of E 80th*

GMC 212.744.0868

hr	rate	specials	rate	enter	exit
1	$22	O/N	$47		after 5am
2	$32	SUV	$10		
10	$37	Month	$725, SUV add $100		
24	$47				

helpful information

7D 6am-2am	AE, MC, V	Max bill $50
94 spaces	5 min grace period	

---

42. 213 E 80th St *bet 3rd/2nd, N side of E 80th*

Elco 212.650.1988

hr	rate	specials	rate	enter	exit
1/2	$6	AM	$14	6-10am	6pm
1	$17	Sa,Su	$10	after 6am	6pm
2	$20	SUV	$10		
3	$24	Month	$500, SUV add $84		
10	$26				
24	$36				

helpful information

24/7	AE, MC, V
51 spaces	Max bill $20

43. 204 E 80th St *bet 3rd/2nd, S side of E 80th*
Central   212.249.8960

hr	rate	specials	rate	enter	exit
1	$19	AM	$18	6-9am	6pm
2	$24	Sa, Su	$13	all day	6pm
10	$31	SUV	$11		
24	$46	Month	$592		

helpful information

24/7	Low clearance	No vans
67 spaces	Max bill $50	
AE, MC, V, Dis	Steep driveway	

44. 239 E 79th St *bet 3rd/2nd, S side of E 80th, near 2nd*
MPG   212.535.2309

hr	rate*	specials	rate	enter	exit
1/2	$6	AM	$6	6am-10am	1/2hr
1	$10	AM	$12	6am-10am	7pm
2	$15	AM	$32	6am-10am	24hr
3	$20	SUV	$10		
MTC	$32	Month	$465, SUV add $43		
10am					
add'l $10					

helpful information

M-Th,Su 6am-12am	AE, MC, V
F-Sa 6am-2am	*M-F 10am to close
42 spaces	

45. 305 E 80th St *bet 2nd/1st, N side of E 80th*
GMC   212.628.3121

hr	rate	specials	rate	enter	exit
1/2	$7	AM 7D	$13	6-11am	7pm
1	$13	O/N	$34		after 9am
2	$19	SUV	$10		
3	$24	Month	$440, SUV add $100		
10	$29				
24	$34				

helpful information

24/7	AE, MC, V	2 elevators
233 spaces	5 min grace period	National, Alamo rental

---

46. 340 E 80th St *bet 2nd/1st, S side of E 80th*
Central   212.650.9569

hr	rate	specials	rate	enter	exit
1	$8	AM 7D	$12	6-10am	7pm
2	$12	SUV	$11		
10	$20				
24	$30				

helpful information
24/7   AE, MC, V
88 spaces

---

47. 345 E 80th St *bet 2nd/1st, N side of E 80th*
Imperial   212.472.1213

hr	rate	specials	rate	enter	exit
1/2	$5	AM	$12	6-11am	7pm
1	$7	Daily	$15	after 11am	by 7pm
2	$12	SUV	$10		
10	$20	Month	$400, SUV add $100		
24	$34				
O/N	$34				

helpful information
24/7   129 spaces   AE, MC, V

---

48. 445 E 80th St *bet 1st/York, N side of E 80th*
Cross Garage Corp   212.535.1184

hr	rate*	specials	rate	enter	exit
1	$9	AM	$10	by 11am	by 6pm
3	$13	PM	$9	6pm-6am	1hr
6	$15	PM	$14	6pm-6am	2hr
24	$25	PM	$16	6pm-6am	7hr
		M-F	$25	all day	
		SUV	$7		
		Month	$380, SUV add $50		

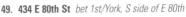

helpful information
24/7   Cash
72 spaces   *6am-6pm

---

49. 434 E 80th St *bet 1st/York, S side of E 80th*
Icon   212.650.0722

hr	rate	specials	rate	enter	exit
1	$13	AM	$10	6-11am	6pm
2	$15	Daily	$5	9am-9pm	1/2hr
3	$17	SUV	$10		
12	$22	Month	$465, O/S add $63		
24	$32				

helpful information
24/7   AE, MC, V   Max bill $20
49 spaces   181" rule for SUV

---

50. 1514 York Ave *bet E 80th/E 81st, E side of York*
Glenwood 212.650.0854

hr	rate	specials	rate	enter	exit
1	$8	AM 7D	$9	6-11am	7pm
2	$13	SUV	$5		12hr
5	$17	Month	$339	tenant, SUV add $38	
9	$21	Month	$363	non-tenant, SUV add $38	
24	$28				

helpful information

M-F 6am-2am   MC, V
Sa,Su 8am-2am   Elevator
100 spaces   181" rule for SUV

---

51. 510 E 80th St *bet York/East End, S side of E 80th*
Ulltra 212.772.9802

hr	rate	specials	rate	enter	exit
2	$13	AM	$9	6-10am	6pm
12	$17	SUV	$10		
24	$23	Month	$398, SUV add $63		
O/N	$23				

helpful information

24/7   Max bill $20
31 spaces
AE, MC, V

---

52. 511 E 80th St *bet York/East End, N side of E 80th*
Bricin Parking Corp 212.650.0904

hr	rate	specials	rate	enter	exit
1	$10	AM m-f	$8	7-10am	6pm
2	$11	Month	$397, SUV or Van add $78		
12	$16				
24	$21				

helpful information

Su-Th 7am-1am   Cash
F-Sa 7am-2am   Max bill $20
50 spaces   No vans

---

53. 525 E 80th St *bet York/East End, N side of E 80th*
MPG 212.988.0629

hr	rate*	specials	rate	enter	exit
1	$12	AM	$6	6-10am	1hr
2	$15	AM	$9	6-10am	7pm
10	$20	SUV	$10		
24	$32	Month	$401, SUV add $42		

helpful information

M-Th 6am-12am   Su 6am-1am   52 spaces
F-Sa 6am-2am   *10am-close   AE, MC, V

---

54. 10 East End Ave *bet York/East End, S side of E 80th, near East End*
Waterview Garage Corp   212.650.1027

hr	rate*	specials	rate	enter	exit
1	$5	Daily	$9	after 6:30am 8pm	
2	$7	SUV	$5		
24	$23	Month	$435		
O/N	$23				

helpful information

Su-Th 6am-1am	Cash
F-Sa 24hr	Steep driveway
60 spaces	*after 8pm

---

55. 30 East End Ave *bet E 80th/E 81th, W side of East End*
Imperial   212.717.5747

hr	rate	specials	rate	enter	exit
1/2	$5	AM 7D	$9	6:30-11am	7pm
1	$10	O/N	$30		
2	$14	SUV	$10		
24	$30	Month	$400, SUV add $100		
MTC	$17				

helpful information

Su-Th 6:30am-1am	AE, MC, V	Max bill $20
F-Sa 6:30am-2am	Lifts	
51 spaces	Eff. 10/05	

---

56. 980 5th Ave *bet Madison/5th, N side of E 79th, near 5th*
980 5th Ave Corp   212.650.1579

hr	rate	specials	rate	enter	exit
1	$16	SUV	$10		
2	$21	Month	$700, Luxury add $200		
10	$30				
24	$42				

helpful information

7D 7am-12am	Elevator
100 spaces	Eff. 11/03
Cash	

---

57. 301 E 79th St *bet 2nd/1st, N side of E 79th*
GMC   212.650.1936

hr	rate	specials	rate	enter	exit
1	$20	AM	$14	8-10am	6pm
2	$25	O/N	$40		after 5am
3	$30	SUV	$10		
8	$35	Month	$510, O/S add $150		
24	$40				

helpful information

24/7	AE, MC, V	Max bill $50
225 spaces	6'6" clearance	

58. 425 E 79th St *bet 1st/York, N side of E 79th*

Ulltra   212.650.1275

hr	rate*	specials	rate	enter	exit
1	$13	AM 7D	$16	6-10am	6pm
2	$18	Sa,Su	$12		1hr
10	$26	Sa,Su	$18		2hr
24	$36	Sa,Su	$28		9hr
O/N	$36	Sa,Su	$37		24h or O/N
		SUV	$10		
		Month	$334	shareholder, O/S add $68	
		Month	$431	non-shareholder, O/S add $68	

helpful information

24/7	AE, MC, V	6'5" clearance
99 spaces	Eff. 3/07	*M-F

---

59. 505 E 79th St *bet York/East End, N side of E 79th*

MPG   212.737.6930

hr	rate*	specials	rate	enter	exit
1/2	$4	AM 7D	$4	6-10am	1/2hr
1	$12	AM 7D	$12	6-10am	7pm
2	$15	AM 7D	$32	6-10am	24hr
10	$20	SUV	$10		
24	$32	Month	$444, O/S add $42		

helpful information

24/7	AE, MC, V
57 spaces	*7D enter 10am-6pm

---

60. 515 E 79th St *bet York/East End, N side of E 79th*

Icon   212.744.9762

hr	rate	specials	rate	enter	exit
1	$14	AM	$8	6-11am	6pm
2	$16	SUV	$10		
3	$19	Month	$506, SUV add $43		
10	$25				
24	$30				

helpful information

24/7	AE, MC, V	No full size vans
125 spaces	181" rule for SUV	

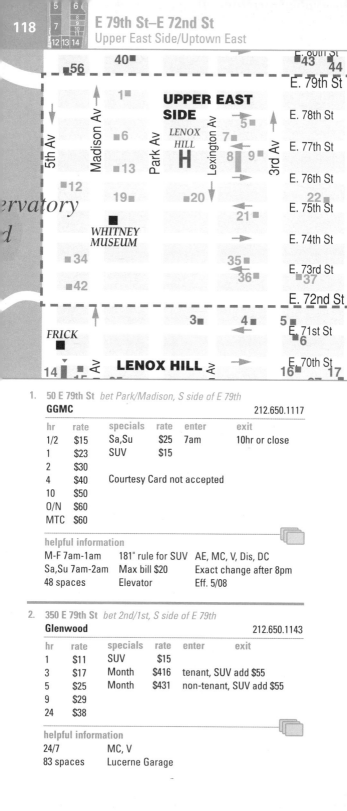

1. 50 E 79th St *bet Park/Madison, S side of E 79th*

GGMC   212.650.1117

hr	rate	specials	rate	enter	exit
1/2	$15	Sa,Su	$25	7am	10hr or close
1	$23	SUV	$15		
2	$30				
4	$40	Courtesy Card not accepted			
10	$50				
O/N	$60				
MTC	$60				

helpful information

M-F 7am-1am	181" rule for SUV	AE, MC, V, Dis, DC
Sa,Su 7am-2am	Max bill $20	Exact change after 8pm
48 spaces	Elevator	Eff. 5/08

2. 350 E 79th St *bet 2nd/1st, S side of E 79th*

Glenwood   212.650.1143

hr	rate	specials	rate	enter	exit
1	$11	SUV	$15		
3	$17	Month	$416	tenant, SUV add $55	
5	$25	Month	$431	non-tenant, SUV add $55	
9	$29				
24	$38				

helpful information

24/7	MC, V
83 spaces	Lucerne Garage

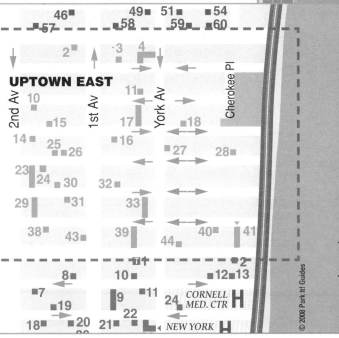

3. **404 E 79th St** *bet 1st/York, N side of E 78th, near 1st*

Flash Parking   212.249.4716

hr	rate	specials	rate	enter	exit
1	$9	PM	$10	after 6pm	10hr, by 3am
2	$14	Sa,Su	$11	6am-9am	10hr, Sun 12am
10	$18	SUV	$10		
24	$26	Month	$422, SUV add $84		

helpful information

24/7	AE, V, MC, DC	Max bill $20
73 spaces	2 elevators	

4. **450 E 79th St** *bet 1st/York, N side of E 78th or W side of York*

Rapid Park   212.650.1178

hr	rate	specials	rate	enter	exit
1/2	$9	AM	$13	4-10am	7pm
1	$15	SUV	$10		
2	$19	Month	$435, O/S add $100		
8	$25	Month	$150	m'cycle	
24	$36				
O/N	$36				
2am	$30				

helpful information

24/7	AE, MC, V	No vans
105 spaces	6'5" clearance	

5. **1356 3rd Ave** *bet Lexington/3rd, S side of E 78th, near 3rd*
   Impark 212.535.4403

hr	rate	specials	rate	enter	exit
1	$26	SUV	$22		
2	$37	Month	$781, SUV add $84		
10	$44				
24	$56				
O/N	$56				

helpful information
24/7	AE, MC, V	Max bill $20
31 spaces	Elevator	

6. **51 E 77th St** *bet Park/Madison, N side of E 77th, near Madison*
   Champion 212.535.0752

hr	rate	specials	rate	enter	exit
1/2	$25	SUV	$10		
1	$35	Month	$832, SUV add $118		
1 1/2	$45				
2	$55				
24	$65				
O/N	$65				

helpful information
24/7	AE, MC, V
113 spaces	Steep driveway

7. **165 E 77th St** *bet 3rd/Lexington, N side of E 77th*
   Rapid Park 212.288.6800

hr	rate	specials	rate	enter	exit
1/2	$10	Sa,Su	$20	6-10am	7pm
1	$27	O/N	$48		
2	$37	SUV	$10		
12	$43	Month	$595, O/S add $100		
24	$48	Lenox Hill Hospital $4-7 discount			

helpful information
24/7	AE, MC, V
200 spaces	Elevator

8. **155 E 76th St** *bet Lexington/3rd, N side of E 76th or S side of E 77th*
   Rapid Park 212.650.0732

hr	rate	specials	rate	enter	exit
1/2	$10	Sa,Su	$20	by 10am	10hr
1	$27	SUV	$10		
2	$37	Month	$600, O/S add $100		
12	$43	Month	$300	m'cycle	
24	$48				
O/N	$48				

helpful information
7D 6am-1am	AE, MC, V	Max bill $20
107 spaces	6'7" clearance	150 E 77th

9. **176 E 77th St** *bet 3rd/Lexington, S side of E 77th*
   Champion 212.650.1280

hr	rate	specials	rate	enter	exit
1/2	$15	AM m-f	$30	by 10am	12hr
1	$27	Sa,Su	$20	all day	6pm
2	$37	SUV	$10		
12	$45	Month	$570, SUV add $254		
24	$55				

helpful information
7D 7am-1am   AE, MC, V   79 spaces

---

10. **300 E 77th St** *bet 1st/2nd, S side of E 77th, near 2nd*
    Impark 212.717.1602

hr	rate	specials	rate	enter	exit
1	$18	AM	$14	6-9am	7pm
2	$24	SUV	$10		
10	$38	Month	$550, SUV add $84		
24	$43				
O/N	$43				

helpful information
24/7   AE, MC, V   Max bill $20
28 spaces   181" rule for SUV

---

11. **439 E 77th St** *bet York/1st, N side of E 77th*
    Lenox Club Garage 212.650.1398

hr	rate*	specials	rate	enter	exit
24	$30	Daily	$13	8am-4pm	6pm
6pm	$13	PM	$20	4pm-8pm	3hr
		PM	$30	4pm-8pm	24hr
		SUV	$10		
		Month	$359, SUV add $84		

helpful information
24/7   Cash, may accept credit cards at end of 2008
96 spaces   *8am-4pm   Surrey Garage

---

12. **4 E 76th St** *bet 5th/Madison, S side of E 76th*
    4 East 76th St Garage Inc 212.988.3628

hr	rate	specials	rate	enter	exit
1/2	$22	SUV	$5		
1	$35	Month	$454	rent-stabilized tenant,	
2	$51			SUV add $60	
3	$47	Month	$659	other tenant, SUV add $60	
24	$56	Month	$800	non-tenant, SUV add $60	
O/N	$56				

helpful information
Su-Th 7am-1am   AE, MC, V   Max bill $50
F-Sa 7am-2am   Eff. 4/08   Car wash
86 spaces   181" rule for SUV

13. **51 E 76th St** *bet Madison/Park, N side of E 76th*

QuikPark   212.570.7182

hr	rate	specials	rate	enter	exit
1/2	$19-25	SUV	$10		
1	$34	Month	$800, SUV add $84		
2	$54				
24	$63				

helpful information
24/7   Elevator
140 spaces   Carlyle Garage
AE, MC, V

14. **332 E 76th St** *bet 2nd/1st, S side of E 76th*

GMC   212.288.6969

hr	rate	specials	rate	enter	exit
1	$13	AM	$13	8-10am	6pm
2	$21	O/N	$36		after 5am
3	$26	SUV	$10		
10	$31	Month	$450, SUV add $100		
24	$36				

helpful information
24/7   5 min grace period   Damage inspection
290 spaces   2 elevators
AE, MC, V   Max bill $50

15. **355 E 76th St** *bet 2nd/1st, N side of E 76th*

Hertz   212.486.5929

hr	rate	specials	rate	enter	exit
1	$10	SUV	$10		
3	$13	Month	$350, O/S add $120		
12	$11-20				
24	$25				

helpful information
M-Th 6:30am-11pm   AE, MC, V
F-Su 6:30am-12am   Elevator
260 spaces

16. **402 E 76th St** *bet 1st/York, S side of E 76th*

Alliance Parking   212.472.8249

hr	rate	specials	rate	enter	exit
1/2	$6	AM	$12	by 11am	12hr
1	$14	Sa,Su	$15	anytime	12hr, by M 5am
2	$18	Event	$35		
3	$22	SUV	$10		
10	$28	Month	$465, O/S add $84		
24	$33	Month	$169	m'cycle	

helpful information
24/7   MC, V   5 min. grace period
58 spaces

17. **433 E 76th St** *bet 1st/York, N side of E 76th or S side of E 77th*
STA Parking Corp   212.737.0050, 212.737.4083

hr	rate	specials	rate	enter	exit
1/2	$6-10	AM	$14	6-11am	7pm
1	$10	AM	add'l $3	6-11am	per hr, 7pm-12am
2	$12	Sa,Su	$10	after 6am	7pm
3	$15	Sa,Su	add'l $3	after 6am	per hr, 7pm-12am
5	$19	SUV	$5		
10	$25	Month	$385, SUV add $90		
24	$30				
O/N	$30				

helpful information		
24/7	AE, MC, V	434 E 77th
90 spaces	Elevator	

---

18. **500 E 77th St** *bet York/FDR, N side of E 76th*
Glenwood   212.650.1433

hr	rate	specials	rate	enter	exit
1	$9	Sa,Su	$12	all day	6pm
2	$13	SUV	$7		12hr
5	$19	Month	$355	tenant, SUV add $38	
9	$25	Month	$389	non-tenant , SUV add $33	
24	$38				

helpful information	
24/7	MC, V
300 spaces	6'6" clearance

---

19. **35 E 75th St** *bet Park/Madison, N side of E 75th*
Rapid Park   212.650.0546

hr	rate	specials	rate	enter	exit
1/2	$25	O/N	$60		after 2am
1	$33	SUV	$10		
2	$50	Month	$750, SUV add $150		
3	$54	Month	$200	m'cycle	
8	$56				
24	$60				

helpful information	
7D 6am-2am	AE, MC, V
73 spaces	Nice interior

---

20. **115 E 75th St** *bet Lexington/Park, N side of E 75th*
GMC   212.628.5770

hr	rate	specials	rate	enter	exit
1	$32	SUV	$10		
2	$37	Month	$695, SUV add $100		
3	$47				
24	$50				
O/N	$50				

helpful information		
7D 6am-2am	AE, MC, V	Elevator
165 spaces	5 min grace period	Max bill $50

---

21. 196 E 75th St *bet 3rd/Lexington, S side of E 75th, near 3rd*

The Berger's Parking Corporation   212.650.1841

hr	rate	specials	rate	enter	exit
1	$20	SUV	$10		
2	$30	Month	$570, SUV add $50		
O/N	$45				

TENANT ONLY

helpful information

7D 7am-1am	Cash	Some casual parking
27 spaces	Very steep driveway	

---

22. 1441 2nd Ave *bet 2nd/3rd, N side of E 75th, near 2nd*

Icon   212.650.1999

hr	rate	specials	rate	enter	exit
1/2	$7	AM m-f	$13	8-10am	6pm
1	$16	Sa,Su	$14	after 6am	6pm
2	$20	SUV	$10		
3	$25	Month	$507, SUV add $84		
24	$34				

helpful information

24/7	181" rule for SUV	245 E 75th
70 spaces	Max bill $20	
AE, MC, V	Short, steep driveway	

---

23. 300 E 75th St *bet 1st/2nd, N side of E 74th or S side of E 75th*

Arwin   212.650.1416

hr	rate	specials	rate	enter	exit
1/2	$9	AM	$14	6-10:30am	7pm
1	$13	Sa,Su	$11	after 7am	7:30pm
2	$16	SUV	$7		14hr
5	$21	Month	$368	tenant, O/S add $38	
10	$27	Month	$433	non-tenant, O/S add $38	
24	$36				

helpful information

24/7	181" rule for SUV
177 spaces	
AE, MC, V	

---

24. 330 E 75th St *bet 1st/2nd, S side of E 75th*

Icon   212.650.1826

hr	rate	specials	rate	enter	exit
1/2	$7	AM	$12	8-10am	6pm
1	$15	Day	$17	10am-6pm	6pm
2	$21	SUV	$10		
10	$30	Month	$507, SUV add $84		
24	$40				

helpful information

24/7	181" rule for SUV
69 spaces	
AE, MC, V	

25. 333 E 75th St *bet 1st/2nd, N side of E 75th*

Jim Dandy 212.249.4794

hr	rate	specials	rate	enter	exit
1	$15	AM	$13	6-11am	8pm
2	$20	PM	$13	after 4pm	12am
10	$26	SUV	$10		
24	$33	Month	$443, SUV add $42		
MTC	$30				

helpful information
M-F 7am-12am   AE, MC, V, Dis, DC
Sa,Su,Hol may open   Steep driveway
25 spaces

---

26. 370 E 76th St *bet 1st/2nd, N side of E 75th*

Champion 212.734.9593

hr	rate	specials	rate	enter	exit
1	$19	Day	$14	4am-6pm	8pm
2	$23	PM 7D	$13	after 4pm	2am
3	$27	SUV	$10		
24	$25-35	Month	$495, SUV add $84		
O/N	$35				

helpful information
24/7   AE, MC, V
104 spaces   341 E 75th

---

27. 1420 York Ave *bet 76th/75th, E side of York*

Ulltra 212.249.2940

hr	rate	specials	rate	enter	exit
1/2	$6	AM	$14	6-11am	7pm
1	$14	Sa,Su	$12	7am-7pm	
2	$17	SUV	$10		
12	$26	Month	$475, SUV add $63		
24	$32				
O/N	$32				

helpful information
24/7
28 spaces
AE, MC, V

---

28. 530 E 76th St *bet York/FDR, N side of E 75th*

Kinney 212.517.4229

hr	rate	specials	rate	enter	exit
1	$18	SUV	$10		
2	$23	Month	$658		
10	$30				
24	$40				

helpful information
24/7   MC, V   Max bill $50
23 spaces   Elevator

29. **300 E 74th St** *bet 2nd/1st, N side of E 73rd or S side of E 74th*
GGMC 212.650.1274

hr	rate	specials	rate	enter	exit
1	$15	AM	$15	6-10am	7pm
2	$19	SUV	$10		
10	$29	Month	$550, O/S add $150		
24	$48				
O/N	$48				

helpful information
24/7 — 6'3" clearance
94 spaces — No vans
AE, MC, V, Dis, DC — Nice interior

30. **319 E 74th St** *bet 2nd/1st, N side of E 74th*
Mega Parking Systems, Inc 212.650.1339

hr	rate	specials	rate	enter	exit
10	$15	M-F	$15		10hr, No O/N
24	$26	Sa,Su	$12	anytime	10hr
		SUV	$10		
		Month	$390		

helpful information
Su-Th 7am-1am — Cash
F-Sa 7am-2am — Nice interior
57 spaces — Takes vans, 4x4

31. **340 E 74th St** *bet 2nd/1st, S side of E 74th*
Fanda Parking LLC 212.249.4724

hr	rate	specials	rate	enter	exit
1	$14	AM	$14	6-11am	6pm
10	$16	Sa,Su	$10		10hr
24	$27	Event	$30		
MTC	$24	SUV	$10		
		Month	$441, SUV add $42		
		Month	$125	m'cycle	

helpful information
7D 7am-1am — Cash — Eff. 6/08
38 spaces — Car wash

32. **401 E 74th St** *bet 1st/York, N side of E 74th*
74th Street Parking LLC 212.288.3025

hr	rate	specials	rate	enter	exit
1	$16	M-F	$12	after 9am	5pm
2	$19	SUV	$5		
3	$22				
5	$25				
12	$29				
24	$36				

helpful information
24/7 — Cash — Eff. 6/06
61 spaces — 5 min grace period — 6'8" clearance

33. **1377 York Ave** *bet 1st/York, N side of E 73rd or S side of E 74th, near York*

Glenwood   212.650.1299

hr	rate	specials	rate	enter	exit
1	$15	AM	$17	6-10am	7:30pm
2	$17	Sa,Su	$11	after 6am	7:30pm
5	$26	SUV	$7		12hr
9	$28	Month	$355	tenant, SUV add $42	
24	$44	Month	$389	non-tenant, SUV add $42	

helpful information

24/7	181" rule for SUV
150 spaces	Eff. 5/07
MC, V	

34. **923 5th Ave** *bet Madison/5th, N side of E 73rd*

MPG   212.249.1947

hr	rate*	specials	rate	enter	exit
1	$22	Sa,Su	$10		1/2hr
1 1/2	$32	Sa,Su	$22		12hr
2	$37	Sa,Su	$35		close
MTC	$45	SUV	$10		
		Month	$718, SUV add $84		

helpful information

7D 7am-12am	AE, MC, V	*7am-close
73 spaces	Hard to see from street	

35. **177 E 73rd St** *bet 3rd/Lexington, N side of E 73rd*

GMC   212.288.1798

hr	rate	specials	rate	enter	exit
1	$20	O/N	$45		after 5am
2	$27	SUV	$10		
8	$35	Month	$690, O/S add $150		
24	$45				

helpful information

24/7	AE, MC, V	Elevator
115 spaces	5 min grace period	Max bill $50

36. **165 E 72nd St** *bet Lexington/3rd, S side of E 73rd, near 3rd*

Imperial   212.744.0264

hr	rate	specials	rate	enter	exit
1/2	$9	AM	$23	6-10am	7pm
1	$18	PM m-f	$15	after 5pm	12am
2	$24	Sa,Su	$15	anytime	12hr, No O/N
8	$30	SUV	$10		
24	$42	Month	$650, SUV add $100		
O/N	$42				

helpful information

24/7	AE, MC, V	Max bill $20
35 spaces	Elevator	Imperial coupons

37. 202 E 73rd St *bet 2nd/3rd, S side of E 73rd, near 3rd*

Kinney 212.650.1417

hr	rate	specials	rate	enter	exit
1	$20	SUV	$11		
2	$26	Month	$550, SUV add $84		
10	$31	MOnth	$168	m'cycle	
24	$45				

helpful information

7D 7am-1am	AE, MC, V	No vans
65 spaces	1257 3rd Ave	Low clearance

38. 315 E 72nd St *bet 1st/2nd, S side of E 73rd*

Icon 212.650.9416

hr	rate	specials	rate	enter	exit
1/2	$7	AM m-f	$15	7-11am	6pm
1	$17	Sa,Su	$12	6am-5pm	5pm
2	$24	SUV	$10		
10	$32	Month	$422	shareholder tenant, SUV add $84	
24	$40	Month	$507	non-tenant, SUV add $84	

helpful information

24/7	AE, MC, V	Max bill $50
60 spaces	181" rule for SUV	

39. 1353 York Ave *bet 1st/York, N side of E 72nd or S side of E 73rd, near York*

Glenwood 212.650.0911

hr	rate	specials	rate	enter	exit
1/2	$9	AM	$17	6-9am	7pm
1	$16	SUV	$7		12hr
3	$23	Month	$380	tenant, SUV add $42	
5	$27	Month	$422	non-tenant, SUV add $42	
9	$29				
12	$37				
24	$42				

helpful information

24/7	AE, MC, V	Somerset Garage
235 spaces	Eff. 5/07	

40. 524 E 73rd St *bet York/FDR, S side of E 73rd*

Icon 212.988.4596

hr	rate	specials	rate	enter	exit
1	$13	AM	$18	4-10am	6pm
2	$19	AM	$27	4-10am	10pm
10	$26	SUV	$10		
24	$31	Month	$380, SUV add $106		
		Month	$211	m'cycle	

helpful information

24/7	AE, MC, V	Car wash
320 spaces	2 elevators	

41. 525 E 72nd St *bet York/FDR, N side of E 72nd or S side of E 73rd, main entrance on E 73rd*

Central 212.650.9887

hr	rate	specials	rate	enter	exit
1	$12	AM m-f	$19	4-10am	12am
2	$23	SUV	$10		
12	$29	Month	$389, SUV add $76		
24	$35				

helpful information

24/7	AE, MC, V	E 72nd not always open
146 spaces	Boom gate at entrance	

---

42. 910 5th Ave *bet Madison/5th, N side of E 72nd*

Imperial 212.650.9262

hr	rate	specials	rate	enter	exit
1	$25	Sa,Su	$16	all day	
2	$30	SUV	$12		
10	$40	Month	$750, SUV add $100		
24	$50				
O/N	$50				

helpful information

Su-Th 7am-1:30am	56 spaces	Max bill $50
F-Sa 7am-2am	AE, MC, V	No full size vans

---

43. 355 E 72nd St *bet E 72nd/E 73rd, W side of 1st*

Imperial 212.396.9714

hr	rate	specials	rate	enter	exit
1/2	$10	AM m-f	$15	7-10am	7pm
1	$16	PM	$10	6pm-2am	4hr
2	$19	Sa,Su	$10	anytime	6pm
3	$24	SUV	$10		
10	$29	Month	$425, SUV add $100		
24	$35				
O/N	$35				

helpful information

7D 7am-2am	AE, MC, V	Eff. 7/07
31 spaces	5'8" clearance	

---

44. 515 E 72nd St *bet York/Dead End-river, N side of E 72nd*

Icon 212.249.8196

hr	rate	specials	rate	enter	exit
1	$20	SUV	$10		
2	$28	Month	$507, SUV add $84		
12	$36				
24	$45				

helpful information

24/7	AE, MC, V	Max bill $50
130 spaces	181" rule for SUV	No full size vans

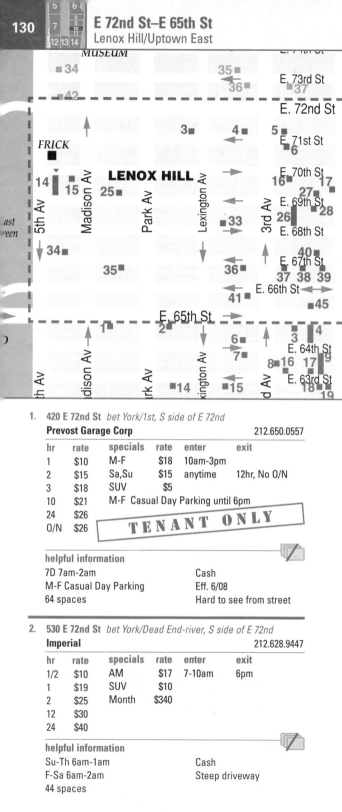

---

1. **420 E 72nd St** *bet York/1st, S side of E 72nd*

Prevost Garage Corp 212.650.0557

hr	rate	specials	rate	enter	exit
1	$10	M-F	$18	10am-3pm	
2	$15	Sa,Su	$15	anytime	12hr, No O/N
3	$18	SUV	$5		
10	$21	M-F Casual Day Parking until 6pm			
24	$26				
O/N	$26				

TENANT ONLY

helpful information

7D 7am-2am	Cash
M-F Casual Day Parking	Eff. 6/08
64 spaces	Hard to see from street

---

2. **530 E 72nd St** *bet York/Dead End-river, S side of E 72nd*

Imperial 212.628.9447

hr	rate	specials	rate	enter	exit
1/2	$10	AM	$17	7-10am	6pm
1	$19	SUV	$10		
2	$25	Month	$340		
12	$30				
24	$40				

helpful information

Su-Th 6am-1am	Cash
F-Sa 6am-2am	Steep driveway
44 spaces	

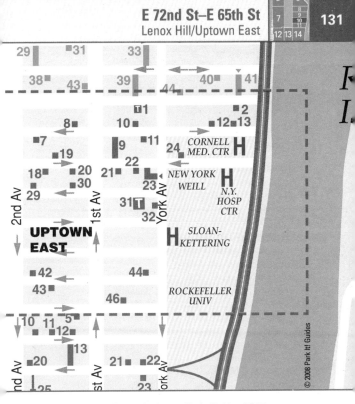

3. **135 E 71st St** *bet Lexington/Park, N side of E 71st*
   GMC   212.879.1801

hr	rate	specials	rate	enter	exit
1	$25	SUV	$10		
2	$35	Month	$790, SUV add $100		
3	$40				
24	$50				
O/N	$50				

helpful information

7D 6am-1am	5 min grace period	Hard to see from street
54 spaces	Max bill $50	Very steep driveway
AE, MC, V		

4. **191 E 71st St** *bet 3rd/Lexington, N side of E 71st*
   GMC   212.249.1090

hr	rate	specials	rate	enter	exit
1	$25	O/N	$45		after 5am
2	$30	SUV	$10		
8	$40	Month	$695, SUV add $100		
24	$45				

helpful information

7D 6am-2am	5 min grace period	Max bill $50
62 spaces	Elevator	No vans
AE, MC, V		

---

5. **203 E 71st St** *bet 2nd/3rd, N side of E 71st, near 3rd*
GMC 212.249.5514

hr	rate	specials	rate	enter	exit
1	$22	O/N	$42		after 5am
2	$29	SUV	$10		
8	$37	Month	$595, SUV add $100		
24	$42				

helpful information
24/7	AE, MC, V
98 spaces	2 elevators

---

6. **211 E 70th St** *bet 2nd/3rd, S side of E 71st, near 3rd*
71st St Garden Garage Inc 212.744.3630

hr	rate	specials	rate	enter	exit
1/2	$9	SUV	$5		
1	$17	Month	$379	rent-stabilized tenant	
2	$23	Month	$519	other tenant	
8	$30	Month	$590	non-tenant	
24	$38				
O/N	$38				

helpful information
Su-Th 7am-1am	MC, V	181" rule for SUV
F-Sa 7am-2am	Max bill $50	Eff. 4/08
150 spaces		

---

7. **300 E 71st St** *bet 1st/2nd, S side of E 71st, near 2nd*
Champion 212.737.4983

hr	rate	specials	rate	enter	exit
1/2	$7-13	AM	$18	6-10am	7pm
1	$17	Sa,Su	$10		10hr, no O/N
2	$21	SUV	$10		
3	$27	Month	$460 , SUV add $84		
24	$35				
O/N	$35				

helpful information
24/7	57 spaces	AE, MC, V	181" rule for SUV

---

8. **355 E 71st St** *bet 1st/2nd, N side of E 71st*
Sylvan 212.650.9725

hr	rate	specials	rate	enter	exit
1	$17	AM	$18	6-9:30am	9pm
2	$20	PM	$17	after 5pm	6am
3	$26	Sa,Su	$17	after 6am	6pm
8	$32	O/N	$40		after 6am
24	$40	SUV	$15		
		Month	$515, SUV add $135		
		Month	$150	m'cycle	

helpful information
24/7	AE, MC, V
268 spaces	Takes 10% coupons

9. 400 E 71st St *bet 1st/York, N side of E 70th or S side of E 71st*
QuikPark   212.650.1061

hr	rate	specials	rate	enter	exit
1/2	$7	PM m-f	$14	after 5:30pm	12am
1	$21	Sa,Su	$16	anytime	12hr, by 12am
2	$26	SUV	$10		
3	$30	Month	$405		
10	$40				
24	$43				

helpful information

24/7	AE, MC, V	6'8" clearance
180 spaces	Max bill $20	181" rule for SUV

---

10. 422 E 72nd St *bet York/1st, N side of E 71st*
Icon   212.288.6874

hr	rate	specials	rate	enter	exit
1/2	$8	Sa,Su	$14	after 6am	6pm
1	$22	SUV	$10		
2	$27	Month	$507, SUV add $84		
10	$36	Month	$169	m'cycle	
24	$45				

helpful information

24/7	AE, MC, V	No full size vans
77 spaces	181" rule for SUV	

---

11. 426 E 71st St *bet York/1st, S side of E 71st, near York*
Rapid Park   212.746.1977

hr	rate*	specials	rate	enter	exit
1/2	$12	SUV	$10		
1	$16	Month	$374 NYPH staff only		
2	$24				
4	$25				
6	$28				
12	$32				

helpful information

24/7	Cash	Eff. 1/08
174 spaces	Accept vans	Max bill $50

---

12. 517 E 71st St *bet York/Dead End-river, N side of E 71st*
MPG

hr	rate*	specials	rate	enter	exit
1	$25	PM m-f	$10	4pm-close	1/2hr
2	$35	PM m-f	$16	4pm-close	close
MTC	$40	Sa,Su	$10	all day	1/2hr
		Sa,Su	$20	all day	close
		SUV	$10		
		Month	$400, SUV add $84		

helpful information

M-Sa 6am-12am	*M-F 6am-4pm	AE, MC, V
Su 7am-12am	50 spaces	

13. 525 E 71st St *bet York Ave/river, N side of E 71st*
Central 212.650.1688

hr	rate	specials	rate	enter	exit
1/2	$16	SUV	$10		
1	$21				
2	$25				
4	$29				
8	$33				
24	$37				

helpful information
24/7   AE, MC, V   Hospital for Special Surgery
248 spaces   Eff. 12/00   6'8" clearance

---

14. 880 5th Ave *bet 5th/Madison, N side of E 69th or S side of E 70th*
Chelnik 212.988.9130

hr	rate	specials	rate	enter	exit
1	$28	SUV	$5		
2	$32	Month	$800, SUV add $51		
10	$42				
24	$50				

helpful information
24/7   AE, MC, V, DC
127 spaces   May take large SUV

---

15. 10 E 70th St *bet 5th/Madison, S side of E 70th*

212.535.9866

hr	rate	specials	rate	enter	exit
1	$20	O/S	$30	after 7pm	
2	$24	SUV	$5		
5	$27	Month	$528 non-tenant		
24hr	$45				

helpful information
7am-7pm   MC, V   Hard to see entrance
24 spaces   No O/S cars or full size vans

---

16. 200 E 70th St *bet 3rd/2nd, S side of E 70th, near 3rd*
Imperial 212.535.5908

hr	rate	specials	rate	enter	exit
1/2	$8	AM m-f	$19	6-9am	6pm
1	$16	PM	$18	after 5pm	12am
2	$20	Sa,Su	$18		12hr, by 12am
2 1/2	$25	SUV	$10		
10	$28	Month	$500, SUV add $100		
24	$32				

helpful information
24/7   72 spaces   MC, V

17. 233 E 69th St *bet E 69th/E 70th, W side of 2nd*

Gemat Parking Corp　　　　　　　　　212.639.1454

hr	rate	specials	rate	enter	exit
1	$11	AM	$18	6-10am	7pm
2	$18	SUV	$11		
10	$23	Month	$445		
24	$30				
O/N	$30				

helpful information

7D 6am-1am	Cash	181" rule for SUV
53 spaces	Eff. 9/06	Takes large vans, pickups

18. 302 E 70th St *bet 2nd/1st, S side of E 70th*

Icon　　　　　　　　　　　　　　　212.650.1930

hr	rate	specials	rate	enter	exit
1/2	$7	Sa,Su	$7		1/2hr
1	$22	Sa,Su	$16		10hr
2	$25	Sa,Su	$26		12hr
12	$34	Sa,Su	$43		24hr
24	$43	SUV	$10		
		Month	$507, SUV add $84		

helpful information

24/7	AE, MC, V	No full size vans
44 spaces	181" rule for SUV	

19. 309 E 70th St *bet 1st/2nd, N side of E 70th*

Imperial　　　　　　　　　　　　　212.879.5434

hr	rate	specials	rate	enter	exit
1/2	$6	AM	$17	5-9am	7pm
1	$13	Daily	$18	10am-3pm	
2	$17	Sa,Su	$15	after 6am	12hr, by 12am
3	$23	SUV	$10		
10	$25	Month	$400	tenant, SUV add $100	
24	$30	Month	$500	non-tenant, SUV add $100	
O/N	$30				

helpful information

24/7	AE, MC, V
49 spaces	Eff. 5/08

---

20. 330 E 70th St *bet 1st/2nd, S side of E 70th*

May Parking Corp 212.734.0142

hr	rate	specials	rate	enter	exit
1/2	$6	AM	$17	6-9:30am	7pm
1	$12	O/N	$32		
2	$20	Daily	$22	after 10am	3pm
3	$23	SUV	$7		
10	$25	Month	$450, SUV add $16		
24	$32	Month	$211	m'cycle	

helpful information

24/7	AE, MC, V	25 spaces

---

21. 400 E 70th St *bet 1st/York, S side of E 70th*

GMC 212.794.9173

hr	rate	specials	rate	enter	exit
1	$25	Sa,Su	$15	anytime	12hr
2	$30	O/N	$50		after 5am
3	$35	SUV	$10		
10	$45	Month	$425, SUV add $100		
24	$50				

helpful information

7D 6am-2am	5 min grace period	Max bill $50	AE, MC, V
56 spaces	7'2" clearance	No vans	

---

22. 430 E 70th St *bet 1st/York, S side of E 70th*

Rapid Park 212.746.0908

hr	rate	specials	rate	enter	exit
1/2	$10	SUV	$0		
1	$15				
2	$20	Monthly only for CUMC staff & students			
4	$22				
8	$25				
24	$30				

helpful information

24/7	Cash	Max bill $100
180 spaces	Lift	Eff. 6/07

---

23. 525 E 68th St *bet 70th/69th, W side of York*

Rapid Park 212.746.1886

hr	rate	specials	rate	enter	exit
1/2	$10	O/N	$30		
1	$15	Month	$327		
2	$20	Month	$210	commuter	
4	$22				
8	$25				
12	$30				

helpful information

24/7	Accept vans
AE, MC, V	Weill Greenberg Pavillion

24. 507 E 70th St *bet York Ave/Dead End-river, N side of E 70th*
Rapid Park   212.746.1974

hr	rate	specials	rate	enter	exit
1/2	$12	PM	$14	after 5pm	1am
1	$16	SUV	$10		
2	$24	Month*	$374, SUV add $25		
4	$25				
8	$28				
24	$32				

helpful information

24/7	6'6" clearance	*New York Presbyterian
175 spaces	Eff. 1/08	Hospital staff only
Cash		

---

25. 700 Park Ave *bet Park/Madison, N side of E 69th*
Chelnik   212.744.4750

hr	rate	specials	rate	enter	exit
1	$28	SUV	$10		
2	$32	Month	$947		
8	$42				
24	$50				

helpful information

24/7	51 spaces	AE, MC, V	Elevator

---

26. 200 E 69th St *bet 2nd/3rd, N side of E 68th or S side of E 69th*
Kingdom   212.744.2277

hr	rate	specials	rate	enter	exit
1/2	$10	AM	$21	6-10am	6pm
1	$19	Sa,Su	$17	anytime	12hr
2	$25	SUV large	$10		
3	$27				
4	$35				
24	$43				

helpful information

24/7	Takes all SUV
200 spaces	Surcharge only for large SUV
AE, MC, V	

---

27. 219 E 69th St *bet 2nd/3rd, N side of E 69th, near 2nd*
219 Garage Corp   212.717.4817

hr	rate	specials	rate	enter	exit
1/2	$8	AM	$18	6-10am	7pm
1	$10	SUV	$10		
3	$18	Month	$495, SUV add $48		
10	$22				
12am	$32				

helpful information

Su-Th 6am-12am	AE, MC, V
F-Sa 6am-2am	
52 spaces	

28. **222 E 69th St** *bet 2nd/3rd, S side of E 69th, near 2nd*

222 East 69th Garage Corp 212.650.1672

hr	rate	specials	rate	enter	exit
1	$12	SUV	$5		
2	$22	Month	$379	rent-stabilized tenant	
10	$29	Month	$512	other tenant	
24	$35	Month	$617	non-tenant	
O/N	$35				

helpful information

Su-Th 7am-1am   MC, V
F-Sa 7am-2am   181" rule for SUV
157 spaces   Eff. 4/08

---

29. **301 E 69th St** *bet 1st/2nd, N side of E 69th, near 2nd*

Central 212.517.2823

hr	rate	specials	rate	enter	exit
1/2	$8	Sa,Su	$19		12hr
1	$18	SUV	$11		
2	$20	Month	$507, SUV add $84		
10	$26	Month	$169	m'cycle	
24	$40				
O/N	$40				

helpful information

Su-Th 7am-2am   40 spaces
F-Sa 7am-3am   AE, MC, V

---

30. **333 E 69th St** *bet 1st/2nd, N side of E 69th, near 1st*

333 Garage Corp 212.650.1529

hr	rate	specials	rate	enter	exit
1	$10	M-F	$18	after 10am	3pm
2	$15	Sa,Su	$15	anytime	12hr, No O/N
3	$18	SUV large	$5		
18	$21	Month	$450	tenant	
24	$30				
O/N	$30				

helpful information

7D 7am-1am   Cash   Eff. 1/06
67 spaces   Hard to see from street

---

31. *bet York/1st, S side of E 69th*

Rapid Park

hr	rate	specials	rate	enter	exit

TENANT ONLY
FOR NYPH

helpful information

6'8" clearance
New York Presbyterian Hospital

32. 1285 York Ave *bet E 68th/E 69th, W side of York*
Rapid Park 212.746.1979

hr	rate	specials	rate	enter	exit
1/2	$12	SUV	$10		
1	$16	Month	$374	NYPH staff only, SUV add $25	
2	$24				
4	$25				
8	$28				
24	$32				

helpful information

7D 7am–12am	Elevator	Damage inspection
77 spaces	Eff. 1/08	Phipps House Garage
Cash	Max bill $20	

---

33. 155 E 68th St *bet Lexington/3rd, N side of E 68th*
Imperial House Parking LLC 212.439.1770

hr	rate	specials	rate	enter	exit
2	$25	AM	$18	6–8:30am	7pm
10	$33	SUV	$10		
24	$39	Event	$40		
		Month	$697		

helpful information

24/7	AE, MC, V	No vans/trucks
139 spaces	Bumper guards	Eff. 5/08

---

34. 860 5th Ave *bet Madison/5th, N side of E 67th*
Imperial 212.650.0996

hr	rate	specials	rate	enter	exit
1/2	$11	AM m-f	$26	4–11am	7pm
1	$28	Sa,Su	$26	after 7am	8pm or 12hr
2	$32	Event	$50		10pm
10	$42	SUV	$10		
24	$52	Month	$850, SUV add $100		
O/N	$52				

helpful information

Su-F 7am–1am	96 spaces	Max bill $20
Sa 7am–2am	AE, MC, V	Bumper guards $50

---

35. 650 Park Ave *bet Park/Madison, S side of E 67th*
Imperial 212.472.2596

hr	rate	specials	rate	enter	exit
1/2	$11	AM m-f	$26	6–10am	7pm
1	$28	SUV	$10		
2	$32	Month	$750, SUV add $100		
10	$42	Parade/Event	$50		
24	$51				
O/N	$51				

helpful information

Su-Th 6am–1am	79 spaces	Elevator
F-Sa 6am–2am	AE, MC, V	

---

36. 166 E 67th St *bet 3rd/Lexington, S side of E 67th*
GGMC   212.628.0620

hr	rate	specials	rate	enter	exit
1/2	$8	AM m-f	$16	6-10am	7pm
1	$20	PM	$12	after 5pm	12am
2	$23	Sa,Su	$13	anytime	12hr, by 12am
3	$28	SUV	$10		
24	$35	Month	$550, SUV add $100		

helpful information
24/7	Max bill $20	Eff. 4/08
120 spaces	Steep driveway	
AE, MC, V	Booth at top of driveway	

---

37. 202 E 67th St *bet 2nd/3rd, S side of E 67th*
Champion   212.861.4160

hr	rate	specials	rate	enter	exit
1/2	$15	AM	$18	3-11am	7pm
1	$17	Sa,Su	$11	anytime	12hr, No O/N
2	$23	SUV	$10		
10	$27	Month	$465, SUV add $84		
24	$35				
O/N	$35				

helpful information
24/7	106 spaces	AE, MC, V

---

38. 220 E 67th St *bet 2nd/3rd, S side of E 67th*
Parking Guys   212.249.4752

hr	rate	specials	rate	enter	exit
1	$16	AM	$17	6-9am	6pm
2	$22	SUV	$10		
10	$27	Month	$456, SUV add $84		
24	$35				

helpful information
24/7	AE, MC, V	Max bill $20
39 spaces	6' clearance	

---

39. 1261 2nd Ave *bet 2nd/3rd, S side of E 67th, near 2nd*
Central   212.650.0702

hr	rate	specials	rate	enter	exit
1	$17	AM m-f	$19	2-10am	12am
2	$26	Sa,Su	$13		10hr
10	$31	SUV	$10		
24	$36	Month	$427, SUV add $76		

helpful information
24/7	6'6" clearance	250 E 67th
197 spaces	Max bill $50	265 Garage
AE, MC, V	Boom gate at entrance	

40. **254 E 68th St** *bet 2nd/3rd, N side of E 67th, near 2nd*
67th St & 2nd Ave Garage Inc 212.861.3603

hr	rate	specials	rate	enter	exit
1	$17	SUV	$5		
2	$24	Month	$379	rent-stabilized tenant	
10	$29	Month	$461	other tenant	
24	$36	Month	$484	non-tenant	
O/N	$36				

helpful information

Su-Th 7am-1am	181" rule for SUV	AE, MC, V
F-Sa 7am-2am	No vans/trucks	Eff. 4/08
150 spaces	Low clearance	

---

41. **181 E 65th St** *bet 3rd/Lexington, S side of E 66th, near 3rd*
MPG

hr	rate*	specials	rate	enter	exit
1/2	$8	Sa,Su	$8		1/2hr
1	$18	Sa,Su	$18		10hr
3	$28	Sa,Su	$40		24hr
10	$32	PM m-f	$8	4pm-12am	1/2hr
24	$40	PM m-f	$15	4pm-12am	2am
		PM m-f	$40	4pm-12am	24hr
		SUV	$10		
		Month	$591, SUV add $84		

helpful information

24/7	AE, MC, V	Hard to see from street
70 spaces	Elevator	*M-F enter 12am-4pm

---

42. **301 E 66th St** *bet 1st/2nd, N side of E 66th, near 2nd*
Kinney 212.744.5511

hr	rate	specials	rate	enter	exit
1	$18	Sa,Su	$14	anytime	12hr
2	$20	SUV	$11		
10	$26	Month	$528, SUV add $84		
24	$40	Month	$169	m'cycle	

helpful information

M-Th 6:30am-1am	Su 7am-12:30am	Max bill $50
F-Sa 6:30am-1am	70 spaces	AE, MC, V, Dis, DC

---

43. **322 E 66th St** *bet 1st/2nd, S side of E 66th*
GMC 212.570.1732

hr	rate	specials	rate	enter	exit
1	$20	Sa,Su	$14	after 6am	by 6pm
2	$27	SUV	$10		
8	$32	Month	$475, SUV add $100		
24	$40				
O/N	$40				

helpful information

7D 6am-2am	AE, MC, V	5 min grace period
50 spaces	Max bill $50	

44. 1231 York Ave *bet York/1st, N side of E 66th*
Memorial Sloan Kettering   212.639.2338

hr	rate	specials	rate	enter	exit
1	$8	SUV	$0		
2	$14				
8	$19				
24	$32				

helpful information
24/7	Eff. 9/05	433 E 66th
263 spaces	Memorial Sloan Kettering	
MC, V	Boom gate at entrance	

---

45. 200 E 66th St *bet 3rd/2nd, N side of E 65th, near 2nd*
Central   212.644.7413

hr	rate	specials	rate	enter	exit
1/2	$5	AM m-f	$15	5-10am	12hr
1	$17	PM	$11	4pm-6am	6am
2	$19	Sa,Su	$13	6am-4pm	12hr
12	$27	SUV	$15		
24	$35	Month	$423, SUV add $84		
		Month	$211	m'cycle	

helpful information
24/7	6'6" clearance
255 spaces	Max bill $50
AE, MC, V, Dis	

---

46. 403 E 65th St *bet 1st/York, N side of E 65th*
Quik Park   212.472.7906

hr	rate	specials	rate	enter	exit
1/2	$9	AM m-f	$17	6-10am	7pm
1	$19	Sa,Su	$14		12hr
2	$21	SUV	$10		
10	$27				
24	$40				

helpful information
24/7	AE, MC, V
180 spaces	Max bill $50

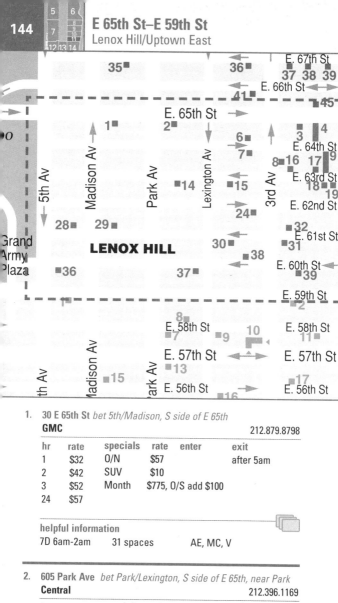

1. **30 E 65th St** *bet 5th/Madison, S side of E 65th*
   GMC   212.879.8798

hr	rate	specials	rate	enter	exit
1	$32	O/N	$57		after 5am
2	$42	SUV	$10		
3	$52	Month	$775, O/S add $100		
24	$57				

   helpful information
   7D 6am-2am   31 spaces   AE, MC, V

2. **605 Park Ave** *bet Park/Lexington, S side of E 65th, near Park*
   Central   212.396.1169

hr	rate	specials	rate	enter	exit
1	$27	SUV	$10		
2	$33	Month	$846, O/S add $211		
10	$43				
24	$56				

   helpful information
   7D 6am-1:45am   Max bill $50
   50 spaces   Hard to see from street
   MC, V

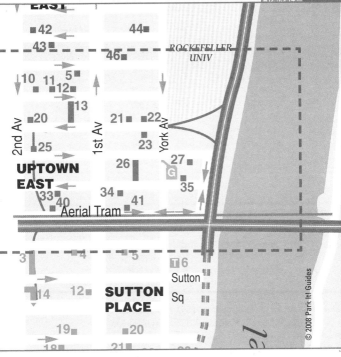

3. **200 E 65th St** *bet 3rd/2nd, S side of E 65th, near 3rd*
   Central   212.308.8421

hr	rate*	specials	rate	enter	exit
1/2	$9	AM m-f	$18	2-10am	2am
1	$18	PM m-f	$15	3pm-2am	2am
2	$20	SUV	$10		
12	$29	Month	$591		
24	$36	10 coupons	$135	AM special	
		10 coupons	$262	24hr	

helpful information

24/7	Near Sloan-Kettering	Long, steep driveway
153 spaces	Near Manhattan Eye	*Enter 2am-3pm
AE, MC, V	Ear & Throat	6'7" clearance

4. **222 E 65th St** *bet 3rd/2nd, N side of E 64th or S side of E 65th*
   Kinney   212.758.8413

hr	rate	specials	rate	enter	exit
1/2	$6	AM	$20	3-8am	6pm
1	$20	AM	$20	6-10am	6pm
2	$21	Sa,Su	$12	anytime	10hr
10	$28	SUV	$11		
24	$40	Month	$507, SUV add $84		

helpful information

24/7	6'3" clearance	Eff. 4/08
300 spaces	No vans	
AE, MC, V	The Concorde	

5. 360 E 65th St *bet 2nd/1st, S side of E 65th, near 1st*
MPG   212.535.1801

hr	rate*	specials	rate	enter	exit
1	$19	AM m-f	$17	6-8am	6pm
2	$21	AM m-f	$40	6-8am	24hr
10	$28	Sa,Su	$15	6am-6pm	7pm
24	$40	Sa,Su	$40	6am-6pm	24hr
		SUV	$10		
		Month	$444 , SUV add $148		
		Month	$211	m'cycle	

helpful information			
24/7	AE, MC, V	*enter M-F 8am-6am	
69 spaces	1189 1st Ave	*enter Sa,Su 6pm-6am	

6. 160 E 65th St *bet Lexington/3rd, N side of E 64th*
Imperial   212.861.9628

hr	rate	specials	rate	enter	exit
1/2	$7	AM	$19	4-10am	9:30am
1	$15	PM m-f	$15	after 5pm	12am
2	$21	Sa,Su	$18	7am	12hr, by 12am
10	$29	SUV	$10		
24	$37	Month	$550, O/S add $100		
O/N	$37	Month	$355	day, 4am-9pm	

helpful information			
24/7	150 spaces	AE, MC, V	Steep driveway

7. 184 E 64th St *bet Lexington/3rd, S side of E 64th*
Icon   212.355.9621

hr	rate	specials	rate	enter	exit
1/2	$6	AM	$19	6-10am	6pm
1	$17	SUV	$10		
2	$23	Month	$507, SUV add $84		
10	$30				
24	$38				

helpful information			
24/7	AE, MC, V	No vans	181" rule for SUV
100 spaces	Max bill $50	Steep, narrow driveway	

8. 1081 3rd Ave *bet E 63rd/E 64th, E side of 3rd*
Imperial   212.750.0253

hr	rate	specials	rate	enter	exit
1/2	$7	AM m-f	$18	4-10am	9pm
1	$15	PM	$15	after 5pm	12am
2	$21	Sa,Su	$16	after 6am	12hr, No O/N
10	$31	SUV	$10		
24	$36	Month	$450, O/S add $100		
O/N	$36				

helpful information			
24/7	AE, MC, V	Max bill $20	
116 spaces	Elevator	181" rule for SUV	

9. **239 E 63rd St** *bet 2nd/3rd, N side of E 63rd or S side of E 64th*
Regency Garage Corp 212.752.0485

hr	rate	specials	rate	enter	exit
1/2	$5	Sa	$10	7-11:30am	11:30pm
1	$15	Su	$10	7am-8pm	by 7pm
2	$20	O/N	$35		after 3am
8	$25	SUV	$10		
24	$35	Month	$350, O/S add $50		

helpful information
24/7	Eff. 1/07
300 spaces	6'2" clearance
AE, MC, V, Dis	Car wash

---

10. **301 E 64th St** *bet 2nd/1st, N side of E 64th, near 2nd*
301 Park Corp 212.717.8285

hr	rate	specials	rate	enter	exit
1	$9-19	AM	$15	4-10am	7pm
2	$23	PM	$22	after 5pm	by 10am
3	$29	Daily	$22	after 6am	10pm
24	$28-35	Sa,Su	$11	after 6am	12hr, No O/N
		SUV	$12		
		Month	$401, SUV add $84		

helpful information
24/7	Cash	12am gate closes
84 spaces	Max bill $20	

---

11. **327 E 64th St** *bet 2nd/1st, N side of E 64th*
Hertz 212.486.5916

hr	rate	specials	rate	enter	exit
1	$7	M-F	$15		12hr, No O/N
2	$10	SUV	$10		
24	$25	Month	$350		
		Month	$250, day, m-f 6:30am-9pm		

helpful information
M-Th 6:30am-11pm	120 spaces	Hertz
F-Su 6:30am-12am	AE, MC, V	

---

12. **337 E 64th St** *bet 2nd/1st, N side of E 64th*
GMC 212.879.9796

hr	rate	specials	rate	enter	exit
1	$17	O/N	$30		after 5am
2	$21	SUV	$10		
8	$26	Month	$425, O/S add $100		
24	$30				

helpful information
24/7	5 min grace period
300 spaces	2 elevators
AE, MC, V	

---

13. 340 E 64th St *bet 2nd/1st, N side of E 63rd or S side of E 64th*
Mutual Parking System 212.888.0637

hr	rate	specials	rate	enter	exit
1	$14	AM 7D	$16	after 8am	6pm
2	$17	O/N	$26		after 5am
8	$21	SUV	$10		
24	$26	Month	$375, O/S add $100		
		Manhattan Grill $20			3hr

helpful information
24/7   AE, MC, V   91 spaces

---

14. 124 E 63rd St *bet Lexington/Park, S side of E 63rd*
GMC 212.838.2720

hr	rate	specials	rate	enter	exit
1	$27	O/N	$50		after 5am
2	$37	SUV	$10		
3	$42	Month	$725, O/S add $200		
24	$50				

helpful information
7D 6am-2am   AE, MC, V   Very clean interior
134 spaces   Elevator

---

15. 166 E 63rd St *bet 3rd/Lexington, S side of E 63rd*
Icon 212.308.8177

hr	rate	specials	rate	enter	exit
1	$21	SUV	$10		
2	$24	Month	$422	tenant, O/S add $84	
12	$37	Month	$549	non-tenant, O/S add $84	
24	$45				

helpful information
24/7   AE, MC, V
56 spaces   181" rule for SUV

---

16. 201 E 63rd St *bet 2nd/3rd, N side of E 63rd, near 3rd*
Icon 212.750.3535

hr	rate	specials	rate	enter	exit
1/2	$8	AM m-f	$17	6-10am	7pm
1	$16	Sa,Su	$15	6am-5pm	12hr
2	$20	Sa,Su	$36	6am-5pm	24hr
12	$26	SUV	$10		
24	$36	Month	$507, O/S add $84		

helpful information
24/7   181" rule for SUV   No full size vans
100 spaces   Max bill $50   1071 3rd Ave
AE, MC, V

17. **225 E 63rd St** *bet 2nd/3rd, N side of E 63rd*
Trito Parking Parking Corp 212.935.5922

hr	rate	specials	rate	enter	exit
1/2	$5	AM	$17	6-10am	6pm
1	$12	PM	$10	after 5pm	2am
2	$17	Sa,Su	$9	anytime	4hr
3	$23	SUV	$5		
10	$29	Month	$371, O/S add $42		
24	$35				

helpful information

24/7	AE, MC, V	Steep driveway
31 spaces	Eff. 10/06	

---

18. **220 E 63rd St** *bet 2nd/3rd, S side of E 63rd*
Imperial 212.752.2178

hr	rate	specials	rate	enter	exit
1/2	$5	AM m-f	$17	6-9am	8pm
1	$10	PM	$10	after 6pm	12am
2	$15	Sa,Su	$10	after 6am	12hr, by 12am
10	$25	SUV	$10		
24	$35	Month	$350, O/S add $100		
O/N	$35				

helpful information

24/7	AE, MC, V	Eff. 11/07
93 spaces	Max bill $20	

---

19. **250 E 63rd St** *bet 2nd/3rd, S side of E 63rd*
Imperial 212.838.3965

hr	rate	specials	rate	enter	exit
1/2	$5	AM m-f	$17	6-9am	8pm
1	$10	PM	$10	after 5pm	12am
2	$15	Sa,Su	$10	after 7am	12am
10	$25	SUV	$10		
24	$35	Month	$350, O/S add $100		
O/N	$35				

helpful information

M-F 6am-12am	39 spaces	Max bill $20
Sa,Su 7am-12am	AE, MC, V	

---

20. **301 E 63rd St** *bet 1st/2nd, N side of E 63rd, near 2nd*
Champion 212.355.9054

hr	rate	specials	rate	enter	exit
1/2	$18	AM	$15	4-10am	7pm
1	$23	Sa,Su	$11	anytime	12hr, No O/N
2	$27	SUV	$10		
3	$32	Month	$401, O/S add $42		
24	$39				
O/N	$39				

helpful information

24/7	AE, MC, V	
39 spaces	181" rule for SUV	

---

21. **405 E 63rd St** *York/1st, N side of E 63rd*
Parking Guys   212.486.8613

hr	rate	specials	rate	enter	exit
1	$10	AM	$13	6-10am	8pm
2	$15	Sa,Su	$12		12hr
12	$19	SUV	$10		
24	$33	Month	$500, SUV add $84		

helpful information

7D 6am-12am 10pm gate closes York Gate Garage
39 spaces 7' clearance
Cash Max bill $20

---

22. **445 E 63rd St** *York/1st, N side of E 63rd*
GGMC   212.223.4219

hr	rate	specials	rate	enter	exit
1	$20	AM m-f	$15	6-10am	9pm
2	$17	Sa,Su	$13	after 6am	close
12	$20	SUV	$10		
MTC $36.50					

helpful information

7D 6am-12am AE, MC, V Riverhouse Garage
94 spaces 6'2" clearance 1175 York Ave

---

23. **450 E 63rd St** *bet York/1st, S side of E 63rd*
Central   212.838.5717

hr	rate	specials	rate	enter	exit
1	$15	AM m-f	$15	8-10am	9pm
2	$17	Sa,Su	$13	after 5am	12hr, by M 2am
12	$19	SUV	$10		
24	$36	Month	$528, SUV add $84		
		Month	$169	m'cycle	

helpful information

24/7 7' clearance
433 spaces Max bill $20
AE, MC, V, Dis

---

24. **162 E 62nd St** *bet Lexington/3rd, S side of E 62nd*
Enterprise 61st LLC   212.759.8333

hr	rate	specials	rate	enter	exit
1/2	$10	AM 7D	$22	5-10am	8pm
1	$21	SUV	$10		
2	$23	Month	$600		
3	$32				
12	$38				
24	$43				

helpful information

24/7 AE, MC, V Trump Plaza
128 spaces 6'9" clearance

25. 301 E 62nd St *bet 2nd/1st, N side of E 62nd*

301 E 62nd Garage Corp 646.414.4242

hr	rate	specials	rate	enter	exit
1/2	$11	SUV	$10		
1	$15	Month	$450		
2	$20				
3	$25				
24	$38				
O/N	$38				
MTC	$30				

helpful information

M-F 7am-7pm	40 spaces	Eff. 8/07
Sa, when open 9am-7pm	Cash	Max bill $50

26. 425 E 61st St *bet 1st/York, N side of E 61st or S side of E 62nd, near York*

QuikPark 212.980.6034

hr	rate	specials	rate	enter	exit
1	$12	AM	$16	6-10am	12hr
2	$17	PM m-f	$11	after 5pm	6am
10	$21	Sa,Su	$11	anytime	10hr, by 12am
24	$29	SUV	$10		
		Dangerfield's discount			

helpful information

24/7	Enterprise rental	Elevator
225 spaces	181" rule for SUV	
AE, MC, V	6:30pm-12am use lobby	

27. 510 E 62nd St *bet York/FDR, S side of E 62nd*

QuikPark 212.223.8491

hr	rate	specials	rate	enter	exit
1	$11	SUV	$5		
2	$13				
3	$15				
10	$17				
MTC	$23				

helpful information

7D 8am-12am	10' clearance	Animal Medical Center
50 spaces	Max bill $50	parking only
Cash	Outdoor under cover	

28. 800 5th Ave *bet Madison/5th, N side of E 61st*

615 Garage Corp 212.838.8869

hr	rate	specials	rate	enter	exit
1	$29	SUV	$10		
2	$35	Month	$650, O/S add $220		
3	$40	Barney's	15% discount	3hr	
8	$45				
12	$51				
24	$57				

helpful information

Su-F 6am-2am	150 spaces	Eff. 10/07
Sa 6am-3am	AE, MC, V	

29. **540 Park Ave** *bet Park/Madison, N side of E 61st*
Icon   212.980.3057

hr	rate	specials	rate	enter	exit
1/2	$20	SUV	$10		
1	$33	Month	$549 tenant, O/S add $84		
2	$40	Month	$676 non-tenant, O/S add $84		
12	$55				
24	$60				

helpful information

24/7	Elevator	Max bill $50
129 spaces	Regency Hotel	No full size vans
AE, MC, V	181" rule for SUV	35 E 61st

---

30. **150 E 61st St** *bet 3rd/Lexington, S side of E 61st*
Imperial   212.308.8291

hr	rate	specials	rate	enter	exit
1/2	$10	AM	$23	7-10am	9pm
1	$20	PM	$15	after 6pm	close
2	$25	Event	$40		10pm
10	$30	SUV	$10		
24	$40				
O/N	$40				
2am	$35				

helpful information

M-Th,Su 7am-2am	AE, MC, V	No vans
F-Sa 7am-3am	Max bill $20	Low clearance
89 spaces	Narrow driveway	

---

31. **200 E 61st St** *bet 2nd/3rd, S side of E 61st, near 3rd*
MPG   212.486.2790

hr	rate*	specials	rate	enter	exit
1/2	$8	AM m-f	$21	6-9am	8pm
1	$22	AM m-f	$45	6-9am	24hr
2	$27	Sa,Su	$17		12hr
12	$36	Sa,Su	$45		24hr
24	$45	SUV	$10		
		Month	$422, O/S add $84		

helpful information

24/7	AE, V, MC
70 spaces	*M-F 9am-6am

32. 203 E 61st St *bet 2nd/3rd, N side of E 61st, near 3rd*

Icon 212.308.9248

hr	rate	specials	rate	enter	exit
1/2	$8	AM	$21	4-10am	8pm
1	$22	PM f-sa	$17	5pm-2am	2am
2	$27	Sa,Su	$17	6am-5pm	12hr
12	$36	SUV	$10		
24	$41	Month	$507, O/S add $84		

helpful information

24/7	AE, MC, V	No full size vans
131 spaces	Max bill $50	

---

33. 330 E 61st St *bet 1st/2nd, S side of E 61st*

Central 212.758.1048

hr	rate	specials	rate	enter	exit
1/2	$8	AM	$20	5-9am	6pm
1	$16	SUV	$11		
2	$20	Month	$528, O/S add $84		
10	$28	LA Sports Club Member Discount			
24	$40				

helpful information

24/7	AE, MC, V, Dis
75 spaces	Max bill $50

---

34. 401 E 60th St *bet York/1st, S side of E 61st*

Bridge Tower Parking LLC 212.355.9133

hr	rate	specials	rate	enter	exit
1	$12	AM	$16	6-10am	12hr
2	$17	Sa,Su	$11	F 12am-Su midnight	10hr
10	$21	SUV	$10		
24	$29				

helpful information

24/7	MC, V	Long driveway
99 spaces	181" rule for SUV	Entrance at 410 E 61st

35. 500 E 62nd St *bet York/FDR, N side of E 62nd*

QuikPark 212.980.7050

hr	rate	specials	rate	enter	exit
1	$12	AM	$15	6-10am	7pm
2	$17	PM	$11	after 5pm	6am
10	$21	Sa,Su	$11	anytime	10hr
24	$29	SUV	$10		
		Month	$338, O/S add $42		

helpful information

24/7	6'8" clearance
120 spaces	181" rule for SUV
Cash	

36. 2 E 60th St *bet Madison/5th, S side of E 60th*

Imperial 212.317.9172

hr	rate	specials	rate	enter	exit
1/2	$28	PM	$26	after 6pm	close
1	$33	Su	$26	by 9am	6pm
2	$44	SUV	$10		
12	$67	Month	$1000, O/S add $100		
24	$87	Harmonie Club	$20-35	6pm	close
O/N	$87				

helpful information

Su-Th 8am-1am	AE, MC, V	Narrow driveway
F,Sa 8am-3am	Hard to see from street	Eff. 5/08
17 spaces		

37. 750 Lexington Ave *bet Lexington/Park, S side of E 60th*

Shoppers Parking Corp 212.754.2678

hr	rate	specials	rate	enter	exit
1/2	$12	SUV	$12		
1	$28	Month	$634, O/S add $127		
2	$39				
3	$48				
10	$51				
24	$64				

helpful information

24/7	181" rule for SUV	Steep driveway
134 spaces	6'6" clearance	
AE, MC, V		

---

38. 169 E 60th St *bet 3rd/Lexington, N side of E 60th*

QuikPark 212.308.4234

hr	rate	specials	rate	enter	exit
1	$25	SUV	$10		
2	$33				
10	$42				
24	$52				
MTC	$47				

helpful information
M-F 7am-12am — AE, MC, V
Sa,Su 8am-12am — Max bill $50
34 spaces

---

39. 220 E 60th St *bet 2nd/3rd, S side of E 60th*

60th Storage Corp 212.223.8482

hr	rate	specials	rate	enter	exit
1/2	$7	AM	$18	5-9am	7pm
1	$17	SUV	$10		
2	$19	Month	$337		
8	$26	Month	$157	m'cycle	
24	$31				

helpful information
24/7 — 6' clearance
55 spaces — Max bill $50
Cash

---

40. 321 E 60th St *bet 1st/bridge ramp, N side of E 60th*

Bridge Parking 212.956.2280

hr	rate	specials	rate	enter	exit
1	$10	AM	$13	6-10:30am	12hr
2	$12	SUV	$10		
10	$17	Month	$325, O/S add $125		
24	$34				

helpful information
Su-Th 6am-11pm — 44 spaces — Outdoor
F-Sa 24hr — Cash

---

41. 403 E 60th St *bet 1st/York, N side of E 60th*

Central 212.421.2298

hr	rate	specials	rate	enter	exit
1	$13	AM m-f	$13	6-10am	12hr
2	$15	Sa	$11	by 6am	12am
10	$20	Su	$11	by 6am	12am
24	$31	SUV	$11		
		Month	$528, SUV add $84		

helpful information
24/7 — 2 elevators
168 spaces — Max bill $50
AE, MC, V

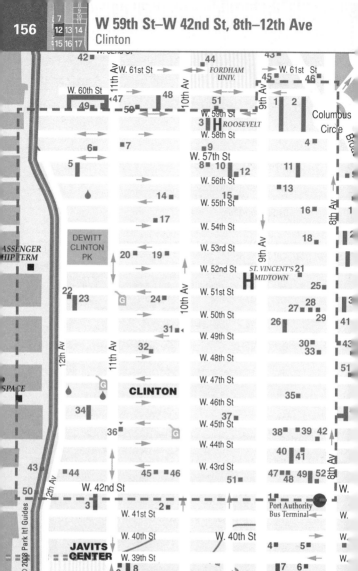

1. **910 9th Ave** *bet 8th/9th, N side of W 58th or S side of W 60th*
   Central   212.582.7110

hr	rate	specials	rate	enter	exit
1	$26	AM 7D	$20	3-10am	12hr
2	$30	Event	$54		
10	$40	SUV	$11		
24	$54	Month	$338, SUV add $84		

helpful information
24/7   Max bill $50
318 spaces   22 W 60th
AE, MC, V

2. **10 Columbus Circle** *bet 8th/9th, N side of W 58th or S side of W 60th*
Central 212.823.6199

hr	rate	specials	rate	enter	exit
1	$26	AM	$20	3-10am	12hr
2	$30	Event	$54		
10	$40	T-giving	$54		
24	$54	Month	$507, SUV add $253		
		SUV	$11		
		Columbus Circle Stores			
			$15	10am-10pm	2hr with $50 minimum purchase

helpful information

24/7	Security inspection
662 spaces	Steep driveway
AE, MC, V	W 58th entrance may be closed

3. **400 W 59th St** *bet 9th/10th, N side of W 58th or S side of W 59th*
1 Columbus Place Garage LLC 212.246.1096

hr	rate	specials	rate	enter	exit
1	$14	PM	$14	1am-10am	14hr
4	$20	Sa,Su	$17	6am-6pm	12hr
12	$22	Event	$15		12hr
24	$26	SUV	$10		
		Month	$378		
		Columbus Circle Stores			
			$10		5hr

helpful information

24/7	181" rule for SUV	No full size vans
294 space	7' clearance	Eff. 9/07
MC, V		

4. **330 W 58th St** *bet 9th/8th, S side of W 58th*
Icon 212.245.9634

hr	rate	specials	rate	enter	exit
1/2	$8	AM m-sa	$17	4-10am	12hr
1	$18	PM 7D	$15	6pm-4am	7am
2	$23	Sa	$20	10am-6pm	12hr
12	$28	Su	$14	4am-6pm	12hr
24	$34	T-giving	$30	5-11am	by 6pm
		SUV	$10		

helpful information

24/7	Across Time Warner Center	No full size vans
95 spaces	181" rule for SUV	
AE, MC, V	Max bill $50	

5. **622 W 57th St** *bet 11th/12th, N side of W 56th or S side of W 57th*
   GMC 212.757.3090

hr	rate*	specials	rate	enter	exit
1	$20	AM	$18	5-10am	7pm
2	$25	PM	$25	5pm-5am	1hr
8	$30	PM	$30	5pm-5am	2hr
24	$35	O/N	$35		after 5am
		SUV	$10		
		Month	$400, SUV add $200		

helpful information
24/7	5 min grace period	MC, V
1000 spaces	Max bill $50	*enter 5am-6pm

6. **601 W 57th St** *bet 11th/12th, N side of W 57th*
   MTP 212.247.0700

hr	rate	specials	rate	enter	exit
1/2	$5	AM	$14	6-9am	12hr
12	$15	Sa,Su	$10	anytime	12hr
24	$20	Event	$25		
		Holiday	$25		
		SUV	$5		
		Month	$249, SUV add $26		
		Month	$199	O/N, SUV add $25	

helpful information
24/7	Cash	100 spaces

7. **838 11th Ave** *bet W 57th/W 58th, E side of 11th*
   Kinney 212.445.0172

hr	rate	specials	rate	enter	exit
1	$16	AM m-f	$20	6-10am	10hr
2	$19	Sa, Su	$20	all day	
10	$28	SUV	$11		
24	$40	Month	$470, SUV add $84		
		Month	$169	m'cycle	

helpful information
24/7	AE, MC, V	No vans/SUVs
84 spaces	Max bill $50	543 W 57th

8. **440 W 57th St** *bet 9th/10th, S side of W 57th*
   Icon 212.765.7069

hr	rate	specials	rate	enter	exit
1/2	$9	AM	$15	4-11am	12hr
1	$13	SUV	$10		
2	$16	T-giving	$30	5-11am	6pm
12	$22	Holiday Inn guest $23			24hr
24	$34				

helpful information
24/7	AE, MC, V	181" rule for SUV
378 spaces	Holiday Inn	Max bill $50

9. 435 W 57th St *bet 9th/10th, N side of W 57th*
Icon 212.664.8520

hr	rate	specials	rate	enter	exit
1	$12	T-giving	$30	5-11am	6pm
2	$16	SUV	$10		
10	$22	Month	$422, SUV add $84		
24	$35				

helpful information
24/7	AE, MC, V	55 spaces	181" rule for SUV

---

10. 408 W 57th St *bet 9th/10th, N side of W 56th or S side of W 57th*
Park It Management 212.586.9182

hr	rate	specials	rate	enter	exit
1/2	$10	AM	$16	5-10am	6pm
1	$14	Event	$35		
2	$19	Parade	$35		
10	$22	Holiday	$35		
24	$33	SUV	$15		
1am	$25	Month	$317-359, SUV add $50		
		Month	$211	m'cycle	
		Month	$106	bicycle	
		Bello Rest	free	after 5pm	3hr by 12am

helpful information
24/7	Car wash	80 spaces	AE, MC, V, Dis, DC

---

11. 316 W 57th St *bet 8th/9th, N side of W 56th or S side of W 57th*
Champion 212.246.8461

hr	rate	specials	rate	enter	exit
1/2	$14	AM 7D	$21	4-11am	12am
1	$25	Event	$35		
2	$28	SUV	$10		
10	$30	Month	$418, SUV add $42		
24	$39				
O/N	$39				

helpful information
24/7	181" rule for SUV AE, MC, V
372 spaces	6'10" clearance

---

12. 401 W 56th St *bet 9th/10th, N side of W 56th*
Park It Mgmt 212.586.9187

hr	rate	specials	rate	enter	exit
1/2	$10	AM	$16	5-10am	6pm
1	$14	Day	$17	10am-4pm	10hr
2	$19	Parade, Event, Hol	$35		
10	$22	SUV	$15		
24	$33	Month	$317-359, SUV add $50		

helpful information
7D 7am-12am	181" rule for SUV	AE, MC, V
25 spaces	Steep driveway	408 W 57th

13. 330 W 56th St *bet 9th/8th, S side of W 56th*
QuikPark   212.586.1021

hr	rate	specials	rate	enter	exit
1/2	$8	AM 7D	$16	4-11am	12am
1	$20	Event	$33		8hr
2	$23	SUV	$10		
10	$29	Month	$338, O/S add $42		
24	$38				
O/N	$38				

helpful information

24/7	10pm gate closes	Damage inspection
115 spaces	Max bill $20	6'10" clearance
AE, MC, V		181" rule for SUV

14. 841 10th Ave *bet 10th/11th, N side of W 55th, near 10th*
MPG   212.315.2462

hr	rate*	specials	rate	enter	exit
1/2	$8	AM 7D	$8	6-10am	1/2hr
1	$11	AM 7D	$11	6-10am	1hr
2	$12	AM 7D	$12	6-10am	2hr
12	$18	AM 7D	$13	6-10am	12hr
24	$28	AM 7D	$28	6-10am	24hr
		SUV	$10		
		Month	$317, O/S add $42		

helpful information

24/7	AE, MC, V	Steep driveway
86 spaces	Near John Jay College	*M-F 10am-6am

15. 411 W 55th St *bet 9th/10th, N side of W 55th*
Rapid Park   212.265.7854

hr	rate	specials	rate	enter	exit
1	$11	AM	$16	4-11am	7pm
2	$20	Sa,Su	$25	4am-4pm	10hr
10	$26	T'giving	$35		
24	$31	SUV	$10		
O/N	$31	Month	$350, O/S add $100		

helpful information

24/7	AE, MC, V	Near Julia Miles Theatre
188 spaces	Elevator	Near Alvin Ailey

16. 300 W 55th St *bet 8th/9th, S side of W 55th, near 8th*
Imperial   212.974.9495

hr	rate	specials	rate	enter	exit
1/2	$5	AM m-f	$17	5-11am	12hr
1	$13	Sa,Su	$12	7am	7pm
2	$18	SUV	$10		
12	$27	Month	$350, O/S add $100		
24	$32				
O/N	$32				

helpful information

24/7	AE, MC, V	Max bill $100
92 spaces	6'6" clearance	

17. 815 10th Ave *bet 10th/11th, N side of W 54th*
Icon — 646.414.4586

hr	rate	specials	rate	enter	exit
1/2	$7	SUV	$10		
1	$12	Month	$422, O/S add $84		
2	$14				
12	$19				
24	$26				

helpful information

24/7	181" rule for SUV
48 spaces	6' clearance
AE, MC, V	Max bill $50

18. 301 W 53rd St *bet 8th/9th, N side of W 53rd*
Imperial — 212.265.1645

hr	rate	specials	rate	enter	exit
1/2	$7	AM	$16	6-10am	7pm
1	$14	Sa,Su	$20	after 10am	7pm
2	$19	Day	$24	10am-5pm	12am
12	$28	SUV	$5-10		
24	$38	Month	$350, O/S add $100		
O/N	$38				

helpful information

24/7	AE, MC, V	Steep driveway
53 spaces	Max bill $50	

19. 520 W 53rd St *bet 10th/11th, S side of W 53rd*
Icon — 212.956.3218

hr	rate	specials	rate	enter	exit
1/2	$7	AM	$13	5-10am	12hr
1	$12	PM	$10	after 5pm	5am
2	$13	Month	$338, SUV add $84		
12	$18				
24	$25				

helpful information

24/7	AE, MC, V	Opened 7/07
83 spaces		

20. 532 W 53rd St *bet 10th/11th, S side of W 53rd*
Rex Parking Corp

hr	rate	specials	rate	enter	exit
		Day	$10	6am-5pm	5pm

helpful information

7D 6am-5pm	Eff. 3/07
78 spaces	Outdoor
Cash	

21. 356 W 52nd St *bet 9th/8th, S side of W 52nd*

Jay B Realty Corp 212.246.7392

hr	rate*	specials	rate	enter	exit
M,T	$15	Su	$20	11am-8pm	2am
W	$20	Event	$40		
Th-Sa	$25	New Year	$40		
		SUV	$5		

helpful information

M-Sa 8am-12am	77 spaces	Damage, security inspection
Su 11am-8pm	Cash	*Rates apply until 6pm,
New Year 8am-2am	Outdoor	then apply again

22. 680 12th Ave *SE corner of 12th/W 51st, E side of 12th or S side of W 51st*

K Park Group LLC 212.265.5376

hr	rate*	specials	rate	enter	exit
1	$17	AM	$13	6-10am	7pm
2	$19	PM	$20	after 6pm	6am
4	$25	Event	$35-40		
6pm	$25	SUV	$0		
24	$30	Month	$300, SUV add $100		

helpful information

24/7	AE, MC, V	*Enter 6am-6pm
170 spaces	Lifts	Outdoor

23. 622 W 51st St *bet 11th/12th, N side of W 50th or S side of W 51st*

Park It 212.245.5910

hr	rate	specials	rate	enter	exit
1	$12	AM m-f	$14	5-10am	12hr
2	$16	Event	$30-35		
3	$19	SUV	$7		
12	$23	Month	$253, SUV add $22		
24	$29				

helpful information

24/7	Cash	Outdoor
181 spaces	Eff. 8/06	

24. 747 10th Ave *bet 10th/11th, S side of W 51st*

Icon 212.974.9608

hr	rate	specials	rate	enter	exit
1	$8	AM m-f	$13	4-9am	12hr
2	$12	PM m-f	$10	6pm-4am	6am
12	$16	Sa,Su	$12	after 6am	Su 6pm, max 12hr
24	$21	SUV	$10		
		Month	$338, SUV add $84		

helpful information

24/7	107 spaces	AE, MC, V	181" rule for SUV

25. 309 W 51st St *NW corner of W 51st/8th, N side of W 51st or W side of 8th*

Icon   212.581.8490

hr	rate	specials	rate	enter	exit
1/2	$10	AM	$15	4-10am	12am
1	$15	m,t,th	$23	10am-5pm	12hr
2	$20	T-giving	$30	5-11am	6pm
12	$28	New Year's	$40	3pm-3am	24hr
24	$34	Times Sq. Church discount			
		SUV	$10		
		Month	$338, SUV add $84		

helpful information

24/7	AE, MC, V	2 Elevators
226 spaces	Hampton Inn	851 8th Ave

---

26. 350 W 50th St *bet 8th/9th, N side of W 49th or S side of W 50th*

Icon

hr	rate	specials	rate	enter	exit
1/2	$8	AM	$15	4-10am	11:59pm
1	$15	SUV	$10		
2	$20	Month	$401, SUV add $84		
10	$32	Month	$169	m'cycle	
24	$40				

helpful information

24/7	New Belvedere Hotel	Boom gate at entrance
473 spaces	6'4" clearance	393 W 49th
AE, MC, V	Max bill $50	

---

27. 331 W 50th St *bet 9th/8th, N side of W 50th*

50th St. Parking   212.258.2997

hr	rate	specials	rate	enter	exit
1/2	$7	SUV	$10		
1	$13	Month	$296		
12	$25				
24	$30				

helpful information

24/7	Cash
124 spaces	Outdoor

164

7	9 10 11
12 13 14	
15 16 17	

W 59th St–W 42nd St, 8th–12th Ave
Clinton

---

28. 311 W 50th St *bet 9th/8th, N side of W 50th*

Imperial 212.265.6275

hr	rate	specials	rate	enter	exit
1/2	$5	AM m-f	$18	5-11am	12am
1	$13	Day m-f	$27	after 11am	12am
2	$16	W	$27		
10	$27	SUV	$7		
24	$31	Month	$389		
O/N	$31				

helpful information

24/7	Max bill $20
60 spaces	Steep driveway
AE, MC, V	

---

29. 305 W 50th St *bet 9th/8th, N side of W 50th*

Impark 212.307.0650

hr	rate	specials	rate	enter	exit
1/2	$9	AM m-f	$16	5-10am	12am
1	$17	Sa,Su	$25		12hr
2	$22	SUV	$10		
10	$32	Month	$317, SUV add $84		
24	$37				

helpful information

24/7	AE, MC, V
87 spaces	181" rule for SUV

---

30. 304 W 49th St *bet 8th/9th, S side of W 49th, near 8th*

304 Associates

hr	rate	specials	rate	enter	exit
1	$15	AM	$16	3-10am	12hr
2	$20	SUV	$10		
12	$30	Month	$313		
24	$37	Discount for: Mayfair Hotel, Time Hotel, New York Inn, Baldonia Restaurant, Ciro Restaurant			

helpful information

24/7	2 elevators
205 spaces	Budget rental
AE, MC, V	7'6" clearance

31. 721 10th Ave *NW corner of W 49th/10th, W side of 10th*

Icon 212.245.1268

hr	rate*	specials	rate	enter	exit
1	$9	AM	$13	2-10am	12hr
2	$14	M,T,Th,F	$16	10am-5pm	12hr
3	$16	PM su-th	$8	5pm-2am	1hr
4	$17	PM su-th	$10	5pm-2am	2hr
12	$20	PM su-th	$12	5pm-2am	3hr
24	$25	PM su-th	$13	5pm-2am	4hr
		PM su-th	$25	5pm-2am	24hr
		PM su-th	$17	5pm-2am	7am
		PM f-sa	$8	5pm-2am	1hr
		PM f-sa	$12	5pm-2am	2hr
		PM f-sa	$15	5pm-2am	3hr
		PM f-sa	$16	5pm-2am	4hr
		PM f-sa	$25	5pm-2am	24hr
		PM f-sa	$20	5pm-2am	7am
		Sa,Su	$9	7am-5pm	1hr
		Sa,Su	$11	7am-5pm	2hr
		Sa,Su	$16	7am-5pm	3hr
		Sa,Su	$17	7am-5pm	4hr
		Sa,Su	$20	7am-5pm	12hr
		Sa,Su	$25	7am-5pm	24hr
		New Year	$20	3pm-3am	2hr
		New Year	$30	3pm-3am	24hr
		SUV	$10		
		Month	$296, SUV add $84		

helpful information

24/7	Skyline Hotel
181 spaces	181" rule for SUV
AE, MC, V	*M-F, 7am-5pm

---

32. 547 W 48th St *bet 10th/11th, N side of W 48th*

MTP 212.957.0797

hr	rate	specials	rate	enter	exit
1/2	$5	Event	$25		12 hr
1	$10	SUV	$5		
12	$12	Month	$220, SUV add $30		
24	$20	Month	$101	m'cycle	

helpful information

24/7	Indoor on W 49th
240 spaces	Outdoor on W 48th
Cash	514 W 49th

33. 305 W 48th St *bet 9th/8th, N side of W 48th*
Bright Management Inc 212.713.1647

hr	rate	specials	rate	enter	exit
		Day m-t	$15	8am-6pm	
		Day w	$23	8am-6pm	
		Day th-sa	$20	8am-6pm	
		PM m-t	$15	6pm-12am	
		PM w-f	$20	6pm-12am	
		PM sa	$23	6pm-12am	
		Su	$15	10am-8pm	
		Event	$35		
		SUV	$6		

helpful information

M-Sa 8am-12am	Cash	No sign, yellow booth
Su 10am-8pm	Eff. 1/02	After 6pm, night rate is
40 spaces	Outdoor	additional

34. 610 W 46th St *bet 11th/12th, N side of W 45th or S side of W 46th*
Car Park Corp 212.957.5340

hr	rate	specials	rate	enter	exit
1	$10	AM	$15	6-9am	12hr
12	$20	PM	$25		12hr
24	$25	SUV	$5		
O/N	$25	Month	$253		

helpful information

24/7	Lifts	Car wash
185 spaces	Outdoor	
Cash	W 45th entrance is nicer	

35. 327 W 46th St *bet 9th/8th, N side of W 46th*
333 W 46th St Corp 212.245.9422

hr	rate	specials	rate	enter	exit
		M,T,Th,F	$15	8am-6pm	7pm*
		W,Sa	$30	8am-6pm	7pm*
		Su	$25	after 11am	8pm
		PM m	$15	6pm-1am	close
		PM t	$25	6pm-1am	close
		PM w-f	$30	6pm-1am	close
		PM sa	$35	6pm-1am	close
		Event	$40		
		SUV	$8		

helpful information

M-Sa 8am-1am	Cash	333 W 46th
Su 11am-8pm	Eff. 11/07	*After 7pm, night rate
95 spaces	Outdoor	is additional

36. 600 11th Ave *SE corner of W 45th/11th, E side of 11th or S side of W 45th*

Park Right   212.459.9003

hr	rate	specials	rate	enter	exit
2	$20	AM m-f	$13	6-9am	12hr
12	$28	Event	$25		
24	$33	SUV	$6		
		Month	$253, SUV add $43		
		Truck/Bus	$90-150 over 14'		24hr

helpful information
24/7   Outdoor
350 spaces Cash

---

37. 413 W 45th St *bet 9th/10th, N side of W 45th*

Theatre Parking LLC   212.265.0774

hr	rate	specials	rate	enter	exit
24	$49	AM	$15	5-10am	7pm
O/N	$49	AM	$9	5-10am	1hr
		AM	$15	5-10am	6pm
		M-F	$17	after 10am	1hr, by 5am
		M-F	$25	after 10am	12am
		M-F	$39	after 10am	5am
		Sa,Su	$29	by 5am	12am
		SUV	$10		

helpful information
24/7   AE, MC, V
100 spaces Budget Truck rental

---

38. 350 W 45th St *bet 8th/9th, S side of W 45th*

344 W 45th St Corp   212.245.9885

hr	rate	specials	rate	enter	exit
		Day m,t,th,f	$15	8am-6pm	
		Day w,sa	$30	8am-6pm	
		PM m	$15	6pm-1am	
		PM t	$25	6pm-1am	
		PM w-f	$30	6pm-1am	
		PM sa	$35	6pm-1am	
		Su	$25	11am-8pm	
		Event	$40		
		SUV	$8		

helpful information
M-Sa 8am-1am   Cash
Su 11am-8pm   Eff. 11/07
41 spaces   Outdoor

39. **344 W 45th St** *bet 8th/9th, S side of W 45th*
344 W 45th St Corp   212.245.9885

hr	rate	specials	rate	enter	exit
		Day m,t,th,f	$15	8am-6pm	
		Day w,sa	$30	8am-6pm	
		PM m	$15	6pm-1am	
		PM t	$25	6pm-1am	
		PM w-f	$30	6pm-1am	
		PM sa	$35	6pm-1am	
		Su	$25	8am-6pm	
		Event	$40		
		SUV	$8		

helpful information

M-Sa 8am-1am	Cash	Outdoor
Su 11am-8pm	Eff. 11/07	
40 spaces	Max bill $50	

40. **332 W 44th St** *bet 8th/9th, N side of W 43rd or S side of W 44th*
Central   212.757.8375

hr	rate	specials	rate	enter	exit
		AM m-sa	$16	3-10am	12hr
		Su,M,T,Th	$18	Su 8am-F 4:59pm	1hr
		Su,M,T,Th	$25	Su 8am-F 4:59pm	2hr
		Su,M,T,Th	$30	Su 8am-F 4:59pm	10hr
		Su,M,T,Th	$52	Su 8am-F 4:59pm	24hr
		W,F,Sa	$18	W, F 5pm-Su 8am	1hr
		W,F,Sa	$28	W, F 5pm-Su 8am	2hr
		W,F,Sa	$41	W, F 5pm-Su 8am	10hr
		F-Su	$52	F 5pm-Su 6am	24hr
		Carmines, Virgil's BBQ, Birdland,			
		Milford Plaza Hotel			
			$10		12hr
		SUV	$11		
		Month	$507, SUV add $42		

helpful information

24/7	Ticket machine
260 spaces	7' clearance
AE, MC, V	Max bill $50

41. 322 W 44th St *bet 9th/8th, S side of W 44th*
MPG   212.399.1030

hr	rate	specials	rate	enter	exit
		AM m,t,th,f,su	$10	6-10am	1/2hr
		AM m,t,th,f,su	$15	6-10am	7pm
		AM m,t,th,f,su	$40	6-10am	24hr
		M,T,Th	$10	10am-12am	1/2hr
		M,T,Th	$15	10am-12am	1hr
		M,T,Th	$22	10am-12am	2hr
		M,T,Th	$25	10am-12am	10hr
		M,T,Th	$40	10am-12am	24hr
		F	$10	10am-6pm	1/2hr
		F	$15	10am-6pm	1hr
		F	$22	10am-6pm	2hr
		F	$25	10am-6pm	10hr
		F	$40	10am-6pm	24hr
		F	$10	6pm-12am	1/2hr
		F	$15	6pm-12am	1hr
		F	$40	6pm-12am	24hr
		W,Sa	$10	all day	1/2hr
		W,Sa	$15	all day	1hr
		W,Sa	$40	all day	24hr
		Su	$10	10am-12am	1/2hr
		Su	$15	10am-12am	1hr
		Su	$30	10am-12am	24hr
		Holiday	$50		
		SUV	$10		
		Month	$338, SUV add $253		

helpful information
24/7   Outdoor
77 spaces
AE, MC, V

---

42. 307 W 44th St *bet 9th/8th, N side of W 44th, near 8th*
Edison/Park Fast   212.664.9126

hr	rate	specials	rate	enter	exit
1/2	$8	AM	$14	4-9am	7pm
1	$16	PM m,t,th,f,su	$26	4pm-4am	12hr
2	$20	PM w,sa	$30	4pm-4am	12hr
24	$35	Su,M,T,Th,F	$26	4am-4pm	12hr
		W,Sa	$35	4am-4pm	12hr
		Event	$35		7pm
		SUV	$10		
		Month	$296, O/S add $84		

helpful information
24/7   AE, MC, V, Dis, DC   Outdoor
71 spaces   Max bill $100

43. **Pier 83/12th Ave @ W 43rd St** *at W 43rd/12th, W side of 12th*
Central-Circle Line

hr	rate	specials	rate	enter	exit
		Day m-f	$25	before 3pm	12am
		PM m-f	$30	after 3pm	12am
		Sa,Su	$30		12am
		Month	$215		

helpful information

7D 7am-7pm	Pay in advance	9'6" clearance
270 spaces	Self parking	
Cash		

44. **627 W 42nd St** *bet 11th/12th, S side of W 43rd, near 12th*
GGMC   212.695.1241

hr	rate	specials	rate	enter	exit
1	$15	AM	$14	6-9am	7pm
2	$18	SUV	$10		
10	$25	Month	$300, SUV add $100		
24	$35				

helpful information

24/7	2 elevators	Near China Embassy
100 spaces	Opened 6/07	181" rule for SUV
AE, MC, V		

45. **520 W 43rd St** *bet 10th/11th, S side of W 43rd*
Imperial   212.244.4786

hr	rate	specials	rate	enter	exit
1/2	$6	AM	$15	6-10am	8pm
1	$10	PM	$15	after 3pm	2am
2	$12	Sa,Su	$16	after 9am	12hr, by 12am
12	$19	Event	$30		
24	$23	SUV	$10		
O/N	$23	Month	$350		

helpful information

24/7	AE, MC, V
75 spaces	

46. **583 10th Ave** *bet 10th/11th, S side of W 43rd*
Alliance Parking   212.502.5268

hr	rate	specials	rate	enter	exit
1/2	$9	AM m-f	$15	by 10am	12hr
1	$11	Event	$25		
2	$13	SUV	$10		
12	$19	Month	$338, SUV add $84		
24	$27	Month	$127	m'cycle	

helpful information
24/7	181" rule for SUV
62 spaces	Max bill $20
MC, V	

47. **360 W 43rd St** *bet 8th/9th, S side of W 43rd, near 9th*
Cosmo Parking, LLC   212.307.1033

hr	rate	specials	rate	enter	exit
1	$5	AM	$12	by 10am	7pm
24	$30	Daily	$14	after 10am	12hr
O/N	$30	SUV	$8		
		Month	$300, O/S add $25		

helpful information
24/7	AE, MC, V
105 spaces	No CC greater than $50

48. **350 W 43rd St** *bet 8th/9th, S side of W 43rd*
GGMC   212.315.1646

hr	rate	specials	rate	enter	exit
1	$13	AM	$12	4-10am	7pm
2	$17	Day m-f	$14	after 10am	12hr, by 12am
10	$20	SUV	$5		
24	$30	Month	$325, O/S add $60		

helpful information
24/7	181" rule for SUV
59 spaces	Max bill $20
AE, MC, V, Dis, DC	

49. 315 W 42nd St *bet 8th/9th, N side of W 42nd or S side of W 43rd*
Impark   212.975.0254

hr	rate	specials	rate	enter	exit
1	$19	SUV	$10		
2	$27	Month	$475		
10	$32				
24	$45				

helpful information
24/7	Max bill $50	Outdoor
80 spaces	7' clearance	314 W 42nd
AE, MC, V		

50. Pier 81/12th Ave @ W 41st *at W 42nd/12th, W side of 12th*
Central - Circle Line   212.630.8821

hr	rate	specials	rate	enter	exit
		Day m-f	$25	before 3pm	12am
		PM m-f	$30	after 3pm	12am
		PM	free	after 10pm	
		Sa,Su	$30	anytime	12am
		Month	$215		

helpful information
7D 6am-10pm	Outdoor	World Yacht parking
Cash	Self parking	
Pay in advance		

51. 401 W 42nd St *bet 9th/10th, N side of W 42nd, across Dyer*
MPG   212.279.5213

hr	rate	specials	rate	enter	exit
		AM su-f	$14	5-8am	1hr
		AM su-f	$18	5-8am	12hr
		AM su-f	$35	5-8am	24hr
		PM m,t	$14	4pm-5am	1hr
		PM m,t	$20	4pm-5am	12hr
		PM m,t	$35	4pm-5am	24hr
		M,T	$14	8am-4pm	1hr
		M,T	$20	8am-4pm	2hr
		M,T	$30	8am-4pm	12hr
		M,T	$35	8am-4pm	24hr
		W-Su	$14	8am-5am	1hr
		W-Su	$20	8am-5am	2hr
		W-Su	$30	8am-5am	12hr
		W-Su	$35	8am-5am	24hr
		Event	$45		
		Month	$335		

helpful information
24/7	6'2" clearance	Pay before getting car
998 spaces	Self parking	Rates change frequently
AE, MC, V, Dis, DC		

52. **305 W 42nd St** *bet 8th/9th, N side of W 42nd*
Impark

hr	rate	specials	rate	enter	exit
1/2	$9	SUV	$10		
1	$19	Month	$338, O/S add $84		
2	$27				
10	$32				
24	$45				

helpful information
24/7   Max bill $20
67 spaces   Outdoor
AE, MC, V

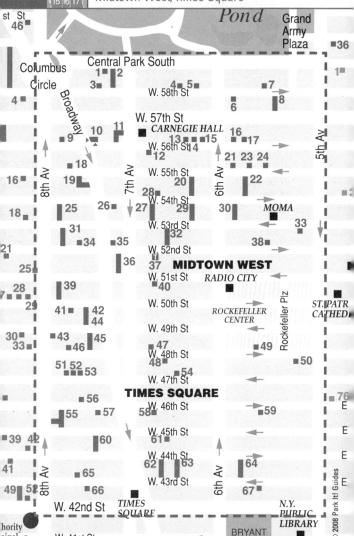

---

1. **210 Central Park South** *bet 7th/Columbus Cir., S side of CPS*
Capable Parking/Ulltra 212.245.5400

hr	rate	specials	rate	enter	exit
1	$21	SUV	$10		
2	$25	Month	$475, O/S add $51		
10	$32				
24	$40				
O/N	$40				

helpful information
Su-Th 7am-1am   25 spaces   Hard to see from street
F,Sa 7am-2am   AE, MC, V

2. **200 Central Park South** *bet Broadway/7th, N side of W 58th or S side of W 59th*

GMC 212.265.1078

hr	rate	specials	rate	enter	exit
1	$25	SUV	$10		
2	$30	Month	$550, O/S add $200		
10	$35	O/N	$45		after 5am
24	$45	NY Athletic Club members can charge to account			

helpful information

24/7	AE, MC, V	8' clearance
198 spaces	5 min grace period	Steep driveway

3. **216 Central Park South** *bet Broadway/7th, N side of W 58th*

Champion 212.765.6258

hr	rate	specials	rate	enter	exit
1	$19	SUV	$10		
2	$23	Month	$431, O/S add $224		
10	$29	Month	$175	m'cycle	
24	$37				
O/N	$37				

helpful information

24/7	Handicapped van OK	Steep driveway
44 spaces	181" rule for SUV	225 W 58th
AE, MC, V		

4. **125 W 58th St** *bet 7th/6th, N side of W 58th*

QuikPark 212.977.7422

hr	rate	specials	rate	enter	exit
1	$26	AM m-f	$26	6-9am	7pm
2	$33	SUV	$10		
10	$40	Month	$507, O/S add $84		
24	$51	Sarabeth	$15		3hr
		NYAC	$9		24hr

helpful information

24/7	58 spaces	AE, MC, V

5. **106 Central Park South** *bet 7th/6th, N side of W 58th*

Parc King Inc 212.956.4430

hr	rate	specials	rate	enter	exit
1/2	$14	AM	$23	7-9:30am	7pm
1	$25	Sa,Su	$20	anytime	8pm
2	$32	SUV	$10		
4	$35	Month	$500		
10	$40				
12	$43				
24	$49				

helpful information

24/7	AE, MC, V	Hard to see from street
107 spaces	2 elevators	Trump Parc Hotel
		105 W 58th

6. **58 W 58 St** *bet 6th/5th, S side of W 58th*
Central 212.593.3867

hr	rate	specials	rate	enter	exit
1/2	$9	AM 7D	$27	6-10am	8pm
1	$20	SUV	$11		
2	$24	Month	$507, O/S add $84		
10	$36				
24	$51				
O/N	$51				

helpful information
24/7   AE, MC, V
160 spaces   181" rule for SUV

7. **33 W 58th St** *bet 6th/5th, N side of W 58th*
Champion 212.223.0056

hr	rate	specials	rate	enter	exit
1/2	$7-20	AM 7D	$27	6-10am	12am
1	$27	SUV	$10		
1 1/2	$37	Month	$465		
2	$47				
24	$59				
O/N	$59				

helpful information
24/7   AE, MC, V   Park Lane Hotel
108 spaces   Elevator   181" rule for SUV

8. **9 W 57th St** *bet 5th/6th, N side of W 57th or S side of W 58th*
Solo 9 W 57th St. 212.754.4077

hr	rate	specials	rate	enter	exit
1/2	$10	AM m-f	$27	5-9am	12am
1	$29	SUV	$10		
2	$35	Month	$465, O/S add $84		
10	$48				
24	$55				

helpful information
24/7   6'4" clearance on W 58th   Nice interior
250 spaces   Max bill $50
AE, MC, V   Hard to see from street

9. **235 W 56th St** *bet 8th/Broadway, N side of W 56th*

QuikPark 212.974.6147

hr	rate	specials	rate	enter	exit
1/2	$8	AM 7D	$17	4-11am	12am
1	$20	SUV	$10		
2	$23	Month	$381, O/S add $84		
10	$31	Nippon Club, Salisbury Hotel, Patsy's			
24	$45	M-F	$17	after 5pm	12am
		Sa,Su	$17	all day	12am
		Carnegie Hall	$20		6hr

helpful information

24/7	146 spaces	AE, MC, V, Dis	Max bill $50

10. **211 W 56th St** *NE corner of Broadway/W 56th, N side of W 56th or E side of Broadway*

GGMC 212.247.8254

hr	rate	specials	rate	enter	exit
1/2	$6	AM 7D	$21	5-11am	12hr
1	$20	SUV	$10		
2	$23	Month	$385, O/S add $100		
10	$30	Carnegie Hall			
24	$42	Guests	$20	after 5pm	11pm, need tkt
		Subscribers	$15	after 5pm	11pm, need tkt*

helpful information

24/7	AE, MC, V, Dis	Elevator
190 spaces		*need Subscriber card

11. **882 7th Ave** *NW corner of 7th/W 56th, N side of W 56th or W side of 7th*

Central 212.586.3665

hr	rate	specials	rate	enter	exit
1	$20	AM 7D	$21	5-10am	12hr
2	$24	SUV	$10		
10	$31	Month	$466, O/S add $84		
24	$51	Event	$50		
		Redeye Grill	$13		3hr
		NY Athletic Club discount			
		Carnegie Hall Subscribers			
		M-F	$20	after 5pm	12am, need tkt
		W	$20	after 11am	12am, need tkt

helpful information

24/7	AE, MC, V	Max bill $50
225 spaces	8' clearance	201 W 56th
		Ticket machine

---

12. 156 W 56th St *bet 7th/6th, S side of W 56th*

GMC   212.265.0841

hr	rate	specials	rate	enter	exit
1	$20	AM	$22	6-10am	7pm
2	$25	O/N	$45		after 5am
10	$35	SUV	$10		
24	$45	Month	$550, O/S add $200		
		City Center 10% discount			

helpful information

24/7	AE, MC, V	Steep driveway
105 spaces	City Spire Garage	

---

13. 145 W 57th St *bet 7th/6th, N side of W 56th*

Central   212.459.8946

hr	rate	specials	rate	enter	exit
1/2	$9	AM	$24	4-10am	7pm
1	$20	SUV	$15		
2	$24	Month	$507, O/S add $84		
10	$31	Carnegie Hall			
24	$51	M-F	$20	after 5pm	12am
		Sa,Su	$20	after 11am	12am
		City Center	$20	Sa,Su	

helpful information

24/7	AE, V, MC, Disc	Hard to see from st. (red brick)
89 spaces	6'9" clearance	No overhead racks, bike racks

---

14. 109 W 56th St *bet 7th/6th, N side of W 56th*

Central   212.245.5000

hr	rate	specials	rate	enter	exit
1	$20	AM	$26	6-9am	7pm
2	$24	SUV	$10		
10	$31	Month	$700, O/S add $84		
24	$51	Carnegie Hall			
		M-F	$14	after 5pm	12am*
		Sa,Su	$14	after 11am	12am*

helpful information

24/7	Parker Meridian Hotel	No vans
87 spaces	6'8" clearance	118 W 57th
AE, MC, V	Damage, security inspection	*Need ticket
	Steep driveway	

15. 1381 6th Ave *bet 7th/6th, N side of W 56th, near 6th*
Central   212.246.4645

hr	rate	specials	rate	enter	exit
1/2	$11	AM	$19	3-8am	8pm
1	$20	AM	$21	8-10am	8pm
2	$24	SUV	$12		
10	$31	Month	$591, O/S add $84		
24	$51	Carnegie Hall	$18		3hr

helpful information

24/7	Max bill $50	2 elevators	Ticket machine
196 spaces	AE, MC, V	6'2" clearance	

16. 65 W 56th *bet 6th/5th, N side of W 56th*
Champion   212.664.9675

hr	rate	specials	rate	enter	exit
1/2	$8	AM	$15	4-10am	9pm
1	$24	SUV	$10		
1 1/2	$34	Month	$752		
2	$44	Buckingham Hotel	$39		24hr
24	$49				

helpful information

24/7	AE, MC, V	6'8" clearance
80 spaces	181" rule for SUV	Steep driveway

17. 51 W 56th St *bet 6th/5th, N side of W 56th*
Icon   212.664.8564

hr	rate	specials	rate	enter	exit
1/2	$8	AM m-f	$20	4-10am	12hr
1	$25	Sa,Su	$15	4-9am	12hr
2	$32	SUV	$10		
12	$35	Month	$507, O/S add $84		
24	$44	New Year	$30	3pm-3am	2hr
		New Year	$40	3pm-3am	24hr

Benihana of Tokyo, Bay Leaf, Zona Rosa,
Joe's Shanghai discount: M-F after 6pm, Sa,Su

helpful information

24/7	AE, MC, V	Steep driveway
140 spaces	181" rule for SUV	

---

18. 1731 Broadway *bet Broadway/8th, N side of W 55th*
Central 212.581.3628

hr	rate	specials	rate	enter	exit
1/2	$11	AM	$19	6-10am	12hr
1	$20	SUV	$12		
2	$24	Month	$507, O/S add $84		
10	$31				
24	$51				

helpful information

24/7	AE, MC, V	Max bill $50
124 spaces	2 elevators	

---

19. 230 W 55th St *bet Broadway/8th, S side of W 55th or W side of Broadway*
Icon 212.246.7218

hr	rate	specials	rate	enter	exit
1/2	$8	AM	$18	3-10am	12hr
1	$15	PM su-th	$10	6pm-12am	12am
2	$21	SUV	$10		
12	$30	Month	$169	m'cycle	
24	$34				

helpful information

24/7	181" rule for SUV	1721 Broadway
109 spaces	Max bill $20	No full size vans
AE, MC, V	Broadway ent closed after 10pm	

---

20. 1345 6th Ave *bet 6th/7th, N side of W 54th or S side of W 55th*
The Fisher & Hawaiian Sixth Ave Co 212.245.8708

hr	rate	specials	rate	enter	exit
1	$19	AM m-f	$18	6-10am	summer 6pm
2	$21	SUV	$9		
4	$26	Month	$465		
10	$33	Month	$169	m'cycle	
24	$42	City Center and Manhattan Theater Club:			
Hourly rates may be higher Nov 15 – Jan 15			$18	M-F	4hr
			$24		7hr
		MoMa member	$18		4hr
		MoMa member	$24		7hr
		MoMa member	$30		24hr
		MoMa non-member	$18		2hr
		MoMa non-member	$21		2hr
		MoMa non-member	$27		2hr
		MoMa non-member	$35		2hr
		Hertz renter discount			

helpful information

24/7	Elevator	Boom gate at entrance
250 spaces	Ziegfeld Theater	Handicapped van OK
AE, MC, V	Damage inspection	

21. 77 W 55th St *bet 5th/6th, N side of W 55th, near 6th*

QuikPark 212.581.4025

hr	rate	specials	rate	enter	exit
1/2	$11	AM 7D	$18	6-10am	12hr
1	$23	PM 7D	$17	after 5pm	12am
2	$28	Sa,Su	$17		8hr, by 12am
24	$44	SUV	$10		
MTC	$40	Month	$400, O/S add $84		
12am	$36				

helpful information

M-Th 6am-12am	Sa 7am-2am	61 spaces
F 6am-2a	Su 7am-12am	AE, MC, V
		Steep driveway

22. 1350 6th Ave *bet 5th/6th, N side of W 54th or S side of W 55th, near 6th*

Icon 212.582.4294

hr	rate	specials	rate	enter	exit
1/2	$11	AM	$24	5-10am	12hr
1	$25	SUV	$10		
2	$29	Month	$507, O/S add $64		
12	$40				
24	$45				

helpful information

24/7	AE, MC, V	Max bill $50
99 spaces	181" rule for SUV	No full size vans

23. 65 W 55th St *bet 5th/6th, N side of W 55th*

Bricin Parking Corp 212.245.9613

hr	rate	specials	rate	enter	exit
1/2	$7	AM m-f	$19	7-10am	7pm
1	$17	PM 7D	$15	after 7pm	close
2	$25	Sa	$17	8am-7pm	7pm
12	$31	Su	$15	10am-10pm	close
24	$37	SUV	$7		
		Month	$354, O/S add $42		

helpful information

M-F 7am-12am	24 spaces	Steep driveway
Sa 8am-12am	Cash	
Su 10am-10pm	Eff. 9/03	

24. 25 W 55th St *bet 5th/6th, N side of W 55th*

Central/Kinney 212.245.9652

hr	rate	specials	rate	enter	exit
1	$22	AM m-f	$19	6-10am	12hr
2	$28	SUV	$11		
12	$34	Month	$508, O/S add $84		
24	$51	Discounts for Shoreham Hotel, Chambers			
		Hotel, MoMa			

helpful information

24/7	150 spaces	AE, MC, V	2 elevators

25. 900 8th Ave *bet 8th/Broadway, N side of W 53rd or S side of W 54th*

Icon 212.956.2856

hr	rate	specials	rate	enter	exit
1/2	$8	AM	$16	4-10am	12hr
1	$15	Su-T,Th,F	$28	10am-4pm	12hr
2	$21	SUV	$15		
12	$35	Month	$338, O/S add $84		
24	$40	T-giving	$30	5-11am	by 6pm
		New Year's	$30	3pm-3am	24hr

helpful information

24/7	AE, MC, V	181" rule for SUV
355 spaces	4 elevators	Max bill $20

---

26. 1700 Broadway *bet Broadway/7th, S side of W 54th*

Icon 212.664.9042

hr	rate	specials	rate	enter	exit
1/2	$9	AM m-f	$18	6-10am	6pm
1	$14	Sa	$16	6-10am	6pm
2	$21	Su	$15	6-12am	12hr
12	$29	SUV	$10		
24	$34	Month	$380, O/S add $84		

helpful information

24/7	181" rule for SUV	Steep driveway
122 spaces	6'3" clearance	People elevator on W 53rd
AE, MC, V	Max bill $50	

---

27. 159 W 53rd St *bet 6th/7th, N side of W 53rd or S side of W 54th*

Champion 212.245.1299

hr	rate*	specials	rate	enter	exit
1/2	$15	AM	$21	5-10am	7:30pm
1	$25	PM m-f, Sa,Su+	$15	5pm-3am	1/2hr
2	$29	PM m-f, Sa,Su+	$27	5pm-3am	1hr
10	$35	PM m-f, Sa,Su+	$32	5pm-3am	2hr
24	$51	PM m-f, Sa,Su+	$42	5pm-3am	10hr
		PM m-f, Sa,Su+	$51	5pm-3am	24hr
		SUV	$10		
		Month	$401, O/S add $211		
		MoMa member	$18		4hr
		MoMa member	$24		7hr
		MoMa non-member	$18		2hr
		MoMa non-member	$21		4hr
		MoMa non-member	$27		7hr

helpful information

24/7	AE, MC, V	*M-F 3am-5pm	156 W 54th
147 spaces	7'6" clearance	+Sa,Su all day	

28. 141 W 54th St *bet 7th/6th, N side of W 54th*

Imperial   212.445.0592

hr	rate	specials	rate	enter	exit
1/2	$8	AM m-f	$19	6-9am	8pm
1	$17	PM 7D	$15	after 5pm	12am
2	$26	Sa,Su	$19	after 8am	5hr
10	$31	Sa,Su	$22	after 8am	all day
MTC	$45	SUV	$10		

helpful information

M-F 6am-12am	Su 8am-8pm	AE, MC, V
Sa 8am-12am	44 spaces	Outdoor

29. 101 W 53rd St *bet 6th/7th, N side of W 53rd or S side of W 54th*

Central   212.977.1054

hr	rate	specials	rate	enter	exit
1/2	$14	AM m-f	$16	6-7am	12hr
1	$17	AM m-f	$20	7-10am	12hr
2	$20	SUV	$10		
10	$30	Month	$359, O/S add $84		
24	$42				

helpful information

24/7	Hilton Hotel	1321 6th Ave
475 spaces	181" rule for SUV	100 W 54th
AE, MC, V	May take O/S vehicles	

30. 1330 6th Ave *bet 5th/6th, N side of W 53rd or S side of W 54th, near 6th*

Icon   212.586.0169

hr	rate	specials	rate	enter	exit
1/2	$11	AM 7D	$23	5-10am	12hr
1	$22	SUV	$10		
2	$26				
12	$39				
24	$45				

helpful information

24/7	AE, MC, V	6'1" clearance
225 spaces	181" rule for SUV	No full size vans

31. 880 8th Ave *bet 8th/Broadway, N side of W 52nd or S side of W 53rd*
Central 212.245.0068

hr	rate	specials	rate	enter	exit
1/2	$6	AM	$18	3-10am	6pm
1	$14	Day m,t,th,f	$36	5am-4pm	10hr
2	$20	Day sa,su,w	$40	4pm-5am	10hr
24	$51	PM su,m	$36	4pm-5am	10hr
		PM t-sa	$40	4pm-5am	10hr

Discounts: Victor Cafe, Russian Samovar, Russian Vodka Room

SUV	$11
Month	$313, O/S add $84

helpful information

24/7	AE, MC, V	6'8" clearance
170 spaces	Dollar rental	

---

32. 140 W 53rd St *bet 6th/7th, N side of W 52nd or S side of W 53rd*
Icon 212.397.9028

hr	rate*	specials	rate	enter	exit
1/2	$10	AM m-f	$19	4-10am	10hr
1	$16	W,Sa,Su & Evenings after 5pm			
2	$21		$10		1/2hr
3	$30		$15		1hr
10	$32		$19		2hr
12	$35		$26		3hr
24	$37		$28		10hr
			$28		12hr
			$30		24hr
		SUV	$10		
		Month	$410, O/S add $68		

Sheraton Hotel $7 Valet charge

helpful information

24/7	2 elevators	*M,T,Th,F enter 10am-5pm
260 spaces	181" rule for SUV	
AE, MC, V	Low clearance	

---

33. 666 5th Ave *bet 5th/6th, S side of W 53rd, near 5th*
Icon 212.581.1154

hr	rate	specials	rate	enter	exit
1/2	$12	AM	$24	6-10am	12hr
1	$26	SUV	$10		
2	$36	Month	$549, O/S add $84		
3	$46				
5	$51				
24	$62				
MTC	$62				

helpful information

Su-Th 7am-12am	AE, MC, V
F-Sa 7am-2am	Elevator
90 spaces	Max bill $50

34. 1675 Broadway *bet 8th/Broadway, N side of W 52nd*

52 Broadway Garage Corp   212.245.2125

hr	rate	specials	rate	enter	exit
1	$14	AM	$17	by 11am	6pm
2	$21	SUV	$5		
24	$34	Month	$350, O/S add $60		
O/N	$34				

helpful information

M 7am-12am	61 spaces	No vans, trucks
T,W,Th 7am-1am	AE, MC, V	Eff. 4/08
F,Sa 7am-2am	2 elevators	181" rule for SUV
Su 11am-12am	Car wash	

---

35. 810 7th Ave *NE corner of Broadway/W 52nd, N side of W 52nd or E side of Broadway*

Central   212.581.5215

hr	rate	specials	rate	enter	exit
1	$14	AM 7D	$18	3-10am	12hr
2	$20	W,Sa	$40		10hr
24	$51	Su-T,Th,F	$36		10hr
		SUV	$11		
		Month	$339, O/S add $42		
		Honor validations from any competitors			

helpful information

24/7	AE, MC, V	6' clearance
210 spaces		Steep driveway

---

36. 200 W 52nd St *bet 7th/Broadway, N side of W 51st or S side of W 52nd*

Icon   212.397.9029

hr	rate*	specials	rate	enter	exit
1/2	$9	AM	$17	4-10am	12hr
1	$13	W,Sa,Su & Evenings after 5pm			
2	$20		$9		1/2hr
3	$26		$13		1hr
10	$27		$23		2hr
12	$29		$30		10hr
24	$32		$31		12hr
			$32		24hr
		SUV	$10		
		Month	$338, O/S add $71		
		Sheraton Hotel guest $37			24hr
		Stardust	$17		4hr
		Ruth's Chris Steakhouse $18			5hr
		Practicing Law Institute $17			12hr
		Times Square Church discounts			
		† also applies to events & theater			

helpful information

24/7	3 elevators	*M,T,Th,F enter 10am-5pm,
440 spaces	181" rule for SUV	non-theater, non-matinee
AE, MC, V	Small vans OK	

37. 787 7th Ave *bet 6th/7th, S side of W 52nd*
Equitable Life Assurance Soc

hr	rate	specials	rate	enter	exit

TENANT ONLY

helpful information
Cash

---

38. 27 W 52nd St *bet 6th/5th, N side of W 52nd*

Central 212.246.9256

hr	rate	specials	rate	enter	exit
1	$25	AM	$22	4-10am	10hr
2	$30	Event	$51		
12	$40	SUV	$11		
24	$51	Month	$507, O/S add $84		

helpful information
24/7   AE, MC, V, Dis   Ticket machine
120 spaces   6'3" clearance

---

39. 1633 Broadway *bet 8th/Broadway, N side of W 50th or S side of W 51st*

QuikPark 212.445.0011

hr	rate	specials	rate	enter	exit
1/2	$9	AM m-f	$15	6-9am	12am
1	$15	Event	$32		10hr
2	$20	SUV	$10		
10	$30	Month	$350, O/S add $42		
24	$35				

helpful information
24/7   6'6" clearance   181" rule for SUV
225 spaces   Max bill $20
AE, MC, V   Security inspection

---

40. 140 W 51st St *bet 6th/7th, S side of W 51st*

Central 212.541.7418

hr	rate*	specials	rate	enter	exit
1/2	$11	AM	$19	3-7am	10hr
1	$26	AM	$25	7-9am	10hr
2	$30	Event	$51	m-f after 5pm, Sa,Su	12hr
12	$40	SUV	$11		
24	$51	Month	$422, O/C add $63		

helpful information
24/7   6'8" clearance   Long, very steep driveway
203 spaces   *Non-events
AE, MC, V   Ticket machine

41. 250 W 50th St *bet 8th/Broadway, S side of W 50th*

Central 212.974.6368

hr	rate	specials	rate	enter	exit
1	$15	AM m-f	$20	4-10am	7pm
2	$15-21	PM	$16	5:01pm-4:59am	1hr
10	$36	PM	$22	5:01pm-4:59am	2hr
24	$51	PM	$37	5:01pm-4:59am	10hr
		PM	$51	5:01pm-4:59am	24hr
		SUV	$10		
		Month	$507, O/S add $84		
		Month	$168	m'cycle	
		Palm	$12	evening	3hr
		Lehman	$17		

helpful information

24/7	AE, MC, V	Max bill $50
120 spaces	Next to Palm restaurant	Steep driveway

42. 218 W 50th St *bet 8th/Broadway, S side of W 50th or N side of W 49th*

GMC 212.262.9779

hr	rate*	specials	rate	enter	exit
1	$15	AM 7D	$21	5-10am	7pm
2	$19	PM	$15	5pm-5am	1hr
12	$27	PM	$22	5pm-5am	2hr
24	$35	PM	$35	5pm-5am	12hr
		PM	$39	5pm-5am	24hr
		O/N	$39	after 5pm	after 5am
		SUV	$10		
		Month	$350, O/S add $200		
		Amsterdam, President, Best Western, Time & Edison Hotels	$25	24hr	
		Caroline's	10% discount	PM, No O/N	
		Ruby Foo, Blue Fin	10% discount		
		Roundabout Theatre	10% discount		

helpful information

24/7	2 elevators	Exit only on W 50th
230 spaces	Max bill $50	*5am-5pm
AE, MC, V, Dis, DC		Damage inspection

43. 790 8th Ave *SE corner of W 49th/8th, S side of W 49th or E side of 8th*

Icon   212.581.8590

hr	rate	specials	rate	enter	exit
1/2	$10	AM	$15	4-10am	12hr
1	$14	M,T,Th	$24	10am-5pm	12hr
2	$20	T-giving	$30	5-11am	6pm
12	$28	New Year's	$25	3pm-3am	2hr
24	$35	New Year's	$40	3pm-3am	24hr
		SUV	$10		
		Month	$380, O/S add $84		

helpful information

24/7	2 elevators	Max bill $20
250 spaces	Days Hotel	No full size vans
AE, MC, V	181" rule for SUV	254 W 49th

---

44. 229 W 49th St *bet Broadway/8th, N side of W 49th*

GMC   212.262.9779

hr	rate*	specials	rate	enter	exit
1	$15	AM 7D	$21	5-10am	7pm
2	$21	PM	$15	5pm-5am	1hr
12	$29	PM	$22	5pm-5am	2hr
24	$39	PM	$35	5pm-5am	12hr
		PM	$39	5pm-5am	24hr
		O/N	$39	after 5pm	after 5am
		SUV	$10		
		Month	$350, O/S add $200		

helpful information

24/7	Elevator	*5am-5pm
175 spaces	Max bill $50	
AE, MC, V, Dis, DC		

---

45. 1601 Broadway *bet Broadway/8th, N side of W 48th or S side of W 49th*

QuikPark   212.586.0665

hr	rate	specials	rate	enter	exit
1/2	$9	AM m,t,th,f	$18	5-10am	12hr
2	$22	SUV	$10		
12	$32	Month	$422, O/S add $42		
24	$39				

helpful information

24/7	AE, MC, V	Max bill $20
159 spaces	Crowne Plaza	

46. 235 W 48th St *bet 8th/Broadway, N side of W 48th*
Icon 212.245.9421

hr	rate	specials	rate	enter	exit
1/2	$8*	AM	$20	5-10am	12hr
1	$13	M,T,Th,F	$25	10am-6pm	
2	$21	SUV	$10		
12	$30	Month	$338, O/S add $84		
24	$33				

helpful information

24/7	AE, MC, V	*Su-T, Th-Su only
94 spaces	181" rule for SUV	No full size vans

47. 153 W 48th St *bet 7th/6th, N side of W 48th, near 7th*
Central 212.354.8904

hr	rate	specials	rate	enter	exit
1	$24	AM	$26	4-11am	8pm
2	$33	SUV	$11		
12	$43	Month	$549, O/S add $84		
24	$51				

helpful information

M-Th 6am-1am	213 spaces	Max bill $50
Sa 6am-2am	AE, MC, V	
Su 10am-12am	2 elevators	

48. 148 W 48th St *bet 7th/6th, S side of W 48th*
GMC 212.575.9133

hr	rate	specials	rate	enter	exit
1/2	$11	AM 7D	$26	5-11am	8pm
1	$23	O/N	$50		5am
2	$28	SUV	$10		
10	$40	Month	$375, O/S add $200		
24	$50				

helpful information

24/7	AE, MC, V	Eff. 8/05
300 spaces	Elevator	Max bill $50

49. 25 W 48th St *bet 6th/5th, N side of W 48th*
Central Parking System 212.698.8530

hr	rate	specials	rate	enter	exit
1/2	$12	AM	$26	4-9:30am	10hr
1	$24	SUV	$11		
2	$33	Month	$528, O/S add $42		
10	$43				
24	$51				

helpful information

24/7	AE, MC, V	Rockefeller Center garage
652 spaces	6'8" clearance	Ticket machine

---

50. 10 W 48th St *bet 5th/6th, S side of W 48th*

Central   212.869.3170

hr	rate	specials	rate	enter	exit
1/2	$11	AM	$26	5:30-9:30am	10hr
1	$24	SUV	$11		
2	$33	Month	$528, O/S add $84		
12	$43				
24	$51				

helpful information

24/7	AE, MC, V	Ticket machine
200 spaces	2 elevators	

---

51. 271 W 47th St *bet Broadway/8th, N side of W 47th, near 8th*

Central   212.977.1876

hr	rate	specials	rate	enter	exit
1	$20	M,T,TH,F	$34	daytime	10hr
2	$26	SUV	$15		
24	$45	Month	$528, O/S add $84		
		Month	$169	m'cycle	
		Parade	$35		

helpful information

24/7	AE, MC, V, Dis	Max bill $50
61 spaces	8" clearance	

---

52. 257 W 47 St *bet Broadway/8th, N side of W 47th*

Central   212.262.9778

hr	rate	specials	rate	enter	exit
1	$20	AM m,t,th,f	$18	5-10am	6pm
2	$26	AM w,sa	$21	3-10am	12hr
24	$40	M,T,Th,F	$30	5am-5pm	10hr
		SUV	$15		
		Olive Garden	$17		6hr

helpful information

24/7	Elevator	AE, V
120 spaces	Max bill $20	

---

53. 253 W 47th St *bet Broadway/8th, N side of W 47th*

Central   212.582.5711

hr	rate	specials	rate	enter	exit
1	$19	AM m,t,th,f	$17	8-10am	7pm
2	$25	SUV	$14		
10	$35				
MTC	$39				

helpful information

M-Sa 8am-12am	41 spaces	Max bill $50
Su 11am-11pm	Cash	Outdoor

54. 145 W 47th St *bet 6th/7th, N side of W 47th*

Icon
212.869.5479

hr	rate	specials	rate	enter	exit
1/2	$8	AM m-f	$26	6-10am	7pm
1	$18	SUV	$10		
2	$25	Month	$465, O/S add $84		
12	$35	Quality Inn	$30		24hr
24	$47	Portland Sq	$30		24hr
		Doubletree	$35		24hr
		Roundabout Theater discount:			
			$14	after 5pm	12hr

helpful information

24/7	AE, MC, V, DC
261 spaces	Max bill $20

---

55. 251 W 45th St *bet Broadway/8th, N side of W 45th or S side of W 46th or E side of 8th*

Champion
212.757.7925

hr	rate	specials	rate	enter	exit
1/2	$14	AM m,t,th,f	$15	5-10am	6pm
1	$25	SUV	$15		
1 1/2	$30	Truck	$80		6hr
2	$35	Month	$503, O/S add $47		
10	$44				
24	$55				

helpful information

24/7	AE, MC, V	256 W 46th
346 spaces	Indoor/outdoor	

---

56. 223 W 46th St *bet 8th/Broadway, N side of W 46th*

QuikPark
212.997.1636

hr	rate*	specials	rate	enter	exit
1/2	$11	AM m	$14	by 10am	close
1	$22	AM t,th,f	$14	by 10am	7pm
2	$27	Day	$22	after 10am	6pm
24	$51	Day	$34	after 10am	12am
MTC	$42	W,Sa	$27		6pm
		W,Sa	$34	after 5pm	12am
		Su	$26		6hr, by 12am
		Event	$50		
		SUV	$10		
		Month	$380, SUV add $50		

helpful information

M-Sa 7am-12am	41 spaces	Outdoor
Su 8am-12a	AE, MC, V	

57. 1535 Broadway *bet 8th/Broadway, S side of W 46th*
Marriott Hotels Inc　　　　　　　　　　　212.298.1900

hr	rate	specials	rate	enter	exit
3	$35	Event	$30		4hr
12	$48	SUV	$10		
		Oversize	$25 add'l		
		Marriott guest	$55		O/N

helpful information

24/7	Eff. 4/08	Security inspection
220 spaces	Enterprise rental	No vans
AE, MC, V	Marriott Hotel	

---

58. 1540 Broadway *bet Broadway/6th, S side of W 46th*
Icon　　　　　　　　　　　　　　　　212.997.9115

hr	rate	specials	rate	enter	exit
1/2	$9	AM	$22	4-10am	7pm
1	$18	SUV	$10		
2	$25	Month	$422, O/S add $84		
12	$32				
24	$40				

helpful information

24/7	Elevator
100 spaces	181" rule for SUV
AE, MC, V	Max bill $50

---

59. 38 W 46th St *bet 6th/5th, S side of W 46th*
Central/Kinney　　　　　　　　　　　212.719.5944

hr	rate	specials	rate	enter	exit
1/2	$12	AM	$24	8-10am	12am
1	$26	SUV	$11		
2	$31	Month	$464, O/S add $84		
10	$40	No entertainment coupons			
24	$51				

helpful information

M-F 6am-12am	AE, MC, V	Max bill $50
Sa,Su 7am-12am	2 elevators	
225 spaces	7' clearance	

60. 1515 Broadway
bet Broadway/8th, N side of W 44th or S side of W 45th

Icon — 212.869.3543

hr	rate*	specials	rate	enter	exit
1/2	$8	AM m-f	$14	6-10am	6pm
1	$10	M,T,Th,F	$18	after 6am	6pm
2	$14	W,Sa	$30	after 6am	6pm
24	$35	Su	$22	after 6am	6pm
		Sa	$35	by 4pm	after 7pm
		PM su-f	$8	6pm-6am	1/2hr
		PM su-f	$10	6pm-6am	1hr
		PM su-f	$14	6pm-6am	2hr
		PM su-t,th	$22	6pm-6am	12hr
		PM su-t,th	$35	6pm-6am	24hr
		PM w,f	$30	6pm-6am	24hr
		PM sa	$35	6pm-6am	12hr
		SUV	$0		
		Month	$275		

helpful information

24/7	6' clearance	Security inspection
225 spaces	No full size vans	
AE, MC, V	*6am-6pm	

61. 120 W 45th St
bet 6th/Broadway, S side of W 45th

MPG — 212.768.1502

hr	rate*	specials	rate	enter	exit
1/2	$8	AM m,t,th,f	$8	7-9am	1/2hr
1	$20	AM m,t,th,f	$20	7-9am	7pm
1 1/2	$30	AM m,t,th,f	$46	7-9am	close
2	$35	Su	$8	8am-close	1/2hr
MTC	$48	Su	$15	8am-close	1hr
		Su	$30	8am-close	close
		SUV	$10		
		Month	$422		

helpful information

M-Th 7am-12am	45 spaces	*M,T,Th,F enter 9am-close
F,Sa 7am-2am	AE, MC, V	*W, Sa enter 7am-close
Su 8am-12am		

62. 141 W 43rd St
bet 6th/Broadway, N side of W 43rd or S side of W 44th

Meyers — 212.997.7690

hr	rate	specials	rate	enter	exit
1	$21	AM m-f	$21	5-10am	8pm
2	$24	Sa,Su	$21	5-7am	8pm
10	$35	SUV	$10		
24	$43	Month	$498, O/S add $105		

helpful information

24/7	AE, MC, V	2 elevators
423 spaces		Car wash

63. **100 W 44th St** *bet 6th/Broadway, N side of W 43rd or S side of W 44th*

Central/Kinney 212.398.0464

hr	rate	specials	rate	enter	exit
1	$24	AM 7D	$21	6-9am	8pm
2	$27	SUV	$11		
10	$37	Month	$700, SUV add $84		
24	$51	No theater discount coupon			

helpful information

24/7	2 elevators	101 W 43rd
187 spaces	6'7" clearance	1211 6th Ave
AE, MC, V, Dis, DC		

64. **1120 6th Ave** *bet 5th/6th, N side of W 43rd or S side of W 44th*

Edison/Park Fast 212.997.9096

hr	rate*	specials	rate	enter	exit
1/2	$11	AM	$24	4-10am	8pm
2	$21	PM m-f	$41	4pm-4am	24hr
12	$35	PM f	$16	5:30pm-4am	12hr
24	$41	PM m-th	$14	5:30pm-4am	12hr
		Sa	$16	Sa 4am-Su 4am	12hr
		Sa	$41	Sa 4am-Su 4am	24hr
		Su	$14	4am-4pm	12hr
		Su	$41	4am-4pm	24hr
		F	$14	5:30pm-4am	12hr
		SUV	$10		
		Month	$359		
		Month	$126	m'cycle	

helpful information

24/7	Main entrance	*M-F enter 4am-4pm
648 spaces	on W 44th	Hippodrome
AE, MC, V, Dis, DC	No sign on W 43rd	50 W 44th
	Boom gates	

65. **249 W 43rd St** *bet 7th/8th, N side of W 43rd*

Icon 212.221.8902

hr	rate	specials	rate	enter	exit
1/2	$10	AM	$18	5-10am	12hr
1	$16	SUV	$10		
2	$22	Month	$422, O/S add $84		
12	$32	Month	$169	m'cycle	
24	$35				

helpful information

24/7	AE, MC, V	181" rule for SUV
225 spaces	2 elevators	Max bill $50

66. 250 W 43rd St *bet 7th/8th, S side of W 43rd*
Good Deal Time Square Parking

hr	rate*	specials	rate	enter	exit
1/2	7	AM	$14	6-10am	6pm
1	$14	PM	$14	after 6pm	1hr
2	$20	PM	$20	after 6pm	2hr
6	$26	PM	$28	after 6pm	12hr
12	$28	SUV	$5		
24	$35	No theatre discount coupons			

helpful information

24/7	80 spaces	Cash	*6am-6pm

---

67. 1114 6th Ave *bet 5th/6th, S side of W 43rd*
Icon   212.575.8986

hr	rate*	specials	rate	enter	exit
1/2	$12	AM	$23	5-10am	12am
1	$19	PM m-f	$12	5pm-5am	1/2hr
2	$23	PM m-f	$15	5pm-5am	1hr
3	$28	PM m-f	$17	5pm-5am	2hr
12	$32	PM m-f	$18	5pm-5am	3hr
24	$40	PM m-f	$19	5pm-5am	12hr
		PM m-f	$40	5pm-5am	24hr
		Sa	$12	Sa 5am-Su 5am	1/2hr
		Sa	$15	Sa 5am-Su 5am	1hr
		Sa	$20	Sa 5am-Su 5am	2hr
		Sa	$21	Sa 5am-Su 5am	3hr
		Sa	$23	Sa 5am-Su 5am	12hr
		Sa	$40	Sa 5am-Su 5am	24hr
		Su	$10	Su 5am-M 5am	1/2hr
		Su	$15	Su 5am-M 5am	1hr
		Su	$17	Su 5am-M 5am	2hr
		Su	$18	Su 5am-M 5am	3hr
		Su	$19	Su 5am-M 5am	12hr
		Su	$40	Su 5am-M 5am	24hr
		SUV	$10		
		Month	$465, O/S add $84		

helpful information

24/7	6' clearance	*Enter M-F 5am-5pm
188 spaces	Long, steep driveway	181" rule for SUV
AE, MC, V	Grace Building	38 W 43rd
	Public bathroom	

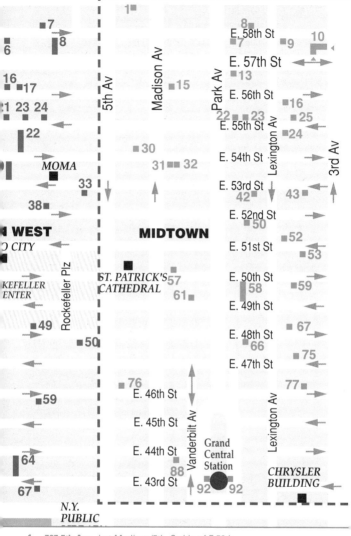

1. **767 5th Ave** *bet Madison/5th, S side of E 59th*

Icon   212.980.7092

hr	rate	specials	rate	enter	exit
1/2	$22	SUV	$10		
1	$32	Month	$676, O/S add $84		
2	$37				
12	$52				
24	$65				

helpful information

24/7	181" rule for SUV	GM Building
136 spaces	Max bill $50	
AE, MC, V	Security inspection	

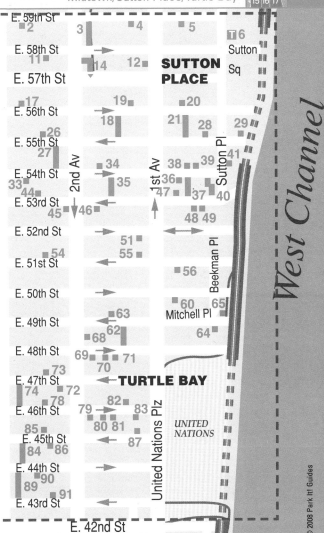

2. **206 E 59th St** bet 3rd/2nd, S side of E 59th
   Impark   212.223.9288

hr	rate	specials	rate	enter	exit
1	$22	AM m-f	$22	3-10am	12hr
2	$30	PM m-sa	$12	5pm-3am	12hr
24	$37	Sa	$18	3am-5pm	12hr
		Su	$12	3am-5pm	12hr
		SUV	$10		
		Month	$422, O/S add $84		
		D&D Bldg	$30	after 10am	6hr
		Imagin Asia discount			

helpful information

24/7   AE, MC, V

225 spaces   6' clearance

---

3. **1104 2nd Ave** *bet 2nd/1st, N side of E 58th or S side of E 59th*

Icon 212.980.0215

hr	rate	specials	rate	enter	exit
1/2	$8	AM m-f	$17	4-11am	8pm
1	$16	PM	$11	after 4pm	4am
2	$20	Sa,Su	$13	4am-4pm	10hr
10	$26	SUV	$10		
24	$35	Month	$422, SUV add $84		

helpful information
24/7   181" rule for SUV
227 spaces   Max bill $50
AE, MC, V   7'1" clearance

---

4. **340 E 59th St** *bet 2nd/1st, S side of E 59th, near 1st*

Champion 212.755.1775

hr	rate	specials	rate	enter	exit
1/2	$17	AM	$16	6-11am	8pm
1	$21	PM 7D	$15	after 5pm	1am
2	$23	Sa, Su	$10	6-11am	8pm
10	$27	SUV	$10		
24	$27-35	Month	$444, O/S add $42		
O/N	$35				

helpful information
24/7   2 elevators
288 spaces
AE, MC, V

---

5. **425 E 58th St** *bet 1st/Sutton Pl, S side of E 59th*

GGMC 212.838.4447

hr	rate	specials	rate	enter	exit
1	$11	M-F	$13	6am-5pm	12hr
2	$16	Sa,Su	$14	6am-12pm	12hr
12	$27	SUV	$9		
24	$35	Truck	$30+ additional		

helpful information
24/7   Max bill $20
AE, MC, V, Dis   Boom gate at entrance

---

6. **35 Sutton Pl** *bet E 58th/E 59th, E side of Sutton Pl*

Sutton Place Garage Corp

hr	rate	specials	rate	enter	exit

TENANT ONLY

helpful information
7D 7am-1am   Eff. 9/05
38 spaces
Cash

7. 110 E 58th St *bet Park/Lexington, S side of E 58th*

Central   212.308.8119

hr	rate	specials	rate	enter	exit
1	$27	AM	$28	6-8am	7pm
2	$34	SUV	$11		
10	$40	Month	$507, O/S add $84		
24	$51				

helpful information

M-F 6:30am-12am	AE, MC, V
Sa 7am-12am	6' clearance
Su 8am-12am	Long, steep driveway
94 spaces	No vans/SUV, park across street

---

8. 109 E 58th St *bet Park/Lexington, N side of E 58th*

Central   212.688.5040

hr	rate	specials	rate	enter	exit
1	$27	AM m-f	$27	4-10am	7pm
2	$34	SUV	$11		
10	$40	Month	$507, O/S add $84		
24	$51	Honors Bridge Club	$24		
		Dr. Celenza, Gerald Bollei,	$24		
		Arrol Cutter, Pierre Michael			

helpful information

24/7	AE, MC, V	7' clearance
150 spaces	12am gate closes	Max bill $50

---

9. 150 E 58th St *bet Lexington/3rd, S side of E 58th*

Central   212.755.8678

hr	rate	specials	rate	enter	exit
1	$27	AM	$26	4-8am	7pm
2	$32	Sa,Su	$18		12hr, by 12am
10	$40	SUV	$10		
24	$50				

helpful information

24/7	AE, MC, V, Dis
260 spaces	Max bill $50

---

10. 153 E 57th St *bet Lexington/3rd, N side of E 57th or W side of 3rd*

Rapid Park   212.223.2838

hr	rate	specials	rate	enter	exit
1/2	$11	AM m-f	$28	7-10am	10hr
1	$26	PM	$21	after 5pm	12am
2	$31	Sa	$20	8-11am	5pm
10	$40	Su	$20	8-11am	12am
24	$45	O/N	$45		
		SUV	$10		
		Month	$475, O/S add $100		
		Month	$150, m'cycle		

helpful information

24/7	AE, MC, V	Steep, narrow driveway
38 spaces	Max bill $20	No vans

11. **220 E 58th St** *bet 3rd/2nd, S side of E 58th*

Central   212.752.8941

hr	rate	specials	rate	enter	exit
1	$26	AM m-f	$19	6-10am	10hr
2	$32	SUV	$11		
10	$40	Month	$507, O/S add $100		
24	$51				

helpful information

24/7	10am gate closes	Steep, narrow driveway
36 spaces	6'10" clearance	
AE, MC, V	Max bill $50	

---

12. **357 E 57th St** *bet E 57th/E 58th, W side of 1st*

Ulltra   212.838.1629

hr	rate	specials	rate	enter	exit
1	$15	AM	$14	7-11am	7pm
2	$20	Sa,Su	$17	after 7am	7pm
12	$28	SUV	$10		
24	$31	Month	$351, O/S add $62		

helpful information

24/7	AE, MC, V
75 spaces	

---

13. **110 E 57th St** *bet Park/Lexington, S side of E 57th*

Champion   212.759.6002

hr	rate	specials	rate	enter	exit
1/2	$22	AM	$32	4-8:30am	7pm
1	$29	PM	$29	after 5pm	4am
1 1/2	$39	Sa,Su	$29	anytime	12hr, by 2am
2	$47	SUV	$10		
24	$55	Month	$570, O/S add $355		
O/N	$55				

helpful information

24/7	AE, MC, V	181" rule for SUV
65 spaces	Eff. 9/05	No full size vans

---

14. **301 E 57th St** *bet E 58th/E 57th, E side of 2nd Ave*

Icon   212.755.6223

hr	rate	specials	rate	enter	exit
1/2	$7	AM m-f	$18	6-10am	12hr
1	$17	PM su-th	$13	6pm-12am	3am
2	$21	Sa,Su	$12	5-11am	12hr
12	$26	SUV	$10		
24	$33	Month	$465, O/S add $84		
		Month	$211	m'cycle	

helpful information

24/7	181	No full size vans
328 spaces	Max bill $50	
AE, MC, V	Exit only on E 57th	

15. 575 Madison Ave *bet Madison/Park, N side of E 56th*
MPG   212.593.5219

hr	rate	specials	rate	enter	exit
1/2	$15	Sa,Su	$15	7-10am	close
1	$26	SUV	$10		
1 1/2	$38	Month	$591, O/S add $42		
2	$43	Lombardy Hotel discount			
MTC	$48				

helpful information
M-Th, Su 7am-12am   AE, MC, V
F,Sa 7am-1am   Low clearance
100 spaces   Damage inspection

---

16. 140 E 56th St *bet Lexington/3rd, S side of E 56th, near Lexington*
QuikPark   212.754.4231

hr	rate	specials	rate	enter	exit
1/2	$16	AM m-f	$20	5-8am	7pm
2	$23	Sa,Su	$17	anytime	10hr, by M 12am
10	$28	SUV	$10		
24	$36	Month	$415, O/S add $42		

helpful information
24/7   181" rule for SUV   7'4" clearance
50 spaces   Long, steep driveway
AE, MC, V   667 Lexington

---

17. 201 E 56th St *bet 3rd/2nd, N side of E 56th*
MPG   212.223.0458

hr	rate*	specials	rate	enter	exit
1/2	$8	AM m-f	$18	6-9am	12hr
1	$20	AM m-f	$45	6-9am	24hr
2	$30	Sa,Su	$8		1/2hr
24	$45	Sa,Su	$30		24hr
		Sa,Su	$12	12am-12pm	12hr
		Sa,Su	$17	12pm-12am	12hr
		SUV	$10		
		Month	$500, O/S add $42		
		Marriott discount			
			$45		24hr

helpful information
24/7   *enter M-F 9am-6am
150 spaces
AE, MC, V

---

18. 300 E 56th St *bet 2nd/1st, N side of E 55th or S side of E 56th*

Glenwood/ 56th Realty LLC   212.308.8107

hr	rate	specials	rate	enter	exit
1	$14	AM	$18	5-10am	8:30pm
3	$17	SUV	$7		14hr
4	$18	Month	$389	tenant, O/S add $42	
5	$20	Month	$418	non-tenant, O/S add $42	
9	$25				
24	$33				

helpful information

24/7	$5 lost claim check fee	Takes large vans
300 spaces	181" rule for SUV	
MC, V	Bristol Garage	

---

19. 333 E 56th St *bet 2nd/1st, N side of E 56th*

Glenwood/ Bamford Realty   212.355.8030

hr	rate	specials	rate	enter	exit
1/2	$6	AM	$16	6-10am	8pm
1	$10	SUV	$7		12hr
3	$13	Month	$338	tenant, O/S add $30	
5	$16	Month	$367	non-tenant, O/S add $30	
9	$18				
24	$30				

helpful information

Su-Th 6am-1am	MC, V	181" rule for SUV
F,Sa 24hr	$5 lost claim check fee	5'11" clearance
150 spaces	Eff. 9/05	

---

20. 405 E 56th St *bet 1st/Sutton Pl South, N side of E 56th*

Little Man Parking/Syd Parking   212.750.4274

hr	rate	specials	rate	enter	exit
1	$10	AM	$15	5-10am	7pm
2	$16	Sa,Su	$11	after 5pm	6pm, no O/N
3	$19	O/N	$21	after 8pm	9am
10	$22	SUV	$10		
24	$32	Month	$390, O/S add $50		
O/N	$21-32				

helpful information

24/7	Max bill $20	Sutton Townhouse Garage
56 spaces	6'11" clearance	Steep driveway
Cash		No full size vans

---

21. 411 E 55th St *bet Sutton Pl South/1st, N side of E 55th or S side of E 56th*

GMC   212.752.2884

hr	rate	specials	rate	enter	exit
1	$14	AM 7D	$17	5-11am	8pm
2	$20	Sa,Su	$11	after 5am	6pm
8	$25	O/N	$35		after 5am
24	$35	SUV	$10		
		Month	$425, O/S add $100		

helpful information

24/7	AE, MC, V	6' clearance on W 56th
571 spaces	5 min grace period	400 E 56th

22. 425 Park Ave *bet Lexington/Park, N side of E 55th*

Champion   212.644.1425

hr	rate	specials	rate	enter	exit
1/2	$13	AM m-f	$26	6-10am	12am
1	$27	PM	$23	after 5pm	12am
1 1/2	$37	Sa	$19	after 7am	12am
2	$43	Su	$10	after 7am	10pm
10	$46	SUV	$10		
24	$53	Month	$465, O/S add $127		
MTC	$53				

helpful information

M-Sa 7am-12am	6'6" clearance
Su 8am-10pm	No vans, full size trucks
Closed some Sa, Su, Hol	181" rule for SUV
130 spaces	Max bill $100
AE, MC, V	Security inspection
12am gate closes	

23. 662 Lexington Ave *bet Lexington/Park, N side of E 55th*

Champion   212.207.8951

hr	rate	specials	rate	enter	exit
1/2	$21	AM m-f	$28	4-10am	12am
1	$27	PM 7D	$23	after 6pm	4am
1 1/2	$37	Sa	$19	4am-5pm	12am
2	$47	Su	$15	4am-5pm	12am
24	$55	SUV	$10		
O/N	$55	Month	$515, O/S add $100		

helpful information

24/7	181" rule for SUV	31 E 55th
67 spaces	6'2" clearance	
AE, MC, V	No full size vans/trucks	

24. 136 E 55th St *bet 3rd/Lexington, S side of E 55th*

Lexington 55th St Garage   212.751.3379

hr	rate	specials	rate	enter	exit
1	$17	AM m-f	$19	by 10am	7pm
2	$20	PM m-th	$19	5pm-1am	
3	$25	Sa	$17	after 7am	6pm
10	$29	Su	$15	after 7am	close
24	$36	SUV	$5		
O/N	$36	Month	$436	tenant, O/S add $60	
		Month	$446	non-tenant, O/S add $60	

helpful information

S-Th 7am-1am	181" rule for SUV	No vans
F,Sa 7am-2am	AE, MC, V	
101 spaces	No sign on street	

25. 155 E 55th St *bet 3rd/Lexington, N side of E 55th*
Bricin Parking Corp   212.319.1470

hr	rate*	specials	rate	enter	exit
1	$15	AM m-f	$18	7-10am	7pm
2	$19	PM m-th	$14	5pm-close	
3	$24	Sa	$16	after 8am	7pm
10	$28	Su	$14	all day	
24	$35	SUV	$7		
		Month	$399		
		Shun Lee	$8.50	after 6pm	

helpful information
M-F 7am-12am	42 spaces	*M-F
Sa 8am-12am	Cash	No vans
Su 10am-10pm		Good rate signs

26. 919 3rd Ave *bet 2nd/3rd, N side of E 55th*
GMC   212.753.2972

hr	rate	specials	rate	enter	exit
1	$15	AM m-f	$19	5-10am	12am
2	$20	Sa,Su	$15	5am-5pm	12am
12	$25	O/N	$32		after 5am
24	$32	SUV	$15		
		Month	$425, O/S add $100		

helpful information
24/7	AE, MC, V
316 spaces	Security inspection

27. 245 E 54th St *bet 3rd/2nd, N side of E 54th or S side of E 55th*
GGMC   212.355.9093

hr	rate	specials	rate	enter	exit
1	$11	AM m-f	$18	6-9am	2am
2	$18	PM su-th	$12	5:30pm-4am	6am
10	$25	Sa,Su	$15	5am-5:30pm	2am
24	$32	SUV	$10		
O/N	$32	Month	$425, O/S add $180		

helpful information
24/7	7'4" clearance
178 spaces	Eff. 4/08
AE, MC, V	No vans

28. 400 E 56th St *bet Sutton Pl South/1st, N side of E 55th*
GMC   212.753.8148

hr	rate	specials	rate	enter	exit
1	$14	AM m-f	$17	5-11am	8pm
2	$20	Sa,Su	$11	after 5am	6pm
8	$24	O/N	$35		after 5am
24	$35	SUV	$10		
		Month	$425, O/S add $100		

helpful information

7D 6am-2am	AE, MC, V	10pm gate closes
571 spaces	5 min grace period	Max bill $50

29. 25 Sutton Pl South *bet river/Sutton Pl South, N side of E 55th*
Imperial   212.355.8007

hr	rate	specials	rate	enter	exit
1	$11	AM m-f	$12	7-11am	7pm
2	$15	SUV	$10		
3	$17				
24	$32				
O/N	$32				
11pm	$20				
2am	$26				
7pm	$19				

helpful information

24/7	12am gate closes
150 spaces	Car wash
AE, MC, V	Bumper guards for residents

30. 13 E 54th St *bet 5th/Madison, N side of E 54th*
Central   212.308.3770

hr	rate	specials	rate	enter	exit
1	$30	AM m-f	$28	3am-10am	10hr
2	$39	SUV	$11		
10	$45	Month	$549, O/S add $84		
24	$51				

helpful information

24/7	3 elevators	311 E 54th
225 spaces	7' clearance	
AE, MC, V	Damage inspection	

31. 527 Madison Ave *bet Madison/Park, S side of E 54th*
Champion   212.355.9564

hr	rate	specials	rate	enter	exit
1/2	$13-22	AM 7D	$27	6:30-9:30am	8pm
1	$29	PM m-f	$23	after 5pm	12am (winter only)
1 1/2	$39	Sa,Su	$18	after 4pm	12am (winter only)
2	$47	SUV	$10		
8am	$55	Month	$625		

helpful information

M-Sa 7am-12am	26 spaces	Elevator
Su 8am-6pm	AE, MC, V	
Summer M-F 6:30am-12am		

206

| 7 | 8 9 10 11 |
| 12 13 14 |
| 15 16 17 |

E 59th St–E 42nd St, 5th Ave–FDR
Midtown/Sutton Place/Turtle Bay

32. 378 Park Ave *bet Madison/Park, S side of E 54th*

QuikPark   212.688.3231

hr	rate	specials	rate	enter	exit
1/2	$13	AM	$27	4-9am	8pm
1	$26	Sa, Su	$18	anytime	12hr
2	$46	SUV	$10		
24	$51	Month	$507, O/S add $42		

helpful information

24/7	AE, MC, V, DC	6'2" clearance
149 spaces	181' rule for SUV	Steep driveway

---

33. 220 E 54th St *bet 3rd/2nd, S side of E 54th, near 3rd Ave*

MPG   212.750.5627

hr	rate*	specials	rate	enter	exit
1/2	$7	Sa	$25	4pm-close	close
1	$22	Sa	$20	7am-4pm	close
2	$29	Su	$20	7am-12am	close
3	$39	Sa, Su	$7		1/2hr
MTC	$42	Sa, Su	$10		1hr
		SUV	$10		
		Month	$400, O/S add $42		

helpful information

M-Th 7am-12am	30 spaces	*M-F
F,Sa 7am-2am	AE, MC, V	

---

34. 300 E 55th St *bet 2nd/1st, N side of E 54th, near 2nd*

Icon   212.486.0387

hr	rate	specials	rate	enter	exit
1/2	$7	AM 7D	$21	6-10am	12hr
1	$12	SUV	$10		
2	$20	Month	$528, O/S add $169		
12	$25				
24	$33				

helpful information

24/7	181" rule for SUV
25 spaces	Max bill $50
AE, MC, V	Very clean interior

---

35. 300 E 54th St *bet 1st/2nd, N side of E 53rd or S side of E 54th, near 2nd*

GGMC   212.223.4891

hr	rate	specials	rate	enter	exit
1	$12	PM su-th	$21	after 6pm	4am
2	$20	O/N	$40	by 12am	after 4am
3	$25	SUV	$15		
10	$30	Month	$450, O/S add $100		
24	$40				

helpful information

24/7	AE, MC, V, Dis, DC	No vans
73 spaces	Low clearance	Connaught Tower

36. 400 E 54th St *bet 1st/Sutton Pl South, S side of E 54th*

Central   212.421.0722

hr	rate	specials	rate	enter	exit
1	$10	AM	$16	6-10am	close
2	$13	SUV	$10		
10	$21	Month	$380, O/S add $84		
24	$27	Month	$169	m'cycle	

helpful information

Su-Th 6am-1am	Cash
Sa 6am-2am	Limited space for SUVs
140 spaces	Eff. 5/07

---

37. 410 E 54th St *bet Sutton Pl South/1st, N side of E 53rd or S side of E 54th*

Icon   212.644.6312

hr	rate	specials	rate	enter	exit
1/2	$7	AM	$17	by 10am	12am
1	$14	Sa,Su	$9	anytime	12hr
2	$20	SUV	$10		
10	$27	Month	$507, O/S add $84		
24	$34				

helpful information

24/7	12am gate closes	River Tower
182 spaces	6'6" clearance	Little signage on E 54th
AE, MC, V	Very clean interior	

---

38. 425 E 54th St *bet 1st/Sutton Pl South, N side of E 54th*

River Edge Sutton Garden Garage   212.223.9532

hr	rate	specials	rate	enter	exit
1	$7	AM	$12.50	7-11am	7pm
2	$12	WE	$8	after 7am	8pm
3	$15	SUV	$10		
10	$17	Month	$380		
24	$23				

helpful information

7am-1am	Cash	Eff. 9/07
68 spaces	181" rule for SUV	

---

39. 50 Sutton Pl South *bet 1st/Sutton Pl South, N side of E 54th*

Gemini Garage Corp   212.223.9532

hr	rate*	specials	rate	enter	exit
1	$7	Sa,Su	$9	anytime	12hr
2	$12	SUV	$10		
3	$15	Month	$425		
10	$17				
10 1/2	$15				
24	$23				

helpful information

24/7	Cash	181" rule for SUV
76 spaces	*M-F	

40. 60 Sutton Pl North /South *bet 1st/Sutton Pl, S side of E 54th or N side of E 53rd*

GMC 212.752.7504
212.752.7529

hr	rate	specials	rate	enter	exit
1	$12	AM m-f	$15	5-10am	6pm
2	$18	Sa,Su	$8	after 5am	7pm
10	$23	SUV	$10		
24	$30	Month	$390, O/S add $100		

helpful information

24/7	AE, MC, V	Hard to see from street
213 spaces	Low clearance	

41. 45 Sutton Pl South *bet E 54th/E 55th, E side of Sutton Pl*

Eastside Parking 212.486.5389

hr	rate	specials	rate	enter	exit
2	$10	AM m-f	$13	6-11am	5pm
24	$22	Sa,Su	$9	after 6am	7pm
MTC	$16	Event	$25		
		SUV	$10		
		Month	$307	tenant, SUV add $84	
		Month	$380	non-tenant, SUV add $84	

helpful information

Su-Th 6am-1am	88 spaces
F,Sa 6am-2am	Cash

42. 375 Park Ave *bet Lexington/Park, S side of E 53rd*

Central 212.644.7429

hr	rate	specials	rate	enter	exit
1/2	$13	Sa,Su	$36		10hr, by 12am
1	$27	SUV	$11		
2	$33	Month	$508, O/S add $84		
10	$44	Lehman	$21		18hr
MTC	$47				

helpful information

Su-Th 6am-1am	AE, MC, V	Very long driveway
F,Sa 24hr	6'5" clearance	Public bathroom
150 spaces	Max bill $50	

43. 154 E 53rd St *bet 3rd/Lexington, S side of E 53rd*

Central 212.759.8689

hr	rate	specials	rate	enter	exit
1	$26	AM	$26	6-9am	12am
2	$33	Sa,Su	$16	anytime	12hr, by 12am
10	$44	SUV	$11		
24	$47	Month	$591		

helpful information

M-F 7am-12am	149 spaces	7' clearance
Sa 8am-12am	AE, MC, V	Max bill $50
Some Su, Hol 8am-12am	2 elevators	Damage inspection

44. 211 E 53rd St *bet 2nd/3rd, N side of E 53rd*

Central   917.369.1137

hr	rate	specials	rate	enter	exit
1/2	$8	AM	$26	7-9:30am	12hr
1	$26	PM	$14	after 5pm	3am
2	$33	Sa, Su	$18	anytime	12hr, by 12am
10	$40	SUV	$11		
24	$45	Month	$507		

helpful information

24/7	12am gate closes	No O/S vans
90 spaces	6'7" clearance	
AE, MC, V	Max bill $50	

45. 248 E 53rd St *bet 2nd/3rd, S side of E 53rd*

MPG   212.230.1413

hr	rate	specials	rate	enter	exit
1	$10	AM m-f	$10	12am-9am	1hr
2	$20	AM m-f	$17	12am-9am	7pm
10	$30	AM m-f	$40	12am-9am	24hr
24	$40	Sa	$15	12am-4pm	12hr
		Su	$15	12am-4pm	12hr
		SUV	$10		
		Month	tenant only		

helpful information

24/7	AE, MC, V	Opened 1/08	Elevator
28 spaces	No vans or O/S	*M-F 9am-12am, Sa 4pm-12am	

46. 310 E 53rd St *bet 1st/2nd, S side of E 53rd*

Icon   212.223.3181

hr	rate	specials	rate	enter	exit
1	$10	AM m-f	$18	5-10am	12hr
2	$20	PM	$14	after 5pm	5am
3	$25	Sa, Su	$11	5am-5pm	12hr
12	$30	SUV	$10		
24	$35	Month	$465, O/S add $169		

helpful information

24/7	AE, MC, V
70 spaces	181" rule for SUV

47. 411 E 53rd St *bet Sutton Pl South/1st, N side of E 53rd, near 1st*

Central   212.644.6312

hr	rate	specials	rate	enter	exit
1	$10	PM	$10	after 7pm	2hr
2	$13	PM	$14	after 7pm	close
10	$21	Sa,Su	$14	anytime	close
24	$27	Sa,Su	$25	anytime	24hr
		SUV	$10		
		Month	$380		

helpful information

M-F 6am-10pm	AE, MC, V	Max bill $50
72 spaces	10pm gate closes	May not accept large cars

48. 420 E 53rd St *bet Sutton Pl South/1st, S side of E 53rd*

GMC 212.759.5290

hr	rate	specials	rate	enter	exit
1	$15	Sa,Su	$11	after 5am	12hr
2	$20	O/N	$35	after 5am	
10	$25	SUV	$10		
24	$35	Month	$415		

helpful information

24/7 5 min grace period
270 spaces 10pm gate closes
AE, MC, V Max bill $50

---

49. 429 E 52nd St *bet Sutton Pl South/1st, S side of E 53rd*

Central 212.223.9500

hr	rate	specials	rate	enter	exit
1	$10	AM	$16	6-10am	close
2	$13	SUV	$10		
10	$21	Month	$380, O/S add $84		
24	$27	Month	$169	m'cycle	

helpful information

Su-Th 6am-1am AE, MC, V
F,Sa 6am-2am 6'6" clearance
225 spaces

---

50. 345 Park Ave *bet Park/Lexington, S side of E 52nd*

Parklex Garage Inc 212.421.0630

hr	rate	specials	rate	enter	exit
1	$25	AM	$23	by 10am	6pm
2	$31	PM	$24	by 6pm	close
3	$35	Sa	$25	after 7:30am	5pm
24	$43	SUV	$5		
O/N	$43	Month	$524, O/S add $40		

helpful information

M-F 6:30am-12am 150 spaces 7' clearance
Sa 7:30am-2am AE, MC, V Max bill $20
Su, Hol closed 181" rule for SUV Eff. 4/08

51. 350 E 52nd St *bet 2nd/1st, S side of E 52nd*

Icon   212.355.8249

hr	rate	specials	rate	enter	exit
1	$20	AM	$18	6-10am	6pm
2	$22	SUV	$10		
12	$30	Month	$507, O/S add $84		
24	$40	July 4	$30	4pm-4am	

helpful information

24/7	181" rule for SUV	No full size vans
80 spaces	6'clearance	
AE, MC, V	Max bill $50	

52. 575 Lexington Ave *bet 3rd/Lexington, N side of E 51st*

MPG   212.888.3422

hr	rate*	specials	rate	enter	exit
1/2	$9	AM	$22	by 9am	12hr
1	$26	AM m-f	$41	by 9am	24hr
2	$31	Sa,Su,Hol	$9	12am-4pm	1/2hr
3	$37	Sa,Su,Hol	$18	12am-4pm	12hr
24	$41	Sa,Su,Hol	$41	12am-4pm	24hr
		SUV	$10		
		Month	$380, O/S add $42		
		Nearby restaurants	$13		4hr

helpful information

24/7	Rent-A-Car, Prestige rental
150 spaces	Bumper Guards for some cars
AE, MC, V	*M-F 9-12am, Sa&Su 4pm-12am

53. 136 E 51st St *bet 3rd/Lexington, S side of E 51st*

Icon   212.308.8474

hr	rate	specials	rate	enter	exit
1/2	$9	AM m-f	$22	5-9am	12hr
1	$26	AM m-f	$25	9-10am	12hr
2	$31	Sa,Su	$18	6am-6pm	12hr
3	$37	SUV	$10		
12	$41	Month	$507, O/S add $84		
24	$42	Month	$211	m'cycle	
		Pickwick Arms, Doubletree Hotel $30 24hr			
		Mr. K's, Al Bustan, Nikki Beach discount			

helpful information

24/7	2 elevators
200 spaces	181" rule for SUV
AE, MC, V	Max bill $50

54. 251 E 51st St *bet 2nd/3rd, N side of E 51st*
Champion 212.223.8649

hr	rate	specials	rate	enter	exit
1/2	$19	AM m-f	$24	7-9:30am	6:30pm
1	$25	Su	$14	anytime	12hr, by 12am
1 1/2	$36	SUV	$10		
2	$46	Month	$486, SUV add $264		
24	$49				
O/N	$49				

helpful information

24/7	Low clearance	181" rule for SUV
54 spaces	No vans	
AE, MC, V	Steep driveway	

55. 351 E 51st St *bet 1st/2nd, N side of E 51st*
Rox Parking 212.486.8603

hr	rate	specials	rate	enter	exit
1	$19	O/N	$38		
2	$23	Event	$45		
10	$29	SUV	$13		
24	$38	Month	$591, O/S add $84		
MTC	$35	Month	$169	m'cycle	

helpful information

Su-Th 7am-1am	AE, V, MC, DC, Disc	181" rule for SUV
F,Sa 7am-2am	Elevator	Eff. 6/08
26 spaces	High clearance	

56. 420 E 51st St *bet Beekman/1st, S side of E 51st*
GMC 212.838.7565

hr	rate	specials	rate	enter	exit
1	$20	O/N	$45		after 5am
2	$25	SUV	$10		
8	$35	Month	$475, O/S add $100		
24	$45				

helpful information

7D 7am-2am	AE, MC, V	5 min grace period
105 spaces	Eff. 9/07	

57. 27 E 50th St *bet Madison/Park, N side of E 50th*
Kinney 212.421.3746

hr	rate	specials	rate	enter	exit
1	$25	AM m-f	$25	6-9am	7pm
2	$30	SUV	$10		
3	$35	Month	$528, O/S add $84		
8	$40				
24	$50				

helpful information

24/7	2 elevators	451 Madison
94 spaces	AE, MC, V	NY Palace Hotel

58. 301 Park Avenue *bet Park/Lexington, N side of E 49th or S side of E 50th*

Central   212.872.4640

hr	rate*	specials	rate	enter	exit
1	$22	Hotel guest	$32		8hr
8	$42	Hotel guest	$50		24hr
12	$60	Hotel guest	$68		26hr
24	$84	Hotel guest	$82		32hr
		Hotel guest	$90		48hr
		Van/Limo	add'l $10		

helpful information

| 24/7 | Waldorf-Astoria | Exit on E 49th |
| AE, MC, V | *Non-guests | |

---

59. 138 E 50th St *bet Lexington/3rd, S side of E 50th*

Central   212.888.2732

hr	rate	specials	rate	enter	exit
1	$26	AM	$22	5-10am	12hr
2	$31	SUV	$11		
10	$40	Month	$507, O/S add $84		
24	$51	San Carlos	$30		24hr
		Hotel Kimberly	$28		24hr

helpful information

| 24/7 | AE, MC, V | 181" rule for SUV |
| 185 spaces | Alamo, National rental | Ticket machine |

---

60. 12 Beekman Pl *bet 1st/Beekman, S side of E 50th ·*

12 Garage Corp   212.755.0171

hr	rate	specials	rate	enter	exit
1/2	$11	SUV	$10		
1	$19	Month	$425		
8	$23				
1am	$28				
24	$35				
O/N	$35				

helpful information

| 7D 7am-1am | Cash |
| 38 spaces | 181" rule for SUV |

---

61. 437 Madison Ave *bet Park/Madison, N side of E 49th*

Sweets Parking   212.486.4121

hr	rate*	specials	rate	enter	exit
1	$29	AM	$29	3-10am	1hr
1 1/2	$39	AM	$38	3-10am	10hr
2	$49	AM	$59	3-10am	O/N to 9am
9am	$59	SUV	$10		
		Month	$549, O/S add $42		

helpful information

24/7	12am gate closes	*enter 10-3am
116 spaces	Eff. 9/05	
AE, MC, V	6'5" clearance	

62. 100 UN Plaza *bet 2nd/1st, N side of E 48th or S side of E 49th*

Icon 212.644.5838

hr	rate	specials	rate	enter	exit
1/2	$7	AM m-f	$17	5-10am	12am
1	$16	PM	$13	after 5pm	5am
2	$19	Sa,Su	$13	anytime	10hr
10	$25	SUV	$10		
24	$33	Month	$422, O/S add $84		

helpful information

24/7	12am gate closes	Steep driveway
150 spaces	6'6" clearance	327 E 48th
AE, MC, V	Damage, security inspection	326 E 49th

63. 333 E 49th St *bet 1st/2nd, N side of E 49th*

Champion 212.223.8675

hr	rate	specials	rate	enter	exit
1/2	$19	AM	$17	4-10am	12am
1	$23	PM	$12	after 4pm	2am
1 1/2	$27	Sa,Su	$12	anytime	12hr, No O/N
2	$33	SUV	$10		
24	$39	Month	$418, O/S add $42		
O/N	$39				

helpful information

24/7	Max bill $50	181" rule for SUV
51 spaces	Damage inspection	
AE, MC, V	Steep driveway	

64. 866 UN Plaza *bet river/1st, S side of E 49th*

Icon 212.223.8787

hr	rate	specials	rate	enter	exit
1/2	$7	AM	$17	6-10am	12hr
1	$15	Sa,Su	$11	6am-6pm	12hr
2	$17	SUV	$10		
3	$19	Month	$390, O/S add $84		
5	$21	July 4	$20	4pm-4am	
12	$24				
24	$32				

helpful information

24/7	181" rule for SUV	No vans, trucks
175 spaces	6'3" clearance	
AE, MC, V	Damage inspection	

65. 443 E 49th St *bet river/1st, N side of E 49th*

GMC 212.688.7666

hr	rate	specials	rate	enter	exit
1/2	$6	AM m-f	$15	6-10am	11pm
1	$15	PM m-f	$8	after 5pm	2am
2	$17	Sa,Su	$9	6am-5pm	11pm
3	$19	O/N	$32		after 5am
12	$24	SUV	$10		
24	$32	Month	$425, O/S add $100		

helpful information

7D 6am-2am	AE, MC, V	Free bumper guards
150 spaces	Lifts	Damage inspection

66. **277 Park Ave** *bet Park/Lexington, S side of E 48th*

Manhattan Parking System Park Ave Corp 212.752.6181

hr	rate*	specials	rate	enter	exit
1	$29	Sa,Su	$28	12am-11am	12hr
1 1/2	$39	O/N add'l	$10		
2	$49	Month	$1014		
2 1/2	$59				
3	$69				
9am	$72				

helpful information

24/7	AE, MC, V	Damage inspection
40 spaces	Max bill $100	*M-F

67. **141 E 48th St** *bet Lexington/3rd, N side of E 48th*

MPG 212.593.3714

hr	rate*	specials	rate	enter	exit
1	$22	PM 7D	$22	6pm-6am	1hr
1 1/2	$32	PM 7D	$32	6pm-6am	1 1/2hr
2	$42	PM 7D	$35	6pm-6am	to 10am
3	$52	PM 7D	$62	6pm-6am	24hr
24	$62	SUV	$10		
		Month	$591, O/S add $42		
		Radisson, Helmsley Hotels	$40		24hr
		Marriott Hotel	$50		24hr

helpful information

24/7	AE, MC, V	*6am-6pm
66 spaces	12am gate closes	

68. **910 2nd Ave** *bet E 48th/E 49th, E side of 2nd*

910 Garage Corp 212.308.1061

hr	rate*	specials	rate	enter	exit
1	$16	PM m-f	$16	after 6pm	6am
2	$17	Sa, Su	$10	Sa 6am-M 6am	1hr
12	$26	Sa, Su	$17	Sa 6am-M 6am	10hr, by M 6am
24	$31	SUV	$10		
		Month	$465, O/S add $84		
		Month	$169	m'cycle	

helpful information

24/7	AE, MC, V	*M-F 6am-6pm
42 spaces	6'6" clearance	

69. **306 E 48th St** *bet 2nd/1st, S side of E 48th*

QuikPark 212.355.8819

hr	rate	specials	rate	enter	exit
1/2	$6	AM m-f	$17	6-10am	12am
1	$15	PM	$12	after 5pm	1am
2	$20	Sa,Su	$11		12am
10	$24	SUV	$10		
24	$35	Month	$435		
		After 12am hourly rates apply			

helpful information

24/7	AE, MC, V	Max bill $20
51 spaces	12am gate closes	

70. 310 E 48th St *bet 2nd/1st, S side of E 48th*

GMC 212.753.0301

hr	rate	specials	rate	enter	exit
1	$17	AM m-f	$18	5-10am	7pm
2	$23	Sa,Su	$12	after 5am	7pm
12	$30	O/N	$35		after 5am
24	$35	SUV	$10		
		Month	$425, O/S add $150		

helpful information		
24/7	2 elevators	
300 spaces	Hertz rental	
AE, MC, V	Handicapped van OK	

71. 318 E 48th St *bet 2nd/1st, S side of E 48th*

GMC 212.755.9253

hr	rate	specials	rate	enter	exit
1	$17	AM m-f	$18	5-10am	7pm
2	$23	Sa,Su	$12	after 5am	7pm
12	$30	O/N	$35		after 5am
24	$35	SUV	$10		
		Month	$425, O/S add $150		

helpful information		
24/7	2 elevators	Damage inspection
250 spaces	Eff. 8/05	May take handicapped van
AE, MC, V	Max bill $50	

72. 240 E 47th St *bet 2nd/3rd, S side of E 47th, near 2nd*

E 47 Parking 212.355.6502

hr	rate	specials	rate	enter	exit
1/2	$7	AM	$18	12-10am	12hr
1	$18	PM	$10	after 5pm	1am
2	$23	Sa,Su	$10	anytime	12hr, No O/N
24	$40	O/N	$40		
12am	$33	SUV	$10		
		Month	$560		

helpful information		
24/7	AE, MC, V	6'6" clearance
37 spaces	Eff. 3/06	

73. 227 E 47 St *bet 2nd/3rd, N side of E 47th*

Kinney 212.421.1865

hr	rate	specials	rate	enter	exit
1	$25	AM	$20	6-10am	close
2	$30	PM	$12	after 3:30pm	1am
10	$38	Sa,Su	$12	7-1am	1am
24	$51	SUV	$10		
		Month	$425	call for special rates	

helpful information		
M-F 6:30am-1am	AE, MC, V	Damage inspection
Sa-Su 7am-1am	12am gate closes	
227 spaces	Max bill $50	

74. 212 E 47th St *bet 3rd/2nd, N side of E 46th or S side of E 47th*

Central
212.843.2362

hr	rate	specials	rate	enter	exit
1	$25	SUV	$11		
2	$31	Month	$507, O/S add $100		
10	$36				
24	$51				

helpful information

24/7	AE, MC, V, Dis, DC	Damage inspection
105 spaces	Max bill $50	Customer recommendation

---

75. 135 E 47th St *bet 3rd/Lexington, N side of E 47th*

Central
212.644.9013

hr	rate	specials	rate	enter	exit
1	$25	AM m-f	$26	6-10am	10hr
2	$30	Sa,Su	$13	6am-6pm	10hr
10	$40	SUV	$11		
24	$51	Month	$528, O/S add $84		

helpful information

24/7	2 elevators	Damage inspection
149 spaces	Enterprise Rental	Check-out machine
AE, MC, V	Max bill $50	

---

76. 380 Madison Ave *bet 5th/Madison, N side of E 46th*

Central
212.983.5876

hr	rate*	specials	rate	enter	exit
1/2	$13	AM	$13	5-11am	1/2hr
1	$26	AM	$26	5-11am	1hr
2	$31	AM	$31	5-11am	2hr
12	$44	AM	$40	5-11am	12hr
24	$49	AM	$49	5-11am	24hr
		SUV	$10		
		Month	$550		

helpful information

24/7	AE, MC, V	Max bill $50
150 spaces	12am gate closes	*enter 11:01am-4:59pm

---

77. 485 Lexington Ave *bet Lexington/3rd, N side of E 46th*

Kinney
212.983.1510

hr	rate	specials	rate	enter	exit
1	$26	PM m-f	$15	after 4:30pm	12am
2	$31	Sa	$13	after 7am	12am
10	$38	SUV	$11		
24	$51	Month	$507, O/S add $84		
MTC	$51				

helpful information

M-Sa 7am-12am	AE, MC, V	Max bill $50
100 spaces	6'6" clearance	

78. **225 E 46th St** *bet 3rd/2nd, N side of E 46th*

Basic Parking Corp   212.980.2006

hr	rate	specials	rate	enter	exit
1	$12	PM	$9	after 5pm	12am
2	$16	Sa,Su	$6		1hr
10	$21	Sa,Su	$9		7pm
24	$29	Sa,Su	$15		12am
O/N	$29	SUV	$8		
12am	$25	Month	$380		

helpful information

M-Sa 7am-12am	Cash
26 spaces	Low clearance

79. **300 E 46th St** *bet 2nd/1st, S side of E 46th, near 2nd*

Icon   212.599.9845

hr	rate	specials	rate	enter	exit
1/2	$8	AM m-f	$18	6-9am	12hr
1	$19	AM m-f	$19	9-10am	12hr
2	$22	PM	$11	5pm-6am	6am
12	$29	Sa,Su	$11	6am-5pm	12hr
24	$32	SUV	$10		
		Month	$422, O/S add $84		
		July 4	$30	4pm-4am	

helpful information

24/7	AE, MC, V	Max bill $20
36 spaces	181" rule for SUV	

80. **312 E 46th St** *bet 2nd/1st, S side of E 46th*

Elco   212.490.9129

hr	rate	specials	rate	enter	exit
1/2	$6	AM	$18	6-10am	7pm
1	$19	PM	$10	after 5pm	by 6am
3	$22	Sa,Su	$10	6am-5pm	10hr
5	$24	SUV	$9		
10	$25	Month	$375		
24	$32				

helpful information

24/7	AE, MC, V	Max bill $20
67 spaces	12am gate closes	May take handicapped van

81. 320 E 46th St *bet 2nd/1st, S side of E 46th*
East 46th Realty   212.599.9495

hr	rate	specials	rate	enter	exit
1/2	$6	AM	$17	6-11am	7pm
1	$14	Sa,Su	$10	anytime	close
3	$16	SUV	$7		14hr
5	$20	Month	$318	tenant, SUV add $38	
9	$22	Month	$343	non-tenant, SUV add $38	
24	$33				

helpful information

M-Th 6am-1am	Sa 7am-2am	49 spaces	MC,V
F 6am-2am	Su 7am-1am	Damage inspection	Eff. 6/07

82. 333 E 46th St *bet 2nd/1st, N side of E 46th*
Icon   212.490.0340

hr	rate	specials	rate	enter	exit
1/2	$7	AM m-f	$16	6:30-9am	12hr
1	$17	AM m-f	$17	9-10am	12hr
2	$19	PM	$9	after 6pm	12am
10	$24	Sa,Su	$9	7am-6pm	all day
24	$32	SUV	$10		
		Month	$380, O/S add $84		
		July 4	$30	4pm-4am	12am

helpful information

M-Sa 7am-12am	12am gate closes	Damage inspection
34 spaces	181" rule for SUV	No full size vans
AE, MC, V	Max bill $50	

83. 330 E 46th St *bet 2nd/1st, S side of E 46th, near 1st*
Imperial   212.599.8937

hr	rate	specials	rate	enter	exit
1/2	$6	M-F	$16	6am	8pm
1	$15	O/N	$30		
2	$18	SUV	$7		
24	$30	Month	$325		

helpful information

M-F 6am-8pm	Max bill $20	Eff. 11/07
155 spaces	No vans	
AE, MC, V	Limited space for tall cars	

84. 711 3rd Ave *bet 2nd/3rd, N side of E 44th or S side of E 45th*
GGMC   212.599.9025

hr	rate	specials	rate	enter	exit
1	$19	AM m-f	$26	6-10am	12hr
2	$25	PM	$13	after 3pm	9am
12	$35	Sa,Su	$12	Sa-Su 9pm	12hr, by M 9am
24	$40	SUV	$10		
O/N	$40	Month	$375		

helpful information

24/7	AE, MC, V, Dis, DC	Damage inspection
165 spaces	6'2" clearance	Very nice interior

85. 235 E 45th St *bet 2nd/3rd, N side of E 45th*

Icon 212.599.9717

hr	rate	specials	rate	enter	exit
1/2	$9	AM m-f	$24	6-9am	12hr
1	$24	AM	$26	9-10am	12hr
2	$28	PM	$13	after 6pm	6am
12	$33	Sa,Su	$13	after 6am	6pm
24	$38	SUV	$10		
		Month	$465, O/S add $84		
		July 4	$20	4pm-4am	

helpful information		
24/7	AE, MC, V	No full size vans
90 spaces	Elevator	181" rule for SUV

86. 825 2nd Ave *bet 2nd/3rd, S side of E 45th*

Icon 212.599.8658

hr	rate	specials	rate	enter	exit
1/2	$9	AM m-f	$26	6-10am	12hr
1	$23	PM	$13	after 6pm	6am
2	$27	Sa,Su	$13	after 6am	6pm
12	$32	SUV	$10		
24	$37	Month	$350, O/S add $84		
		July 4	$30	4pm-4am	

helpful information		
24/7	11pm gate closes	No full size vans
126 spaces	181" rule for SUV	246 E 45th
AE, MC, V	Olympia House	

87. 333 E 45th St *bet 1st/2nd, N side of E 45th, near 1st*

45 East LLC/Enterprise 212.681.9212

hr	rate	specials	rate	enter	exit
1/2	$14	AM	$22	6-10am	7pm
1	$21	PM	$14	after 6pm	1am
2	$25	Sa,Su	$14	after 7am	12am
3	$32	SUV	$10		
12	$36	Month	$450		
24	$39				

helpful information		
7D 7am-1am	35 spaces	Low clearance
Su 11pm close	AE, MC, V	Damage inspection

88. 335 Madison Ave *bet Madison/Vanderbilt, S side of E 44th*

Central 212.697.1814

hr	rate	specials	rate	enter	exit
1/2	$17	AM m-f	$31	4-9am	9pm
1	$25	PM	$15	after 5pm	8am
2	$30	SUV	$10	for 16'+	
3	$35	Month	$392-540, O/S add $51		
10	$40	Yale Club	$28		24hr
24	$45				

helpful information		
24/7	AE, MC, V	5 min grace period
90 spaces	Damage, security inspection	

89. 213 E 43rd St bet 3rd/2nd, N side of E 43rd or S side of E 44th, near 3rd

Central   212.843.8765

hr	rate	specials	rate	enter	exit
1/2	$10	AM m-f	$25	by 11am	12hr
1	$19	PM	$13	3pm-3am	9am
2	$25	Sa,Su	$13	after 6am	12am
12	$36	SUV	$11		
24	$51	Month	$507, SUV add $100		
		Month	$169	m'cycle	

helpful information

24/7	AE, MC, V	Eff. 11/06
250 spaces	2 elevators	6'10" clearance

90. 230 E 44th St bet 3rd/2nd, S side of E 44th

Park on 44 Corp   212.599.8851

hr	rate	specials	rate	enter	exit
1	$17	AM m-f	$25	6-10am	12hr
2	$22	PM	$12	after 7pm	3am
4	$25	Sa,Su	$12	anytime	12am
10	$30	SUV	$10		
24	$33	Month	$390, SUV add $118		
O/N	$33	Month	$220	m'cycle	
		Ben & Jack's	$10+	PM,Sa,Su	4hr

helpful information

24/7	150 spaces	Cash

91. 231 E 43rd St bet 2nd/3rd, N side of E 43rd

Icon   212.682.5393

hr	rate	specials	rate	enter	exit
1/2	$9	AM m-f	$24	6-10am	12hr
1	$21	PM	$13	4pm-6am	8am
2	$27	Sa,Su	$13	6am-4pm	12am
12	$35	SUV	$10		
24	$37	Month	$401		

helpful information

24/7	AE, MC, V	181" rule for SUV
250 spaces	Elevator	Max bill $50

92. 200 Park Ave above Grand Central Station, enter via Park Ave overpass

Standard   212.599.0184

hr	rate	specials	rate	enter	exit
1	$21	AM m-f	$26	5-9am	7pm
2	$32	PM m-f	$20	after 5pm	12hr
10	$43	Sa,Su	$20	anytime	12hr
24	$50	SUV	$15		

helpful information

24/7	No large vans	Grand Central Station
265 spaces	Security inspection	Hyatt Hotel
AE, MC, V	People access at top of escalator of Met Life building, N entrance of Grand Central Station	

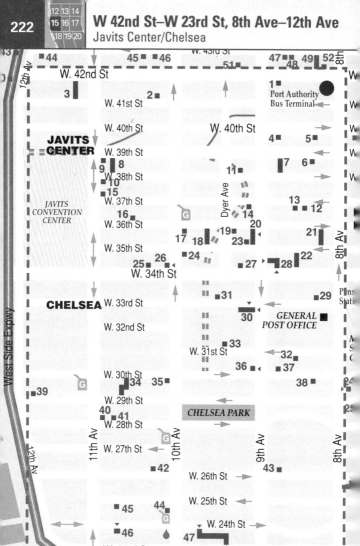

1. **350 W 42nd St** *bet 9th/8th, S side of 42nd*
   Icon   212.594.4546

hr	rate	specials	rate	enter	exit
1/2	$10	AM m-f	$15	6-10am	12hr
1	$15	T'giving	$30	6-11am	12hr
2	$20	SUV	$10		
12	$30	Month	$380, O/S add $169		
24	$40				

helpful information

24/7	AE, MC, V	181" rule for SUV
200 spaces	2 elevators	No full size vans, O/S, trucks
		Opened 4/07

W 42nd St–W 23rd St, 8th Ave–12th Ave
Javits Center/Chelsea

12 13 14
15 16 17
18 19 20

223

2. 561 10th Ave *bet 10th/11th, N side of W 41st*
Icon 212.564.9152

hr	rate	specials	rate	enter	exit
1/2	$8	AM	$15	6-10am	12hr
1	$16	PM	$15	after 6pm	6am
2	$18	Event, Hol	$30		
12	$22	SUV	$10		
24	$35	Month	$338, SUV add $84		
		Month	$169	m'cycle	

helpful information
24/7	181" rule for SUV
71 spaces	Max bill $50
AE, MC, V	

---

3. 601 W 41st St *bet 11th/12th, N side of W 41st or S side of W 42nd*
QuikPark 212.868.3107

hr	rate	specials	rate	enter	exit
1/2	$10	Event	$45		8hr
2	$15	SUV	$10		
12	$22	Month	$350		
24	$29	Month	$148	m'cycle	

helpful information
24/7	AE, MC, V, Dis	181" rule for SUV
194 spaces	7' clearance	River Place Bldg

---

4. 346 W 40th St *bet 9th/8th, S side of W 40th*
Peach Parking 212.695.3862

hr	rate	specials	rate	enter	exit
1/2	$8	SUV	$10		
1	$13	Month	$253, O/S add $42, call for special rates		
12	$15-18	Month	$165	m'cycle	
24	$28				

helpful information
24/7	MC, V	Opened 7/08
250 spaces	181" rule for SUV	2 elevators

---

5. 310 W 40th St *bet 9th/8th, S side of W 40th*
Best Parking 212.695.1018

hr	rate	specials	rate	enter	exit
1	$15	AM	$15	4-10am	12hr
12	$25	Event	$50+		
		SUV	$10+		
		Month	$350, O/S add $150		

helpful information
24/7	Lifts
50 spaces	Outdoor
Cash	SUV surcharge applies to 4x4s

---

6. **310 W 39th St** *bet 8th/9th, S side of W 39th*
Icon   212.695.3472

hr	rate	specials	rate	enter	exit
1/2	$10	AM m-f	$15	6-7am	close
1	$22	AM m-f	$25	7-10am	close
2	$27	Daily	$28	after 10am	close
24	$40	T'giving	$30	6-11am	12hr
MTC	$32	SUV	$15		
		Month	$507, SUV add $127		

helpful information

M-Sa 7am-12am	171 spaces	2 elevators
Su 10am-7pm	AE, MC, V	181" rule for SUV

---

7. **328 W 39th St** *bet 8th/9th, N side of W 38th or S side of W 39th*
Icon   212.502.4595

hr	rate	specials	rate	enter	exit
1/2	$10	AM m-f	$15	6-7am	close
1	$22	AM m-f	$25	7-10am	close
2	$27	T'giving	$30	6-11am	12hr
MTC	$38	Daily	$28	after 10am	close
24	$32	SUV	$15		
		Month	$507, O/S add $84		

helpful information

7D 7am-7pm	Lifts	Max bill $20
130 spaces	181" rule for SUV	Outdoor
AE, MC, V		

---

8. **541 W 38th St** *bet 10th/11th, N side of W 38th or S side of W 39th*
Central   212.502.4390

hr	rate	specials	rate	enter	exit
1	$30	Event	$50-$60		
10	$51	SUV	$15		
24	$65	Month	$310		

helpful information

24/7	AE, MC, V	536 W 39th
221 spaces	Outdoor	

---

9. **346 W 40th St** *SE corner of W 39th/11th, E side of 11th*
Central

hr	rate	specials	rate	enter	exit

OPEN SA, SU ONLY

helpful information
Outdoor

10. 470 11th Ave *SE corner of W 38th/11th, S side of W 38th or E side of 11th*

Mutual

hr	rate	specials	rate	enter	exit
		Event	$50		
		SUV	$10		

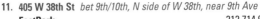

helpful information

Open on Javits show days 8am-5pm   Outdoor
90 spaces
Cash

---

11. 405 W 38th St *bet 9th/10th, N side of W 38th, near 9th Ave*
FastPark   212.714.9239

hr	rate*	specials	rate	enter	exit
1/2	$10	Sa,Su	$20	after 7am	12am
1	$20	Daily	$25	7am-12am	12am
2	$30	Event	$20-$60		
10	$60	O/N add'l	$20		7am
MTC	$75	SUV	$10		
add'l hr $10		Month	$165		

helpful information

7D 7am-12am   MC, V, DC   *7am-7pm
30 spaces   Outdoor

---

12. 312 W 37th St *bet 8th/9th, S side of W 37th*
S & R Parking Inc   212.502.4637

hr	rate	specials	rate	enter	exit
1	$17	Month	$423		
2	$24				
MTC	$33				
6:30pm	$33				

helpful information

Su-F 7:30am-6:30pm Cash   Outdoor
Sa 7:30am-2:30pm   Lifts
77 spaces   Eff. 9/07

---

13. 326 W 37th St *bet 8th/9th, S side of W 37th*
Glenwood   212.695.6402

hr	rate	specials	rate	enter	exit
1/2	$6	AM m-f	$25	by 9am	7pm
1	$12	Sa,Su	$15	all day	
2	$18	Event	$45		8hr
24	$32	SUV	$5		
MTC	$30				

helpful information

M-Th 6am-12am	Su 7am-12am	Lifts
F 6am-1am	130 spaces	Outdoor
Sa 7am-1am	MC, V	

---

14. 404 W 37th St *bet 9th/Dyer/10th, S side of W 37th, near 9th*
Enterprise   212.629.6397

hr	rate	specials	rate	enter	exit
1/2	$10	Daily	$20	7-9:30am	7pm
1	$17	Event/Javits	$36		1/2hr
2	$20	Event/Javits	$40		1hr
10	$28	Event/Javits	$52		2hr
24	$38	Event/Javits	$60		all day
		SUV	$10		
		Month	$450 , O/S add $150		
		Month	$300	m'cycle	

helpful information

24/7	166 spaces	AE, MC, V

---

15. 456 11th Ave *NE corner of W 37th/11th, N side of W 37th or E side of 11th*
Westside Express Corp   212.695.6262

hr	rate	specials	rate	enter	exit
1	$20	SUV	$10		
2	$25	Event	$25-$60		15hr
3	$30				
4	$35				
6pm	$40				
add'l hr	$10				

helpful information

7D 8am-6pm	MC, V	Outdoor
20 spaces	Eff. 5/03	

W 42nd St–W 23rd St, 8th Ave–12th Ave
Javits Center/Chelsea

12	13	14
15	16	17
18	19	20

227

16. 517 W 36th St *bet 11th/10th, N side of W 36th*
E/Z Sprint　　　　　　　　　　　　　　　　　　　212.736.8240

hr	rate	specials	rate	enter	exit
		Event	$15-50		
		SUV	$10		
		Month	$350		

helpful information
7D 7am-7pm　　25 spaces　　　　　Cash

---

17. 452 10th Ave *SE corner of W 36th/10th, S side of W 36th or E side of 10th*
Impark　　　　　　　　　　　　　　　　　　　646.733.5926

hr	rate	specials	rate	enter	exit
1/2	$5	AM	$16	5-10am	7pm
1	$17	Event	$40-50		
2	$22	Special Event	$45		
10	$27	SUV	$10		
24	$37	Month	$300		

helpful information
24/7　　　　　　AE, MC, V　　　　　Outdoor
121 spaces　　Max bill $20

---

18. 447 W 35th St *bet 9th/10th, N side of W 35th or S side of W 36th*
Enterprise Parking

hr	rate	specials	rate	enter	exit
1/2	$10	AM m-f	$17	3-10am	7pm
1	$17	Daily	$15	6am-12am	12hr
2	$20	Event	$60		
10	$28	SUV	$10		
24	$52	Month	$400 , O/S add $105		
12am	$38	Truck	$60		

helpful information
24/7　　　　　　Lifts　　　　　　　Outdoor
65 spaces　　　Max bill $50　　　Takes trucks
AE, MC, V

---

19. 416 W 36th St *SE corner of W 36th/Dyer, S side of W 36th, at Dyer*
Central

hr	rate	specials	rate	enter	exit
1/2	$7	AM	$16	3-10am	7pm
1	$16	SUV	$11		
2	$19	Event	$50		
10	$32	Month	$423 , O/S add $84		
24	$51				

helpful information
M-F 7am-10pm　　　　　　AE, MC, V
Sa,Su for special events　Max bill $50
28 spaces　　　　　　　　Outdoor

20. 451 9th Ave *bet W 35th/W 36th, W side of 9th*
Edison ParkFast   212.502.4885

hr	rate*	specials	rate	enter	exit
1/2	$9	AM	$22	4-9am	7pm
1	$15	PM m-f	$15	5pm-4am	10hr, non-event
2	$18	PM m-f	$38	5pm-4am	24hr, non-event
10	$31	Sa,Su	$10	after Sa 4am	1hr
24	$38	Sa,Su	$16	after Sa 4am	10hr, by M 4am
		Sa,Su	$36	after Sa 4am	24hr, by M 4am
		Event	$30		10hr
		Event	$38		24hr
		Auto Show	$45		10hr
		SUV	$10		
		Month	$346 , O/S add $101		
		Month	$321 , O/S add $101, m-f 4am-8pm		

helpful information
24/7	Lifts
154 spaces	Outdoor
AE, MC, V	*M-F, enter 4am-5pm non-event days Eff. 2/08

21. 320 W 36th St *bet 8th/9th, N side of W 35th or S side of W 36th*
Ulltra   212.594.7894

hr	rate	specials	rate	enter	exit
1	$19	AM m-f	$19	6-8am	6pm
2	$22	PM	$17	after 6pm	2pm
12	$32	Event	$23		
24	$37	SUV	$10		
O/N	$37	Month	$321 , O/S add $51		

helpful information
24/7	AE, MC, V
150 spaces	

22. 323 W 34th St *bet 8th/9th, N side of W 34th or S side of W 35th*
Meyers/Central   212.279.7310

hr	rate	specials	rate	enter	exit
1	$21	AM	$19	3-8am	7pm
2	$24	Event	$34		
10	$34	Spec event	$39		
24	$44	SUV	$10		
		Month	$397 , O/S add $105		

helpful information
24/7	AE, MC, V	6'8" clearance
500 spaces	Max bill $50	Hertz

23. 415 W 35th St *bet 9th/10th, N side of W 35th*
Central   646.674.1888

hr	rate	specials	rate	enter	exit
1	$16	AM m-f	$16	3-10am	7pm
2	$20	Event	$51		
10	$33	Truck/Van	$60		
24	$51	SUV	$11		
		Month	$338 , O/S add $92		

helpful information

24/7	AE, MC, V	Outdoor
52 spaces	Max bill $50	Takes trucks

24. 444 10th Ave *SE corner of W 35th/10th, S side of W 35th or E side of 10th*
Enterprise Parking   212.564.1965

hr	rate	specials	rate	enter	exit
1/2	$10	AM	$17	3-10am	7pm
1	$17	Event	$60		
2	$20	SUV	$10		
10	$28	Month	$400 , O/S add $50		
24	$52	Van, SUV	$60		
MTC	$38				

helpful information

M-F 7am-10pm	AE, MC, V	Outdoor
Sa,Su when open	Lifts	
25 spaces	Max bill $50	

25. 509 W 34th St *bet 10th/11th, N side of W 34th*
GGMC   212.967.2771

hr	rate	specials	rate	enter	exit
1	$18	SUV	$20		
2	$30				
10	$50				
MTC	$60				

helpful information

M-F 6am-11pm	181" rule for SUV	Near FedEx, Channel 13
AE, MC, V, Dis, DC	200 spaces	

26. 435 10th Ave *NW corner of W 34th/10th, W side of 10th*
Imperial   212.967.3522

hr	rate	specials	rate	enter	exit
1	$15	Daily	$15		10pm
2	$20	SUV	$10		
10	$35	Javits	$20-45		
24	$60	Garden event	$25		
2am	$50	Copacabana	$20-30		

helpful information

24/7	AE, MC, V	Outdoor
99 spaces	Lifts	

27. **441 9th Ave** *bet 9th/10th, N side of W 34th, near 9th*
Central 212.594.5242

hr	rate	specials	rate	enter	exit
1	$19	Event	$24-$32		
2	$22	Javits	$60		
10	$27	Garden Event	$40		
24	$52	Special Event	$40		
		SUV	$11		
		Month	$422, O/S add $63		

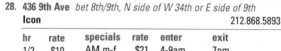

helpful information

24/7	160 spaces	AE, MC, V

---

28. **436 9th Ave** *bet 8th/9th, N side of W 34th or E side of 9th*
Icon 212.868.5893

hr	rate	specials	rate	enter	exit
1/2	$10	AM m-f	$21	4-9am	7pm
1	$22	Daily	$30	9am-5pm	7pm
2	$24	T'giving	$30	5-11am	12hr
10	$35	SUV	$10		
24	$39	Month	$380 , O/S add $84		

helpful information

24/7	AE, MC, V	181" rule for SUV
140 spaces	Lifts	Outdoor

---

29. **305 W 33rd St** *bet 8th/9th, N side of W 33rd*
Central 212.947.0727

hr	rate	specials	rate	enter	exit
1	$21	AM m-f	$21	3-11am	7pm
2	$25	Event	$21		1hr
10	$36	Event	$45		10hr
24	$52	Event	$52		24hr
		SUV	$11		
		Month	$359 , O/S add $84		

helpful information

24/7	Max bill $50
250 spaces	Very long, steep driveway
AE, MC, V	Public driveway

30. 401 9th Ave *SW corner of W 33rd/9th, W side of 9th or S side of W 33rd*

Edison/Park Fast
212.695.4290

hr	rate*	specials	rate	enter	exit
1/2	$9	AM m-f	$22	4-8am	7pm
1	$20	PM m-f+	$14	3pm-4am	1hr
2	$23	PM m-f+	$20	3pm-4am	10hr
12	$32	PM m-f+	$42	3pm-4am	24hr
24	$42	Sa,Su	$14	Sa 4am-M 4am	1hr
		Sa,Su	$20	Sa 4am-M 4am	10hr
		Sa,Su	$42	Sa 4am-M 4am	24hr
		Event	$35-40		12hr
		SUV	$10		
		Month	$363 , O/S add $55		
		Month	$317	m-f 6am-10pm	

helpful information

24/7	Outdoor	+Non-event
207 spaces	*enter M-F 4am-3pm	
AE, MC, V	412 W 33rd	

31. 431 W 33rd St *bet 9th/10th, N side of W 33rd, near Tunnel entrance*

Enterprise/33 W LLC
646.473.0944

hr	rate	specials	rate	enter	exit
1/2	$10	AM m-f	$16	5-11am	7pm
1	$15	Event	$22		1hr
2	$16	Event	$30		2hr
10	$22	Event	$35		10hr
24	$27	SUV	$10		
		Month	$375, O/S add $50		

helpful information

7D 7am-12am	AE, MC, V	Outdoor
Some Sa,Su,Hol closed	Lifts	
77 spaces	Max bill $20	

32. 340 W 31st St *bet 8th/9th, S side of W 31st*

Meyers
212.594.1915

hr	rate	specials	rate	enter	exit
1/2	$6	AM	$13	3-10am	7pm
1	$17	Event	$42		
2	$21	SUV	$10		
10	$29	Month	$400, O/S add $105		
24	$42				

helpful information

24/7	Rates change annually
255 spaces	Low clearance
AE, MC, V	Max bill $50

---

33. 425 W 31st St *bet 9th/10th, N side of W 31st*
Imperial   212.695.6460

hr	rate	specials	rate	enter	exit
1/2	$5	AM	$16	3-10am	7pm
1	$14	Event	$25		
2	$18	SUV	$10		
10	$22	Month	$300 , O/S add $100		
24	$32				
O/N	$32				

helpful information

24/7	Outdoor
145 spaces	Accepts trucks 14'-35'
AE, MC, V	

---

34. 506 W 30th St *bet 10th/11th, N side of W 29th or S side of W 30th*
Enterprise

hr	rate*	specials	rate	enter	exit
1/2	$8	AM m-f	$12	6-10am	7pm
1	$13	PM	$8	after 7pm	1/2hr
2	$14	PM	$13	after 7pm	1hr
3	$20	PM	$14	after 7pm	2hr
10	$25	PM	$20	after 7pm	3hr
24	$27	PM	$27	after 7pm	24hr, by 7am
		Event	$22		1/2hr
		Event	$27		1hr
		Event	$35		2hr
		Event	$40		3hr
		Event	$48		12am
		Club	$30		
		SUV	$10		
		Month	$350		

helpful information

24/7	Takes trucks
213 spaces	*enter 7am-7pm
AE, MC, V	505 W 29th

W 42nd St–W 23rd St, 8th Ave–12th Ave
Javits Center/Chelsea

12 13 14
15 16 17
18 19 20

233

35. 343 10th Ave *SW corner of W 30th/10th, S side of W 30th or W side of 10th*

Enterprise

hr	rate*	specials	rate	enter	exit
1/2	$8	AM	$12	6-10am	7pm
1	$13	PM	$8	after 7pm	1/2hr
2	$14	PM	$13	after 7pm	1hr
3	$20	PM	$14	after 7pm	2hr
10	$26	PM	$20	after 7pm	3hr
24	$27	PM	$27	after 7pm	24hr, by 7am
		Event	$22		1/2hr
		Event	$27		1hr
		Event	$35		2hr
		Event	$40		3hr
		Event	$48		12am
		Club	$30		
		SUV	$10		
		Month	$300 , Van add $75		
		Truck	$50-80		24hr

helpful information

24/7	Max bill $20	*enter 7am-7pm
50 spaces	Outdoor	
AE, MC, V	Takes trucks	

---

36. 359 9th Ave *NW corner of W 30th/9th, W side of 9th*
Ulltra   212.564.1851

hr	rate	specials	rate	enter	exit
1/2	$7	AM m-f	$13	3-10am	7pm
1	$13	O/N	$12	10pm-12am	9am
2	$17	Event	$26		
10	$22	Special event	$30		
24	$29	SUV	$10		
O/N	$29	Month	$232 , O/S add $46		

helpful information

24/7	40 spaces	AE, MC, V	Outdoor

---

37. 363 W 30th St *bet 9th/8th, N side of W 30th*
Icon   212.239.8656

hr	rate	specials	rate	enter	exit
1/2	$8	AM m-f	$16	7-10am	12hr
1	$19	SUV	$10		
2	$22	Month	$338 , O/S add $84		
10	$27				
24	$33				

helpful information

7D 7am-12am	AE, MC, V	Max bill $50
18 spaces	181" rule for SUV	No street signage

---

38. 320 W 30th St *bet 9th/8th, S side of W 30th*

Ulltra   212.967.7102

hr	rate*	specials	rate	enter	exit
1/2	$10	AM m-f	$16	6-10am	6pm
1	$17	PM	$19	7pm-12am	1hr
2	$19	PM	$25	7pm-12am	2hr
3	$25	PM	$28	7pm-12am	3hr
7pm	$28	PM	$35	7pm-12am	24hr
12am	$30	Sa,Su	$12	5am-12pm	8pm
24	$35	Event	$28-36		
O/N	$35	SUV	$10		
		Month	$400		
		Month	$300	m-f 8am-6pm	

helpful information

24/7	AE, MC, V	*enter 7am-7pm
82 spaces	Max bill $50	

---

39. 613 W 29th St *bet 11th/12th, N side of W 29th*

MTP   212.560.9497

hr	rate	specials	rate	enter	exit
1/2	$5	SUV	$5		
12	$10	Month	$169		
24	$15				

helpful information

7D 6am-12am	Cash
89 spaces	Outdoor

---

40. 282 11th Ave *NE corner of W 28th/11th, N side of W 28th or E side of 11th*

Parking Management Inc   212.502.4236

hr	rate*	specials	rate	enter	exit
1	$20	PM	$30	6pm-6am	1hr
2	$25	PM	$40	6pm-6am	12hr
3	$30	PM	$50	6pm-6am	6am
10	$40	SUV	$10		
6pm	$50	Month	$338 , O/S add $105		
		Event, Javits	$50		

helpful information

24/7	Lifts	553 W 28th
80 spaces	Outdoor	Pay in advance
Cash	*enter 6am-6pm	

W 42nd St–W 23rd St, 8th Ave–12th Ave
Javits Center/Chelsea

12	13	14
15	16	17
18	19	20

235

---

41. 553 W 28th St *bet 11th/10th, N side of W 28th*
Parking Management Inc 212.502.4236

hr	rate*	specials	rate	enter	exit
1	$20	PM	$30	6pm-6am	1hr
2	$25	PM	$40	6pm-6am	12hr
3	$30	PM	$50	6pm-6am	6am
10	$40	SUV	$10		
6pm	$50	Month	$338 , O/S add $105		
		Event, Javits $50			

helpful information

24/7	Cash	Outdoor
57 spaces	Lifts	*6am-6pm

---

42. 279 10th Ave *bet 11th/10th, N side of W 26th*
Park It Mgmt 212.967.2705

hr	rate*	specials	rate	enter	exit
1/2	$8	AM	$14	6-9am	12hr
1	$12	PM th-sa	$20	6pm-6am	1hr
2	$17	PM th-sa	$30	6pm-6am	24hr
3	$21	SUV	$10		
12	$25	Month	$296 , SUV add $43, O/S add $127		
24	$30				

helpful information

M-F 6am-7pm	AE, MC, V	*7D 6am-6pm
140 spaces	Outdoor	*Su-W 6pm-6am

---

43. 333 W 26th St *bet 9th/8th, N side of W 26th*
Ulltra

hr	rate*	specials	rate	enter	exit
1	$15	PM	$15	after 6pm	2am
2	$18	Sa,Su	$15	after 7am	6pm
12	$20	SUV	$8		
24	$29	Month	$279 , O/S add $42		
O/N	$29				

helpful information

24/7	Max bill $20	Large SUVs OK
839 spaces	Outdoor	*Enter 7am-7pm
AE, MC, V		Zipcar site

44. 249 10th Ave *bet W 24th/W 25th, W side of 10th*
249 Parking Corp 212.645.7548

hr	rate	specials	rate	enter	exit
1	$12	AM m-f	$16	5-9am	12hr
2	$17	PM su-th	$12	5pm-5am	1hr
3	$21	PM su-th	$17	5pm-5am	2hr
12	$25	PM su-th	$21	5pm-5am	10hr
24	$30	PM su-th	$30	5pm-5am	24hr
		F,Sa	$15		1hr
		F,Sa	$25		2hr
		SUV	$5-10		
		Month	$380, O/S add $42		
		Month	$190	m'cycle	

helpful information
24/7	120 spaces	AE, MC, V	Elevator

45. 550 W 25th St *bet 10th/11th, S side of W 25th*
GGMC 212.929.0443

hr	rate	specials	rate	enter	exit
1	$20	AM	$20	4-10am	8pm
2	$25	Sa,Su	$15	7am-7pm	10hr
12	$32	SUV	$10		
24	$34	Month	$400, O/S add $100		

helpful information
24/7	163 spaces	AE, MC, V, Dis

46. 549 W 23rd St *bet 11th/10th, S side of W 24th*
Imperial 646.486.0767

hr	rate	specials	rate	enter	exit
1/2	$5	Sa,Su	$13	after 4am	7pm
1	$15	Month	$400, O/S add $100		
2	$20	Month	$175	m'cycle	
10	$25				
24	$30				
O/N	$30				

helpful information
24/7	70 spaces	MC, V	Lifts

47. 423 W 23rd St *bet 9th/10th, N side of W 23rd near 9th or S side of W 24th near 10th*

QuikPark   212.352.0514

hr	rate	specials	rate	enter	exit
1/2	$5	AM m-f	$16	5-10am	7pm
1	$13	Sa,Su	$17	anytime	12hr
2	$19	SUV	$10		
10	$25	Month	$350 , O/S add $50		
24	$30				

helpful information

24/7	AE, MC, V
185 spaces	181" rule for SUV

■65
■66
62 63
■64
W. 43rd St
67

8th Av
52
W. 42nd St
TIMES SQUARE
N.Y. PUBLIC LIBRARY

W. 41st St ■1
BRYANT PARK

W. 40th St
■4
■2
■3
W. 39th St
■5

W. 38th St
Broadway
■6

W. 37th St
■7
■8

FASHION DISTRICT
■10
W. 36th St
■11 ■9

7th Av
Av of the Americas (6th Av)
■12

W. 35th St
5th Av

W. 34th St
■13

MIDTOWN SOUTH
■14
Penn Station

W. 33rd St
■15
■16
EMPIRE STATE BLDG.

MADISON SQUARE GARDEN
W. 32nd St
■17
■22

■18
W. 31st St
■19 ■20 ■21

■24
W. 30th St
■23

■26 ■28 ■29
W. 29th St
■30 ■31

■25 ■27
■35

■32
W. 28th St
■34

FLATIRON
■33

W. 27th St
■36

■38
W. 26th St
■41

■37 ■39
■40 ■42

■43
W. 25th St
■45
■44

W. 24th St
■48
■46
■47

■49
■50

W. 23rd St
■1

EA
■3
■2

W. 22nd St
■3

■10
W. 21st St
■7

■9 ■8
■14

■11 ■12 ■13
W. 20th St
■15

W. 19th St

■7
FLATIRON
W. 18th St

■16
■17

© 2008 Park Itl Guides

W 42nd St–W 23rd St, 5th–8th Ave
Fashion Center/Midtown South/Flatiron

12	13	14
15	16	17
18	19	20

239

---

1. **220 W 41st St** *bet 7th/8th, S side of W 41st*
Times Square 41st Street Garage LLC   212.730.1777

hr	rate	specials	rate	enter	exit
1/2	$10	AM m-f	$23	6-9am	7pm
1	$19	SUV	$10		
2	$24	Month	$400, O/S add $100		
12	$30	Month	$175	m'cycle	
24	$37				

helpful information
24/7	AE, MC, V	Max bill $20
124 spaces	Elevator	

---

2. **252 W 40th St** *bet 8th/7th, S side of W 40th*
Central/Kinney   212.840.2270

hr	rate	specials	rate	enter	exit
1/2	$8	AM	$22	3-10am	12am
1	$20	PM 7D	$22	3pm	11pm
2	$26	SUV	$11		
12	$32	Month	$486, O/S add $84		
24	$51	Month	$300	m'cycle	

helpful information
24/7	AE, MC, V	Alamo, National rental
300 spaces	2 elevators	

---

3. **136 W 40th St** *bet 7th/Broadway, S side of W 40th*
Icon   212.221.9827

hr	rate	specials	rate	enter	exit
1/2	$12	AM m-f	$25	6-10am	12am
1	$23	PM m-f	$10	6pm-12am	1/2hr
2	$28	PM m-f	$14	6pm-12am	1hr
3	$31	PM m-f	$16	6pm-12am	2hr
12	$34	PM m-f	$19	6pm-12am	12hr
24	$37	PM m-f	$22	6pm-12am	close
MTC	$35	PM m-f	$37	6pm-12am	24hr
		Sa	$10	Sa 1am-Su 6pm	1/2hr
		Sa	$14	Sa 1am-Su 6pm	1hr
		Sa	$15	Sa 1am-Su 6pm	2hr
		Sa	$16	Sa 1am-Su 6pm	3hr
		Sa	$20	Sa 1am-Su 6pm	12hr
		Sa	$24	Sa 1am-Su 6pm	close
		Sa	$37	Sa 1am-Su 6pm	24hr
		Su	$10	6pm-12am	1/2hr
		Su	$13	6pm-12am	1hr
		Su	$14	6pm-12am	2hr
		Su	$19	6pm-12am	3hr
		Su	$22	6pm-12am	close
		Su	$37	6pm-12am	24hr
		SUV	$10		
		Month	$422, O/S add $84		
		Month	$300	m'cycle	$380

helpful information
7D 7am-12am	2 elevators	Max bill $50
150 spaces	181" rule for SUV	*M-F 7am-6pm
AE, MC, V	Low clearance	

240

12	13	14
15	16	17
18	19	20

W 42nd St–W 23rd St, 5th–8th Ave
Fashion Center/Midtown South/Flatiron

4. **143 W 40th St** *bet 7th/Broadway, N side of W 40th*

Icon 212.221.9485

hr	rate*	specials	rate	enter	exit
1/2	$12	AM	$25	7-10am	close
1	$23	PM m-f	$10	6pm-12am	1/2hr
2	$28	PM m-f	$14	6pm-12am	1hr
3	$31	PM m-f	$16	6pm-12am	2hr
12	$34	PM m-f	$19	6pm-12am	12hr
24	$37	PM m-f	$22	6pm-12am	close
close	$35	PM m-f	$37	6pm-12am	24hr
		Sa	$10	7am-close	1/2hr
		Sa	$14	7am-close	1hr
		Sa	$15	7am-close	2hr
		Sa	$16	7am-close	3hr
		Sa	$20	7am-close	12hr
		Sa	$24	7am-close	close
		Sa	$37	7am-close	24hr
		SUV	$10		
		Month	$422, SUV add $84		

helpful information

M-Sa 7am-12am 2 elevators 181" rule for SUV
150 spaces Max bill $20
AE, MC, V *M-F enter 7am-6pm

---

5. **13 W 39th St** *bet 5th/6th, N side of W 39th*

GGMC 212.768.8038

hr	rate	specials	rate	enter	exit
1/2	$10	AM m-f	$35	5:30-9am	12am
1	$25	PM	$10	5pm-close	1hr
2	$35	PM	$26	5pm-close	close
3	$40	Sa,Su	$10		1hr
10	$50	Sa,Su	$26		close
		SUV	$15		

helpful information

M-F 5:30am-12am 76 spaces 181" rule for SUV
Sa 7am-12am AE, MC, V, Dis, DC Outdoor
Su 9am-6pm 13 W 39th Large vans/SUVs OK

---

6. **102 W 39th St** *bet 6th/Broadway, S side of W 39th*

Champion 212.852.9033

hr	rate	specials	rate	enter	exit
1/2	$15	AM	$32	5-9am	12am
1	$29	Sa,Su	$25	7am-12pm	
2	$37	Event	$30		
10	$41	SUV	$15+		
24	$55	Month	$655, O/S add $148		
O/N	$55				

helpful information

24/7 AE, MC, V Opened 6/08
75 spaces Steep driveway

7. **515 7th Ave** *bet 7th/Broadway, S side of W 38th*
Central   212.398.0547

hr	rate	specials	rate	enter	exit
1/2	$10	AM	$30	6-10am	7pm
1	$26	PM	$18	after 5pm	12am
2	$32	Sa,Su	$24	all day	
10	$39	SUV	$10		
24	$31	Month	$507		

helpful information

M-Th 6am-12am	AE, MC, V
F, Sa 8am-12am	Self-retrieve after 7pm
450 spaces	Ticket machine

---

8. **1010 6th Ave** *bet 6th/5th, S side of W 38th*
Imperial   212.221.8857

hr	rate	specials	rate	enter	exit
1/2	$13	PM	$16	after 6pm	close
1	$26	Sa,Su	$19	after 7am	close
2	$34	SUV	$15		
10	$37	Month	$500, O/S add $100		
24	$47				
O/N	$47				

helpful information

Su-Th 6am-1am	Sa 7am-2am	AE, MC, V
F 6am-2am	86 spaces	2 elevators

---

9. **59 W 36th St** *bet 5th/6th, N side of W 36th or S side of W 37th*
Icon   212.502.5188

hr	rate	specials	rate	enter	exit
1/2	$15	PM	$16	6pm-close	1/2hr
1	$31	PM	$25	6pm-close	close
2	$36	Sa,Su	$16	7am-6pm	1hr
24	$46	Sa,Su	$22	7am-6pm	close
MTC	$42	T-giving	$30	6-11am	12hr
		SUV	$10		
		Month	$507, O/S add $84		

helpful information

M-F 7am-10pm	150 spaces	No full size vans
Sa 7am-7pm	AE, MC, V	181" rule for SUV
Su,Hol closed	Max bill $50	58 W 37th

10. **161 W 36th St** *bet 7th/Broadway, N side of W 36th*
Icon   212.502.5324

hr	rate	specials	rate	enter	exit
1/2	$16	PM m-f	$22	6pm-12am	12am
1	$32	Sa,Su	$16	after 7am	1hr
2	$34	Sa,Su	$22	after 7am	close, by 7pm
24	$47	SUV	$10		
MTC	$42	Month	$591, O/S add $84		

helpful information

M-F 7am-12am	149 spaces	181" rule for SUV
Sa,Su 7am-7pm	AE, MC, V	Max bill $20

11. **990 Avenue of the Americas** *bet 6th/5th, N side of W 36th*
Pace Parking LLC   212.502.5908

hr	rate	specials	rate	enter	exit
1/2	$13	AM m-f	$27	6-10am	12hr
1	$31	T-giving	$30	6-11am	12hr
2	$36	SUV	$10		
3	$42	Month	$591, O/S add $84		
24	$46				

helpful information

24/7	AE, V, MC	6'5" clearance
120 spaces	181" rule for SUV	

12. **12 W 36th St** *bet 5th/6th, N side of W 35th or S side of W 36th*
Meyers   212.268.8572

hr	rate	specials	rate	enter	exit
1	$20	AM m-f	$26	3-9am	7pm
2	$24	SUV	$10		
10	$33	Month	$486, O/S add $105		
24	$42				

helpful information

24/7	AE, MC, V	9 W 35th
225 spaces	7' clearance	

13. **74 W 35th St** *bet 5th/6th, S side of W 35th*
Icon   212.695.9685

hr	rate	specials	rate	enter	exit
1/2	$10	AM	$25	5-10am	12hr
1	$20	PM	$16	5pm-5am	5am
2	$25	SUV	$10		
12	$35	Month	$507, O/S add $84		
24	$45				

helpful information

24/7	AE, MC, V	
149 spaces	1328 Broadway	

W 42nd St–W 23rd St, 5th–8th Ave
Fashion Center/Midtown South/Flatiron

12	13	14
15	16	17
18	19	20

243

---

14. 1 Penn Plaza *bet 7th/8th, N side of W 33rd or S side of W 34th*
Central   212.563.1131

hr	rate	specials	rate	enter	exit
1	$20	AM m-f	$21	3-10am	8pm
2	$24	Event	$20		1hr
10	$34	Spec Event	$45-51		10hr-24hr
24	$51	SUV	$11		
		Month	$507, O/S add $63		

helpful information
24/7   6'7" clearance   Self parking & valet
665 spaces   Max bill $50   Boom gate at entrance
AE, MC, V

---

15. 35 W 33rd St *bet 5th/6th, N side of W 33rd*
MTP   212.947.7778

hr	rate	specials	rate	enter	exit
1/2	$11	AM	$25	6-9:30am	12hr
1	$20	Event	$35		
2	$23	New Year	$35		
12	$30	SUV	$10		
24	$35	Month	$406		

helpful information
7D 6am-1am   Cash   No vans
34 spaces   Elevator

---

16. 38 W 33rd St *bet 5th/6th, S side of W 33rd*   212.947.3398
GGMC   212.502.4410

hr	rate	specials	rate	enter	exit
1/2	$13	AM m-f	$25	6-9:30am	close
1	$22	Sa,Su	$26	after 3pm	close
2	$26	O/N	$38	by 12am	after 6am
10	$35	SUV	$10		
24	$38	Month	$400, SUV add $50		
MTC	$36				

helpful information
M-Sa 6am-12am   224 spaces   Max bill $20
Su 7am-11pm   AE, MC, V   Eff. 4/08

---

17. 1250 Broadway *bet Broadway/5th, S side of W 32nd*
Central   212.695.4568

hr	rate	specials	rate	enter	exit
1/2	$11	AM	$20	3-10am	8pm
1	$20	SUV	$11		
2	$26	Month	$591, SUV add $63		
10	$36				
24	$51				

helpful information
24/7   La Quinta Inn discount
150 spaces
AE, MC, V

18. 218 W 31st St *bet 7th/8th, N side of W 30th or S side of W 31st*
Meyers 212.736.8233

hr	rate	specials	rate	enter	exit
1	$19	AM m-f	$20	3-10am	7pm
2	$22	Garden Event	$37		
10	$33	Special Event	$43		
24	$45	SUV	$10		
		Month	$401, O/S add $105		

helpful information

24/7	Avis rental	No exit on W 30th
1500 spaces	7' clearance	227 W 30th
AE, MC, V	Self parking	

19. 148 W 31st St *bet 6th/7th, S side of W 31st, near 7th*
Imperial 646.473.1531

hr	rate	specials	rate	enter	exit
1/2	$8	AM m-f	$22	4-9am	7pm
1	$19	PM	$12	by 6pm	12am
2	$22	Event	$25-35		
10	$30	SUV	$10		
24	$42	Month	$425		
O/N	$42	Month	$150	m'cycle	
		Affinia Hotel	$44		24hr

helpful information

24/7	AE, MC, V	371 7th Ave
94 spaces	6' clearance	Very steep driveway

20. 124 W 31st St *bet 6th/7th, S side of W 31st*
Flash 31 Mgmt 212.244.1043

hr	rate*	specials	rate	enter	exit
1	$20	AM m-f	$21	by 9am	6pm
2	$24	PM	$23	after 4pm	close (non-events)
10	$24	Sa,Su	$15	after 8am	5pm (non-events)
24	$28	Event	$25		
MTC	$34†	SUV	$10		
6pm	$25	Month	$371, O/S add $84		
9pm	$32†	MTC	$40	Event days	
		Garden event/hockey, basketball	$23		
		Garden event/circus, concerts	$25		
		Garden event/play-offs	$35		

helpful information

24/7	Cash	*enter 7am-4pm
Not always open	Outdoor	†non-event days
34 spaces		

---

21. 1251 Broadway *bet Broadway/6th, S side of W 31st*
Central   212.684.0292

hr	rate	specials	rate	enter	exit
1/2	$11	SUV	$11		
1	$20	Month	$422, O/S add $170		
2	$25				
MTC	$33				

helpful information

M-Sa 7am-11pm	80 spaces	Max bill $50
Su 9am-7pm	AE, MC, V	Outdoor
Some Hol closed	Lifts	Busy on weekends

---

22. 9 W 31st St *bet 5th/Broadway, N side of W 31st, near 5th*
Central   212.868.1682

hr	rate	specials	rate	enter	exit
1/2	$11	SUV	$10		
1	$21	Month	$507, O/S add $63		
2	$27				
10	$37				
24	$52				

helpful information

24/7	AE, MC, V
101 spaces	No vans

---

23. 42 W 30th St *bet 6th/Broadway, S side of W 30th*
Pater Realty   212.779.7337

hr	rate	specials	rate	enter	exit
1	$18	AM	$27	8-10am	6:30pm
2	$25	SUV	$10		
3	$33				
MTC	$33				

helpful information

M-F 8am-6:30pm	100 spaces	7' clearance
Sa 8am-5pm	AE, MC, V, Dis, DC	
Su 8am-3pm	Eff. 3/07	

---

24. 384 8th Ave *bet W 29th/W 30th, E side of 8th*
QuikPark   212.947.5805

hr	rate	specials	rate	enter	exit
1/2	$9	AM m-f	$17	5-10am	7pm
1	$17	Sa,Su	$14	anytime	10hr
3	$22	Event	$32		
12	$26	SUV	$5		
24	$38	Month	$295		
MTC	$32				

helpful information

7D 7am-12am	AE, MC, V	No vans/trucks
35 spaces	Outdoor	

25. **245 W 28th St** *bet 7th/8th, N side of W 28th or S side of W 29th*
Edison   212.695.4221

hr	rate*	specials	rate	enter	exit
1/2	$9	AM m-f	$21	5-8am	12am
2	$23	PM m-f	$15	after 5pm	6am (non-events)
12	$28	PM m-f	$36	after 5pm	24hr
24	$36	Sa,Su	$15	6am-6pm	12hr(non-events)
		Sa, Su	$36	6am-6pm	24hr(non-events)
		Event	$25-35		7am
		SUV	$15		
		Month	$285		

helpful information

24/7	AE, MC, V	Outdoor
131 spaces	Lifts	*enter 5am-5pm

---

26. **253 W 29th St** *bet 7th/8th, N side of W 29th*
QuikPark   212.947.5808

hr	rate	specials	rate	enter	exit
1/2	$9	AM m-f	$16	5-10am	7pm
1	$17	Garden event	$30		10hr
3	$21	SUV	$5		
12	$26	Month	$296		
24	$38				
MTC	$32				

helpful information

M-F 7am-11pm	Cash	Outdoor
Sa 9am-7pm	Lifts	No full size vans
Su closed	Max bill $20	25 spaces

---

27. **241 W 28th St** *bet 7th/8th, N side of W 28th or S side of W 29th*
Icon   212.563.4620

hr	rate	specials	rate	enter	exit
1/2	$10	AM m-f	$22	5-10am	12hr
1	$22	Sa,Su	$18	after 6pm	6pm
2	$25	FIT	$16		12hr
12	$28	District School	$16		12hr
24	$38	SUV	$10		
		Month	$422, O/S add $84		
		Hotel Pennsylvania	$40		24hr

helpful information

24/7	AE, MC, V	Max bill 50
240 spaces	2 elevators	181" rule for SUV

---

28. 217 W 29th St *bet 7th/8th, N side of W 29th*
Little Man Parking 212.629.4504

hr	rate	specials	rate	enter	exit
1/2	$10	AM m-f	$18	7-10am	7pm
1	$18	Sa,Su	$15	(non-event)	close, no O/N
2	$21	Event	$20		
12	$26	Playoff	$25		
24	$32	SUV	$10		
		Month	$350, O/S add $84		

helpful information

M-F 7am-9pm	Cash
Sa 9am-5pm	Outdoor
48 spaces	Lot closes 30 min after event

---

29. 211 W 29th St *bet 7th/8th, N side of W 29th*
Little Man Parking 212.564.9409

hr	rate	specials	rate	enter	exit
1/2	$10	AM m-f	$18	6-10am	7pm
1	$18	PM m-f	$15	after 3pm	10pm
2	$21	Sa,Su	$15		
12	$26	Event	$20		
24	$32	Playoff	$25		
		SUV	$10		
		Month	$350, O/S add $100		

helpful information

M-F 7am-9pm	50 spaces	Outdoor
Sa 8am-6pm	Cash	Lot closes 30 min after event
Some Su,Hol closed	Lifts	

---

30. 32 W 29th St *bet Broadway/6th, S side of W 29th*
Central 212.252.5993

hr	rate	specials	rate	enter	exit
1	$20	SUV	$11		
2	$25	Month	$380, O/S add $42		
MTC	$36				

helpful information

M-F 7am-7pm	35 spaces	Max bill $50
Sa,Su 8am-5pm	AE, MC, V	Outdoor

---

31. 11 W 28th St *bet 5th/Broadway, N side of W 28th or S side of W 29th*
Central 212.889.1032

hr	rate	specials	rate	enter	exit
1/2	$11	SUV	$11		
1	$21	Month	$380, O/S add $51		
2	$27				
MTC	$37				

helpful information

M-F 8am-10pm	112 spaces	6 W 29th
Sa,Su 8am-5pm	AE, MC, V	Max bill $50
Some Sa,Su,Hol closed	Lifts	Outdoor

248

12 13 14
15 16 17
18 19 20

W 42nd St–W 23rd St, 5th–8th Ave
Fashion Center/Midtown South/Flatiron

32. 217 W 28th St *bet 8th/7th, N side of W 28th*
Park Here

hr	rate	specials	rate	enter	exit
1	$14	AM	$19	by 10am	7pm
2	$18	Sa,Su	$10		1hr
MTC	$23	Sa,Su	$14		close
		SUV	$10+		
		Month	$275		

helpful information
M-F 7am-7pm Closed some Sa, Su, Hol Cash
Sa 7am-6pm 25 spaces Outdoor

---

33. 140 W 28th St *bet 7th/6th, S side of W 28th*
Central   212.414.4640

hr	rate	specials	rate	enter	exit
1/2	$12	PM m-f	$16	after 4pm	close
1	$21	SUV	$11		
2	$25	Month	$422, O/S add $63		
MTC	$32				

helpful information
M-F 6am-6pm   AE, MC,V
Sa 6am-6pm when open   60 spaces
Su 6am-4pm when open   Outdoor

---

34. 800 6th Ave *bet 6th/Broadway, S side of W 28th*
Central   212.779.2272

hr	rate	specials	rate	enter	exit
1/2	$9	SUV	$11		
1	$21	Month	$591, O/S add $84		
2	$27				
10	$37				
24	$52				

helpful information
24/7   AE, MC, V   Steep driveway
56 spaces   Limited space for SUVs

---

35. 33 W 28th St *NW corner of W 28th/Broadway, N side of W 28th*
or W side of Broadway
Central/Kinney   212.532.3370

hr	rate	specials	rate	enter	exit
1	$21	AM	$22	6-9am	6pm
2	$25	SUV	$11		
10	$33	Month	$401, O/S add $84		
24	$40				

helpful information
24/7   AE, MC, V
224 spaces   6' clearance

---

36. 132 W 27th St *bet 6th/7th, S side of W 27th*

SPI Operating Corp

hr	rate	specials	rate	enter	exit
1	$17	Sa,Su	$16	after 6am	close
2	$20	O/N	$12	7pm	7am
MTC	$25	SUV	$10		
		Month	$338, O/S add $42		

helpful information

M-F 7am-7pm	85 spaces	Outdoor
Sa,Su 7am-4pm	Cash	
Some Sa,Su,Hol closed	Lifts	

---

37. 252 W 26th St *SE corner of W 26th/8th, S side of W 26th or E side of 8th*

Park It Mgmt 212.807.8208

hr	rate	specials	rate	enter	exit
1	$14	AM	$19	5-9am	7pm
2	$18	PM	$29	after 5pm	8am
3	$20	PM th-sa	$15	8pm-5am	1hr
10	$23	PM th-sa	$21	8pm-5am	3hr
24	$29	PM th-sa	$25	8pm-5am	10hr
		PM th-sa	$29	8pm-5am	24hr
		Sa,Su	$18	anytime	12 hr, No O/N
		Event	$40		
		SUV	$9		
		Month	$317		

helpful information

M-F 7am-12am	82 spaces	Outdoor
Sa,Su 8am-6pm	Cash	

---

38. 241 W 26th St *bet 8th/7th, N side of W 26th, near 8th*

Park It Mgmt 212.242.9559

hr	rate*	specials	rate	enter	exit
1/2	$8	AM	$19	5-9am	7pm
1	$15	PM	$18	after 4pm	12am
2	$20	PM	$16	8pm-5am	1hr
3	$22	PM	$23	8pm-5am	3hr
10	$25	PM	$26	8pm-5am	10hr
24	$35	PM	$35	8pm-5am	24hr
		Sa,Su	$17	anytime	12hr, No O/N
		Event	$40		
		SUV	$15		
		Month	$359, O/S add $42		
		Month	$232	m'cycle	

helpful information

24/7	2 elevators	Large vans/SUVs OK
225 spaces	Car wash	*5:01am-7:59pm
AE, MC, V		

39. 220 W 26th St *bet 8th/7th, S side of W 26th*
Imperial 646.336.6574

hr	rate	specials	rate	enter	exit
1/2	$6	AM	$21	6-9:30am	8pm
1	$19	PM	$11	after 6am	1am
2	$21	Sa,Su	$17		12hr
10	$26	SUV	$10		
24	$31	Month	$450, O/S add $100		
O/N	$31				

helpful information		
M-Th 6am-1am	Sa 7am-2am	120 spaces
F 6am-2am	Su 7am-1am	AE, MC, V

40. 100 W 26th St *bet 7th/6th, S side of W 26th*
Olympic Parking Systems 212.675.6122

hr	rate*	specials	rate	enter	exit
1/2	$9	PM	$16	7pm-7am	7am
1	$16	Sa,Su	$18	after 7am	7pm
2	$19	Club	$15		
3	$25	SUV	$14		
7pm	$33	Month	$470, O/S add $100		
24	$49	Month	$224	m'cycle	

helpful information		
24/7	AE, MC, V	
49 spaces	*7am-7pm	

41. 55 W 26th St *bet 6th/Broadway, N side of W 26th*
Central 212.252.1673

hr	rate	specials	rate	enter	exit
1	$20	AM m-f	$22	5-10am	12hr
2	$26	SUV	$11		
10	$36	Month	$591, O/S add $84		
24	$51	Month	$211	m'cycle	

helpful information		
24/7	92 spaces	AE, MC, V

42. 55 W 25th St *bet 6th/Broadway, S side of W 26th, near 6th*
Icon 212.206.8749

hr	rate	specials	rate	enter	exit
1/2	$8	AM	$25	5-10am	12hr
1	$20	Daily	$30	10am-6pm	12hr
2	$25	SUV	$10		
12	$35	Monthly	$506, O/S add $84		
24	$40				

helpful information			
24/7	85 spaces	AE, MC, V	Opened August 07

W 42nd St–W 23rd St, 5th–8th Ave
Fashion Center/Midtown South/Flatiron

12 13 14
15 16 17
18 19 20

251

---

43. 252 7th Ave *bet 7th/8th, S side of W 25th*
Imperial   212.807.1819

hr	rate	specials	rate	enter	exit
1/2	$7	AM	$23	4-9am	8pm
1	$20	Sa,Su	$20	after 6am	6pm
2	$25	SUV	$10		
12	$35				
24	$45				
O/N	$45				

helpful information
24/7	AE, MC, V	Max bill $20
175 spaces	6'4" clearance	

---

44. 112 W 25th St *bet 6th/7th, S side of W 25th*
IR Parking Inc   212.242.9755

hr	rate	specials	rate	enter	exit
1	$18	PM m-f	$15	after 7pm	7am
2	$23	SUV	$12		
7pm	$28	Month	$548		

MAY BE CLOSING

helpful information
24/7	290 spaces	AE, MC, V

---

45. 25 W 25th St *bet Broadway/6th, N side of W 25th*
MPG   212.255.3440

hr	rate	specials	rate	enter	exit
1/2	$15	AM m-f	$21	6-9am	close
1	$21	SUV	$17		
2	$24	Month	$400, O/S add $84		
MTC	$28				

helpful information
M-F 6am-8pm	AE, MC, V
Sa,Su,Hol closed	After close $25 transfer fee to other
180 spaces	location plus new location fees
Outdoor	

---

46. 160 W 24th St *bet 7th/6th, S side of W 24th*
W.K. Parking Corp   212.242.9537

hr	rate	specials	rate	enter	exit
1/2	$7	AM	$17	6-10am	12hr
1	$13	SUV	$10		
2	$17	Month	$340		
3	$19				
12	$21				
24	$29				
O/N	$29				

helpful information
24/7	Cash	Outdoor
93 spaces	Max bill $50	

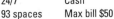

47. 724 6th Ave *bet 6th/Broadway, S side of W 24th, at 6th*
Car Park 29 LLC 212.627.0667

hr	rate*	specials	rate	enter	exit
1/2	$10	AM	$20	6:30-8am	7pm
1	$19	PM su-w	$16	after 7pm	7am
2	$26	PM th-sa	$32	7pm-7am	10hr
7pm	$33	Event	$32		
		SUV	$10		
		Month	$465		
		Masonic Hall member discount			

helpful information

24/7	Max bill $20	*7am-7pm
150 spaces	Outdoor	
Cash	Accepts large SUVs	

48. 750 6th Ave *bet 6th/Broadway, N side of W 24th, near 6th*
Impark 212.691.8562

hr	rate	specials	rate	enter	exit
1/2	$10	AM	$22	6-8am	8pm
1	$20	PM th-sa	$38	10pm-4am	10hr
2	$27	SUV	$10		
10	$38	Month	$507, O/S add $84		
24	$48				
O/N	$48				

helpful information

24/7	AE, MC, V
73 spaces	Max bill $20

49. 101 W 23rd St *bet 7th/6th, N side of W 23rd, near 6th*
Ulltra 212.242.7181

hr	rate	specials	rate	enter	exit
1/2	$10	PM	$20	after 6pm	7am
1	$22	Sa,Su	$19	after 7am	6pm
2	$26	SUV	$10		
10	$29	Month	$372, SUV add $63		
24	$36				
O/N	$36				

helpful information

24/7	140 spaces	AE, MC, V

W 42nd St–W 23rd St, 5th–8th Ave
Fashion Center/Midtown South/Flatiron

12	13	14
15	16	17
18	19	20

253

50. 39 W 23rd St *bet 5th/6th, N side of W 23rd*

Park It Mgmt 212.727.4101

hr	rate	specials	rate	enter	exit
1/2	$14	AM	$22	by 7am	7pm
1	$19	PM	$18	after 5pm	close
2	$24	Sa,Su	$18		10hr
10	$29	Event	$40		
24	$39	Holiday	$40		
12am	$32	SUV	$15		
		Month	$422, O/S add $42		

helpful information

| M-Sa 7am-12am | 92 spaces | Outdoor |
| Su 8am-7pm | AE, MC, V, Dis | |

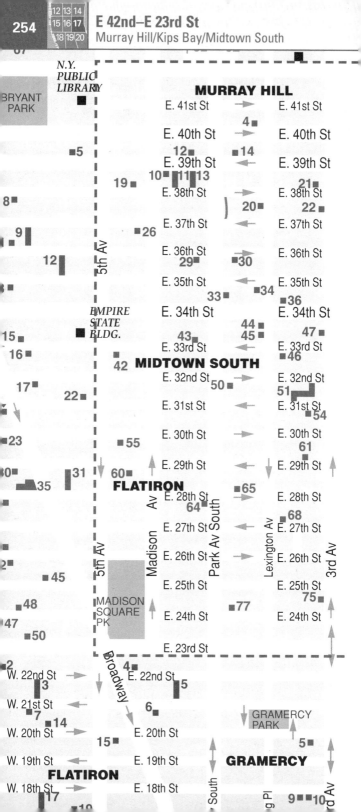

254

12 13 14
15 16 17
18 19 20

E 42nd–E 23rd St
Murray Hill/Kips Bay/Midtown South

N.Y. PUBLIC LIBRARY

BRYANT PARK

MURRAY HILL

E. 41st St → E. 41st St

■4

E. 40th St → E. 40th St

■5

■12 ■14

E. 39th St ← E. 39th St

19■ 10■ ■11 ■13

■21

E. 38th St → E. 38th St

8■ ■20 ■22

9■

E. 37th St ← E. 37th St

■26

12■ 5th Av

E. 36th St E. 36th St
■29 ■30

E. 35th St ← E. 35th St

33■ ■34

■36

EMPIRE STATE BLDG. E. 34th St E. 34th St

15■ 44■

16■ 43■ 45■ 47■

42■ E. 33rd St ← E. 33rd St
■46

MIDTOWN SOUTH

17■ E. 32nd St 50■ → E. 32nd St

22■ 51

E. 31st St ← E. 31st St
■54

23■ E. 30th St → E. 30th St

30■ ■55 61

■35 31■ E. 29th St ← E. 29th St ↑

60■

FLATIRON ■65

Av E. 28th St

64■ 68

2■ 45■ Madison E. 27th St ← Lexington Av E. 27th St

Park Av South

48■ E. 26th St → E. 26th St

47■ E. 25th St E. 25th St
75■

50■ **MADISON SQUARE PK** ■77 3rd Av

↑ E. 24th St E. 24th St

E. 23rd St

2■ Broadway
W. 22nd St → 4■ E. 22nd St 5■

3■

W. 21st St ← 6■

7■ E. 20th St ↓ GRAMERCY PARK

14■

15■ E. 20th St 5■

W. 19th St ← E. 19th St **GRAMERCY**

FLATIRON

W. 18th St → E. 18th St

9■ ■10

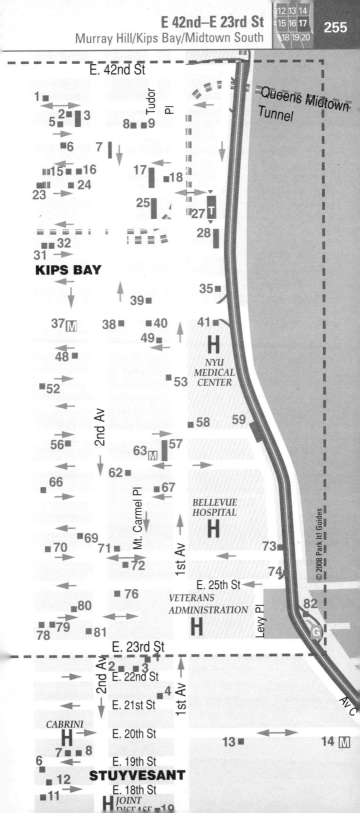

E 42nd–E 23rd St
Murray Hill/Kips Bay/Midtown South

12 13 14
15 16 17
18 19 20

255

E. 42nd St

Queens Midtown Tunnel

1
2 3
5
6
7
8 9
Tudor Pl

15 16
17 18
23 24

25
27 T
28

31 32

KIPS BAY

35

39
37 M
38 40
41
49
48

H
NYU MEDICAL CENTER

52
53

59
56 58

2nd Av

63 M 57
62
66
67

Mt. Carmel Pl

BELLEVUE HOSPITAL
H

70 69
71
73
72
74

1st Av

E. 25th St

76

VETERANS ADMINISTRATION
H

Levy Pl

80
78 79 81

82
G

E. 23rd St

2nd Av
2 3
E. 22nd St
4
E. 21st St

1st Av

CABRINI
H
E. 20th St

7 8
E. 19th St
6
12
STUYVESANT
11
E. 18th St
H *JOINT DISEASE* 19

13
14 M

Av C

© 2008 Park It! Guides

1. **214 E 42nd St** *bet 2nd/3rd, N side of E 41st, across Tunnel Exit*
   Champion   212.490.1205

hr	rate	specials	rate	enter	exit
1/2	$8	AM m-f	$25	4-10am	7pm
1	$27	Sa,Su	$11	6am-4pm	12am
2	$37	SUV	$10		
3	$47	Month	$507, O/S add $89		
24	$59				
O/N	$59				

   helpful information

24/7	11pm gate closes	6'6" clearance
115 spaces	NY Helmsley Hotel	Damage, security inspection
AE, MC, V	181" rule for SUV	No large vans

2. **240 E 41st St** *bet 2nd/3rd, S side of E 41st, E of Tunnel Exit*
   Quik Park   212.983.4450

hr	rate	specials	rate	enter	exit
1	$19	AM m-f	$19	5-10am	all day
2	$23	PM	$11	after 2:45pm	3am
3	$25	SUV	$10		
10	$28	Month	$350, SUV add $42		
24	$36				

   helpful information

24/7	6'8" clearance	Limited space for tall cars
74 spaces	Max bill $20	No vans
AE, MC, V	181" rule for SUV	

3. **245 E 40th St** *bet 3rd/2nd, N side of E 40th or S side of E 41st, E of Tunnel Exit*

   Icon   212.599.9485

hr	rate	specials	rate	enter	exit
1/2	$9	AM m-f	$21	5-10am	12hr
1	$22	PM m-f	$12	5pm-5am	6am
2	$26	Sa,Su	$12	6am-1am	1am
12	$35	July 4	$30	4pm-4am	4am
24	$40	SUV	$10		
		Month	$400		

   helpful information

24/7	181" rule for SUV
130 spaces	Max bill $50
AE, MC, V	

E 42nd–E 23rd St
Murray Hill/Kips Bay/Midtown South

12 13 14
15 16 17
18 19 20

257

4. **101 Park Ave** *bet Park/Lexington, N side of E 40th*
Quik Park 212.661.7493

hr	rate	specials	rate	enter	exit
1/2	$20	AM m-f	$28	by 8:30am	7pm
1	$31	Sa,Su	$18	anytime	12am
2	$46	SUV	$10		
10	$48	Month	$600		
MTC	$51				
24	$60				

helpful information

M-F 6am-12am	AE, MC, V, DC	Damage inspection
Sa,Su 8am-12am	6'2" clearance	No vans, campers, trucks
124 spaces	Max bill $50	

---

5. **222 E 41st St** *bet 3rd/2nd, N side of E 40th*
Icon 212.867.9847

hr	rate	specials	rate	enter	exit
1/2	$9	AM m-f	$22	5-10am	12hr
1	$21	PM	$13	after 5pm	5am
2	$25	Sa,Su	$13	5am-5pm	12hr
3	$28	July 4	$30	4pm-4am	4am
12	$36	SUV	$10		
24	$38				

helpful information

24/7	181" rule for SUV	Elevator
76 spaces	Max bill $50	
AE, MC, V	No full size vans	

---

6. **222 E 40th St** *bet 3rd/Tunnel Exit/2nd, S side of E 40th*
Gemini Garage 212.689.8030

hr	rate	specials	rate	enter	exit
1	$15	AM 7D	$20	4-10am	12hr
2	$18	SUV	$10		
3	$21	Month	$287		
10	$27.50				
24	$35.75				

helpful information

24/7	12am gate closes
750 spaces	Hertz
AE, MC, V	Gemini Garage

7. **310 E 40th St** *bet 2nd/1st, N side of E 39th or S side of E 40th, W of Tunnel Entrance*

Icon 212.599.9762

hr	rate	specials	rate	enter	exit
1	$19	AM m-f	$17	5-10am	12hr
2	$23	PM 7D	$10	3pm-5am	6am
10	$26	Sa,Su	$9	6am-3pm	12hr
24	$36	July 4	$20	4pm-4am	4am
		SUV	$10		
		Month	$325		

helpful information

24/7	181" rule for SUV	12am gate closes
235 spaces	Max bill $50	
AE, MC, V	No full size vans	

8. **301 E 40th St** *bet 2nd/1st, N side of E 40th, across Tunnel Entrance*

Icon 212.888.1265

hr	rate*	specials	rate	enter	exit
1/2	$8	AM m-f	$17	5-10am	12hr
1	$18	PM	$10	3pm-5am	5am
2	$21	Sa,Su	$9	5am-3pm	12hr
12	$25	Sa,Su	$31	5am-3pm	24hr
24	$33	July 4	$20	4pm-4am	4am
		SUV	$10		
		Month	$380		

helpful information

24/7	12am gate closes
108 spaces	181" rule for SUV
AE, MC, V	*M-F

9. **315 E 40th St** *bet 2nd/1st, N side of E 40th*

Imperial 212.697.7773

hr	rate	specials	rate	enter	exit
1/2	$5	AM m-f	$17	4-11am	12hr
1	$14	PM m-f	$10	after 3pm	1am
2	$17	Sa,Su	$10	anytime	10hr
12	$22	SUV	$10		
24	$31	Month	$340		
O/N	$31				

helpful information

24/7	Max bill $20
334 spaces	
AE, MC, V	

E 42nd–E 23rd St
Murray Hill/Kips Bay/Midtown South

12	13	14
15	16	17
18	19	20

259

---

10. 247 Madison Ave *bet Park/Madison, S side of E 39th*
Icon   212.599.9024

hr	rate*	specials	rate	enter	exit
1/2	$11	AM m-f	$27	6-9am	12am
1	$28	AM m-f	$31	9-10am	12am
2	$35	PM m-f	$18	6pm-close	close
10	$43	Sa	$18	after 7am	12am
24	$45	SUV	$10		
		Month	$507, O/S add $84		

helpful information
M-Sa 7am-12am	AE, MC, V	No full size vans
Su, Hol closed	181" rule for SUV	*M-Sa 7am-12am
80 spaces	Max bill $50	

---

11. 23 E 38th St *bet Park/Madison, N side of E 38th (alley) or
S side of E 39th*

Icon   212.599.9024

hr	rate	specials	rate	enter	exit
1/2	$11	AM m-f	$27	6-9am	12am
1	$28	AM m-f	$31	9-10am	12am
2	$35	PM m-f	$18	6pm-close	close
3	$43	Sa	$18	after 7am	12am
24	$45	SUV	$10		
		Month	$507, O/S add $84		

helpful information
M-Sa 7am-7pm	181" rule for SUV
25 spaces	Max bill $50
AE, MC, V	Outdoor

---

12. 90 Park Ave *bet Park/Madison, N side of E 39th*
MPG   212.682.6884

hr	rate	specials	rate	enter	exit
1/2	$10	Sa,Su	$10	after 6am	1hr
1	$24	Sa,Su	$15	after 6am	2hr
2	$42	Sa,Su	$25	after 6am	close
MTC	$46	SUV	$10		
		Month	$444, SUV add $42		

helpful information
Su-Th 6am-12am	AE, MC, V	*M-F 6am-close
F,Sa 6am-2am	Elevator	
150 spaces	Damage inspection	

13. 80 Park Ave *bet Madison/Park, N side of E 38th or S side of E 39th*
Rapid Park 212.599.9714

hr	rate	specials	rate	enter	exit
1/2	$10	AM	$28	6-10am	12am
1	$27	Sa,Su	$25		
2	$46	SUV	$10		
24	$50	Month	$510, O/S add $100		
12am	$48				
O/N	$50				

helpful information
24/7	AE, MC, V	Damage inspection
79 spaces	Max bill $20	35 E 38th

---

14. 99 Park Ave *bet Lexington/Park, N side of E 39th*
RapidPark 212.661.3495

hr	rate	specials	rate	enter	exit
1/2	$15	AM	$28	6-10am	6pm
1	$27	O/N	$50		8am
1 1/2	$36	SUV	$10		
2	$46	Month	$510, O/S add $100		
12am	$48	Month	$150	m'cycle	

helpful information
M-F 6am-12am	AE, MC, V	70 spaces
Sa,Su 7am-12am	Elevator	

---

15. 222 E 39th St *bet 3rd/2nd, S side of E 39th, E of Tunnel Exit*
LAZ 212.867.4365

hr	rate	specials	rate	enter	exit
1	$15	AM m-f	$20	6-11am	12hr
2	$19	PM m-f	$10	after 5pm	3am
12	$24	Sa,Su	$10	anytime	12hr, No O/N
24	$34	Event	$34		
		SUV	$10		
		Month	$338, SUV add $42		
		Month	$168	m'cycle	

helpful information
M-F 6am-3am	86 spaces	Largest van-Tahoe
Sa,Su 7am-3am	AE, MC, V, Dis	with no carrier

---

16. 250 E 39th St *bet 3rd/2nd, S side of E 39th*
LAZ 212.922.0746

hr	rate	specials	rate	enter	exit
1/2	$5	Daily	$17	anytime	close
1	$15	PM	$10	after 5pm	1am
2	$19	Sa,Su	$10	all day	
12	$22	Event	$34		
24	$34	SUV	$10		
		Month	$338, SUV add $42		
		Month	$127	m'cycle	

helpful information
M-F 6am-1am	35 spaces	Steep driveway
Sa,Su 7am-1am	AE, MC, V, Dis	

---

17. 315 E 38th St *bet 2nd/1st, N side of E 38th or S side of E 39th, E of Tunnel Entrance*

Icon   212.599.8670

hr	rate	specials	rate	enter	exit
1/2	$10	AM m-f	$16	5-10am	12hr
1	$17	Sa,Su	$11	Sa after 6am	12 hr, by Su 6pm
2	$22	July 4	$30	4pm-4am	4am
12	$25	SUV	$10		
24	$35	Month	$422, SUV add $84		

helpful information

24/7	AE, MC, V	6'4" clearance	330 E 59th
208 spaces	181" rule for SUV	Max bill $50	

---

18. 333 E 38th St *bet E 38th/E 39th, W side of 1st*

Rapid Park   212.818.9435

hr	rate	specials	rate	enter	exit
1/2	$9	AM	$16	6-10am	12hr
1	$18	PM	$11	after 3pm	6am
2	$20	Sa,Su	$10	6am-3pm	12hr
12	$22	SUV	$10		
24	$31	Month	$380		

helpful information

24/7	AE, MC, V	6'9" clearance
146 spaces	181" rule for SUV	Very steep driveway

---

19. 250 Madison Ave *bet 5th/Madison, N side of E 38th*

Icon   212.725.9319

hr	rate	specials	rate	enter	exit
1/2	$11	AM m-f	$28	5-9am	12hr
1	$29	AM m-f	$32	9-10am	12hr
2	$36	PM	$18	6pm-5am	8am
3	$40	Sa,Su	$18	6am-6pm	12hr
24	$45	SUV	$10		
		Month	$507, SUV add $84		

helpful information

24/7	AE, MC, V	Max bill $50
155 spaces	181" rule for SUV	No full size vans

---

20. 310 Lexington Ave *bet E 38th/E 37th, W side of Lexington*

LAZ   212.681.2044

hr	rate	specials	rate	enter	exit
1/2	$11	Sa,Su	$13	anytime	10hr
1	$18	Event	$40		
2	$22	SUV	$10		
10	$28	Month	$422, SUV add $84		
24	$32	Month	$148, m'cycle		

helpful information

M-Sa 7am-1am	AE, MC, V, Dis, DC	6'10" clearance
Su 7am-12am	Hard to see from street	Steep driveway
26 spaces		

262

12	13	14
15	16	17
18	19	20

E 42nd–E 23rd St
Murray Hill/Kips Bay/Midtown South

21. 155 E 38th St *bet Lexington/3rd, N side of E 38th*
Icon 212.599.9140

hr	rate	specials	rate	enter	exit
1/2	$11	July 4	$30	4pm-4am	4am
1	$24	SUV	$10		
2	$26	Month	$422, SUV add $84		
3	$29				
12	$32				
24	$36				

helpful information

7D 7am-12am	AE, MC, V	181" rule for SUV
67 spaces	Elevator	Max bill $20

22. 560 3rd Ave *bet E 37th/E 38th, W side of 3rd*
Icon 212.599.9807

hr	rate	specials	rate	enter	exit
1/2	$12	AM m-f	$23	5-10am	12hr
1	$26	Sa,Su	$18	anytime	12hr
2	$28	July 4	$30	4pm-4am	4am
12	$34	SUV	$10		
24	$36	Month	$422, SUV add $84		

helpful information

24/7	AE, MC, V	No full size vans
300 spaces	Max bill $50	

23. 205 E 38th St *bet 3rd/2nd, N side of E 38th, near 3rd*
Icon 212.684.9138

hr	rate	specials	rate	enter	exit
1/2	$11	PM 7D	$15	5pm-6am	6am
1	$24	Sa,Su	$15	6am-5pm	12hr
2	$26	July 4	$30	4pm-4am	4am
12	$33	SUV	$10		
24	$36				

helpful information

24/7	181" rule for SUV	Elevator
125 spaces	Max bill $50	
AE, MC, V	No full size vans	

24. 221 E 38th St *bet 3rd/2nd, N side of E 38th, E of Tunnel Exit*
Glenwood 212.599.8610

hr	rate	specials	rate	enter	exit
1	$11	AM	$15	5:30-9am	6:30pm
3	$15	Sa,Su	$11	after 7am	7pm
5	$19	SUV	$7		
9	$23	Month	$359	tenant, O/S add $42	
24	$38	Month	$380	non-tenant, O/S add $42	

helpful information

24/7	181" rule for SUV	Paramount Tower
95 spaces	Damage inspection	Eff. 5/07
AE, MC, V		

E 42nd–E 23rd St
Murray Hill/Kips Bay/Midtown South

12	13	14
15	16	17
18	19	20

263

25. **345 E 37th St** *bet 2nd/1st, N side of E 37th or S side of E 38th*
Corinthian Garage Corp 212.599.8659

hr	rate	specials	rate	enter	exit
1/2	$10	AM m-f	$15	5-10am	7pm
1	$16	Sa,Su	$10	by 12pm	12hr
2	$20	SUV	$10		
3	$23	Month	$375, SUV add $40		
12	$24	Month	$230	7am-7pm	
24	$33	Month	$175	m'cycle	

helpful information

24/7	186 spaces	AE	330 E 38th	Eff. 10/07

26. **220 Madison Ave** *bet Madison/5th, S side of E 37th*
MPS 212.684.8207

hr	rate*	specials	rate	enter	exit
1/2	$15	AM m-f	$29	7-9:30am	7pm
1	$30	Sa	$10	after 7am	1hr
1 1/2	$34	Sa	$15	after 7am	7pm
2	$37	O/N	add'l $12		9am
MTC	$39	SUV	$10		
		Month	$359	tenant, SUV add $42	
		Month	$401	non-tenant, SUV add $42	

helpful information

M-F 7am-10pm	45 spaces	*M-F, 9:30am-close
Sa 7am-7pm	AE, MC, V	
Su,Hol closed	Eff. 9/06	

27. **415 E 37th St** *bet 1st/FDR, S side of E 38th*

212.679.8414

hr	rate	specials	rate	enter	exit
1	$10	SUV	$10		
2	$14	Month	$450, O/S add $100		
3	$16	July 4th	$35	4am	
12	$23				
24	$35				

TENANT ONLY

helpful information

60 spaces	Max bill $20	2 elevators
Cash	Car wash	Exit only on E 37th

28. **630 1st Ave** *bet 1st/river, N side of E 36th or S side of E 37th*
Imperial 212.684.9347

hr	rate	specials	rate	enter	exit
1	$12	AM	$15	4-11am	12hr
2	$17	Sa,Su	$10	after 7am	7pm
10	$24	SUV	$10		
24	$28	Month	$375, O/S add $100		
O/N	$28	Month	$150	m'cycle	

helpful information

24/7	AE, MC, V	
100 spaces	6'8" clearance	

29. 30 Park Ave *bet Madison/Park, S side of E 36th*
Champion 212.684.8576

hr	rate	specials	rate	enter	exit
1/2	$14	AM m-f	$27	5-10am	8pm
1	$27	Sa,Su	$25	after 7am	8pm
2	$34	SUV	$10		
10	$39	Month	$395	rent-stabilized tenant,	
24	$45			O/S add $211	
O/N	$45	Month	$498	other tenant, O/S add $211	

helpful information
24/7	AE, MC, V	6'6" clearance
142 spaces	Elevator	181" rule for SUV

30. 35 Park Ave *bet Park/Lexington, S side of E 36th*
QuikPark 212.684.9229

hr	rate	specials	rate	enter	exit
1/2	$10-14	AM m-f	$23	6-10am	8pm
1	$24	Sa, Su	$18	anytime	12hr, by 12am
4	$30	SUV	$10		
24	$42	Month	$152	m'cycle	
O/N	$42				
MTC	$34				

helpful information
7D 7am-2am	AE, MC, V, DC	Steep driveway
47 spaces	181" rule for SUV	

31. 221 E 36th St *bet 3rd/2nd, N side of E 36th, just before Tunnel exit*
QuikPark 212.481.2870

hr	rate	specials	rate	enter	exit
1/2	$7	AM 7D	$14	5-11am	8pm
1	$15	Event	$50		
3	$23	SUV	$10		
10	$24	Month	$338		
24	$36				

helpful information
24/7	AE, MC, V, Dis
64 spaces	Max bill $50

32. 245 E 36th St *bet 3rd/2nd, N side of E 36th, just before Tunnel exit*
245 East 36th Street Garage Corp 212.684.6619

hr	rate*	specials	rate	enter	exit
1	$13	AM	$13	6:30-10am	7pm
2	$17	Event	$30		
3	$22	SUV	$10		
8	$25				
MTC	$35				
O/N	$38				

helpful information
M-Sa 6:30am-7pm	Cash	Outdoor
35 spaces	Max bill $50	*after 10am

33. 9 Park Ave *bet E 34th/E 35th, E side of Park*
Icon   212.725.5081

hr	rate	specials	rate	enter	exit
1/2	$10	AM m-f	$24	5-10am	12hr
1	$24	PM	$16	5pm-5am	7am
2	$28	Sa,Su	$15	7am-5pm	12hr
10	$35	July 4	$30	4pm-4am	4am
24	$42	SUV	$10		
		Month	$500		

Mendy's discount, Wolfgang's discount

helpful information

24/7	AE, MC, V	181" rule for SUV
150 spaces	2 elevators	

---

34. 132 E 35th St *bet Lexington/Park, S side of E 35th*
Icon   212.684.8430

hr	rate	specials	rate	enter	exit
1/2	$10	Sa,Su	$11	6am-5pm	3hr
1	$23	Sa,Su	$13	6am-5pm	8hr
2	$25	Sa,Su	$15	6am-5pm	12hr
12	$33	Sa,Su	$41	6am-5pm	24hr
24	$43	July 4	$30	4pm-4am	4am
		SUV	$10		
		Month	$376		

helpful information

24/7	AE, MC, V	181" rule for SUV
85 spaces	Elevator	No full size vans

---

35. 400 E 35th St *bet FDR/1st, S side of E 35th*
Icon   212.684.8311

hr	rate	specials	rate	enter	exit
1/2	$7	AM	$17	6-10am	6pm
1	$19	July 4	$30	4pm-4am	4am
2	$20	SUV	$10		
10	$27	Month	$422		
24	$33				

helpful information

24/7	AE, MC, V	181" rule for SUV
80 spaces	5'11" clearance	Eff. 9/07

---

36. 155 E 34th St *bet Lexington/3rd, N side of E 34th*
QuikPark   212.683.2928

hr	rate	specials	rate	enter	exit
1/2	$9	AM	$19	6-10am	12hr
1	$16	PM	$12	after 4pm	6am
2	$20	Su	$15	anytime	12hr, by 12am
10	$30	SUV	$10		
24	$35	Month	$380		
		NYU Medical Center	$17		8hr

helpful information

24/7	66 spaces	AE, MC, V, DC, Disc	Steep driveway

---

37. 222 E 34th St *bet 3rd/2nd, S side of E 34th*

Icon 212.689.2730

hr	rate	specials	rate	enter	exit
		Month	$380, O/S add $84		

MONTHLY ONLY

helpful information

24/7	AE, MC, V	Max bill $50
107 spaces	181" rule for SUV	No left turn from E 34th exit

---

38. 300 E 34th St *bet 2nd/Tunnel Approach/1st, S side of E 34th*

GMC 212.481.6016

hr	rate	specials	rate	enter	exit
1/2	$10	AM	$17	by 9am	8pm
1	$23	Sa,Su	$15	6am-6pm	6pm
2	$30	O/N	$40		after 5am
10	$35	SUV	$10		
24	$40	Month	$375, O/S add $100		

helpful information

7D 6am-2am	AE, MC, V	min grace period
148 spaces	Elevator	6'6" clearance

---

39. 333 E 34th St *bet 2nd/Tunnel Approach/1st, N side of E 34th*

MPG 212.686.2508

hr	rate*	specials	rate	enter	exit
1/2	$9	AM m-f	$17	12-8am	12hr
1	$18	PM m-f	$9	4pm-12am	1/2hr
2	$22	PM m-f	$10	4pm-12am	6am
24	$30	PM m-f	$30	4pm-12am	24hr
		Sa,Su	$9	anytime	1/2hr
		Sa,Su	$10	anytime	12hr
		Sa,Su	$30	anytime	24hr
		SUV	$10		
		Month	$400, SUV add $42		

helpful information

24/7	AE, MC, V	*M-F, 8am-4pm
56 spaces	Damage inspection	

---

40. 332-342 E 34th St *bet 2nd/Tunnel Approach/1st, S side of E 34th*

Imperial 212.252.8726

hr	rate	specials	rate	enter	exit
1/2	$9	AM	$17	5-9am	12hr
1	$18	PM m-f	$10	after 4pm	12am
2	$22	Sa,Su	$10	anytime	12hr
10	$28	SUV	$10		
24	$34	Month	$350		
O/N	$34				

helpful information

24/7	AE, MC, V	7'2" clearance
41 spaces	Lift	

E 42nd–E 23rd St
Murray Hill/Kips Bay/Midtown South

12 13 14
15 16 17
18 19 20

267

---

41. 400 E 34th St *bet 1st/river, S side of E 34th*
Central   212.686.1620

hr	rate	specials	rate	enter	exit
1/2	$12	SUV	$10		
1	$18				
2	$24				
3	$27				
10	$32				
24	$35				

NYU HOSPITAL VISITORS ONLY

helpful information

24/7	AE, MC, V	Outdoor
114 spaces	Max bill $50	Eff. 6/08

---

42. 325 5th Ave *bet Madison/5th, S side of E 33rd*
Impark   212.725.4102

hr	rate	specials	rate	enter	exit
1/2	$13	AM m-f	$24	5-9am	12am
1	$25	PM m-f	$15	after 6pm	1am
2	$33	Sa,Su	$30		12hr
10	$38	SUV	$10		
24	$50	Month	$634, O/S add $84		
		Month	$232	m'cycle	

helpful information

24/7	174 spaces	AE, MC, V

---

43. 4 Park Ave *bet Park Ave South/Madison, N side of E 33rd*
Champion   212.679.8111

hr	rate	specials	rate	enter	exit
1/2	$11	AM	$23	5-10am	11pm
1	$27	Sa,Su	$17	7am-4pm	12am
2	$35	SUV	$10		
10	$41	Month	$423, O/S add $84		
24	$47				
O/N	$47				

helpful information

24/7	AE, MC, V	6'6" clearance
150 spaces	181" rule for SUV	53 E 33rd

---

44. 230 Lexington Ave *bet E 34th/E 33rd, W side of Lexington*
Murray Park Garage Co   212.684.9312

hr	rate	specials	rate	enter	exit
1/2	$12	AM m-f	$18	by 11am	8pm
1	$17	PM	$12	after 5pm	10am
2	$19	Sa,Su	$10	anytime	1am
10	$30	Event	$25		
24	$36	SUV	$10		
O/N	$36	Month	$329, SUV add $84		

helpful information

M-Th 6am-1am	123 spaces	15 spots for casual
F 6am-3am	AE, MC, V	parking M-F
Sa,Su 7am-3am	181" rule for SUV	120 E 34th

45. **220 Lexington Ave** *bet E 34th/E 33rd, W side of Lexington*
Central   212.725.3927

hr	rate	specials	rate	enter	exit
1/2	$5	AM m-f	$20	3-10am	7pm
1	$20	Sa,Su	$13	anytime	12hr
2	$24	SUV	$11		
10	$32	Month	$422, O/S add $84		
24	$46	Month	$169	m'cycle	

helpful information
24/7	AE, MC, V, Dis	Max bill $50
125 spaces	2 elevators	135 E 33rd

---

46. **148 E 33rd St** *bet 3rd/Lexington, S side of E 33rd*
RapidPark   212.686.0861

hr	rate	specials	rate	enter	exit
1/2	$7	AM	$17	6-10am	7pm
1	$18	Sa,Su	$11	7am-6pm	6pm
2	$22	July 4	$30		
3	$26	SUV	$10		
12	$28	Month	$385, O/S add $100		
24	$32				
O/N	$32				

helpful information
24/7	AE, MC, V	Max bill $20
149 spaces	Elevator	

---

47. **488 3rd Ave** *bet E 33rd/E 34th, W side of 3rd*
Icon   212.725.9679

hr	rate	specials	rate	enter	exit
1/2	$10	Sa	$10	7am-close	12hr, by 6pm
1	$16	Su	$10	7am-close	12hr, by 6pm
2	$21	July 4	$30	4pm-close	
24	$26	SUV	$10		
MTC	$33	Month	$380, O/S add $84		
		Month	$169	m'cycle	

helpful information
24/7	AE, MC, V	Max bill $20
55 spaces	181" rule for SUV	No full size vans

---

48. **200 E 33rd St** *bet 2nd/3rd, S side of E 33rd*
Laurence Towers Garage   212.696.1194

hr	rate	specials	rate	enter	exit
1	$16	AM 7D	$17	6:30-10am	7pm
2	$18	Sa,Su	$10	anytime	12hr
3	$22	Event	$30	after 3pm	1am
12	$25	SUV	$10		
1am	$29	Month	$351, O/S add $84		
O/N	$29				

helpful information
M-F 6am-1am	AE, MC, V, Dis	5 min grace period
Sa,Su,Hol 7am-1am	181" rule for SUV	Rent-a-Car
157 spaces		

49. 377 E 33rd St *bet 1st/2nd, N side of E 33rd*

Impark 646.935.1109

hr	rate	specials	rate	enter	exit
1	$21	AM	$17	6-9:30am	7pm
2	$27	Event	$32		
10	$36	SUV	$10		
24	$40	Month	$465, O/S add $84		
O/N	$40				

helpful information
M-F 6am-12am   AE, MC, V   Eff. 6/07
Sa,Su 7am-12am   45 spaces

---

50. 475 Park Avenue South *bet Park Ave South/Lexington, S side of E 32nd*

Icon 212.684.8352

hr	rate	specials	rate	enter	exit
1/2	$13	AM m-f	$21	6-9am	12hr
1	$25	PM m-f	$12	after 4pm	12am
2	$27	Sa,Su	$12	after 7am	12am
12	$34	SUV	$10		
24	$42	Month	$422, O/S add $84		
12am	$42	Ramada, Grand Union, Roger Williams,			
		Quality Hotels	$20		24hr

helpful information
M-F 6am-12am   Su 8am-12am   AE, MC, V
Sa 7am-12am   150 spaces   181" rule for SUV

---

51. 135 E 31st St *bet Lexington/3rd, N side of E 31st or S side of E 32nd*

Central 212.951.4800

hr	rate	specials	rate	enter	exit
1/2	$8	AM m-f	$20	6-10am	8pm
1	$16	Event	$20		
2	$22	SUV	$10		
10	$28	Month	$342	tenant, O/S add $84	
24	$36	Month	$363	non-tenant, O/S add $84	

helpful information
24/7   AE, MC, V   Boom gate on E 32nd
141 spaces   Max bill $50   Windsor Court Garage

---

52. 200 E 32nd St *bet 3rd/2nd, S side of E 32nd*

Icon 212.684.2481

hr	rate	specials	rate	enter	exit
1/2	$10	AM 7D	$16	7-10am	7pm
1	$16	PM 7D	$9	after 6pm	close
2	$18	Sa,Su	$8	7am-6pm	to 6pm
24	$28	Sa,Su	$12	7am-6pm	close
MTC	$23	July 4	$30	4pm-close	close
		SUV	$10		
		Month	$380, O/S add $84		

helpful information
Su-Th 7am-12am   33 spaces   181" rule for SUV
F,Sa 7am-1am   Cash   No full-size vans

---

53. 575 1st Ave *bet E 32nd/E 33rd, W side of 1st Ave*
RapidPark   212.684.2762

hr	rate	specials	rate	enter	exit
1/2	$12	AM m-sa	$20	3am-9am	12am
1	$23	Su	$15	after 6pm	by 7pm
2	$33	SUV	$10		
3	$35	Month	$375, O/S add $100		
10	$37	Month	$150	m'cycle	
24	$40				

helpful information		
24/7	AE, MC, V	300 E 33rd
300 spaces	Max bill $20	

---

54. 142 E 31st St *bet 3rd/Lexington, S side of E 31st*
GMC   212.683.2056

hr	rate	specials	rate	enter	exit
1	$17	AM 7D	$20	5-10am	12am
2	$28	O/N	$40		after 5am
10	$32	SUV	$10		
24	$40	Month	$375, O/S add $200		

helpful information		
24/7	5 min grace period	Max bill $50
550 spaces	2 elevators	Large vans, O/S OK
AE, MC, V	Alamo, National rental	

---

55. 10 E 30th St *bet 5th/Madison, S side of E 30th*
RapidPark   212.725.9250

hr	rate	specials	rate	enter	exit
1	$26	PM	$25	after 5pm	12am
2	$35	Sa,Su	$25	6am-6pm	6pm
3	$37	O/N	$50		
10	$40	SUV	$10		
12	$45	Month	$575, O/S add $100		
24	$45				

helpful information	
24/7	2 elevators
200 spaces	Max bill $20
AE, MC, V	

---

56. 230 E 30th St *bet 3rd/2nd, S side of E 30th*
Supreme Parking   212.683.4976

hr	rate	specials	rate	enter	exit
1	$12	SUV	$5+		
3	$18	Month	$350		
10	$24				
24	$28				

helpful information
24/7
25 spaces
Cash

57. 350 E 30th St *bet 2nd/1st, N side of E 29th or S side of E 30th*
Central 212.779.8311

hr	rate	specials	rate	enter	exit
1/2	$8	AM m-f	$16	6-9am	10hr, by 7pm
1	$16	PM	$16	after 6pm	6am
2	$20	Sa,Su	$20	anytime	24hr, by 12am
10	$30	SUV	$10		
24	$39	Month	$422, SUV add $63		
		Month	$148	m'cycle	

helpful information

24/7	AE, MC, V	Max bill $50
68 spaces	7'6" clearance	

58. 530 1st Ave *bet E 30th/E 33rd, E side of 1st*
Rapid Park 212.263.7304

hr	rate	specials	rate	enter	exit
1/2	$12	Curbside parking:	$15		1/2hr
1	$18	Curbside parking:	$25		1hr
2	$24	Curbside parking:	$30		2hr
3	$27	Curbside parking:	$40		3hr
10	$32	Curbside parking:	$50		24hr
24	$35	SUV	$10		

helpful information

7D 6am-12am	Eff. 6/08	No vans/SUVs
130 spaces	NYU Medical Center	Eff. 6/08
AE, MC, V	Low clearance	

59. end of E 30th St *FDR Service Road from E 29th to E 31st*
Impark

hr	rate	specials	rate	enter	exit
1	$10	SUV	$5		
2	$12				
8	$15				

helpful information

6am-12am	Rates repeat after 8hr	Hospital employee
230 spaces	Outdoor	parking above E
Cash	NYU Hospital parking	31st St

60. 10 E 29th St *bet Madison/5th, S side of E 29th*
Champion 212.684.4394

hr	rate	specials	rate	enter	exit
1/2	$23	AM m-f	$32	4-9am	7pm
1	$33	Sa,Su	$29	after 6am	7pm
2	$43	SUV	$10		
3	$53	Month	$655, O/S add $148		
24	$59				
O/N	$59				

helpful information

24/7	60 spaces	AE, MC, V	6'4" clearance

---

61. 155 E 29th St *bet 3rd/Lexington, N side of E 29th*

Icon   212.684.8259

hr	rate	specials	rate	enter	exit
1/2	$10	AM 7D	$20	6-10am	12hr
1	$19	PM 7D	$15	after 6pm	6am
2	$23	July 4	$30	4pm-4am	4am
12	$26	SUV	$10		
24	$36	Month	$422, O/S add $84		
		Month	$169	m'cycle	

helpful information

24/7	123 spaces	AE, MC, V

---

62. 500 2nd Ave *bet 1st/2nd, S side of E 29th*

Icon   212.684.9526

hr	rate	specials	rate	enter	exit
1/2	$8	AM m-f	$17	5-10am	12hr
1	$14	PM	$10	after 4pm	by 6am
2	$16	Sa,Su	$10	6am-4pm	12hr
10	$18	Sa,Su	$20	6am-4pm	24hr
24	$24	July 4	$30	4pm-4am	
		SUV	$10		
		Month	$338, SUV add $84		
		Month	$211	m'cycle	

helpful information

24/7	AE, MC, V	Max bill $50
169 spaces	181" rule for SUV	No full size vans

---

63. 331 E 29th St *bet 2nd/1st, N side of E 29th*

Icon   212.686.9800

hr	rate	specials	rate	enter	exit

MONTHLY ONLY

helpful information

Cash

---

64. 398 Park Avenue South *SW corner of Park Ave South/E 28th, W side of Park Ave South or S side of E 28th*

Champion   212.532.4818

hr	rate	specials	rate	enter	exit
1/2	$23	AM m-f	$34	by 9am	7pm
1	$33	PM m-f	$34	after 4:30pm	close
1 1/2	$39	Sa,Su	$32	anytime	close
2	$48	SUV	$10		
MTC	$59	Month	$718, O/S add $106		

helpful information

M-Sa 7:30am-1am	90 spaces	Outdoor
Su 8am-6pm	AE, MC, V	

65. 119 E 28th St *bet Park Ave South/Lexington, N side of E 28th*

Park It Mgmt 212.725.9747

hr	rate	specials	rate	enter	exit
1/2	$15	AM 7D	$28	by 9:30 am	11hr
1	$22	PM 7D	$22	after 4:30pm	close
2	$28	Sa,Su	$24	anytime	12hr
3	$30	Daily	$35	all day	
24	$40	SUV	$10		
		Month	$465, O/S add $84		

helpful information

M-F 6am-12am	138 spaces	Outdoor
Sa 8am-12am	AE, V, MC	
Su 8am-6pm	Lift	

---

66. 201 E 28th St *bet 3rd/2nd, N side of E 28th*

Imperial

hr	rate	specials	rate	enter	exit
1/2	$9	AM m-f	$18	6-10am	7pm
1	$17	F,Sa	$15	after 6pm	close
2	$20	SUV	$7		
10	$23				
24	$35				
O/N	$35				

helpful information

M-Th 6am-1am	Sa 7am-3am	61 spaces
F 6am-3am	Su 7am-1am	AE, MC, V, Dis, DC

---

67. 479 1st Ave *bet 1st/Mt. Carmel on N side of E 28th*

Icon 212.725.7246

hr	rate	specials	rate	enter	exit
1	$18	Sa,Su	$10		12hr
2	$20	Sa,Su	$18		24hr
10	$24	July 4	$30	4pm-4am	4am
24	$27	SUV	$10		
		Month	$380, O/S add $84		
		Month	$169 m'cycle		

helpful information

24/7	AE, MC, V	Max bill $50
42 spaces	181" rule for SUV	No full size vans

---

68. 145 E 27th St *bet 3rd/Lexington, N side of E 27th*

Townsway Garage Co 212.684.9675

hr	rate	specials	rate	enter	exit
1	$15	AM	$15	7:30-9:30am	6pm
2	$16	PM	$11	by 6pm	1am
24	$26	Month	$319		

helpful information

M-F 7am-1am	48 spaces	Steep driveway
Sa,Su closed	Cash	

69. 240 E 27th St *bet 2nd/3rd, S side of E 27th*

Central   212.684.8934

hr	rate	specials	rate	enter	exit
1/2	$8	AM m-f	$15	6-10am	12hr
1	$15	PM	$10	6pm-6am	6am
2	$16	Sa,Su	$10	6am-6pm	12hr
10	$18	SUV	$15		
24	$30	Month	$507, O/S add $84		
		Month	$211	m'cycle	

helpful information

24/7	Max bill $50
65 spaces	Steep driveway
AE, MC, V	

70. 200 E 27th St *bet 3rd/2nd, N side of E 26th*

Chelnik   212.684.9704

hr	rate	specials	rate	enter	exit
1	$16	AM	$16	6-10am	10hr
2	$18	Sa,Su	$16	7-10am	10hr
10	$23	Baruch	$16		10hr with valid ID
24	$33	SUV	$5		
		Month	$413, SUV add $35		

helpful information

M-Th 6am-12am	Su 7am-12am	Lifts
F 6am-2am	68 spaces	Max bill $20
Sa 7am-2am	AE, MC, V	Indoor/Outdoor

71. 460 2nd Ave *bet 2nd/1st, N side of E 26th*

Icon   212.252.8038

hr	rate	specials	rate	enter	exit
1/2	$8	AM m-f	$16	6-10am	12hr
1	$14	PM	$9	after 4pm	6am
2	$16	Sa,Su	$10	6am-4pm	12hr
10	$18	Sa,Su	$20	6am-4pm	24hr
24	$24	July 4	$30	4pm-4am	4am
		SUV	$10		
		Month	$338, SUV add $84		
		Month	$211	m'cycle	

helpful information

24/7	Max bill $50
192 spaces	Steep driveway
AE, MC, V	

E 42nd–E 23rd St
Murray Hill/Kips Bay/Midtown South

12	13	14
15	16	17
18	19	20

275

72. 442 2nd Ave *bet 2nd/1st, S side of E 26th*

Icon 212.213.6049

hr	rate	specials	rate	enter	exit
1/2	$8	AM m-f	$16	6-10am	12hr
1	$14	PM	$9	after 4pm	6am
2	$16	Sa,Su	$10	6am-4pm	12hr
10	$18	Sa,Su	$20	6am-4pm	24hr
24	$24	July 4	$30	4pm-4am	4am
		SUV	$10		
		Month	$338	, SUV add $84	
		Month	$211	m'cycle	

helpful information

24/7	AE, MC, V	Max bill $50
98 spaces	181" rule for SUV	

---

73. *Corner of E 26th/FDR Service Road, enter from E 29th St to FDR Service Road*

Impark

hr	rate	specials	rate	enter	exit
1	$10	Month	Rates upon request		
2	$12				
8	$15				

helpful information

Cash	Outdoor	Bellevue Hospital parking
		Rates repeat after 8hr

---

74. 2500 FDR Dr *under FDR bet E 25th/E 26th, turn left from E 23rd onto FDR*

Five Star Parking 212.532.9268

hr	rate*	specials	rate	enter	exit
1/2	$6	AM m-f	$13	6-10am	7pm
1	$12	F,Sa,Su	$6	F after 5pm	1/2hr
2	$14	F,Sa,Su	$12	F after 5pm	1hr
12	$17	F,Sa,Su	$14	F after 5pm	2hr, by Su 5pm
24	$25	F,Sa,Su	$21	F after 5pm	24hr, by Su 5pm
		Event	$30		to 2am
		Month	$228	tenant	
		Month	$241	non-tenant	
		Month	$127	day	

$10 coupon with purchase of $100 coupon book

helpful information

24/7	Eff. 1/08	Self parking
735 spaces	6'3" clearance	*Su after 5pm - F 5pm
MC, V	Max bill $50	Waterside Plaza

276

12	13	14
15	16	17
18	19	20

E 42nd–E 23rd St
Murray Hill/Kips Bay/Midtown South

75. 330 3rd Ave *bet E 24th/E 25th, W side of 3rd*
KC Parking LLC/Park Here   212.665.5773

hr	rate	specials	rate	enter	exit
1	$12	AM m-f	$17	by 9am	6pm
2	$15	PM	$10	after 5pm	12am
10	$19	Sa,Su	$11		10hr
24	$30	SUV	$10		
		Month	$401, SUV add $84		
		Month	$169	m'cycle	

helpful information
24/7   42 spaces   AE, MC, V

---

76. 300 E 25th St *bet 1st/2nd, S side of E 25th, near 2nd*
Impark   212.213.1349

hr	rate	specials	rate	enter	exit
1	$13	AM	$15	6-9am	7pm
2	$15	Event	$25		
10	$20	SUV	$10		
24	$25	Month	$325, O/S add $84		

helpful information
24/7   AE, MC, V   Car wash $15
146 spaces

---

77. 111 E 24th St *bet Park Ave South/Lexington, N side of E 24th*
24 Parking Corp   212.995.2430

hr	rate	specials	rate	enter	exit
1	$20	SUV	$10		
MTC	$31	Month	$401, O/S add $21		

helpful information
M-F 7am-11pm   Cash   45 spaces
Sa 7am-7pm   Outdoor   Large SUVs OK

---

78. 200 E 24th St *bet 3rd/2nd, S side of E 24th, near 3rd*
GGMC   212.725.0225

hr	rate	specials	rate	enter	exit
1	$12	AM	$19	6-9am	7pm
2	$14	SUV	$10		
12	$21				
24	$27				

helpful information
7D 6am-12am   54 spaces   AE, MC, V

E 42nd–E 23rd St
Murray Hill/Kips Bay/Midtown South

12 13 14
15 16 17
18 19 20

277

79. 214 E 24th St bet 3rd/2nd, S side of E 24th
Park It/East 24 Garage Corp 212.448.0725

hr	rate	specials	rate	enter	exit
1	$8	SUV	$5		
2	$10				
10	$14				
12	$17				
24	$23				

helpful information

M-F 6am-8pm	37 spaces	Cash	Car wash

80. 215 E 24th St bet 3rd/2nd, N side of E 24th
GGMC 212.684.8687

hr	rate	specials	rate	enter	exit
1	$12	AM	$17	6-10am	7pm
2	$14	Sa,Su	$6	6am-6pm	1hr
12	$21	Sa,Su	$8	6am-6pm	2hr
24	$27	Sa,Su	$10	6am-6pm	6pm
		SUV	$10		
		Month	$385		

helpful information

24/7	AE, MC, V	6'2" clearance
99 spaces	Very nice interior	

81. 401 2nd Ave bet E 24th/E 23rd, W side of 2nd
Icon 212.683.4009

hr	rate	specials	rate	enter	exit
1/2	$7	AM	$16	6-10am	7pm
2	$14	PM m-f	$16	2:30pm-6am	6am
10	$20	Sa,Su	$10	6am-6pm	10hr
24	$25	Sa,Su	$25	6am-6pm	24hr
		July 4	$25		10hr
		July 4	$30		24hr
		SUV	$10		
		Month	$380, O/S add $84		

helpful information

24/7	AE, MC, V	6'4" clearance
72 spaces	181" rule for SUV	

82. E 23rd St & East River East end of E 23rd
New York Skyports Inc 212.686.4546

hr	rate	specials	rate	enter	exit
12	$25	SUV	$10		
24	$35	Month	$380	indoor parking, O/S add $84	
O/N	$35	Month	$338	roof parking, O/S add $84	
		Month	TBD	outdoor (50 spaces)	

helpful information

24/7	Cash	Self parking
515 spaces	6'3" clearance	Indoor/Outdoor

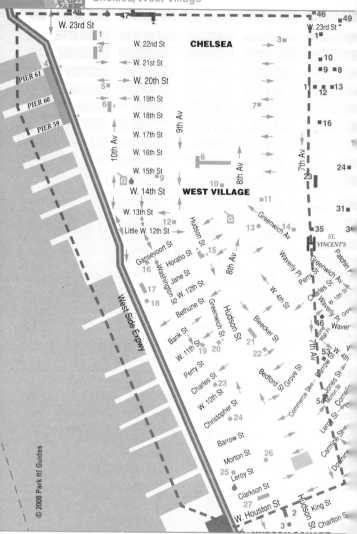

1. **514 W 23rd St** *bet 10th/11th, N side of W 22nd or S side of W 23rd, near 10th*

Park It Mgmt 212.807.8207

hr	rate*	specials	rate	enter	exit
1/2	$8	AM	$16	5-9am	12hr
1	$12	PM	$8	5pm-6am	1/2hr
2	$16	PM	$12	5pm-6am	1hr
3	$20	PM	$16	5pm-6am	2hr
12	$25	PM	$20	5pm-6am	12hr
24	$30	PM	$25	5pm-6am	24hr
		SUV	$5-10		
		Month	$329, SUV add $30, O/S add $93		

helpful information

24/7	AE, MC, V	Outdoor
81 spaces	Lifts	*5am-5pm

2. **507 W 21st St** *bet 10th/11th, N side of W 21st or S side of W 22nd, near 10th*

Edison/Park Fast
212.929.3560

hr	rate*	specials	rate	enter	exit
1/2	$6	PM 7D	$6	4pm-4am	1/2hr
2	$20	PM 7D	$12	4pm-4am	4am
12	$28	PM 7D	$30	4pm-4am	24hr
24	$30	Sa,Su	$6	4am-4pm	1/2hr
		Sa,Su	$12	4am-4pm	12hr
		Sa,Su	$30	4am-4pm	24hr
		Event	$30	9pm-4am	11am
		SUV	$12		
		Month	$359, O/S add $84		

helpful information

24/7	AE, MC, V	*M-F, enter 4am-4pm
49 spaces	Outdoor	

3. **235 W 22nd St** *bet 8th/7th, N side of W 22nd*

Quik Park
646.638.4213

hr	rate	specials	rate	enter	exit
1/2	$9	AM	$20	6-10am	12hr
1	$18	SUV	$10		
2	$26	Month	$450, O/S add $42		
10	$30	Month	$169	m'cycle	
24	$38				

helpful information

24/7	6'8" clearance
85 spaces	
AE, MC, V	

4. **Pier 59-61 @ Chelsea Piers** *bet W 18th/W 20th, W side of Westside Highway*

Pier 59-61

hr	rate	specials	rate	enter	exit
1	$12	7D	free		20 min
2	$16				
3	$20				
4	$28				
5	$38				
6	$40				
8	$46				
add'l hr $9					

helpful information

24/7	Enter via W 24th
AE, MC, V	Self parking
Chelsea Piers	

5. **161 10th Ave** *bet W 20th/W 19th, W side of 10th, near W 20th*
Edison/Park Fast   212.633.6259

hr	rate*	specials	rate	enter	exit
1/2	$6	PM 7D	$6	after 4pm	1/2hr
2	$20	PM 7D	$12	after 4pm	4am
12	$28	PM 7D	$30	after 4pm	24hr
24	$30	Sa,Su	$6	4am-4pm	1/2hr
		Sa,Su	$12	4am-4pm	10hr
		Sa,Su	$30	4am-4pm	24hr
		Event/club	$30	9pm-4am	11am
		SUV	$20		
		Month	$359, O/S add $100		

helpful information

24/7	80 spaces	Outdoor
Some Sa,Su,Hol closed	AE, MC, V, Dis, DC	
*M-F enter 4am-4pm	Lifts - 4 levels	

6. **511 W 18th St** *W 18th/W 19th, W side of 10th*
MTP   212.675.7759

hr	rate	specials	rate	enter	exit
1/2	$5	AM	$17	6-8am	12hr
12	$20	SUV	$10		12hr
24	$39	Month	$245	outdoor	
		Month	$278	indoor	
		Club	$20-25		pay in advance

helpful information

24/7	Cash	508 W 19th St
250 spaces	Outdoor	

7. **250 W 19th St** *bet 7th/8th, S side of W 19th*
Imperial   646.638.3558

hr	rate	specials	rate	enter	exit
1/2	$7	AM	$21	7-10am	7pm
1	$15	SUV	$10		
2	$21	Month	$425, O/S add $100		
10	$27				
24	$33				
O/N	$33				

helpful information

24/7	7' clearance
61 spaces	Eff. 5/07
AE, MC, V, Dis, DC	

W 23rd St–W Houston, 7th Ave–West St
Chelsea/West Village

15 16 17
18 19 20
21 22
23

281

8. **111 8th Ave** *bet 8th/9th, N side of W 15th or S side of W 16th*

Icon 212.929.8164

hr	rate*	specials	rate	enter	exit
1/2	$15	AM	$25	5-10am	12hr
1	$25	PM 7D	$25	4pm-5am	1hr
2	$28	PM 7D	$50	4pm-5am	24hr
12	$33	PM su-w	$18	4pm-5am	6am
24	$50	PM th-sa	$40	4-10pm	6am
		Su	$17	5am-4pm	12hr
		SUV	$15		
		Month	$507, O/S add $84		
		Month	$169	m'cycle	

helpful information

24/7	Eff. 5/07	Max bill $50
342 spaces	181" rule for SUV	Long driveway
AE, MC, V	*enter 5am-4pm	Eff. 3/08

9. **422 W 15th St** *bet 9th/10th, S side of W 15th*

212.255.4693

hr	rate	specials	rate	enter	exit
1/2	$10	AM	$22	6-10m	7pm
1	$19	Sa,Su	$17	7am-7pm	
2	$23	SUV	$10		
3	$28	Month	$475, O/S add $75		
24	$43				
12am	$37				

helpful information

24/7	AE, MC, V	2 elevators
374 spaces	Takes large vans	

10. **85 8th Ave** *bet 8th/9th, N side of W 14th, near 8th*

Icon 212.807.8125

hr	rate	specials	rate	enter	exit
1/2	$15	PM su-th	$15	4pm-12am	12am
1	$28	Sa,Su	$14	7am-7pm	
2	$29	SUV	$10		
12	$35	Month	$464, O/S add $84		
24	$40				

helpful information

24/7	AE, MC, V	No full size vans
47 spaces	181" rule for SUV	

11. 222 W 14th St *bet 7th/8th, S side of W 14th*

222 W 14th St Parking Corp — 212.243.9102

hr	rate	specials	rate	enter	exit
1	$18	SUV	$10		
2	$22	Month	$465, O/S add $84		
12	$28	Month	$169	m'cycle	
24	$35				

helpful information

24/7	AE, MC, V, Disc, DC
80 spaces	Eff. 3/08

---

12. 9 9th Ave *bet Little W 12th/W 13th, W side of 9th*

Olympia Garage Inc — 212.255.0864

hr	rate	specials	rate	enter	exit
24	$40	PM	$25	7pm	1am
		Daily m-f	$20		

helpful information

M-F 24hr	100 spaces	Cash

---

13. 11 Jane St *bet Greenwich Ave/W 4th, N side of Jane*

Park It Mgmt — 212.462.4585

hr	rate	specials	rate	enter	exit
1/2	$10	AM	$17	6-9am	12hr
1	$14	Event	$40		
2	$18	Holiday	$40		
3	$20	SUV	$10		
10	$23	Month	$444	small car, SUV add $42	
12	$25	Month	$486	large car, SUV add $42	
24	$32	Month	$411	m'cycle	

helpful information

24/7	AE, MC, V, Dis, DC
92 spaces	Car wash

---

14. 203 W 12th St *bet Greenwich/7th, N side of W 12th*

Central — 212.604.8538

hr	rate	specials	rate	enter	exit
1	$17	SUV	$10		
2	$20	Month	$422 , O/S add $51		
10	$24	Month	$169	m'cycle	
24	$27				

helpful information

7D 6am-10pm	AE, MC, V	Hard to see from street
48 spaces	Max bill $50	Saint Vincent Catholic Medical Center

15. 61 Jane St *bet Jane/Horatio, W side of Hudson*

Imperial   212.243.6303

hr	rate*	specials	rate	enter	exit
1/2	$7	PM su-th	$7		1/2hr
1	$15	PM su-th	$16		1hr
2	$20	PM su-th	$21		2hr
10	$25	PM su-th	$25		3hr
24	$36	PM su-th	$35		24hr
		PM f,sa	$7		1/2hr
		PM f,sa	$18		1hr
		PM f,sa	$23		2hr
		PM f,sa	$38		24hr
		SUV	$10		
		Month	$550, O/S add $100		
		Month	$150	m'cycle	

helpful information

24/7	Eff. 6/08	623 Hudson
110 spaces	Exit only from Horatio	*7D 5am-5pm
MC, V		

16. 82 Gansevoort *bet Washington/West St, S side of Gansevoort closer to Washington*

West-Coast Garage Corp   212.929.8447

hr	rate*	specials	rate	enter	exit
1/2	$7	O/N	$17		by 9am
1	$10	O/N	$20		after 9am, to 24hr
7pm	$14	PM	$8	after 7pm	close
		SUV	$7		
		Month	$400		

helpful information

7D 5am-2am	Cash	302 Washington
46 spaces	*5am-7pm	

17. 99 Jane St *bet Washington St/West St, N side of Jane or S side of Horatio*

Icon   212.243.4436

hr	rate	specials	rate	enter	exit
1/2	$11	AM m-f	$17	6-10am	6pm
1	$16	Sa,Su	$16	6am-6pm	12hr
2	$21	Daily m-f	$19	10am-6pm	by 7pm
12	$27	SUV	$10		
24	$37	Month	$422		

helpful information

24/7	AE, MC, V	Max bill $50
100 spaces	7'1" clearance	No full size vans

18. 497 West St *SE corner of Jane/West, S side of Jane or*
E side of West

Icon 212.206.9498

hr	rate	specials	rate	enter	exit
1/2	$8	AM, m-f	$17	6-10am	7pm
1	$16	Sa,Su	$16	6am-6pm	12hr
2	$21	Daily m-f	$19	10am-6pm	7pm
12	$27	SUV	$10		
24	$35				

helpful information

24/7	AE, MC, V	Outdoor
120 spaces	181" rule for SUV	134 Jane St

---

19. 332 W 11th St *bet Greenwich St/Washington, S side of W 11th*

Apple 212.741.9079

hr	rate	specials	rate	enter	exit
1	$15	AM	$20	6-9am	6pm
2	$22	PM su-th	$27	after 5pm	10am
3	$27	SUV	$10	(over 17' long)	
24	$35	Month	$591, O/S add $178		

helpful information

24/7	Cash	Car wash
150 spaces	Elevator	

---

20. 738 Greenwich St *NW corner of Greenwich & Perry,*
W side of Greenwich

Perry Garage Co Inc 212.242.8762

hr	rate	specials	rate	enter	exit
1	$15	AM	$20	6-10am	6pm
2	$22	Event	$25		1hr
3	$27	Event	$35		2hr
24	$35	Event	$45		3hr
		Event	$60		24hr
		SUV	$10		
		Month $465-501, SUV add $63			

helpful information

24/7	Cash	Battery boost $15
240 spaces	Elevator	Tire change $15

21. 97 Charles St *bet Hudson/Bleecker, N side of Charles or S side of Perry*

Charles Street Garage, Inc   212.242.9723

hr	rate	specials	rate	enter	exit
1	$18	AM m-f	$18	6-10am	6pm
2	$23	SUV	$10		
4	$28	Month	$549, O/S add $126		
10	$37				
24	$48				

helpful information

24/7	AE, MC, V	Elevator
206 spaces	5 min grace period	

22. 235 W 10th St *bet Hudson/Bleeker, N side of W 10th*

212.929.9677

hr	rate*	specials	rate	enter	exit
1/2	$7	PM m-f	$13	6pm-6am	1hr
1	$12	PM m-f	$14	6pm-6am	2hr
2	$14	PM m-f	$19	6pm-6am	3hr
3	$17	PM m-f	$26	6pm-6am	10hr
10	$23	PM m-f	$32	6pm-6am	24hr
24	$32	Sa,Su	$13		1hr
		Sa,Su	$14		2hr
		Sa,Su	$19		3hr
		Sa,Su	$26		10hr
		Sa,Su	$32		24hr
		SUV	$10		
		Month	$380		
		Month	$199	m'cycle	

helpful information

24/7	Cash	Takes vans
150 spaces	*6am-6pm	Hard to see from street
		350 Bleeker St

23. 140 Charles St *bet Charles/W 10th St, E side of Washington*

Standard   212.929.9170

hr	rate	specials	rate	enter	exit
1	$16	SUV	$10		
2	$20	Month	$465, O/S add $63		
24	$32	Month	$296	day	
		Month	$211	m'cycle	

helpful information

7D 6:30am-1am	AE, MC, V
20 spaces	Eff. 4/08

---

24. 666 Greenwich St *bet Christopher/Barrow, E side of Washington*

Archives Garage Corp 212.741.8524

hr	rate*	specials	rate	enter	exit
1	$13	AM	$17	7-10am	6pm
2	$16	PM	$16	6pm-7am	1hr
3	$17	PM	$19	6pm-7am	2hr
24	$38	PM	$38	6pm-7am	24hr
6pm	$31	SUV	$10		
		Month	$550		
		Month	$250	m'cycle	

helpful information		
24/7	AE. MC, V	No vans
97 spaces	Low clearance	*7am-6pm

---

25. 100 Morton St *bet Washington/West, N side of Leroy*

Central 646.638.1781

hr	rate	specials	rate	enter	exit
1	$13	Daily m-f	$16	by 10am	7pm
2	$19	SUV	$10		
7	$21	Month	$591, O/S add $50		
24	$40	Month	$211	m'cycle	

helpful information		
24/7	AE, MC, V	No signage on street
140 spaces	Max bill $50	

---

26. 115 Leroy St *NE corner of Leroy/Greenwich, N side of Leroy or E side of Greenwich*

Ulltra 212.352.3494

hr	rate	specials	rate	enter	exit
1	$16	AM 7D	$20	by 9am	7pm
2	$18	PM 7D	$12	after 5pm	by 2am
12	$23	SUV	$10		
24	$28	Month	$291, O/S add $63		

helpful information		
24/7	98 spaces	AE, MC, V Outdoor

---

27. 575 Washington St *bet Clarkson/W Houston, E side of Washington or W side of Greenwich*

Elba Operating Corp 212.645.1132

hr	rate	specials	rate	enter	exit
1/2	$10	AM	$22	5-9am	7pm
1	$16	PM	$17	after 6pm	by 8am
2	$19	SUV	$5-10		
12	$25	Month	$525, O/S add $50		
24	$30				

helpful information		
24/7	400 spaces	AE, MC, V

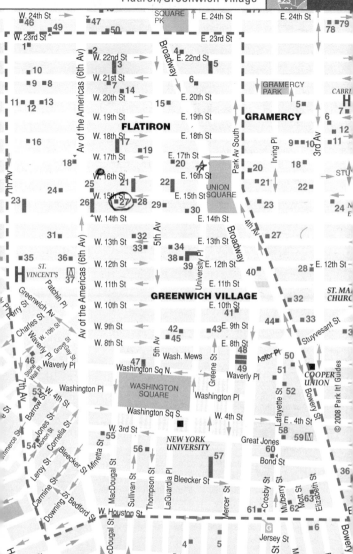

1. **170 W 23rd St** *bet 6th/7th, S side of W 23rd*

Icon					212.741.9410

hr	rate	specials	rate	enter	exit
1/2	$10	SUV	$10		
1	$23	Month	$420, O/S add $80		
2	$27				
3	$29				
12	$31				
24	$37				

helpful information

24/7   AE, MC, V

105 spaces   181" rule for SUV

2. 60 W 23rd St *bet 6th/5th, N side of W 22nd, near 6th*
Icon   646.230.7263

hr	rate	specials	rate	enter	exit
1/2	$12	AM	$27	6-10am	12hr
1	$25	SUV	$10		
2	$32	Month	$465, O/S add $84		
12	$36	Arezzo Rest.	$15	after 6pm	4hr
24	$43				

helpful information
24/7   AE, MC, V   Long, steep driveway
195 spaces   181" rule for SUV

---

3. 7 W 21st St *bet 5th/6th, N side of W 21st or S side of W 22nd*
GMC   212.243.6540

hr	rate*	specials	rate	enter	exit
1	$25	PM su-th	$25	5pm-5am	1hr
2	$35	PM su-th	$35	5pm-5am	2hr
24	$45	PM su-th	$45	5pm-5am	24hr
		Sa,Su	$21	5am-5pm	6pm
		F,Sa	$30	5pm-5am	1hr
		F,Sa	$40	5pm-5am	2hr
		O/N	$45		after 5am
		SUV	$10		
		Month	$475, O/S add $150		

helpful information
24/7   AE, MC, V   Outdoor
180 spaces   Lift   *5am-5pm

---

4. 5 E 22nd St *bet Broadway/Park Ave South, N side of E 22nd,*
Icon   *near Broadway*   212.674.9002

hr	rate	specials	rate	enter	exit
1/2	$16	Sa	$15	6-11am	7pm
1	$31	Su	$15	after 6am	6pm
2	$34	SUV	$10		
12	$42	Month	$507		
24	$45				

helpful information
24/7   AE, MC, V   Max bill $50
86 spaces   181" rule for SUV   No full size vans

5. **41 E 21st St** *bet Park Ave South/Broadway, N side of E 21st or S side of E 22nd*

Icon 212.674.9528

hr	rate	specials	rate	enter	exit
1/2	$18	AM m-f	$33	5-9am	12hr
1	$32	Sa,Su	$17	6-11am	7pm
2	$34	SUV	$10		
12	$42	Month	$676, O/S add $84		
24	$47	Month	$211	m'cycle	
		Gramercy Tavern		$20	4hr
		Gramercy Park Hotel		$20	4hr
		Radiology Diagnostic		$20	4hr

helpful information

24/7	AE, MC, V	Max bill $50
175 spaces	2 elevators	

6. **34 E 21st St** *bet Park Ave South/Broadway, S side of E 21st*

Champion 212.473.9365

hr	rate	specials	rate	enter	exit
1/2	$19	AM m-f	$32	by 9am	close
1	$27	PM	$25	6pm	close
2	$33	Sa,Su	$15	all day	7pm
24	$41	SUV	$10		
MTC	$41	Month	$549, SUV add $151		

helpful information

M-W 8am-7pm	36 spaces	Lift
Th-F 8am-11pm	AE, MC, V	Outdoor
Sa 9am-11am		

7. **4 W 21st St** *bet 5th/6th, S side of W 21st*

GMC 212.529.9614

hr	rate*	specials	rate	enter	exit
1	$25	AM	$25	5-10am	6pm
2	$35	PM	$25	5pm-5am	1hr
24	$45	PM	$35	5pm-5am	2hr
		PM	$45	5pm-5am	24hr or O/N
		F,Sa	$30	5pm-5am	1hr
		F,Sa	$40	5pm-5am	2hr
		F,Sa	$45	5pm-5am	24hr or O/N
		Sa,Su	$21	5am-5pm	6pm
		O/N	$45	8am-5pm	
		SUV	$10		
		Month	$475, O/S add $150		

helpful information

Su-Th 6am-2am	65 spaces	*5am-5pm
F,Sa 24hr	AE, MC, V	Opened 10/06

---

8. **120 W 21st St** *bet 6th/7th, S side of W 21st*
Central   212.633.6488

hr	rate	specials	rate	enter	exit
1/2	$11	AM	$20	5-10am	12hr
1	$20	Club	$20	after F 4pm	Sa 8am pre-pay
2	$22	Club	$20	after Sa 4pm	Su 8am pre-pay
10	$27	SUV	$11		
24	$40	Month	$465, O/S add $42		
		Month	$211	m'cycle	

helpful information

24/7	AE, MC, V, Dis, DC	
152 spaces	8' clearance	

---

9. **142 W 21st St** *bet 6th/7th, S side of W 21st*
Elbert Holding Corp   212.929.3677

hr	rate*	specials	rate	enter	exit
1	$16	AM	$20	5-10am	12hr
24	$44	PM	$16	after 6pm	1hr
6pm	$28	PM	$28	after 6pm	8am
		SUV	$5		
		Month	$400, O/S add $100		

helpful information

24/7	Cash	No sign, blue & white building
129 spaces	*enter 8am-6pm	

---

10. **159 W 21st St** *bet 6th/7th, N side of W 21st*
Access   212.675.7985

hr	rate*	specials	rate	enter	exit
1/2	$9	AM	$18	5-10am	12hr
1	$16	PM	$19	after 6pm	6am
2	$19	Sa,Su	$9	after 7am	6pm
10	$23	SUV	$10		
24	$33	Month	$380, O/S add $84		
		Month	$150	m'cycle	

helpful information

24/7	Cash	
78 spaces	No signage	

---

11. **180 W 20th St** *bet 7th/6th, S side of W 20th*
Central   646.638.0695

hr	rate*	specials	rate	enter	exit
1/2	$10	AM m-f	$18	3-10am	12hr
1	$19	Sa	$11	8am-4pm	12am
2	$21	Su	$11	8am-12am	12am
10	$26	SUV	$11		
24	$40	Month	$591, O/S add $42		
		Month	$211	m'cycle	

helpful information

24/7	55 spaces	AE, MC, V

---

12. 148 W 20th St *bet 7th/6th, S side of W 20th*
Little Man Parking 212.627.4505

hr	rate	specials	rate	enter	exit
1/2	$9	AM	$20	6-10am	12hr
1	$17	SUV	$10		
2	$19	Month	$400, O/S add $100		
10	$24	MOnth	$175	m'cycle	
24	$30				

helpful information
24/7   AE, MC, V
150 spaces   Elevator

---

13. 124 W 20th St *bet 7th/6th, S side of W 20th*
Rapid Park 212.627.7739

hr	rate	specials	rate	enter	exit
1/2	$10	AM	$20	6-9am	6pm
1	$19	SUV	$10		
2	$21	Month	$425, O/S add $100		
8	$27	Month	$150	m'cycle	
24	$35				
O/N	$35				
12am	$31				

helpful information
24/7   AE, MC, V
155 spaces   Max bill $20

---

14. 21 W 20th St *bet 6th/5th, N side of W 20th*
Icon 212.243.9384

hr	rate	specials	rate	enter	exit
1/2	$14	PM	$13	6pm-6am	1hr
1	$25	PM	$37	6pm-6am	24hr
2	$26	PM su-th	$20	6pm-6am	6am
12	$32	PM su-th	$28	6pm-6am	12hr
24	$42	PM f,sa	$26	6pm-6am	2hr
		PM f,sa	$31	6pm-6am	12hr
		SUV	$10		
		Month	$465, O/S add $84		
		Month	$169	m'cycle	

helpful information
24/7   AE, MC, V   181" rule for SUV
306 spaces   2 elevators

---

15. 6 E 20th St *bet 5th/Broadway, S side of E 20th*
Champion   212.473.9186

hr	rate	specials	rate	enter	exit
1/2	$19	AM m-f	$32	by 10am	close
1	$27	Sa,Su	$15		1hr
2	$33	Sa,Su	$23		close
MTC	$41	SUV	$10		
		Month	$549, O/S add $151		

helpful information
M-F 7am-7pm   29 spaces   Outdoor
Sa, when open 8am-3pm   AE, MC, V
Su Closed   Lift

---

16. 140 W 18th St *bet 7th/6th, S side of W 18th*
18th Street Parking Corp   212.929.0739

hr	rate	specials	rate	enter	exit
1	$14	SUV	$10		
2	$20				
24	$37				
MTC	$30				

helpful information
M-F 6am-12am   21 spaces   High clearance
Sa,Su 7am-12am   Cash

---

17. 41 W 17th St *bet 5th/6th, N side of W 17th or S side of W 18th*
Impark   212.255.7713

hr	rate	specials	rate	enter	exit
1	$22	Sa,Su	$25	by 7am	7pm
2	$33	SUV	$10		
10	$38	Month	$549, O/S add $84		
24	$45				

helpful information
Su-Th 6am-11pm   54 spaces   Outdoor
F,Sa 24hr   AE, MC, V

---

18. 587 6th Ave *SW corner of W 17th/6th Ave, S side of W 17th*
Olympic Parking System

hr	rate	specials	rate	enter	exit
1	$19	Event	$30		
2	$25	SUV	$10		
3	$35	Month	$469		
7pm	$35				

helpful information
M-F 7am-7pm   44 spaces   Outdoor
Some Sa,Su,Hol may open   AE, MC, V

19. 7 W 17th St *bet 5th/6th, N side of W 17th, near 5th*

Champion   212.242.5372

hr	rate	specials	rate	enter	exit
1/2	$19	Sa,Su	$13		1hr
1	$27	Sa,Su	$19		close
2	$33	SUV	$10		
24	$41	Month	$549, O/S add $151		

helpful information

M-F 7am-7pm	25 spaces
Sa 7am-3pm	AE, MC, V
Some Sa,Hol closed	Outdoor

---

20. 6 E 17th St *bet Union Sq W-Broadway/5th, S side of E 17th*

Champion   212.242.9173

hr	rate	specials	rate	enter	exit
1/2	$19	AM m-f	$32	6-9:30am	12am
1	$27	PM m-f	$23	after 5pm	12am
2	$33	Sa,Su	$15		1hr
MTC	$41	Sa,Su	$23		all day
		SUV	$10		
		Month	$549, O/S add $151		

helpful information

M-Th 7am-10pm	74 spaces	Outdoor
F,Sa 7am-7pm	AE, MC, V	
Su 8am-6pm	Lifts	
Some Sa,Su,Hol closed		

---

21. 16 W 16th St *bet 5th/6th, N side of W 15th or S side of W 16th, near 5th*

Icon   212.242.9635

hr	rate	specials	rate	enter	exit
1	$21	SUV	$10		
3	$26	Month	$422, O/S add $84		
12	$28	Month	$169	m'cycle	
24	$38				

helpful information

24/7	AE, MC, V
99 spaces	7' clearance

---

22. 21 E 15th St *bet 5th/Union Sq W, N side of E 15th or S side of E 16th*
Central   212.741.5163

hr	rate	specials	rate	enter	exit
1/2	$9	PM m-th	$15	5pm-12am	10hr
1	$20	F,Sa,Su	$20	5pm-5am	1hr
2	$22	F,Sa,Su	$33	5pm-5am	10hr
10	$31	F,Sa,Su	$51	5pm-5am	24hr
24	$51	Su	$20		10hr
		SUV	$11		
		Month	$507, O/S add $42		
		Month	$211	m'cycle	

helpful information
24/7	AE, MC, V	Max bill $50
48 spaces	7' clearance	

---

23. 77 7th Ave *bet 6th/7th, N side of W 14th or S side of W 15th*
Fleur Garage Corp   212.956.2280

hr	rate	specials	rate	enter	exit
1	$14	O/N	$31	1am	7am
10	$18	SUV	$10		
		Month	$360		

helpful information
7D 7am-2am	Cash
94 spaces	No sign on W 15th

---

24. 101 W 15th St *bet 6th/7th, N side of W 15th, near 6th Ave*
Central   212.604.2739

hr	rate	specials	rate	enter	exit
1/2	$8	AM	$13	3-9am	10hr
1	$17	PM m-f	$12	5pm-12am	10hr
2	$20	SUV	$10		
10	$24	Month	$422, O/S add $51		
24	$27	Month	$169	m'cycle	

helpful information
24/7	AE, MC, V	Long, steep driveway
90 spaces	6'6" clearance	

---

25. 552 6th Ave *bet 5th/6th, N side of W 15th, near 6th Ave*
Impark   212.366.4632

hr	rate	specials	rate	enter	exit
1/2	$7	SUV	$10		
1	$19	Month	$422, O/S add $84		
2	$22				
10	$28				
24	$33				

helpful information
24/7	MC, V
42 spaces	65 W 15th

26. **55 W 14th St** *bet 5th/6th, N side of W 14th or S side of W 15th, near 6th Ave*

Icon   212.242.9218

hr	rate	specials	rate	enter	exit
1/2	$11	SUV	$10		
1	$21				
2	$24				
12	$26				
24	$32				

helpful information

24/7	181" rule for SUV	Elevator
129 spaces	6'8"clearance	
AE, MC, V	Max bill $20	

---

27. **10 W 15th St** *bet 5th/6th, S side of W 15th*

Champion   212.243.9112

hr	rate	specials	rate	enter	exit
1/2	$17	AM m-f	$20	5-10am	12hr
1	$21	SUV	$10		
2	$25	Month	$363, O/S add $186		
10	$31				
24	$32-37				
O/N	$37				

helpful information

24/7	AE, MC, V	181" rule for SUV
117 spaces	Eff. 10/06	

---

28. **96 5th Ave** *bet 5th/6th, S side of W 15th*

Imperial   212.675.0335

hr	rate	specials	rate	enter	exit
1/2	$10	AM	$21	7-9am	11pm
1	$20	SUV	$10		
2	$24	Month	$350		
10	$29	Imperial coupons			
24	$33				
O/N	$33				

helpful information

M-F 7am-11pm	75 spaces
Sa,Su 8am-8pm, when open	AE, MC, V

29. 69 5th Ave *bet E 15th/E 14th, E side of 5th*
Central   212.627.5805

hr	rate	specials	rate	enter	exit
1/2	$7	PM m-th,su	$15	after 5pm	close
1	$15	PM f,sa	$18	after 5pm	close
3	$23	Sa,Su	$11	after 6am	6pm
24	$33	SUV	$10		
MTC	$30	Month	$450		

helpful information

M-Th 6am-12am	Su 8am-12am	6'11" clearance
F 6am-1am	32 spaces	No signage
Sa 7am-1am	AE, MC, V	Next to Pier 1 store
		Eff. 7/05

30. 7 E 14th St *bet 5th/Union Sq W, N side of E 14th*
Imperial   212.929.8529

hr	rate	specials	rate	enter	exit
1/2	$10	AM m-f	$20	6-10am	7pm
1	$18	Sa,Su	$14	after 7 am	6pm
2	$21	SUV	$10		
10	$27	Month	$450, O/S add $100		
24	$34	Month	$170	m'cycle	
O/N	$34				

helpful information

24/7	AE, MC, V
112 spaces	

31. 107 W 13th St *bet 6th/7th, N side of W 13th, near 6th Ave*
Imperial   212.243.3943

hr	rate	specials	rate	enter	exit
1/2	$6	AM	$15	4-9:30am	9pm
1	$14	PM	$10	after 6pm	12am
2	$17	SUV	$10		
24	$35				
O/N	$35				
10	$21				
12	$26				

helpful information

24/7	AE, MC, V	Max bill $20
96 spaces	Elevator	No vans

32. 25 W 13th St *bet 5th/6th, N side of W 13th*

Ronel Parking Corp   212.229.0548

hr	rate	specials	rate	enter	exit
1/2	$8	AM	$16	7-10am	12hr
1	$12	PM	$14	after 5pm	12am
2	$15	SUV	$5		
3	$19	Month	$450		
12	$25	Month	$275	day	
24	$30				

helpful information

M-F 7am-11pm	Cash
62 spaces	Hard to see from street

---

33. 20 W 13th St *bet 5th/6th, S side of W 13th, near 5th*

Kinney   212.352.8628

hr	rate	specials	rate	enter	exit
1	$15	AM	$14	6:30-9:30am	10hr
2	$19	Sa,Su	$12	all day	12am
10	$26	SUV	$12		
24	$40	Month	$350, O/S add $42		

helpful information

24/7	AE, MC, V	Steep driveway
55 spaces	Max bill $50	Butterfield House Garage

---

34. 12 E 13th St *bet University Pl/5th, S side of E 13th*

Hertz   212.486.5915

hr	rate	specials	rate	enter	exit
1/2	$7	Sa,Su	$14		10hr, no O/N
1	$10	SUV	$10		
2	$14	Month	$375, O/S add $100		
24	$34				
10	$18, no O/N				

helpful information

7D 6:30am-11pm	2 elevators
250 spaces	Hertz
AE, MC, V, Dis, DC	

35. **173 W 12th St** *bet 7th/6th, N side of W 12th*
Quik Park 646.336.6225

hr	rate	specials	rate	enter	exit
1/2	$8	SUV	$10		
1	$11				
4	$25				
24	$32				
MTC	$30				

helpful information
M-Th 6am-12am	Su 8am-12am	AE, MC, V
F 6am-1am	43 spaces	Max bill $50
Sa 7am-1am	AE, MC, V	No vans/SUVs

36. **101 W 12th St** *bet 7th/6th, N side of W 12th*
Chivian Garage Corp 212.929.8322

hr	rate	specials	rate	enter	exit
1	$11	AM	$15	7-9am	7pm
3	$17	SUV	$10		
6	$25	Month	$415		
12	$30	James Beard discount			
24	$41				

helpful information
24/7	181" rule for SUV
98 spaces	Eff. 9/07
MC, V	

37. **100 W 12th St** *bet 7th/6th, S side of W 12th*
Mark Twain Garage Corp 212.929.8322

hr	rate	specials	rate	enter	exit

MONTHLY ONLY

helpful information
24/7
40 spaces
Cash

38. **17 E 12th St** *bet 5th/University Pl, N side of E 12th*
12th Street Garage Corp 212.929.9879

hr	rate	specials	rate	enter	exit
1/2	$6	SUV	$10		
1	$22	Month	$465, O/S add $84		
2	$28				
10	$32				
24	$40				

helpful information
24/7	AE, MC, V	Alamo car rental
285 spaces	2 elevators	

39. 21 E 12th St *bet 5th/University Pl, N side of E 12th or W side of University Pl*

GMC 212.924.1604

hr	rate	specials	rate	enter	exit
1	$27	O/N	$45		after 5am
2	$35	SUV	$10		
10	$40	Month	$475, O/S add $200		
24	$45				

helpful information

24/7	AE, MC, V	National car rental
200 spaces	5 min grace period	Max bill $50

40. 60 E 12th St *bet Broadway/4th Ave-Bowery, S side of E 12th*

Impark 212.539.0251

hr	rate	specials	rate	enter	exit
1	$19	Th-Sa	$19	9pm-6am	1hr
2	$27	Th-Sa	$40	9pm-6am	24hr
10	$35	SUV	$10		
24	$42	Month	$620, O/S add $84		
O/N	$42				

helpful information

24/7	AE, MC, V	Clean interior
27 spaces	Lifts	

41. 63 E 9th St *bet University Pl/Broadway, S side of E 10th*

Icon 212.979.5380

hr	rate	specials	rate	enter	exit
1/2	$6	AM m-f	$17	7-10am	6pm
1	$13	PM m-f	$12	after 5pm	7am
2	$17	Sa,Su	$15	7am-5pm	12hr
12	$23	Graduation	$30		
24	$30	SUV	$10		
		Month	$380, O/S add $84		

helpful information

24/7	AE, MC, V, Dis, DC	
112 spaces	7'7" clearance	

42. 12 E 9th St *bet University Pl/5th, S side of E 9th*

Icon 212.473.9751

hr	rate	specials	rate	enter	exit
1	$15	Graduation	$30		
2	$19	SUV	$10		
3	$20	Month	$380, O/S add $84		
12	$25	Month	$169	m'cycle	
24	$35				

helpful information

24/7	181" rule for SUV	No full size vans
134 spaces	Max bill $20	
AE, MC, V	Steep driveway	

43. 26 E 9th St *bet Broadway/University Pl, S side of E 9th*
Icon   212.674.7291

hr	rate	specials	rate	enter	exit
1	$15	AM m-f*	$16	5-10am	6pm
2	$20	M-F*	$20	10am-6pm	12am
12	$26	Sa,Su*	$16	after 6am	12am
24	$33	SUV	$10		
		Month	$422, O/S add $84		
		Graduation	$28		
		NYU	$14		12hr, by 12am

helpful information
24/7	AE, MC, V	No full size vans
272 spaces	Max bill $50	*Not graduation day

---

44. 70 E 10th St *bet 4th Ave/Broadway, N side of E 9th*
GGMC   212.995.1940

hr	rate	specials	rate	enter	exit
1	$13	AM	$19	6-10am	8pm
2	$16	O/N	$32	by 12am	after 4am
10	$25	SUV	$10		
24	$32	Month	$475, O/S add $200		

helpful information
24/7	AE, MC, V, Dis, DC	6'6" clearance
255 spaces	Eff. 12/04	

---

45. 11 5th Ave *bet 5th/University Pl, N side of E 8th*
Icon   212.475.9562

hr	rate	specials	rate	enter	exit
1/2	$8	AM	$18	5-10am	6pm
1	$16	Graduation	$30		
2	$19	SUV	$10		
3	$20	Month	$401		
12	$26				
24	$35				

helpful information
24/7	AE, MC, V	Max bill $50
113 spaces	181" rule for SUV	No full size vans

46. **160 W 10th St** *bet 7th Ave/Waverly, S side of W 10th*
GMC 212.929.3041

hr	rate*	specials	rate	enter	exit
1	$17	AM	$19	6-10am	5pm
2	$22	PM	$25	5pm-2am	1hr
10	$32	PM	$35	5pm-2am	2hr
24	$45	PM	$45	5pm-2am	24hr
		PM	$45	5pm-2am	O/N, after 5am
		SUV	$10		
		Month	$490, O/S add $200		

helpful information

Su-Th 6am-2am	200 spaces	5 min grace period
F,Sa 24hr	AE, MC, V	*6am-5pm

---

47. **2 5th Ave** *bet 5th/MacDougal, N side of Washington Sq N*
GMC 212.533.8312

hr	rate*	specials	rate	enter	exit
1	$16	PM	$18	5pm-5am	1hr
2	$23	PM	$20	5pm-5am	2hr
10	$30	PM	$25	5pm-5am	24hr
24	$40	PM	$35	5pm-5am	O/N, after 5am
O/N	$40	SUV	$10		
		Month	$450, O/S add $200		

helpful information

24/7	AE, MC, V	*5am-5pm
146 spaces		

---

48. **60 E 8th St** *bet E 8th/Waverly, E side of Mercer or W side of Broadway, at Astor Pl*
Champion 212.473.9061

hr	rate*	specials	rate	enter	exit
1/2	$15	AM	$17	6-9:30am	12hr
1	$21	PM	$17	5pm-6am	1/2hr
2	$23	PM	$23	5pm-6am	1hr
10	$27	PM	$25	5pm-6am	2hr
24	$35	PM	$28	5pm-6am	3hr
O/N	$35	PM	$35	5pm-6am	24hr
		SUV	$10		
		Month	$380, O/S add $42		
		Halloween	$30	after 5pm	
		Graduation	$30	all day	
		NYU w/ID	$15		until 12am

helpful information

24/7	AE, MC, V	No vans, full size trucks
169 spaces	181" rule for SUV	*6am-5pm

49. 300 Mercer St *bet E 8th/Waverly, E side of Mercer or W side of Broadway*

Hilary Gardens Garage   212.473.8752

hr	rate*	specials	rate	enter	exit
1/2	$14	AM	$14	6-9:30am	12hr
1	$18	PM	$15	5pm-6am	1/2hr
2	$20	PM	$22	5pm-6am	1hr
10	$25	PM	$23	5pm-6am	2hr
24	$32	PM	$27	5pm-6am	3hr
		PM	$32	5pm-6am	24hr
		Parade, Halloween	$30 after 5pm		
		Holiday, Graduation	$30		
		NYU	$13	after 6am	12hr
		SUV	$10		
		Month	$346, O/S add $42		

helpful information
24/7	No O/S or trucks	Action Car Rental
225 spaces	*6am-5pm	741 Broadway
AE, MC, V	181" rule for SUV	

---

50. 445 Lafayette St *bet E 8th/E 6th, E side of Bowery-4th Ave, just S of Astor Pl*

Icon   212.777.1659

hr	rate*	specials	rate	enter	exit
1/2	$6	AM	$17	6-10am	6pm
1	$11	SUV	$10		
2	$16	Month	$400	tenant, O/S add $84	
12	$26	Month	$422	non-tenant, O/S add $84	
24	$31				

helpful information
24/7	AE, MC, V
14 spaces	* 6am-6pm, $3/hr additional after 7pm

---

51. 410 Lafayette St *bet E 4th/Astor Pl, W side of Lafayette*

Park It Mgmt   212.260.9122

hr	rate	specials	rate	enter	exit
1/2	$7	AM	$17	6-10am 12hr	
1	$12	SUV	$7-12		
2	$17	Month	$338		
3	$21				
12	$25				
24	$35				

helpful information
24/7	AE, MC, V
53 spaces	Outdoor

52. 403 Lafayette St *bet E 4th/Astor Pl, E side of Lafayette*
Park It Mgmt 212.254.1263

hr	rate*	specials	rate	enter	exit
1/2	$8	AM	$17	3-10am	10hr
1	$12	PM su-th	$8	5pm-5am	1/2hr
2	$17	PM su-th	$12	5pm-5am	1hr
3	$21	PM su-th	$17	5pm-5am	2hr
12	$25	PM su-th	$21	5pm-5am	3hr
24	$35	PM su-th	$25	5pm-5am	12hr
		PM su-th	$35	5pm-5am	24hr
		F-Sa	$8		1/2hr
		F-Sa	$13		1hr
		F-Sa	$17		2hr
		F-Sa	$25		12hr
		F-Sa	$35		24hr
		SUV	$7-15		
		Month	$422, O/S add $43		

helpful information
24/7   267 spaces
AE, MC, V   *enter 5am-5pm

---

53. 3 Sheridan Sq *bet 7th Ave/W 4th, N side of Barrow*
3 Sheridan Square Parking Corp 212.242.9791

hr	rate*	specials	rate	enter	exit
1	$15	PM	$23	4pm-5am	1hr
2	$21	PM	$30	4pm-5am	2hr
10	$27	PM	$40	4pm-5am	8hr
24	$42	PM	$42	4pm-5am	24hr
		Event	$41		
		SUV	$10		
		Month	$414, O/S add $84		

helpful information
24/7   Cash   No sign on street
51 spaces   Max bill $100   *enter after 5am, exit by 5pm

54. **18 Morton St** *just East of 7th Ave, N side of Morton*
Central 212.242.8451

hr	rate*	specials	rate	enter	exit
1	$14	AM m-f	$19	5-10am	7pm
2	$18	PM su-th	$19	6pm-2am	1hr
10	$26	PM su-th	$26	6pm-2am	2hr
24	$46	PM su-th	$28	6pm-2am	10hr
		PM su-th	$46	6pm-2am	24hr
		F,Sa	$21	4pm-6am	1hr
		F,Sa	$27	4pm-6am	2hr
		F,Sa	$46	4pm-6am	24hr
		Event	$46		
		Parade	$46		
		SUV	$11		

helpful information

24/7	Max bill $50
180 spaces	*M-Th 2am-6pm, F-Sa 6am-4pm, Su 6am-6pm
AE, MC, V, Dis	Hertz rental

55. **122 W 3rd St** *bet MacDougal/6th, S side of W 3rd*
GMC 212.777.3530

hr	rate*	specials	rate	enter	exit
1	$20	AM m-f	$19	5-9:30am	7pm
2	$25	PM su-th	$21	5pm-5am	1hr
10	$30	PM su-th	$25	5pm-5am	2hr
24	$40	PM su-th	$40	5pm-5am	24hr or O/N
O/N	$40	F,Sa	$28	4pm-5am	1hr
		F	$35	4pm-5am	2hr
		F	$40	4pm-5am	24hr or O/N
		Sa	$30	4pm-5am	1hr
		Sa	$40	4pm-5am	2hr
		Sa	$50	4pm-5am	24hr or O/N
		SUV	$10		
		Month	$425, O/S add $200		

helpful information

24/7	5 min grace period	Minetta Garage
300 spaces	Max bill $50	Near Blue Note
AE, MC, V	*5am-5pm	

56. 221 Thompson St *bet W 3rd St/Bleeker, W side of Thompson*
Thompson Street Parking 212.677.8741

hr	rate*	specials	rate	enter	exit
1	$12	AM m-f	$18	6-10am	7pm
2	$17	PM su-th	$14	5pm-5am	1hr
3	$20	PM su-th	$19	5pm-5am	2hr
12	$25	PM su-th	$24	5pm-5am	8hr
24	$38	PM su-th	$38	5pm-5am	24hr
O/N	$38+	PM f,sa	$17	4pm-4am	1hr
		PM f,sa	$25	4pm-4am	2hr
		PM f,sa	$33	4pm-4am	8hr
		Event	$30		
		SUV	$10		
		Month	$418, O/S add $84		
		Month	$190	m'cycle	
		NYU Student, Faculty, or Employee Rates:			
		Su-F	$15	6am-12am	
		F	$15	6am-8pm	12hr

helpful information

24/7	Elevator	+O/N rate applies after 5am
235 spaces	Enterprise rental	
AE, MC, V	*5am-5pm	

---

57. 91 Bleeker St *bet La Guardia/Mercer, N side of Bleeker*
Central 212.253.9061

hr	rate	specials	rate	enter	exit
1	$18	SUV	$10		
2	$22	Month	$371	non-tenant, O/S add $42	
10	$27	Month	$237	tenant, O/S add $42	
24	$40				

helpful information

24/7	6'4" clearance	Near NYU
670 spaces	Max bill $50	
AE, MC, V	Long entrance	

---

58. 375 Lafayette St *NE corner of Lafayette/Great Jones, E side of Lafayette or N side of Great Jones*

Edison/Park Fast

hr	rate*	specials	rate	enter	exit
1/2	$7	PM 7D	$7	after 4pm	1/2hr
1	$16	PM 7D	$25	after 4pm	4am
2	$19	PM 7D	$33	after 4pm	24hr
10	$27	SUV	$30		
24	$33	Month	$401		
		Month	$334	day	
		10 coupons	$195		24hr

helpful information

24/7	AE, MC, V, Dis, DC	Outdoor
67 spaces	Lift	*4am-4pm

59. 32 Great Jones St *bet Lafayette/Bowery, N side of Great Jones*
Edison/Park Fast

hr	rate	specials	rate	enter	exit
		Month	$380		

MONTHLY ONLY

helpful information

24/7	AE, MC, V	Outdoor
60 spaces	Lifts - 4 levels	

---

60. 358 Lafayette St *NW corner of Bond/Lafayette, W side of Lafayette*

AJS Vella　　　　　　　　　　　　　　　212.529.3616

hr	rate*	specials	rate	enter	exit
1	$15	PM	$15	4pm-4am	1hr
2	$18	PM	$21	4pm-4am	to 8am
10	$24	PM	$29	4pm-4am	24hr
24	$29	SUV	$10		
		Month	$400, O/S add $50		

helpful information

24/7	Cash	*4am-4pm
30 spaces	Outdoor	Lift

---

61. 610 Broadway *NW corner of Houston/Crosby, W side of Crosby*

Icon　　　　　　　　　　　　　　　　　212.253.2129

hr	rate	specials	rate	enter	exit
1	$15	Sa,Su	$10	6-10am	12hr
2	$20	SUV	$10		
12	$30	Month	$591, O/S add $84		
24	$35				

helpful information

24/7	181" rule for SUV
126 spaces	6'6" clearance
AE, MC, V	No full size vans

62. 298 Mulberry St *bet Houston/Bleeker, E side of Mulberry, near Houston*

VIP Capital Parking Corp.   212.925.3331

hr	rate	specials	rate	enter	exit
1/2	$6	AM m-f	$15	6-10am	6pm
1	$18	Event	$35		
2	$20	SUV	$10		
10	$28	Month	$422, O/S add $127		
24	$35	Month	$210	m'cycle	

helpful information
24/7
Cash

63. 303 Elizabeth St *bet Houston/Bleeker, W side of Elizabeth*

Icon   212.219.9562

hr	rate	specials	rate	enter	exit
1/2	$7	SUV	$10		
1	$13	Month	$422, O/S add $84		
2	$16				
12	$21				
24	$31				

helpful information
24/7   Cash
39 spaces   1-2 spaces for casual parking

308

E 23rd St–E Houston, FDR–Park Ave S
East Village

15 16 17
18 19 20
21 22
23

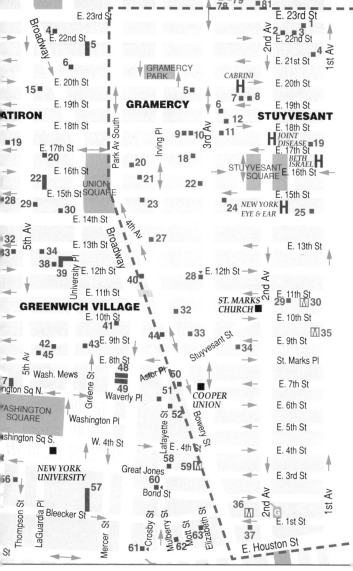

1. **318 E 23rd St** *bet 2nd/1st, S side of E 23rd*

   Icon 212.674.2918

hr	rate	specials	rate	enter	exit
1/2	$10	SUV	$10		
1	$17	Month	$422, O/S add $84		
2	$21	Month	$190	m'cycle	
10	$27				
12	$31				
24	$40				

   helpful information

24/7	AE, MC, V	Max bill $50
53 spaces	181" rule for SUV	Steep driveway

E 23rd St–E Houston, FDR–Park Ave S
East Village

15	16	17
18	19	20
21	22	
23		

309

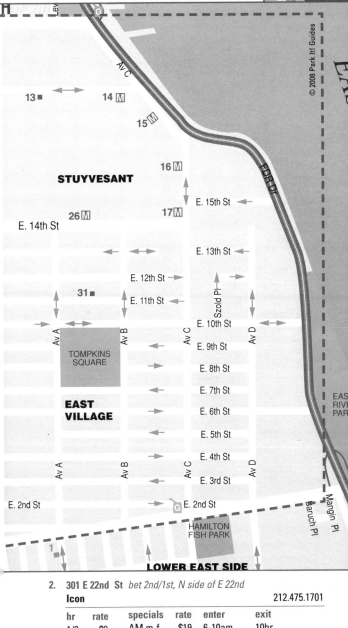

© 2008 Park It! Guides

STUYVESANT

E. 14th St

TOMPKINS SQUARE

EAST VILLAGE

E. 2nd St

Av A   Av B   Av C   Av D

13 ■   14 Ⓜ
15 Ⓜ
16 Ⓜ
E. 15th St ←
17 Ⓜ
26 Ⓜ
E. 13th St ←
E. 12th St →
Szold Pl
E. 11th St ←
31 ■
E. 10th St
E. 9th St
E. 8th St
E. 7th St
E. 6th St
E. 5th St
E. 4th St
E. 3rd St
E. 2nd St

Av C

FDR Dr

EAST RIVER PARK

Margin Pl   Baruch Pl

HAMILTON FISH PARK

LOWER EAST SIDE

---

2. 301 E 22nd St *bet 2nd/1st, N side of E 22nd*

| Icon | | | | | 212.475.1701 |

hr	rate	specials	rate	enter	exit
1/2	$9	AM m-f	$19	6-10am	10hr
1	$14	Sa,Su	$12		12hr
2	$17	Sa,Su	$33		24hr
10	$23	SUV	$10		
24	$33	Month	$380, O/S add $84		

helpful information

24/7	AE, MC, V	Max bill $50
53 spaces	181" rule for SUV	

---

3. **329 E 22nd St** *bet 2nd/1st, N side of E 22nd*
   22 East   212.254.5444

hr	rate	specials	rate	enter	exit
1/2	$10	AM	$20	6-10am	7pm
1	$16	SUV	$8		
2	$17	Month	$500, O/S add $150		
3	$25				
4	$28				
10	$30				
24	$38				

helpful information
24/7	AE, MC, V
160 spaces	2 elevators

---

4. **329 E 21st St** *bet 1st/2nd, N side of E 21st, near 1st*
   Kinney   212.473.0400

hr	rate	specials	rate	enter	exit
1/2	$8	AM m-f	$21	5-10am	10hr
1	$14	Sa,Su	$16		12hr, last exit 12am
2	$16	SUV	$11		
10	$22	Month	$380, O/S add $63		
24	$40				

helpful information
24/7	AE, MC, V	Max bill $50
180 spaces	2 elevators	

---

5. **32 Gramercy Park South** *bet Irving Pl/3rd Ave, S side of E 20th*
   MPG   212.533.0863

hr	rate*	specials	rate	enter	exit
1/2	$10	Sa,Su	$10	after 6am	1/2hr, by close
1	$16	Sa,Su	$12		1hr, by close
2	$18	Sa,Su	$15		10hr, by close
MTC	$25	Sa,Su	$25		close
		SUV	$10		
		Month	$450, O/S add $42		

helpful information
M-Th 6am-12am	38 spaces	Tire inflation
F,Sa 6am-1am	AE, MC, V	Jump start
Su 6am-12am	*M-F enter 6am-close	Steep driveway

---

6. **205 3rd Ave** *bet 2nd/3rd, S side of E 19th*
   Icon   212.674.9645

hr	rate	specials	rate	enter	exit
1/2	$10	SUV	$10		
1	$18	Month	$465, O/S add $84		
12	$25				
24	$35				

helpful information
24/7	AE, MC, V	No full size vans
96 spaces	181" rule for SUV	

7. 237 E 19th St *bet 2nd/3rd, N side of E 19th*
Standard

hr	rate*	specials	rate	enter	exit
		Daily	$19		

helpful information

M-F 6am-6pm	Pay in advance	Cabrini Medical Center
30 spaces	Outdoor	Eff. 5/08
Cash	*M-F	

8. 245 E 19th St *bet 2nd/3rd, N side of E 19th, near 2nd*
Icon   212.228.7973

hr	rate	specials	rate	enter	exit
1/2	$12	SUV	$10		
1	$20	Month	$422, O/S add $84		
12	$26				
24	$36				

helpful information

24/7	AE, MC, V	Max bill $50
106 spaces	181" rule for SUV	No full size vans

9. 130 E 18th St *bet Irving Pl/3rd, S side of E 18th*
Imperial   212.475.8091

hr	rate	specials	rate	enter	exit
1/2	$5	AM	$20	6-9am	7pm
1	$12	PM m-f	$10	by 6pm	12am
2	$20	Sa	$11	after 6am	close
8	$25	SUV	$10-15		
24	$32	Month	$500, O/S add $150		
O/N	$32	Month	$200	m'cycle	
12am	$28	Filmmakers	$19		

helpful information

M-F 6am-12am	84 spaces	Max bill $20
Sa,Su,Hol closed	AE, MC, V	Eff. 11/07

10. 150 E 18th St *bet Irving Pl/3rd, S side of E 18th*
Precise Parking Corp   212.254.3955

hr	rate	specials	rate	enter	exit
1	$11	PM	$11	after 6pm	12am
2	$14	Sa	$11	8-12am	7pm
3	$16	SUV	$5		
7pm	$18	Month	$440, O/S add $30		
24	$24				
O/N	$24				
MTC	$20				
12am	$20				

helpful information

M-Sa 7am-12am	58 spaces	Steep driveway
Su, Hol closed	Cash	6' clearance

11. 201 E 17th St *bet 3rd/2nd, S side of E 18th, near 3rd*

Icon   212.473.9869

hr	rate	specials	rate	enter	exit
1	$16	Sa,Su	$12	6am-6pm	12hr
2	$21	SUV	$10		
10	$26	Month	$422, O/S add $84		
24	$35				

helpful information

24/7	108 spaces	AE, MC, V	No full size vans

12. 211 E 18th St *bet 3rd/2nd, N side of E 18th*

Park It Mgmt   212.473.9345

hr	rate	specials	rate	enter	exit
1	$15	Sa,Su	$14	anytime	12hr, No O/N
2	$21	SUV	$12		
10	$25	Month	$444, O/S add $54		
12	$29				
24	$35				

helpful information

24/7	70 spaces	AE, MC, V

13. 420 E 20th St *bet 1st/Ave C, S side of E 20th*

Impark   212.614.5861

hr	rate	specials	rate	enter	exit
1	$8	AM	$15	by 10am	7pm
2	$12	SUV	$10		
10	$25	Month	$372, O/S add $42		
24	$30	Month	$136	m'cycle	

helpful information

24/7	510 spaces	AE, MC, V	Eff. 5/08

14. 528 E 20th St *bet 1st/Ave C, S side of E 20th*

Impark

hr	rate	specials	rate	enter	exit
1	$8	SUV	$10		
2	$12	Month	$372, O/S add $42		
10	$25	Month	$136	m'cycle	
24	$30				

helpful information

24/7	MC, V	Limited space for
320 spaces	Eff. 1/08	casual parking

15. 325 Avenue C *bet E 14th/E 20th, W side of Avenue C*

Central   212.473.9739

hr	rate	specials	rate	enter	exit
		Month	$325		

MONTHLY ONLY

helpful information

24/7	210 spaces	Cash	Eff. 11/06

16. 279 Avenue C *bet FDR/E 15th, W side of Avenue C*
Central   212.674.9765

hr	rate	specials	rate	enter	exit
		Month	$300		

MONTHLY ONLY

helpful information

24/7	Cash	320 spaces	Eff. 11/06

---

17. 251 Avenue C *bet E 15th/E 14th, W of Avenue C*
Central   212.777.9615

hr	rate	specials	rate	enter	exit
		Month	$300		

MONTHLY ONLY

helpful information

24/7	580 spaces	Cash

---

18. 144 E 17th St *bet 3rd/Irving Pl, S side of E 17th*
GMC   212.533.7362

hr	rate	specials	rate	enter	exit
1	$14-25	Sa	$20	after 6am	12hr
2	$35	Su	$16	after 6am	12hr
10	$38	O/N	$44		after 5am
24	$44	SUV	$10		
		Month	$490	non-tenant, O/S add $200	

helpful information

7D 7am-2am	Max bill $50	5 min grace period
47 spaces	Steep driveway	
AE, MC, V	No vans	

---

19. 347 E 17th St *bet 1st/2nd, N side of E 17th*
Propark   212.420.2505

hr	rate	specials	rate	enter	exit
1	$14	SUV	$10		
2	$18	Month	$312		
10	$23				
24	$28				

helpful information

24/7	Cash	Beth Israel Medical Center
67 spaces	6'10" clearance	

---

20. 101 E 16th St *bet Union Sq E-Park Ave South/Irving Pl, N side of E 16th*
Champion   212.358.1476

hr	rate	specials	rate	enter	exit
1	$25	AM	$25	5-9:30am	12hr
2	$33	Sa,Su	$15	6-10am	6pm
10	$41	SUV	$10		
24	$47	Month	$448, O/S add $355		
O/N	$47				

helpful information

24/7	61 spaces	AE, MC, V	181" rule for SUV

21. 110 E 16th St *bet Union Sq E-Park Ave South/Irving Pl,*
S side of E 16th

Icon 212.473.9056

hr	rate	specials	rate	enter	exit
1/2	$11	AM m-f	$21	6-9am	12hr
1	$24	PM	$18	5pm-5am	7am
2	$26	Sa,Su	$17	5am-5pm	12hr
12	$31	SUV	$10		
24	$40	Month	$422, O/S add $84		
		Union Sq Theater, Century Theater,			
			$14	5pm-12am	
		Irving Pl Theater	$14		5pm-4am
		Irving Mill	$14	5pm-1am, m-f	

helpful information

24/7	AE, MC, V	181" rule for SUV
275 spaces	2 elevators	Max bill $50

22. 146 3rd Ave *bet E 16th/E 15th, W side of 3rd*

Icon 212.475.9159

hr	rate	specials	rate	enter	exit
1/2	$11	SUV	$10		
1	$20	Month	$380, O/S add $84		
2	$21				
12	$25				
24	$38				

helpful information

7D 7am-12am	55 spaces	AE, M, V	Steep driveway

23. 1 Irving Pl *bet Irving Pl/Union Sq E-Park Ave South,*
S side of E 15th

GGMC 212.677.2026

hr	rate	specials	rate	enter	exit
1/2	$11	SUV	$10		
1	$22	Month	$475, O/S add $100		
2	$26				
10	$32				
24	$40				
O/N	$40				

helpful information

24/7	AE, MC, V, Dis, DC	Long driveway
198 spaces	8' clearance	

---

24. 200 E 15th St *bet 2nd/3rd, S side of E 15th*

Nice Park 22 LLC   212.228.6734

hr	rate	specials	rate	enter	exit
1	$13	O/N	$38		after 10am
2	$17	PM add'l $1.69			per hour, after 12am
3	$21	SUV	$5-10		
7pm	$24	Month	$444, O/S add $42		
12am	$31				
24	$38				

helpful information

24/7 | AE, MC, V | Hard to see from street
43 spaces

---

25. 333 E 14th St *bet 2nd/1st, N side of E 14th*

Gema Parking Corp   212.477.4043

hr	rate	specials	rate	enter	exit
1/2	$12	PM	$27	after 5pm	by 5am
1	$19	SUV	$5-10		
2	$24	Month	$410, O/S add $50		
8	$29				
12	$33				
24	$42				
O/N	$42				

helpful information

M-F 6am-12am | Su 8am-12am | Cash | Eff. 1/07
Sa 7am-12am | 44 spaces | 4 min grace period

---

26. 527 E 14th St *bet Avenue B/Avenue A, N side of E 14th*

Central

hr	rate	specials	rate	enter	exit
1/2	$7	Month	$350		
1	$9				
2	$12				
3	$16				
24	$29				

MONTHLY ONLY

helpful information

24/7 | 125 spaces | Payment unkown

---

27. 101 E 13th St *bet 3rd/4th Aves, N side of E 13th, near 4th*

Icon   212.674.9706

hr	rate*	specials	rate	enter	exit
1/2	$9	PM m-w	$18	7pm-7am	1hr
1	$17	PM m-w	$25	7pm-7am	3hr
3	$22	PM m-w	$29	7pm-7am	12hr
8	$25	PM m-sa	$40	7pm-7am	24hr
12	$29	PM th-sa	$14	7pm-7am	1hr
24	$40	PM th-sa	$40	7pm-7am	24hr
		SUV	$10		
		Month	$465		

helpful information

24/7 | AE, MC, V | 181" rule for SUV | *7am-7pm
46 spaces | Steep driveway | No full size vans

28. 74 3rd Ave *bet 4th/3rd Ave, S side of E 12th, near 3rd*
MPG 212.388.0759

hr	rate*	specials	rate	enter	exit
1/2	$8	AM	$20	6-10am	7pm
1	$14	PM su-w	$8	6pm-6am	1/2hr
2	$17	PM su-w	$17	6pm-6am	12hr
12	$23	PM su-w	$35	6pm-6am	24hr
24	$35	PM th-sa	$8	4pm-6am	1/2hr
		PM th-sa	$35	4pm-6am	24hr
		SUV	$10		
		Month	$400, SUV add $48		

helpful information
24/7	AE, MC, V	*enter 10am-4pm
80 spaces	Outdoor	

29. 311 E 11th St *bet 1st/2nd, S side of E 11th*
Nice Park 212.475.5262

hr	rate*	specials	rate	enter	exit
1/2	$11	AM	$14	6-10am	7pm
1	$13	PM 7D	$14	6pm-6am	1hr
2	$18	PM 7D	$19	6pm-6am	2hr
7pm	$22	PM 7D	$24	6pm-6am	3hr
		PM 7D	$29	6pm-6am	4hr
		PM 7D	$38	6pm-6am	24hr
		PM f-sa	$41		
		O/N su-th	$32		
		O/N f-sa	$38		
		SUV	$10		
		Month	$380, O/S add $84		
		Hospital	$2 discount		

helpful information
24/7	AE, MC, V, Dis, DC	*6am-6pm, $3/hr additional
350 spaces	Elevator	after 7pm

30. 324 E 11th St *bet 1st/2nd, S side of E 11th*
Fraclac Realty Corp

hr	rate	specials	rate	enter	exit
		Month	$265		

MONTHLY ONLY

helpful information
24/7	Cash	Outdoor
7 spaces	Eff. 9/04	

31. 525 E 11th St *bet Avenue B/Avenue A, N side of E 11th*

212.388.1030

hr	rate	specials	rate	enter	exit
12	$9	Month	$296		

MOSTLY MONTHLY ONLY

helpful information

7D 6am-11pm	Cash	1-2 casual spots

---

32. 85 4th Ave *bet 4th/3rd Ave, N side of E 10th, near 4th Ave*
S.D. Barron

212.505.6669

hr	rate	specials	rate	enter	exit
O/N	$50	Daily	$15	after 7am	6pm
		SUV	$5		
		Month	$320, O/S add $50		
		Month	$240	day	
		Month	$105	m'cycle	

helpful information

M-F 7am-6pm	48 spaces	Cash

---

33. 115 E 9th St *bet 3rd/4th Ave, N side of E 9th*
Icon

212.473.9643

hr	rate*	specials	rate	enter	exit
1/2	$8	AM	$15	5-10am	12am
1	$13	PM	$8	6pm-5am	1/2hr
2	$16	PM	$15	6pm-5am	1hr
12	$21	PM	$19	6pm-5am	2hr
24	$27	PM	$24	6pm-5am	12hr
		PM	$27	6pm-5am	24hr
		SUV	$10		
		Month	$422, O/S add $84		
		Month	$169	m'cycle	

helpful information

24/7	AE, MC, V	No full size vans
87 spaces	181" rule for SUV	*5am-6pm

---

34. 220 E 9th St *bet 2nd/3rd Ave, S side of E 9th*
Kinney

212.979.5708

hr	rate	specials	rate	enter	exit
1/2	$8	AM m-f	$15	by 11am	7pm
1	$16	PM th-sa	$19	5pm-3am	1hr
2	$19	PM th-sa	$21	5pm-3am	2hr
10	$24	PM th-sa	$40	5pm-3am	24hr
24	$40	SUV	$11		
		Month	$422, O/S add $84		
		Month	$169	m'cycle	

helpful information

24/7	AE, MC, V	Max bill $50
175 spaces	Elevator	

35. **327 E 9th St** *bet 1st/2nd Ave, N side of E 9th*
Ubo Realty Corp

hr	rate	specials	rate	enter	exit
		Month	$350		

MONTHLY ONLY

helpful information
24/7	Eff. 11/04
10 spaces	Outdoor
Cash	Self parking

36. **22 E 1st St** *bet 2nd Ave/Bowery, N side of E 1st*
Central

hr	rate	specials	rate	enter	exit
		Month	$350, O/S add $84		
		Month	$169	m'cycle	

helpful information
Su-Th 6am-12am
F,Sa 6am-2am

37. **1 E 1st St** *bet 2nd Ave/Bowery, S side of E 1st*
Central   646.602.9723

hr	rate*	specials	rate	enter	exit
1/2	$7	PM, su-th	$15	6pm-4am	4am
1	$10	F,Sa	$20	6pm-4am	4am
2	$14	SUV	$10		
3	$18	Month	$380, O/S add $84		
12	$20	Month	$169	m'cycle	
24	$25				

helpful information
24/7	AE, MC, V
131 spaces	Opened 11/07

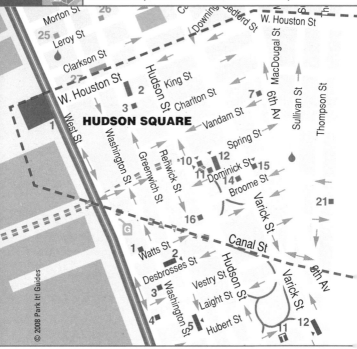

© 2008 Park It! Guides

---

1. **Pier 40 West Street/West Houston** *across W Houston,*
W side of West

Standard 212.989.9536

hr	rate*	specials	rate	enter	exit
4	$15	PM 7D	$30	9pm-4am	24hr
12	$24	Event	$30		
24	$30	SUV	$0		
		Month	$257-274 roof		
		Month	$329-378 indoor, SUV add $63		

helpful information

24/7	AE, MC, V	Self parking	Pay at pay stations
3500 spaces	Eff. 4/08	*4am-9pm	on Level 1

---

2. **375 Hudson St** *bet Greenwich St/Hudson, N side of King or*
S side of W Houston

Icon 212.645.4084

hr	rate*	specials	rate	enter	exit
1/2	$10	AM m-f	$25	5-10am	7pm
1	$22	PM	$10	4pm-6am	1/2hr
2	$25	PM	$25	4pm-6am	12hr
12	$35	PM	$40	4pm-6am	24hr
24	$40	PM	$15	4pm-6am	6am
		Sa,Su	$12	6am-4pm	12hr
		SUV	$10		
		Month	$465, SUV add $84		

helpful information

24/7	AE, MC, V	Max bill $50
100 spaces	181" rule for SUV	*6am-4pm

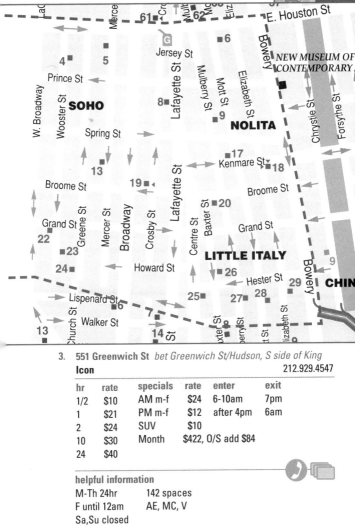

3. **551 Greenwich St** *bet Greenwich St/Hudson, S side of King*
   Icon   212.929.4547

hr	rate	specials	rate	enter	exit
1/2	$10	AM m-f	$24	6-10am	7pm
1	$21	PM m-f	$12	after 4pm	6am
2	$24	SUV	$10		
10	$30	Month	$422, O/S add $84		
24	$40				

helpful information
M-Th 24hr   142 spaces
F until 12am   AE, MC, V
Sa,Su closed

4. **146 Wooster St** *bet Houston/Prince, E side of Wooster*
   Albro Parking Alignment Corp   212.473.2660

hr	rate	specials	rate	enter	exit
1	$24	Sa,Su	$29	when open	
2	$29	SUV	$10		
6pm	$34				

helpful information
7D 8am-6pm   Cash   Outdoor
34 spaces

W Houston–Canal St, Bowery–West St

Hudson Square/SoHo/NoLita/Little Italy

---

5. 165 Mercer St *bet Houston/Prince, W side of Mercer*
Mercer Parking Garage Corp   212.226.5578

hr	rate	specials	rate	enter	exit
1	$15	O/N	add'l $20		
2	$23	SUV	$15		
3	$32	Month	$600, O/S add $200		
MTC	$44				

helpful information
M-F 5am-7:30pm   120 spaces   Takes trucks 18'-22'
Sa 8am-12am   Cash
Su 9am-11pm   Elevator

---

6. 284 Mott St *Houston/Prince, E side of Mott*
Mott Park LLC   212.625.9221

hr	rate*	specials	rate	enter	exit
1/2	$12	AM	$20	6-9am	7pm
1	$17	PM	$17	7pm-7am	1hr
2	$23	PM	$23	7pm-7am	2hr
3	$25	PM	$28	7pm-7am	3hr
7pm	$28	PM	$40	7pm-7am	24hr
		Event/Feast	$40		
		SUV	$10		
		Month	$500, O/S add $100		

helpful information
24/7   AE, MC, V   Steep driveway
62 spaces   *7am-7pm

---

7. 14 Charlton St *bet 6th Ave/Varick, N side of Vandam, near 6th*
Kinney   212.691.3109

hr	rate	specials	rate	enter	exit
1	$20	Event	$32		
2	$21	SUV	$11		
MTC	$31	Month	$317 tenant, O/S add $63		
		Month	$328 non-tenant, O/S add $63		
		Month	$148 m'cycle		

helpful information
M-F 7am-8pm   Cash
63 spaces   Max bill $50

---

8. 258 Lafayette St *bet Spring/Prince, W side of Lafayette*
                                                  646.613.1186

hr	rate	specials	rate	enter	exit
1	$22	Festival	$35		
2	$25	SUV	$10		
MTC	$30	Month	$380		

helpful information
M-F 7am-12am   60 spaces   Lift
Sa,Su 7am-10pm   Cash   Outdoor

9. **224 Mulberry St** *bet Spring/Prince, E side of Mulberry*

Kinney   212.343.8401

hr	rate	specials	rate	enter	exit
1/2	$6	AM m-f	$20	6-9am	7pm
1	$15	PM su-w	$15	after 5pm	2am
2	$18	PM th-sa	$15	after 5pm	1hr
10	$26	PM th-sa	$22	after 5pm	2hr
24	$41	PM th-sa	$41	after 5pm	24hr
		SUV	$11		

helpful information

24/7	AE, MC, V, Dis, DC	Max bill $50
150 spaces	Elevator	Customer recommendation

---

10. **272 Hudson St** *SE corner of Spring/Hudson, S side of Spring or E side of Hudson*

Central   212.337.8537

hr	rate*	specials	rate	enter	exit
1/2	$11	PM	$11	4pm	close
1	$15	SUV	$10		
MTC	$31	Month	$401, O/S add $63		

helpful information

M-F 8am-6pm	AE, MC, V	Outdoor
43 spaces	*7am-6pm	

---

11. **43 Dominick St** *bet Varick/Hudson, N side of Dominick*

Central   212.620.0104

hr	rate*	specials	rate	enter	exit
1/2	$11	PM	$11	after 4pm	
1	$15	SUV	$11		
MTC	$31	Month	$401, O/S add $63		

helpful information

M-F 8am-6pm	49 spaces	Outdoor
Sa,Su may open	AE, MC, V	

12. 272 Spring St *bet Hudson/Varick, N side of Dominick or S side of Spring*

Edison/Park Fast 212.675.8910

hr	rate*	specials	rate	enter	exit
1/2	$8	PM 7D	$8	4pm-4am	1/2hr
2	$22	PM 7D	$35	4pm-4am	24hr
24	$35	Sa,Su	$8	4am-4pm	1/2hr
		Sa,Su	$15	4am-4pm	12hr
		Sa,Su	$35	4am-4pm	24hr
		SUV	$20		
		Month	$444, O/S add $84		
		Month	$401. m-f 4am-8pm, O/S add $17		

helpful information

24/7	Outdoor	Lift
63 spaces	No large SUVs	Good Sa,Su parking
AE, MC, V, Dis, DC	*M-F 4am-4pm	

---

13. 81 Mercer St *bet Spring/Broome, W side of Mercer*

Aspire One 212.966.3484

hr	rate*	specials	rate	enter	exit
1	$23	SUV	$10		
10	$35	Month	$650, O/S add $84		
24	$45				

helpful information

M-Sa 7am-10pm	AE, MC, V	21 spaces
Su 8am-8pm	Outdoor	

---

14. 111 Varick St *bet Dominick/Broome, W side of Varick*

Crown/Pine Parking 212.675.3719

hr	rate*	specials	rate	enter	exit
1/2	$10	AM m-f	$22	4-9am	12hr
1	$14	Sa,Su	$10		12hr
2	$21	Sa,Su	$32		24hr
12	$28	SUV	$10		
24	$34	Month	$435, O/S add $63		
		Month	$182	m'cycle	

helpful information

24/7	MC, V	*M-F	Eff. 7/08
183 spaces	Elevator	Outdoor	

---

15. 114 Varick St *SE corner of Dominick/Broome, S (left) side of Dominick or E side of Varick*

Icon 212.925.9297

hr	rate	specials	rate	enter	exit
1/2	$8	AM m-f	$25	7-10am	12hr
1	$20	PM	$13	after 4pm	12am
12	$27	Sa,Su	$10	6am-4pm	12hr
24	$35	SUV	$10		
		Month	$422, O/S add $84		

helpful information

24/7	AE, MC, V	181" rule for SUV
86 spaces	Lift	Outdoor

---

16. 489 Canal St *NW corner of Canal/Hudson, W side of Hudson*

hr	rate	specials	rate	enter	exit
1/2	$10	Month	$338		
1	$13				
2	$20				
Close	$25				

helpful information

M-F 6am-6:30pm	Payment unknown	Eff. 3/08
25 spaces	Outdoor	

---

17. 75 Kenmare St *bet Mott/Mulberry, N side of Kenmare*

Park In Auto Services 212.966.1186

hr	rate	specials	rate	enter	exit
1	$10	PM su-th	$10	after 8pm	12am, no Hol
2	$12	Feast	$50		1am
3	$14	SUV	$5		
6	$15	Month	$385, O/S add $53		
9	$17				
12	$19				
16	$25				
20	$27				
24	$29				

helpful information

24/7	Cash	196 Mulberry St
175 spaces	2 Elevators	Eff. 10/07

18. **152 Elizabeth St** *SE corner of Kenmare/Elizabeth, S side of Kenmare or E side of Elizabeth*

Park Here 212.226.8567

hr	rate*	specials	rate	enter	exit
1/2	$9	AM	$20	6-10am	12hr
1	$17	Sa,Su	$17	before 9pm	1hr
2	$20	Sa,Su	$25	before 9pm	3hr
3	$22	Sa,Su	$29	before 9pm	12hr
12	$26	Sa,Su	$50	before 9pm	24hr
24	$50	Sa,Su	$35	after 9pm	
		Festival	$50		
		Holiday	$35		
		SUV	$10		
		Month	$506, O/S add $84		

helpful information
24/7	AE, MC, V	14 Kenmare
100 spaces	Elevator	*M-F

19. **432 Broome St** *NW corner of Crosby/Broome, W side of Crosby*
LAZ 212.334.3978

hr	rate	specials	rate	enter	exit
1	$18	Event	$45		
2	$29	SUV	$10		
3	$34	Month	$507, O/S add $84		
24	$40				

helpful information
M-F 7am-12am	AE, MC, V, Dis
Sa,Su 8am-12am	Outdoor
40 spaces	

20. **395 Broome St** *bet Mulberry/Baxter, S (left) side of Broome*
Park It Mgmt 212.226.9797

hr	rate*	specials	rate	enter	exit
1/2	$8	AM m-f	$19	6-10am	12hr
1	$12	PM sa	$12	5pm-5am	1hr
2	$17	PM sa	$20	5pm-5am	2hr
3	$20	PM sa	$25	5pm-5am	12hr
12	$25	PM sa	$35	5pm-5am	24hr
24	$35	PM su-f	$8	5pm-5am	1/2hr
12am	$25	PM su-f	$12	5pm-5am	1hr
		PM su-f	$17	5pm-5am	2hr
		PM su-f	$21	5pm-5am	3hr
		PM su-f	$25	5pm-5am	12am
		PM su-f	$35	5pm-5am	24hr
		Event	$40		
		SUV	$5-10		

helpful information
24/7	AE, MC, V	Angelo's discount
85 spaces	Outdoor	*5am-5pm

21. 360 W Broadway *bet Broome/Grand, W side of W Broadway*
Crown   212.966.6774

hr	rate	specials	rate	enter	exit
1/2	$13	AM m-f	$28	6-10am	7pm
1	$22	PM su-w	$15	5pm-12am	2am
2	$28	SUV	$10		
3	$39	Month	$520, O/S add $64		
12	$45	Month	$182	m'cycle	
24	$52				

helpful information

24/7	MC, V	Eff. 6/07
180 spaces	181" rule for SUV	

---

22. 61 Grand St *SW corner of Grand/Wooster, S side of Grand or W (right) side of Wooster*
Crown   212.925.2751

hr	rate*	specials	rate	enter	exit
1	$22	PM su-w	$10	5pm-12am	1hr
2	$28	PM su-w	$12	5pm-12am	close/12am
3	$39	PM th-sa	$10	5pm-12am	1hr
MTC	$45	PM th-sa	$15	5pm-12am	close/12am
		SUV	$10		
		Month	$444, O/S add $63		

helpful information

7D 7am-12am	MC, V	*enter 7am-5pm
Some Sa,Su,Hol closed	181" rule for SUV	Eff. 7/08
45 spaces	Outdoor	

---

23. 349 Canal St *bet Grand/Canal, E (left) side of Wooster*
Wooster Parking Corp   212.226.8541

hr	rate	specials	rate	enter	exit
1/2	$12	O/N	$42		
1	$18	SUV	$5-10		
2	$24	Month	$507, O/S add $84		
12am	$31	Month	$189	m'cycle	
24	$42				

helpful information

24/7	AE, MC, V	Takes vans, trucks
225 spaces	6 Wooster	

24. 335 Canal St *NW corner of Canal/Greene, N side of Canal across Church or W side of Greene*

Canal Development Corp

hr	rate	specials	rate	enter	exit
1	$15	Event	$40		
2	$20	SUV	$7		
3	$26	Month	$338, O/S add $84		
6pm	$31				

helpful information

7D 7am-6pm	Cash	Eff. 4/05
89 spaces	Outdoor	

25. 174 Centre St *bet Canal/Hester, E (right) side of Centre*

Edison/Park Fast 212.226.2950

hr	rate*	specials	rate	enter	exit
1/2	$13	PM m-th	$13	4pm-4am	1/2hr
1	$23	PM m-th	$20	4pm-4am	12hr
2	$27	PM m-th	$36	4pm-4am	24hr
12	$32	PM f-su	$13	4pm-4am	1/2hr
24	$36	PM f-su	$23	4pm-4am	1hr
		PM f-su	$29	4pm-4am	2hr
		PM f-su	$36	4pm-4am	24hr
		Sa,Su	$13	4am-4pm	1/2hr
		Sa,Su	$23	4am-4pm	1hr
		Sa,Su	$29	4am-4pm	2hr
		Sa,Su	$36	4am-4pm	24hr
		SUV	$15		
		Month	$465		

helpful information

24/7	AE, MC, V	Outdoor
93 spaces	*M-F 4am-4pm	

26. 123 Baxter St *bet Grand/Hester, E (left) side of Baxter*

Automation Parking 212.920.2439

hr	rate*	specials	rate	enter	exit
1/2	$12	Event	$48		
1	$22	Month	$500, O/S add $150		
3	$26				
12	$30				
24	$35				

AUTOMATED

helpful information

24/7	AE, MC, V, Disc
68 spaces	2 elevators
	Eff. 2/08

27. 114 Mulberry St *bet Canal/Hester, E (right) side of Mulberry*
Pine   917.237.1317

hr	rate*	specials	rate	enter	exit
1/2	$12	AM m-f	$22	by 10am	close
1	$22	PM m-th	$10	5pm-10pm	1/2hr
2	$26	PM m-th	$15	5pm-10pm	close
MTC	$34	F,Sa,Su	$15	after 10pm	close
		Sa,Su	$12	8am-5pm	1/2hr
		Sa,Su	$22	8am-5pm	1hr
		Sa,Su	$29	8am-5pm	2hr
		Sa,Su	$36	8am-5pm	close
		SUV	$10		
		Month	$380		

helpful information

M-Th 8am-10pm	42 spaces	*M-F 8am-5pm
F,Sa 8am-12am	MC, V	Eff. 7/08
Su 8am-10pm	Outdoor	

28. 106 Mott St *bet Hester/Canal, E side of Mott*
Pine Parking   212.219.8940

hr	rate*	specials	rate	enter	exit
1/2	$10	AM m-f	$15	5-10am	7pm
1	$16	PM m-th	$10	5pm-12am	1hr
2	$20	PM m-th	$16	5pm-12am	12hr
12	$26	PM m-th	$29	5pm-12am	24hr
24	$29	SUV	$10		
		Month	$401, O/S add $63		

helpful information

24/7	*M-F
154 spaces	181" rule for SUV
AE, MC, V	

29. 44 Elizabeth St *bet Canal/Hester, E (right) side of Elizabeth*
Rapid Park   212.226.9425

hr	rate*	specials	rate	enter	exit
1/2	$12	AM	$15-18	7-10am	7pm
1	$23	F,Sa,Su	$24	5pm-1am	1hr
2	$27	F,Sa,Su	$30	5pm-1am	2hr
3	$30	F,Sa,Su	$32	5pm-1am	3hr
24	$35	F,Sa,Su	$35	5pm-1am	24hr or close
O/N	$35	SUV	$10		
MTC	$32	Month	$400, O/S add $100		
		Feast, Holiday	$20		1hr
		Feast, Holiday	$40		close

helpful information

Su-Th 7am-11pm	AE, MC, V	*enter M-Th all day
F,Sa 7am-1am	Max bill $20	*enter F,Sa,Su 5pm-close
120 spaces		

E. 2nd St

E. 2n

36

E. 1st St

37

E. Houston St

Bowery

NEW MUSEUM OF CONTEMPORARY ART

Stanton St

LOWER EA

Rivington S

Attorney St

Ridge St

Clinton St

Suffolk St

Norfolk St

Essex St

Ludlow St

Orchard St

Allen St

Eldridge St

Forsythe St

Chrystie St

beth St

LITA

re St

18

Delancey St

3

Broome St

and St

ITALY

Hester St

28

29

9

Bowery

CHINATOWN

10

Hester St

TENEMENT MUSEUM

Broome St

5 6

4

8

Grand St

GOUVERNEUR

H

E. Broadway

Jefferson St

Rutgers St

Canal St

11

Forsythe St

Pike St

13

Mott St

Elizabeth St

9

Bayard St

Pell St

BUS

Park St

26

Division St

12

Henry St

14

15

Market St

Madison St

17

Monroe St

Oliver St

Catherine St

Rutgers Slip

16

19

ROW

Pearl St

James St

Cherry St

Water St

18

Manhattan

St. James Pl

South St

FDR Br

Wagner St

JLTON

17

18

Beekman St

24

Pearl St

Dover St

Water St

Peck Slip

19

20

21

Brooklyn Br

Bowery–FDR
Lower East Side/Chinatown

5 16 17
18 19 20
21 22
23

331

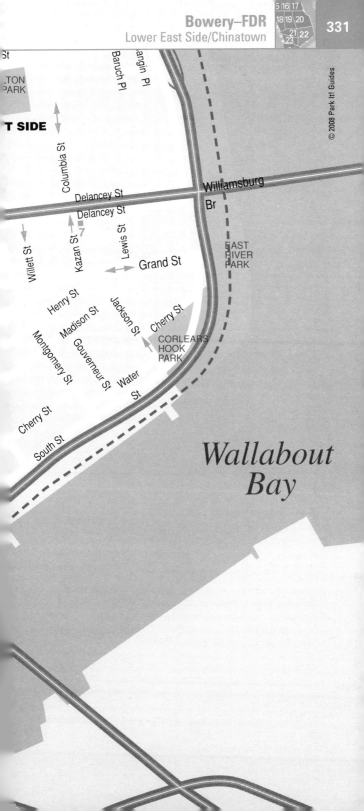

© 2008 Park It! Guides

St

LTON
PARK

T SIDE

Baruch Pl

angin Pl

Columbia St

Delancey St

Delancey St

Williamsburg

Br

Willett St

Kazan St

7

Lewis St

Grand St

EAST
RIVER
PARK

Henry St

Madison St

Jackson St

Cherry St

Montgomery St

Gouverneur St

Water
St

CORLEARS
HOOK
PARK

Cherry St

South St

*Wallabout
Bay*

1. **184 Ludlow St** *bet Houston/Stanton, W side of Essex*
Edison 212.253.6891

hr	rate*	specials	rate	enter	exit
1/2	$10	PM su-t,th	$10	4pm-4am	1/2hr
1	$13	PM su-t,th	$25	4pm-4am	4am
2	$18	PM su-t,th	$35	4pm-4am	24hr
10	$27	PM w,f,sa	$10	4pm-4am	1/2hr
24	$35	PM w,f,sa	$32	4pm-4am	4am
		PM w,f,sa	$35	4pm-4am	24hr
	,	Sa,Su	$10	4am-4pm	1/2hr
		Sa,Su	$15	4am-4pm	1hr
		Sa,Su	$20	4am-4pm	2hr
		Sa,Su	$30	4am-4pm	10hr
		Sa,Su	$35	4am-4pm	24hr
		Month	$401, O/S add $127		

helpful information

24/7	AE, MC, V, Dis	Outdoor
92 spaces	Eff. 8/05	*M-F 4am-4pm

2. **107 Essex St** *bet Rivington/Delancey, W side of Essex*
Muni 2, Delancey & Essex Garage 212.529.8824

hr	rate	specials	rate	enter	exit
1	$3	Month	$250		
24	$43.25				
add'l hr	$1.75				

helpful information

24/7	Cash	Self parking
357 spaces	Eff. 4/07	8 handicapped spaces

3. **Broome & Ludlow** *bet Delancey/Broome, E side of Ludlow or*
W side of Essex
Muni 1, Broome & Ludlow Garage

hr	rate	specials	rate	enter	exit
1	$1				
15 min	$.25				

helpful information

M-Sa 8am-10pm	Meter parking, 4 hr limit	Outdoor
66 spaces	Accepts quarters,	Self parking
Cash, credit cards	NYC Parking Card,	3 handicapped spaces
	credit cards	

4. **135 Delancey St** *bet Suffolk/Norfolk/Broome/Delancey, S side of Delancey*

Central   212.505.7153

hr	rate*	specials	rate	enter	exit
1	$5	Sa,Su,Hol	$6.50	8am	1hr
2	$8	Sa,Su,Hol	$9	8am	2hr
12	$13	Sa,Su,Hol	$15	8am	12hr
24	$23	Sa,Su,Hol	$23	8am	24hr
		SUV	$10		
		Month	$148		

helpful information

M-F 7am-10pm	294 spaces	*M-F 7am-10pm
Sa 8am-10pm	Cash	
Su 8am-10pm	Outdoor	

5. **163 Delancey St** *bet Suffolk/Clinton, N side of Broome*
Central

hr	rate	specials	rate	enter	exit
		Trucks only			

MONTHLY ONLY

helpful information

M-F 5am-9pm	Su 7am-7pm	Trucks only
Sa 5am-7am	Outdoor	

6. **178 Broome St** *NE corner of Broome/Clinton*
Broome Street Parking Lot   718.648.6410

hr	rate	specials	rate	enter	exit
		Month	$177		

MONTHLY ONLY

helpful information
48 spaces
Outdoor

7. **24 Columbia St** *bet Columbia/Lewis, E side of Columbia*
Park It Mgmt   212.228.9200

hr	rate	specials	rate	enter	exit
1	$10	Daily	$15	6am-7pm	
2	$12	SUV	$8		
10	$15	Month	$296		
24	$22	Month	$169	m'cycle	

helpful information

24/7	Cash
475 spaces	275 Delancey

---

8. **54 Suffolk St** *bet Broome/Grand, E side of Suffolk*
Suffolk Parking   212.674.9804

hr	rate	specials	rate	enter	exit
1	$12	SUV	$0		
2	$15	Month	$253, O/S add $43		
3	$18				
12	$20				

helpful information
24/7   Outdoor   Cash   90 spaces   Large truck pays double

---

9. **89 Chrystie St** *bet Grand/Hester, W side of Chrystie*
MTP   212.431.7778

hr	rate	specials	rate	enter	exit
1	$10	SUV	$5-10		
12	$18	Month	$395, O/S add $30		
24	$30	Month	$150	m'cycle	

helpful information
7D 6am-2am   Cash   Indoor and Rooftop
116 spaces   Elevator

---

10. **59 Allen St** *bet Grand/Hester, W side of Allen*
Imperial   212.226.1793

hr	rate	specials	rate	enter	exit
1/2	$8	AM 7D	$15	4-10am	7pm
1	$11	PM	$13	after 6pm	2am
2	$15	Sa,Su	$16	anytime	12hr, by 12am,
10	$20				no O/N
24	$27	O/N	$27		to 9am
		SUV	$10		
		Month	$375, O/S add $100		
		Blue Moon Hotel	$25		24hr

helpful information
24/7   AE, MC, V   Max bill $20
200 spaces   Elevator   Eff. 11/07

---

11. **26 Forsythe St** *bet Canal/Division, E side of Forsythe*
Bridge View Auto Service Center Inc   212.226.6465

hr	rate	specials	rate	enter	exit
1/2	$6.50	SUV	$5-8		
1	$8				
2	$12				
3	$15				
4	$17				
5	$19				
O/N	$10				
add'l hr	$8				
MTC	$20				

helpful information
7D 8am-12am   Cash
52 spaces   Outdoor

12. 2 Division St *bet Catherine/Market, N side of Division at Market*

Champion   212.274.8644

hr	rate*	specials	rate	enter	exit
1/2	$6	AM 7D	$17	4-11am	10pm
1	$14	Sa-M	$15		1hr
3	$19	Sa-M	$21		3hr
10	$27	Sa-M	$26		4hr
24	$35	Sa-M	$35		24hr
O/N	$35	SUV	$5		
		Month	$346, O/S add $85		

helpful information

24/7	AE, MC, V	*T-F
300 spaces	6'11" clearance	181" rule for SUV

13. 85 Henry St *bet Forsythe/Pike, N side of Henry*

Lan Tian Garage, Inc   212.385.9600

hr	rate	specials	rate	enter	exit
1/2	$5	O/N	add'l $10		
1	$8				
2	$10				
24	$12				

helpful information

7D 11:30am-5pm	Cash
50 spaces	Outdoor

14. 49 Henry St *bet Catherine/Market Slip, N side of Henry*

MTP   212.285.1583

hr	rate*	specials	rate	enter	exit
1	$12	Th-Sa	$15		12hr
12	$18	Th-Sa	$25		24hr
24	$30	SUV	$5		
		Month	$253, O/S add $43		

helpful information

7D 6am-1am	Max bill $50
114 spaces	Outdoor
Cash	*Su-W

15. 38 Henry St *bet Catherine/Market, S side of Henry or N side of Madison*

MTP 212.619.1777

hr	rate*	specials	rate	enter	exit
1/2	$5	AM f	$10	6-9am	12hr
1	$12	Th-Sa	$15		12hr
12	$18	Holiday	$21		
24	$30	SUV	$5		
		Month	$295, O/S add $20		

helpful information

24/7	Cash	Outdoor
150 spaces	Lift	*W-F

16. 148 Madison St *bet Market/Pike, N side of Monroe, near Pike*

Ulltra 212.566.8944

hr	rate	specials	rate	enter	exit
1/2	$6	AM	$13	5am-12pm	12hr
1	$11	PM	$14	after 6pm	12hr
2	$15	Sa,Su	$9	after 7am	7pm
12	$18	SUV	$10		
24	$30	Month	$275, O/S add $20		
O/N	$30	Month	$148	m'cycle	

helpful information

24/7	Cash	Max bill $50
66 spaces	Eff. 9/06	

17. 88 Madison St *bet Catherine/Market, S side of Madison St*

MTP 212.962.9805

hr	rate	specials	rate	enter	exit
1	$12	Sa	$15		12hr
12	$18	SUV	$5		
24	$30	Month	$223, O/S add $63		

helpful information

7D 6am-11pm	Cash	Max bill $20
50 spaces	Lift	Outdoor

Bowery–FDR
Lower East Side/Chinatown

5 16 17
18 19 20
21 22
23

337

18. **220 South St** *SW corner of Market Slip/Water, enter via Market near South St*

Edison   212.374.1704

hr	rate	specials	rate	enter	exit
1/2	$7	PM m-f	$17	4pm-6am	24hr
1	$13	Sa,Su	$10		1hr
12	$19	Sa,Su	$16		12hr
24	$26	Sa,Su	$18		24hr
		SUV	$10		
		Month	$258, O/S add $65		

helpful information

24/7	AE, MC, V	*enter M-F 6am-4pm
63 spaces	Outdoor	

19. **227 Cherry St** *bet Pike/Rutgers Slip, N side of South*

Central   212.619.4749

hr	rate	specials	rate	enter	exit
1	$9	AM	$11	3-10am	12hr
2	$12	SUV	$10		
10	$15	Month	$591		
24	$25	Pathmark	free		1 1/2hr

helpful information

24/7	AE, MC, V	Pathmark Supermarket
100 spaces	Max bill $50	

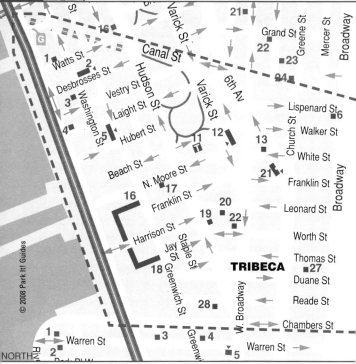

1. 281 West St *bet West/Washington, N side of Watts,*
enter via West St

Erik Parking					212.274.9225
hr	rate	specials	rate	enter	exit
1	$12	SUV	$10		
2	$18	Month	$380, O/S add $50		
Close	$22				

helpful information

M-F 8am-6pm	75 spaces	Outdoor
Sa,Su,Hol closed	Cash	Eff. 6/07

2. 454 Greenwich St *NW corner of Greenwich/Desbrosses,*
W side of Greenwich

EZ Park					212.274.8513
hr	rate	specials	rate	enter	exit
1/2	$9	SUV	$5		
1	$14	Month	$499, O/S add $50		
2	$21				
24	$44				
7pm	$24				
12am	$27				

helpful information

M-Sa 5am-12am	Eff. 6/07
Cash	

---

3. **432 Washington St** *bet Vestry/Desbrosses, W (left) side of Washington*

West Side Parking Corp   no telephone

hr	rate	specials	rate	enter	exit
1/2	$11	SUV	$5		
1	$14	Month	$499, O/S add $50		
2	$21				
7pm	$24				
Close	$27				
MTC	$27				

helpful information
M-F 7am-9pm   Cash
25 spaces   Eff. 6/06

---

4. **90 Laight St** *bet Washington/West, N side of Laight*
Empire Parking   212.925.1350

hr	rate	specials	rate	enter	exit
1/2	$6	AM	$24	6-10am	12hr
1	$14	Sa,Su	$10	after 6am	6pm
2	$21	SUV	$7		
12	$24-29	Month	$583, O/S add $177		
24	$39				

helpful information
24/7   AE, MC, V, DC
90 spaces

---

5. **412 Greenwich St** *bet Laight/Hubert, W (right) side of Greenwich*
Crown   212.219.3349

hr	rate	specials	rate	enter	exit
1/2	$10	SUV	$10		
1	$20	Month	$591, O/S add $63		
2	$27				
24	$45				
12am	$35				

helpful information

M-F 6am-12am	23 spaces	Lifts
Sa,Su may open	MC, V	67 Laight St

---

6. **411 Broadway** *SW corner of Broadway/Lispenard, S side of Lispenard or W side of Broadway*
Champion   212.226.9226

hr	rate	specials	rate	enter	exit
1/2	$18	Event	$55		
1	$29	SUV	$10		
1 1/2	$35	Month	$594, O/S add $84		
2	$39				
MTC	$44				

helpful information

M-F 7:30am-9pm	60 spaces	64 Lispenard
Sa 8am-9pm	AE, MC, V	Closed some Sa,Su,Hol
Su 9am-8pm	Outdoor	

---

7. **88 Walker St** *bet Broadway/Lafayette, N side of Walker*
Chinatown Parking Corp   212.941.6942

hr	rate	specials	rate	enter	exit
1/2	$12	SUV	$10		
1	$18	Month	$359, O/S add $42		
2	$24				
3	$30				
MTC	$36				

helpful information

7D 7am-7pm	AE, MC, V	5 min grace period
35-40 spaces	Outdoor	

---

8. **95 Baxter St** *bet Walker/Bayard, E (left) side of Baxter*
Chung Pak Parking Corp   no telephone

hr	rate*	specials	rate	enter	exit
1/2	$12	PM	$8	6-10pm	1/2hr
1	$16	PM	$10	6-10pm	1hr
2	$19	PM	$12	6-10pm	2hr
3	$22	PM	$15	6-10pm	4hr
4	$24	SUV	$5		
6pm	$26	Feast	$26		
		Forlini's	$12	M-F after 5pm, Sa,Su	

helpful information

7D 8am-10pm	Cash	Outdoor
28 spaces	Eff. 6/08	*8am-6pm

9. **38 Bowery** *bet Canal/Bayard, W side of Bowery*
QuikPark   212.732.3399

hr	rate	specials	rate	enter	exit
1/2	$10	AM m-f	$15	6-11am	12am
1	$22	PM m-th	$25	after 5pm	12am
2	$25	SUV	$10		
3	$28	Feast	$25		1hr
8	$31	Feast	$32		6hr
add'l hr	$4	Feast	$4		add'l 1hr

helpful information

24/7	AE, MC, V, DC	Max bill $20	2 Elizabeth
140 spaces	181" rule for SUV	42 Bayard	

---

10. **98 Bayard St** *bet Baxter/Mulberry, N (left) side of Bayard*
Pescatore Parking Inc   no telephone

hr	rate*	specials	rate	enter	exit
1	$8				
1 1/2	$10				
2	$12				
3	$15				
4	$18				
6pm	$24				

helpful information

7D 8am-6pm	Outdoor
12 spaces	No vans/large SUV
Cash	*8am-6pm

---

11. **27 North Moore St** *bet Hudson/Varick, S (right) side of Beach*
Park It Mgmt   212.966.1984

hr	rate	specials	rate	enter	exit
1/2	$7	AM	$20	5-10am	12hr
1	$12	O/N	$18	after 5pm	by 8am
2	$17	SUV	$5-10		
3	$22	Month	$498, O/S add $42		
12	$28				
24	$33				

TENANTS & VISITORS ONLY

helpful information

24/7	Cash	Ice House Garage
76 spaces	No sign on street	

12. **20 Varick St** *bet Beach/N Moore, E (left) side of Varick*
Kinney   212.625.0323

hr	rate	specials	rate	enter	exit
1	$20	AM	$24	by 8:30am	close
MTC	$31	PM	$11	after 4pm	close
		SUV	$11		
		Month	$401, O/S add $51		
		Month	$211	m'cycle	

helpful information
M-F 7am-9pm   92 spaces   Max bill $50
Sa,Su, Hol may open AE, MC, V   Outdoor

---

13. **14 White St** *bet White/Walker, W side of 6th*
512 Parking Corp   212.343.7277

hr	rate	specials	rate	enter	exit
1	$19	PM	$23	when open	
2	$26	Sa,Su	$23	when open	
MTC	$36	SUV	$10		
		Month	$465		

helpful information
M-F 7am-5:30pm   Cash   Outdoor
42 spaces   Eff. 5/07   Sa may open

---

14. **84 White St** *bet Lafayette/Broadway-Cortlandt, N (right) side of White*
Central   212.925.9309

hr	rate	specials	rate	enter	exit
1/2	$7	PM m-f	$16	after 4pm	7pm
1	$24	Sa,Su	$19		all day
2	$28	SUV	$11		
MTC	$44	Month	$422, O/S add $63		
		Month	$211	m'cycle	

helpful information
M-F 7am-8pm   59 spaces   Max bill $50
Sa,Su 9am-5pm AE, MC, V   Outdoor

---

15. **Lafayette & Centre St** *bet Franklin/Leonard, E side of Lafayette or W side of Centre*
Muni 3, Leonard St

hr	rate	specials	rate	enter	exit
1/2	$2.50				
1	$5				

helpful information
M-Sa 6am-10pm   Cash, Credit Cards   Outdoor
45 spaces   Eff. 2/04   2 hr limit
Meter parking. Accepts quarters, NYC Parking Card,
Credit Cards

16. 350 Greenwich St *bet N Moore/Harrison, W (right) side of Greenwich or N side of Harrison*

Icon 212.608.2780

hr	rate	specials	rate	enter	exit
1/2	$9	AM m-f	$25	5-9am	7pm
1	$18	Sa,Su	$10	5am-4pm	12hr
2	$24	SUV	$10		
12	$29	Month	$507, O/S add $84		
24	$35	BMCC	$20		12hr
		Tribeca Film Festival $16			12hr

helpful information

7D 5am-12am   181" rule for SUV   34 Harrison
318 spaces   Max bill $50
AE, MC, V

---

17. 56 North Moore St *bet Hudson/Greenwich, S (left) side of N Moore*

Central 212.941.7633

hr	rate	specials	rate	enter	exit
1/2	$8	AM 7D	$24	5-9am	7pm
1	$20	SUV	$11		
2	$26	Month	$676, O/S add $84		
10	$32	Month	$211	M'cycle	
24	$46				

helpful information

24/7   AE, MC, V   Max bill $50
220 spaces   2 elevators

---

18. 308 Greenwich St *after Harrison, W (right) side of Greenwich or S side of Harrison*

Icon 212.619.2790

hr	rate	specials	rate	enter	exit
1/2	$9	AM m-f	$25	5-9am	7pm
1	$18	Sa,Su	$10	5am-4pm	12hr
2	$24	SUV	$10		
12	$29	Month	$507, O/S add $84		
24	$35	BMCC	$20		12hr

helpful information

24/7   AE, MC, V   Max bill $50
232 spaces   181" rule for SUV

19. **74 Hudson St** *bet Leonard/Worth, E side of Hudson*
Park It Mgmt   212.966.9837

hr	rate	specials	rate	enter	exit
1/2	$12	AM	$30	by 9am	7pm
1	$20	SUV	$10		
2	$25	Month	$422, O/S add $84		
3	$30				
7pm	$35				

helpful information
M-F 7am-7pm   AE, MC, V, Dis, DC   Outdoor
99 spaces   Lifts

20. **24 Leonard St** *bet W Broadway/Hudson, S (left) side of Leonard*
Provenzano   212.226.3327

hr	rate	specials	rate	enter	exit
1	$15	AM	$23	5-9am	7pm
2	$23	Sa,Su	$11	anytime	12hr
12	$30	Sa,Su	$22	anytime	24hr
24	$44	SUV	$5-10		
		Month	$475, O/S add $24		

helpful information
24/7   AE, MC, V   Eff. 7/08
217 spaces   Pay in advance   Car wash

21. **98 Franklin St** *bet Franklin/White, W (left) side of 6th*
512 Parking Corp   212.431.5732

hr	rate	specials	rate	enter	exit
1	$19	PM	$23	when open	
2	$26	Sa,Su	$23	when open	
MTC	$36	SUV	$10		
		Month	$465		

helpful information
7D 8am-5:30pm   Cash
Sa,Su may close   Eff. 5/07
36 spaces   Outdoor

22. 16 Worth St *NW corner of Worth/W Broadway , W side of W Broadway or N side of Worth*

Edison/Park Fast   212.226.1981

hr	rate*	specials	rate	enter	exit
1	$18	PM m-f	$15	after 3:30pm	10hr, by 4am
2	$33	PM m-f	$38	after 3:30pm	24hr, by 4am
24	$38	Sa,Su	$15	4am-4pm	10hr
		Sa,Su	$38	4am-4pm	24hr
		Event	$20		10hr
		SUV	$30		
		Month	$444		

helpful information

24/7	Lifts - 4 Levels
98 spaces	Outdoor
AE, MC, V, Dis, DC	*Enter 4am-3:30pm

23. 336 Broadway *bet Broadway/Lafayette, N side of Worth or E side of Broadway*

Icon   212.784.1467

hr	rate	specials	rate	enter	exit
1	$22	AM m-f	$28	6-10am	12hr
2	$30	PM	$10	4pm-6am	6am
12	$35	Sa,Su	$10	6am-4pm	12hr
24	$45	Sa,Su	$44	6am-4pm	24hr
		SUV	$10		
		Month	$549, O/S add $84		

helpful information

24/7	2 elevators
114 spaces	95 Worth St
AE, MC, V, DC	

24. 101 Worth St *bet Broadway/Lafayette, N side of Worth*

Central   212.619.0415

hr	rate	specials	rate	enter	exit
1	$22	AM m-f	$28	3-9am	12hr
2	$29	PM	$10	4pm-3am	10hr
10	$35	Sa,Su	$10		
24	$50	SUV	$10		
		Month	$591, O/S add $64		
		Month	$253	m'cycle	

helpful information

24/7	Max bill $50
226 spaces	
AE, MC, V	

25. 62 Mulberry St *bet Bayard/Worth, E (right) side of Mulberry*
Champion   212.385.8449

hr	rate	specials	rate	enter	exit
1/2	$17	AM m-f	$23	5-11am	7pm
1	$24	O/S	$45		after 5am
2	$30	T-giving	$40		10hr
10	$35	SUV	$10		
24	$45	Month	$465, O/S add $127		
		Feast	$40		10hr
		Nearby restaurants discount			

helpful information
24/7   2 elevators
191 spaces
AE, MC, V

26. 180 Park Row *bet Pearl/Mott across Mulberry, S side of Worth*
Chatham Parking Systems   212.513.7143

hr	rate*	specials	rate	enter	exit
1/2	$14	PM m-th	$9	4pm-1am	1hr
1	$23	PM m-th	$16	4pm-1am	1am
2	$30	Sa,Su	$17	1am-4pm	1hr
24	$36	Sa,Su	$21	1am-4pm	1am
		F,Sa,Su	$12	4pm-1am	1hr
		F,Sa,Su	$20	4pm-1am	1am
		SUV	$8		
		Month	$380		
		Feast m-f	$22	4pm-2am	
		Feast sa-su	$22	all day	
		Peking Duck House	$10	after 4pm	3hr

helpful information
24/7   Eff. 2/06   *M-F enter 1am-4pm
130 spaces   7'3" clearance
AE, MC, V, Dis, DC   Damage inspection

27. 105 Duane St *bet Church/Broadway, enter L from Duane*
MPG   212.964.4968

hr	rate*	specials	rate	enter	exit
1/2	$10	Sa,Su	$10		1/2hr
1	$26	Sa,Su	$16		12hr
2	$32	Sa,Su	$25		24hr
24	$40	SUV	$10		
		Month	$591, O/S add $63		
		Month	$211	m'cycle	

helpful information
24/7   *M-F
72 spaces
AE, MC, V

28. 121 Reade St *bet Hudson/Greenwich, S (left) side of Reade*
MPG   212.608.3060

hr	rate*	specials	rate	enter	exit
1/2	$8	AM m-f	$8	6-9am	1/2hr
1	$15	AM m-f	$15	6-9am	1hr
2	$23	AM m-f	$24	6-9am	12hr
3	$30	AM m-f	$40	6-9am	9am
24	$40	Sa	$8	12am-4pm	1/2hr
		Sa	$13	12am-4pm	1hr
		Sa	$24	12am-4pm	12hr
		Sa	$40	12am-4pm	9am
		Su	$8		1/2hr
		Su	$15		1hr
		Su	$17		12hr
		Su	$25		24hr
		SUV	$10		
		Month	$591, O/S add $63		
		Month	$211	m'cycle	

helpful information
24/7   *M-F enter 9am-6am, Sa 4pm-12am
89 spaces
AE, MC, V

29. 280 Broadway *bet Centre/Broadway, S (left) side of Reade*
GGMC   212.566.2247

hr	rate	specials	rate	enter	exit
1/2	$15	AM	$28	5:30-9am	1am/close
1	$27	Sa,Su	$12	6am-8pm	1am/close
2	$32	SUV	$10		
MTC	$38	Month	$444, O/S add $150		

helpful information
7D 6am-1am   Enter at 35 Reade St
149 spaces   95 Worth St
AE, MC, V

18 19 20
21 22
23
24

Chambers St–Southern tip of Island
Battery Park/Financial District/Fulton

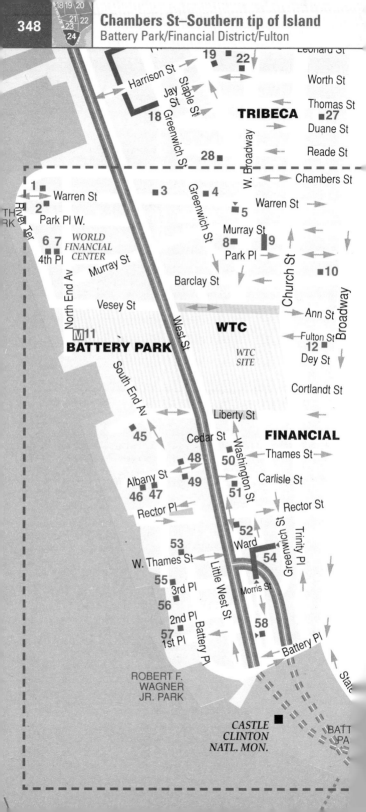

Leonard St

Harrison St

Jay St

Staple St

19

22

Worth St

TRIBECA

Thomas St

27

18

Greenwich St

Duane St

W. Broadway

28

Reade St

Chambers St

1

Warren St

3

Greenwich St

4

Warren St

River Ter

2

Park Pl W.

5

6 7

Murray St

8

9

4th Pl

WORLD FINANCIAL CENTER

Murray St

Park Pl

Church St

10

North End Av

Barclay St

Broadway

Vesey St

West St

M 11

WTC

BATTERY PARK

Ann St

Fulton St

12

WTC SITE

Dey St

Cortlandt St

South End Av

Liberty St

45

Cedar St

Washington St

FINANCIAL

Thames St

48

50

Albany St

49

51

Carlisle St

46 47

Rector Pl

Rector St

52

Greenwich St

Trinity Pl

53

Ward

54

W. Thames St

55

3rd Pl

Morris St

56

2nd Pl

Little West St

58

57

1st Pl

Battery Pl

Battery Pl

ROBERT F. WAGNER JR. PARK

Stat

CASTLE CLINTON NATL. MON.

BATT PA

COLUMBUS PARK

Catherine Ln

23 24

ROLEY SQUARE

Park St

Hayes Pl

26

Henry St 15

Oliver St

Madison St 17

Catherine St

Monro

Pearl St

CIVIC CENTER

Elk St

29

Park Row

Pearl St

James St

St. James Pl

South St

CITY HALL

Centre St

Av of the Finest

Frankfort St

Wagner St

Park Row

Spruce St

13 NYU

Beekman St

14 15

Ann St

Nassau St

Dutch St

John St

Maiden Ln

Liberty St

DISTRICT

H

FULTON

Gold St

16

Pearl St

Dover St

19

17

18

Beekman St

Water St

Speck Slip

20

Fulton St 24

Ryder St 23

Cliff St

26

25

29

Front St

21

27

SOUTH STREET SEAPORT

22

28

William St

Platt St

30

33 34

31

Cedar St

36

Pine St

Pearl St

John St

Fletcher St

Maiden Ln

32

35

NEW YORK STOCK EX.

Wall St

38

37

Exchange Pl

Hanover St

New St

Water St

Front St

New St

South St

New St

Beaver St

40

39

S. William St

William St

Pearl St

Old Slip

41 42

Stone St

Bridge St

Broad St

Coenties Slip

43

Whitehall

State St

44

EAST RIV

BATTERY PARK

FERRY TERMINAL

© 2008 Park It! Guides

---

1. **400 Chambers St** *bet North End Ave/river, N side of Warren*
Central 212.566.9783

hr	rate	specials	rate	enter	exit
1/2	$11	AM 7D	$26	5-9am	7pm
1	$18	SUV	$11		
2	$24	Month	$718, O/S add $63		
10	$33				
24	$51				

helpful information
24/7   AE, MC, V
123 spaces   Max bill $50

---

2. **325 North End Ave** *bet North End Ave/river, S side of Warren*
MPG 212.786.9545

hr	rate	specials	rate	enter	exit
1	$17	SUV	$10		
2	$23	Month	$634, O/S add $84		
10	$32	Month	$211	m'cycle	
24	$50				

helpful information
24/7   AE, MC, V
55 spaces   2 elevators

---

3. **200 Chambers** *bet West/Greenwich, N side of Warren*
Central 212.587.6942

hr	rate	specials	rate	enter	exit
1/2	$11	AM	$26	5-9am	7pm
1	$22	PM	$20	after 5pm	5am
2	$28	Sa,Su	$20		12hr
10	$38	SUV	$11		
24	$60	Month	$776, O/S add $51		
		Month	$253	m'cycle	

helpful information
24/7   AE, MC, V   Takes vans
60 spaces   Opened 5/07   Steep driveway

---

4. **86 Warren St** *bet Greenwich/W Broadway, N (left) side of Warren*
Pine 212.766.2230

hr	rate	specials	rate	enter	exit
1/2	$11	PM m-f	$12	after 4pm	2am
1	$19	Sa,Su	$17		12hr, by 12am
2	$25	SUV	$10		
12	$34	Month	$486, O/S add $63		
MTC	$48				

helpful information
24/7   MC, V   Outdoor
52 spaces   Lift

5. **69 Warren St** *SW corner of Warren/W Broadway, S side of Warren*

69 Warren St Parking Corp/Speedy Park 917.748.1561

hr	rate	specials	rate	enter	exit
1/2	$11	Sa	$16	all day	when open
1	$16	SUV	$5		
2	$24	Month	$444		
MTC	$32				
7pm	$26				

helpful information

M-F 8am-7pm	Cash	Speedy Park garage
Sa,Su may open	Eff. 5/06	
50 spaces	Outdoor	

---

6. **20 River Terr.** *bet North End/river-dead end, N side of 4th Pl*

Impark 212.571.0538

hr	rate	specials	rate	enter	exit
1	$20	AM	$25	6-8:30am	8pm
2	$29	SUV	$10		
10	$38	Month	$620, O/S add $84		
24	$50				
O/N	$50				

helpful information

24/7	AE, MC, V
41 spaces	8'9" clearance

---

7. **211 North End Ave** *bet North End Ave/river-dead end, N side of 4th Pl*

Impark 212.964.0236

hr	rate	specials	rate	enter	exit
1	$20	AM	$25	6-8:30pm	8pm
2	$29	SUV	$10		
10	$38	Month	$620, O/S add $84		
24	$50				
O/N	$50				

helpful information

24/7	AE, V, MC	Eff. 7/07
25 spaces		

---

8. **75 Park Pl** *bet Murray/Park Pl, W (right) side of W Broadway*

Central 212.732.6637

hr	rate	specials	rate	enter	exit
1	$22	PM m-f	$20	after 5pm	10hr
2	$28	Sa,Su	$20	anytime	12hr
10	$40	SUV	$11		
24	$59	Month	$675, O/S add $51		
		Month	$211	m'cycle	

helpful information

24/7	AE, MC, V	Security inspection M-F
100 spaces	Damage inspection	

9. **110 Church St** *bet Church/W Broadway, N side of Park or S side of Murray*

Icon 212.962.9011

hr	rate	specials	rate	enter	exit
1/2	$11	PM	$12	5pm-5am	5am
1	$26	Sa,Su	$15	5am-5pm	12hr
2	$31	SUV	$10		
12	$36	Month	$507, O/S add $84		
24	$46				

helpful information

24/7 181" rule for SUV   Steep driveway
88 space   Park Pl entrance closed Sa
AE, MC, V   No full size vans

10. **233 Broadway** *bet Broadway/Church, N side of Barclay*

Icon 212.732.2943

hr	rate	specials	rate	enter	exit
1/2	$11	PM	$12	5pm-5am	5am
1	$26	SUV	$10		
2	$31	Month	$507, O/S add $84		
12	$36				
24	$46				

helpful information

24/7   AE, MC, V   Max bill $50
150 spaces   181" rule for SUV

11. **250 Vesey St** *at end of Vesey towards water, E side of Vesey*

Standard 212.786.4245

hr	rate	specials	rate	enter	exit

PERMIT ONLY
MONTHY ONLY

helpful information

24/7   Cash
371 spaces   Self parking

12. **47 Church St** *bet Broadway/Church, S side of Fulton*

Central 212.693.2001

hr	rate	specials	rate	enter	exit
1	$22	SUV	$10		
2	$29	Month	$675, O/S add $51		
10	$35	Month	$211	m'cycle	
O/N	$48				
MTC	$48				

helpful information

M-W 6am-12am   65 spaces   2 elevators
Th-Su 24hr   AE, MC, V   Millenium Hilton

13. 2 Spruce St *bet Nassau/Gold, S side of Spruce*
Nassau Street Garage Corp 212.608.6153

hr	rate*	specials	rate	enter	exit
1	$15	PM	$10	by 5pm	1hr
2	$20	PM	$13	by 5pm	13hr, by 6am
12	$25	PM	$33	by 5pm	24hr, by 6am
24	$30	Sa,Su	$18	after Sa 6am	1hr
		Sa,Su	$23	after Sa 6am	12hr, by M 6am
		Sa,Su	$33	after Sa 6am	24hr, by M 6am
		SUV	$10		
		Month	$465		
		Month	$169	m'cycle	

helpful information

24/7	Elevator	*M-F 6am-5pm
25 spaces	No O/S vehicles	
AE, MC, V	6' clearance	

---

14. 25 Beekman St *bet William/Nassau, S (left) side of Beekman*
RapidPark 212.766.0871

hr	rate	specials	rate	enter	exit
1/2	$12	AM m-f	$24	7-10am	10pm
1	$22	PM	$15	after 4pm	close
2	$27	Daily	$24	6am-4pm	12am
6	$40	Sa	$15	8am-6pm	
24	$42	Su	$15	9am-5pm	
O/N	$42	SUV	$10		
MTC	$42	Month	$425, O/S add $100		

helpful information

M-F 7am-12am	Su 9am-5pm	AE, MC, V
Sa 8am-8pm	149 spaces	2 elevators

---

15. 57 Ann St *bet Nassau/William, N (left) side of Ann,*
enter via Nassau
Enterprise/Little Man Parking 212.608.4740

hr	rate	specials	rate	enter	exit
1/2	$10	AM	$23	6-9am	9pm
1	$21	Sa,Su	$15		
2	$25	SUV	$10		
10	$35	Month	$400, O/S add $100		
24	$40	J&R Music World: 2hr free w/$100 purchase			

helpful information

24/7	AE, MC, V
276 spaces	Elevator

16. 80 Gold St *bet Beekman/Spruce, E side of Gold*

Chelnik   212.964.5250

hr	rate	specials	rate	enter	exit
1/2	$10	AM	$23	6-10am	10hr
1	$21	PM	$15	4pm-12am	12am
2	$25	Sa,Su	$15	6am-3am	3am
10	$30	SUV	$5		
24	$35	Month	$400, O/S add $25		

helpful information

24/7	AE, MC, V, DC	Boom gate at entrance
351 spaces	Max bill $50	

17. 299 Pearl St *bet Beekman/Peck Slip, W side of Pearl*

Chelnik   212.227.2215

hr	rate	specials	rate	enter	exit
1/2	$8	AM	$23	2-10am	12hr
1	$17	PM	$15	4pm-12am	12am
2	$22	Sa,Su	$15	after 6am	3am
10	$28	SUV	$5		
24	$34	Month	$380, O/S add $25		

helpful information

24/7	AE, MC, V, DC
310 spaces	Boom gate at entrance

18. 288 Pearl St *SE corner of Pearl/Peck Slip, S side of Peck Slip or E side of Pearl*

Central   212.766.9456

hr	rate	specials	rate	enter	exit
1/2	$8	AM m-f	$23	by 10am	2am
1	$19	SUV	$10		
2	$24				
10	$29				
24	$35				
O/N$302am					

helpful information

24/7	AE, MC, V	228 Water St
286 spaces	Outdoor	10 Peck Slip

19. Lot 5 *at Dover (Col 33-43), E side of Marginal*

Propark   212.732.2670

hr	rate	specials	rate	enter	exit
1	$15	PM	$20		
24	$25	Event	$36		
		SUV	$5		
		Month	$224, O/S add $50		

helpful information

24/7	MC, V
315 spaces	Eff. 4/08

20. Peck Slip *at Marginal St/FDR/South St, S side of Peck Slip*
Propark   212.732.2670

hr	rate	specials	rate	enter	exit
1	$15	PM	$20		
24	$25	Event	$36		
		SUV	$5		
		Month	$275, O/S add $42		

helpful information

24/7	MC, V	South St Seaport sign
58 spaces	Outdoor	

---

21. Lot 3 *North of Beekman St, E side of South*
Propark   212.732.2670

hr	rate	specials	rate	enter	exit
1	$16	Event	$36		
24	$25	SUV	$5		
		Month	$262, O/S add $42		

helpful information

24/7	MC, V
242 spaces	Outdoor

---

22. 85 John St *bet Fulton/John, W (right) side of Gold*
GMC   212.385.9182

hr	rate*	specials	rate	enter	exit
1	$20	AM 7D	$22	5-9am	7pm
2	$25	Sa,Su	$13		12 hr, no O/N
10	$35	O/N	$40		after 5am
24	$40	SUV	$10		
		Month	$475, O/S add $150		

helpful information

24/7	Elevator
32 spaces	*6am-12am
AE, MC, V	

---

23. 99 John St *bet John/Fulton, W (left) side of Cliff*
Icon   212.751.3987

hr	rate	specials	rate	enter	exit
1/2	$10	AM m-f	$23	5-10am	12hr
1	$17	PM m-f	$12	4pm-5am	6am
2	$22	WE	$12	Sa 6am-M 6am	12hr
12	$27	SUV	$10		
24	$35	Month	$422, O/S add $84		

helpful information

24/7	AE, MC, V	Max bill $50
87 spaces	181" rule for SUV	

24. **56 Fulton St** *bet Cliff/Gold, S side of Fulton*
Marlo Towers Garage Corp 212.227.5185

hr	rate*	specials	rate	enter	exit
1	$16	AM m-f	$22	6-10am	10pm
2	$20	PM m-f	$10	4pm-12am	2am
12	$26	PM m-f	$22	4pm-12am	12hr
24	$30	PM m-f	$30	4pm-12am	24hr
		Sa,Su	$10	Sa after 6am	10hr, by M 6am
		Sa,Su	$15	Sa after 6am	12hr, by M 6am
		Sa,Su	$30	Sa after 6am	24hr, by M 6am
		SUV	$10		
		Month	$550		

helpful information

24/7	2 Elevators	No vans
280 spaces	Enterprise rental	*M-F 12am-4pm
AE, MC, V, Dis	8'3" clearance	Eff. 11/07

25. **243 Pearl St** *bet Fulton/John, E side of Cliff or W side of Pearl*
Icon 212.962.8374

hr	rate	specials	rate	enter	exit
1/2	$10	AM m-f	$25	by 10am	close
1	$18	PM m-f	$12	after 4pm	close
2	$23	Sa,Su	$12	all day	
12	$28	SUV	$10		
24	$33	Month	$444, O/S add $63		

helpful information

M-Sa 6am-8pm	AE, MC, V
Su 8am-6pm	Outdoor
90 spaces	

26. **251 Pearl St** *bet Fulton/John, W side of Pearl*
GMC 212.406.1938

hr	rate	specials	rate	enter	exit
1	$20	AM	$24	6-10am	8pm
2	$25	PM	$11	after 4pm	8pm
10	$35	O/N	$40		after 5am
24	$40	Sa	$11	after 8am	8pm
		SUV	$10		
		Month	$375, O/S add $100		

helpful information

M-F 6am-8pm	AE, MC, V
92 spaces	Outdoor

---

27. Lot 2 *South of Beekman St, E side of South, just N of Fulton Cross*
Propark, Col 23-26 212.732.2670

hr	rate	specials	rate	enter	exit
1	$16	Event	$36		
24	$25	SUV	$5		
		Month	$262, O/S add $42		

helpful information
24/7   MC, V
242 spaces   Outdoor

---

28. 72 John St *bet William/Gold, N (left) side of Platt*
Imperial 212.480.4210

hr	rate	specials	rate	enter	exit
1/2	$11	AM	$24	5-10am	9pm
1	$22	PM	$15	after 4pm	12am
2	$25	Sa,Su	$12	anytime	10hr by 12am
10	$31	SUV	$10-20		
24	$40	Month	$500, O/S add $100		
		Gildhall Hotel $45			24hr, valet

helpful information
24/7   AE, MC, V
43 spaces   Eff. 4/08

---

29. 199 Water St *bet Front/Water, N side of John*
Central 212.785.4552

hr	rate	specials	rate	enter	exit
1	$21	PM	$15	after 4pm	close
2	$27	Sa,Su	$17	all day	
10	$38	SUV	$11		
24	$49	Month	$465		

helpful information
24/7   AE, MC, V
99 spaces   Long, steep driveway

---

30. 13 Gold St *bet Platt/Maiden, W (right) side of Gold*
MC Parking, LLC 212.747.8786

hr	rate	specials	rate	enter	exit
1	$19	AM	$23	7-9am	6pm
2	$22	PM	$12	after 4pm	11pm
10	$28	SUV	$10		
24	$33	Month	$380, O/S add $84		

helpful information
M-F 7am-11pm   19 spaces   Outdoor
Sa 7am-7pm when open   MC, V
Su 7am-7pm when open   Lift

31. 2 Gold St *bet Maiden/Platt, W (right) side of Pearl*
Imperial 212.487.1072

hr	rate	specials	rate	enter	exit
1/2	$10	AM	$23	5-10am	9pm
1	$21	Sa,Su	$12		
2	$24	SUV	$10		
10	$30	Month	$464, O/S add $100		
24	$35				
O/N	$35				

helpful information
24/7	6'10" clearance
98 spaces	
AE, MC, V	

32. 167 Front St *SE corner of Front/John, S side of John*
Edison/Park Fast 212.509.9576

hr	rate*	specials	rate	enter	exit
1	$20	AM m-f	$27	6-9am	close
3	$35	PM 7D	$8	after 4pm	1/2hr
MTC	$40	PM su-w	$15	after 4pm	close
		PM th-sa	$17	after 4pm	close
		Sa,Su	$8	by 4pm	1/2hr
		Sa,Su	$19	by 4pm	close
		Event	$25		
		SUV	$10		
		Month	$402, O/S add $65		

helpful information
Oct-May M-F 6am-9pm	72 spaces
Oct-May Sa,Su 9am-7pm	AE, MC, V, Dis
June-Sept M-F 6am-10pm	Outdoor
June-Sept Sa,Su 9am-10pm	*M-F enter by 4pm
Closed some Sa,Su,Hol	

33. 10 Liberty St *bet William/Pearl, S (right) side of Liberty*
Glenwood 212.509.5278

hr	rate	specials	rate	enter	exit
1/2	$11	AM	$22	6-9am	8pm
1	$18	Sa,Su	$15	after 6am	7pm
3	$24	SUV	$15		
10	$29	Month	$422	tenant	
24	$36	Month	$444	non-tenant	

helpful information
24/7	AE, MC, V
200 spaces	181" rule for SUV

---

34. 100 Maiden Lane *bet Pearl/William, N side of Cedar*
Imperial   212.514.5026

hr	rate	specials	rate	enter	exit
1/2	$10	AM	$23	5-9am	8pm
1	$21	PM	$15	after 4pm	12am
2	$24	Sa,Su	$12	after 6am	10hr, by 12am
10	$30	SUV	$10		
24	$35	Month	$464, O/S add $100		
		Month	$200	m'cycle	

helpful information

24/7	AE, MC, V	Steep driveway
67 spaces	Eff. 12/07	

---

35. Lot 1 *at Maiden (Col. 19-21), E side of South*
Propark   212.732.2670

hr	rate	specials	rate	enter	exit
1/2	$9	Event	$36		
1	$22	SUV	$5		
2	$28	Month	$351, O/S add $42		
3	$35				
24	$40				

helpful information

7D 8am-10pm	AE, MC, V	Eff. 4/08
60 spaces	Outdoor	

---

36. 80 Pine St *bet Maiden/Pine, W side of Water*
Pine Water Garage LLC   212.425.6136

hr	rate	specials	rate	enter	exit
1	$20	SUV	$5		
2	$23	Month	$483, O/S add $60		
3	$27				
24	$37				
O/N	$37				

helpful information

M-F 6am-12am	178 spaces	Security inspection
Sa,Su 8am-6pm	AE, MC, V	Eff. 4/08 Car wash

---

37. 45 Wall St *left off William into one-way, N side of Exchange*
Wall Street Parking Corp   212.825.0700

hr	rate	specials	rate	enter	exit
1/2	$15	AM m-f	$25	6-9am	7pm
1	$26	SUV	$10		
2	$30	Month	$484, O/S add $66		
12	$38	Month	$211	m'cycle	
24	$43				

helpful information

24/7	AE, MC, V, DC
137 spaces	Takes vans/4x4/trucks

38. 67 Wall St *bet Wall/Exchange Pl, turn R on Wall,*
L side of Hanover

John St. Parking Corp 212.785.4594

hr	rate	specials	rate	enter	exit
1/2	$15	AM	$25	6-9am	7pm
1	$26	SUV	$10		
2	$30	Month	$464, O/S add $66		
12	$38	Month	$211	m'cycle	
24	$43				

helpful information

24/7	AE, MC, V
85 spaces	7'10" clearance

39. 2 Broadway / 9 Stone St *bet Broad/Broadway/Whitehall,*
N side of Stone

Kura River Management 212.363.7700

hr	rate	specials	rate	enter	exit
1	$22	Sa,Su	$16	all day	
2	$26	SUV	$10		
10	$34	Month	$475, O/S add $84		
24	$40				

helpful information

M-F 7am-12am	56 spaces
Sa 7am-6pm	AE, MC, V
Su Summer 8am-6pm	Hard to see from street

40. 14 South William St *bet Broad/Old Slip, Left side of William*

Icon 212.269.5056

hr	rate	specials	rate	enter	exit
1/2	$15	AM m-f	$28	6-10am	12am
1	$26	AM sa-su	$18	6-10am	12am
2	$30	PM m-th	$18	after 4pm	6am
12	$38	SUV	$10		
24	$43	Month	$549, O/S add $84		
		Month	$211	m'cycle	

helpful information

24/7	Elevator	Max bill $50
400 spaces	181" rule for SUV	
AE, MC, V	6'5" clearance	

41. 7 Hanover Sq *bet Hanover Sq/Coenties Alley, E (left) side of Pearl*

Central 212.668.8630

hr	rate*	specials	rate	enter	exit
1	$15	AM	$22	6-7:30am	7pm
2	$25	PM m-f	$16	after 4pm	close
3	$30	Sa	$15	all day	7pm, close
MTC	$35	SUV	$10		
		Month	$414, O/S add $46		

helpful information

M-F 6am-12am	67 spaces	6'6" clearance
Sa 7am-7pm	AE, MC, V	*M-F before 4pm

42. 55 Water St *SW corner of Old Slip/South, W side of South or S side of Old Slip*

Impark 212.809.6789

hr	rate	specials	rate	enter	exit
1	$19	AM m-f	$25	5-10am	7pm
2	$28	PM m-f	$15	after 5pm	1am
10	$39	Sa,Su	$15	5am-10am	12hr
24	$45	SUV	$10		
O/N	$45	Month	$549, O/S add $84		
		Month	$253	O/N m-f 6pm-8am, Sa,Su	
		Month	$169	m'cycle	

helpful information

24/7	Car wash
545 spaces	Security inspection
AE, MC, V	Self parking
Pay at machine before leaving	Boom gate at entrance
6'8" clearance	Exit only from Old Slip

---

43. 1 Battery Park Plaza *bet Whitehall/State, N (right) side of Pearl*

State Pearl Garage Inc 212.248.5752

hr	rate	specials	rate	enter	exit
1	$21	Sa	$19	after 8am	6pm
2	$25	SUV	$5		
10	$35	Month	$490, O/S add $60		
24	$42				
O/N	$42				

helpful information

M-F 6:30am-8pm	AE, MC, V	Security inspection
Sa 8am-6pm	181" rule for SUV	2 elevators
150 spaces	6'1" clearance	Eff. 4/08

---

44. 1 NY Plaza *bet Water/South St, 2nd right turn onto Whitehall, entrance on right*

QuikPark 212.514.8630

hr	rate	specials	rate	enter	exit
1/2	$15	AM m-f	$25	5-10am	10hr
1	$25	SUV	$10		
2	$29	Month	$507		
10	$38				
24	$44				

helpful information

24/7	181" rule for SUV
150 spaces	6'8" clearance
AE, MC, V	Long driveway

45. 345 South End Ave *W side of South End Ave, bet Liberty/Albany, small dead end*

Chelnik   212.321.2360

hr	rate	specials	rate	enter	exit
1	$22	AM	$30	2-10am	12hr
2	$25	SUV	$5		
10	$40	Month	$370	tenant	
24	$50	Month	$450	non-tenant	

helpful information

24/7	Eff. 9/07	Gateway Garage
678 spaces	Avis rental	
AE, MC, V	6'6" clearance	

46. 333 Rector Pl *bet South End/dead end, S side of Albany at end*

GMC   212.945.0028

hr	rate	specials	rate	enter	exit
1	$10	AM	$25	7-10am	6pm
2	$22	O/N	$37		after 5am
10	$30	SUV	$10		
24	$37	Month	$503, O/S add $118		

helpful information

7D 7am-2am	5 min grace period	Separate entrance and exit
46 spaces	Elevator	Rector Garage
AE, MC, V	Max bill $50	

47. 398 Albany St *bet South End/dead end, S side of Albany, left at curve*

GMC   212.945.3646

hr	rate	specials	rate	enter	exit
1	$10	AM m-f	$25	7-10am	6pm
2	$22	O/N	$37		after 5am
10	$30	SUV	$10		
24	$37	Month	$425, O/S add $100		

helpful information

24/7	AE, MC, V	Max bill $50
49 spaces	5 min grace period	Hudson Tower Garage

48. 200 Liberty St *bet South End Ave/West, N side of Albany*

1 World Financial Center Garage   212.786.9564

hr	rate	specials	rate	enter	exit
1	$14	SUV	$5		
2	$20	Month	$380		
MTC	$32				

helpful information

M-F 6am-10pm for casual parking   AE, MC, V
232 spaces

49. 225 Rector Pl *bet South End Ave/West, S side of Albany*
MPG 212.945.1876

hr	rate*	specials	rate	enter	exit
1/2	$11	AM m-f	$11	by 10am	1/2hr
1	$20	AM m-f	$20	by 10am	1hr
2	$24	AM m-f	$28	by 10am	12hr
12	$34	AM m-f	$40	by 10am	24hr
24	$40	PM m-f	$11	4pm-12am	1/2hr
		PM m-f	$18	4pm-12am	6am
		PM m-f	$40	4pm-12am	24hr
		Sa,Su	$11		1/2hr
		Sa,Su	$17		12hr
		Sa,Su	$38		24hr
		SUV	$10		
		Month	$422, O/S add $84		
		Month	$211	m'cycle	

helpful information

24/7	AE, MC, V	*enter M-F 10am-4pm
114 spaces	2 elevators	

50. 90 West St *bet West/Washington, N side of Albany, enter from West St*
Icon 212.227.8854

hr	rate	specials	rate	enter	exit
1/2	$9	AM	$20	5-8am	12hr
1	$18	PM m-f	$14	4pm-5am	5am
2	$21	SUV	$10		
12	$28	Month	$591, O/S add $169		
24	$45				

helpful information

24/7	AE, MC, C
65 spaces	No full size vans

51. 75 West St *bet Washington/West, S (left) side of Carlisle*
Icon 212.619.4235

hr	rate	specials	rate	enter	exit
1/2	$9	AM	$18	5-8am	12hr
1	$18	PM m-f	$14	4pm-5am	5am
2	$21	SUV	$10		
12	$28	Month	$591, O/S add $169		
24	$45				

helpful information

24/7	AE, MC, V	Max bill $50
38 spaces	181" rule for SUV	

52. 90 Washington St *just S of Rector, E (right) side of West*
GGMC 212.344.4800

hr	rate	specials	rate	enter	exit
1/2	$10	AM 7D	$24	6-9am	7pm
1	$19	PM m-f	$16	after 3pm	close
2	$25	SUV	$10		
10	$31	Month	$450, O/S add $100		
24	$42				
close	$37				

helpful information
M-F 6am-12am   79 spaces
Sa,Su 8am-1am   AE, MC, V

---

53. 200 Rector Pl *E of South End Ave, N side of W Thames*
Central 212.766.9762

hr	rate	specials	rate	enter
1/2	$7	AM m-f	$20	4-10am
1	$18	SUV	$10	
2	$22	Month	$465	tenant
10	$31	Month	$507	non-tenant
24	$38	10 coupons	$237	

exit: 8pm

helpful information
24/7   2 Elevators
134 spaces   Liberty Court Parking
AE, MC, V

---

54. 56 Greenwich St *corner of Morris/Washington & corner of Joseph Ward/Washington, N side of Morris or S side of Washington, enter on Greenwich*
Central 212.425.1065

hr	rate*	specials	rate	enter	exit
1	$16	PM	$12	6pm-2am	1hr
2	$19	PM	$14	6pm-2am	2hr
12	$26	PM	$18	6pm-2am	12hr
24	$38	PM	$38	6pm-2am	24hr
		Sa,Su	$14	2am-6pm	1hr
		Sa,Su	$20	2am-6pm	12hr
		Sa,Su	$38	2am-6pm	24hr
		July 4	$30		12hr
		Event	$30	pm,sa,su	12hr
		SUV	$0		
		Month	$371	non-tenant	
		Jewish Museum	$20		pm,sa,su

helpful information
24/7   Eff. 4/08   Morris St entrance open M-F 6am-8pm, Sa,Su 9am-5pm
988 spaces   Hertz
AE, MC, V   Self parking   *M-F 2am-6pm
Clean public bathroom   15 min grace period
Pay at cashier booth

---

55. 2 South End Ave *bet Battery/South End Ave, N side of 3rd Pl*
GGMC 212.786.0666

hr	rate	specials	rate	enter	exit
1	$14	AM m-f	$21	5-9am	6pm
2	$20	SUV	$10		
3	$23	Month	$450		
10	$33				
24	$35				
O/N	$35				

helpful information
24/7   AE, MC, V, DC, CB
69 spaces   7' clearance

---

56. 70 Battery Pl *bet Battery Pl/South End Ave, S side of 3rd Pl*
River Watch Garage LLC 212.577.9862

hr	rate	specials	rate	enter	exit
1	$14	AM	$21	5-9am	6pm
2	$20	SUV	$5		12hr
3	$23	Month	$425		
10	$33	Jewish Museum $3 discount			10hr
24	$35				
O/N	$35				

helpful information
M-Th 6:30am-1am   Su 7am-2am   Cash
F-Sa 7am-2:30am   36 spaces   181" rule for SUV

---

57. 50 Battery Pl *bet Battery Pl/dead end, S side of Second*
GGMC 212.945.3109

hr	rate	specials	rate	enter	exit
1	$16	SUV	$10		
2	$22	Month	$450, O/S add $250		
3	$25				
10	$35				
24	$37				

helpful information
M-F 6am-12am   AE, MC, V, Dis, DC   Max bill $20
Sa,Su 7am-1am   42 spaces

---

58. 17 Battery Pl *bet Battery Pl/Morris, E (right) side of West*
GGMC 212.742.1848

hr	rate	specials	rate	enter	exit
1/2	$10	AM m-f	$22	6-10am	8pm
1	$21	Sa,Su	$19		1hr
2	$25	Sa,Su	$38		3hr
10	$38	Sa,Su	$45		10hr
24	$45	Sa,Su	$50		24hr
		SUV	$10		
		Month $450, O/S add $106			

helpful information
24/7   Elevator   Steep driveway
98 spaces   Max bill $50   6'6" clearance
AE, MC, V

NOTES

My Favorite Garages

Page_____ Location_____

Notes_____

Page_____ Location_____

Notes_____

Page_____ Location_____

Notes_____

Page_____ Location_____

Notes_____

Page_____ Location_____

Notes_____

Page_____ Location_____

Notes_____

Page_____ Location_____

Notes_____

Page_____ Location_____

Notes_____

Page_____ Location_____

Notes_____

NOTES

My Favorite Garages

Page_____ Location_____

Notes_____

Page_____ Location_____

Notes_____

Page_____ Location_____

Notes_____

Page_____ Location_____

Notes_____

Page_____ Location_____

Notes_____

Page_____ Location_____

Notes_____

Page_____ Location_____

Notes_____

Page_____ Location_____

Notes_____

Page_____ Location_____

Notes_____

LANDMARKS

Museums	Address
American Museum of Natural History	Central Park West @ 79th St
Cooper Hewitt	2 E 91st St
Frick Collection	1 E 70th St
Guggenheim Museum	1071 5th Ave @ 78th St
International Center of Photography	1133 6th Ave @ 43rd St
The Jewish Museum	1109 5th Ave
Metropolitan Museum of Art	1000 5th Ave @ 82nd St
Museum of the City of New York	1220 5th Ave @ 103rd St
Museum of Jewish Heritage	36 Battery Pl
MoMa: Museum of Modern Art	11 W 53rd St
New Museum of Contemporary Art	235 Bowery St @ Prince
New York Historical Society	170 Central Park West @ 77th St
Whitney Museum of American Art	945 Madison Ave @ 75th St

Shopping

Bloomingdales	Lexington Ave @ 59th St
Bergdorf Goodman	57th St @ 5th Ave
Saks Fifth Avenue	5th Ave @ 49th St
Lord & Taylor	5th Ave @ 38th St
Barney's	Madison Ave @ 60th St
Macy's	Broadway @ 34th St

Tourist Attractions

Empire State Building	5th Ave @ 34th St
Rockefeller Center	5th Ave @ 48th St
Time Warner Center	Broadway @ 59th St

Other

Javits Center	11th Ave @ 37th St
Lincoln Center	Broadway @ 63rd St
Chrysler Building	42nd St & Lexington Ave
City Hall	Broadway & Chambers
United Nations	1st Ave @ 45th St
World Trade Center Site	West St & Vessey
New York Public Library	Fifth Ave @ 42nd St
Madison Square Garden	7th Ave @ 32nd St

Education

Columbia University	Broadway @ 116th St
Hunter College	Lexington Ave @ 68th St
New York University	Washington Square
Parsons School of Design	5th Ave @ 13th St
Fashion Institute of Technology	7th Ave @ 27th St

Religious

St. Patrick's Cathedral	5th Ave @ 51st St
Temple Emanu-El	1 E 65th St

NYC TAX

Most people wonder why the rates posted on the garage signs seem like they are plucked out of thin air. They're not. NYC charges an additional 18.375% tax on all parking, which brings these seemingly random rates to even dollar amounts. The tax rate used to be 18.25%, so you will notice that the 'pre-tax' rates are not always consistent. The chart below lists the range of pre-tax rates and the final figure that you will pay.

Pre-Tax	Post-Tax	Pre-Tax	Post-Tax
$.83 - .87	$ 1	$28.66 - 28.76	$34
$1.69 - 1.74	$ 2	$29.52 - 29.68	$35
$2.53 - 2.56	$ 3	$30.34 - 30.42	$36
$2.94 - 2.98	$ 3.50	$31.19 - 31.26	$37
$3.38 - 3.42	$ 4	$32.04 - 32.11	$38
$4.20 - 4.24	$ 5	$32.88 - 32.95	$39
$5.05 - 5.09	$ 6	$33.73 - 33.82	$40
$5.71	$ 6.75	$34.59 - 34.75	$41
$5.90 - 5.93	$ 7	$35.41 - 35.48	$42
$6.73 - 6.77	$ 8	$36.26 - 36.50	$43
$7.57 - 7.62	$ 9	$37.10 - 37.26	$44
$8.41 - 8.46	$10	$37.94 - 38.01	$45
$9.25 - 9.30	$11	$38.79 - 38.86	$46
$10.01- 10.15	$12	$39.63 - 39.70	$47
$10.95 - 10.99	$13	$40.48 - 40.55	$48
$11.79 - 11.84	$14	$41.32 - 41.44	$49
$12.63 - 12.69	$15	$42.15 - 42.28	$50
$13.48 - 13.54	$16	$43.04 - 43.10	$51
$14.33 - 14.38	$17	$43.88	$52
$15.14 - 15.29	$18	$44.73	$53
$15.59 - 16.07	$19	$45.67	$54
$16.85 - 16.99	$20	$46.46	$55
$17.70 - 17.74	$21	$47.32	$56
$18.55 - 18.65	$22	$48.10	$57
$19.39 - 19.43	$23	$48.94	$58
$20.22 - 20.30	$24	$49.84	$59
$21.08 - 21.16	$25	$50.63	$60
$21.91 - 21.99	$26	451.53	$61
$22.75 - 22.83	$27	$52.32	$62
$23.61 - 23.68	$28	$53.17	$63
$24.45 - 24.50	$29	$54.01	$64
$25.30 - 25.38	$30	$54.85	$65
$26.13 - 26.19	$31	$55.70	$66
$26.98 - 27.03	$32	$56.60	$67
$27.82 - 27.88	$33	$65.06	$77

GARAGE CUSTOMER SERVICE NUMBERS

If you do report a problem to a garage company, provide as much information as possible: garage, date, time you parked, time you retrieved your car, anyone who can verify your complaint, and whether you spoke with anyone at the garage. Listed below are the phone numbers and websites for the major companies.

Central Parking 800.836.6666 *www.parking.com*

Champion 212.308.5959 *www.championparking.com*

Chelnik 212.751.1080

Edison/Park Fast 888.727.5327 *www.parkfast.com*

Elco 212.661.6702

GGMC 212.987.2791 *www.ggmcparking.com*

GMC 212.888.7400 *www.gmcparking.com*

Icon Parking 877.727.5464 *www.iconparking.com*

Impark 212.937.8660 *www.impark.com*

Imperial 212.736.7171 *www.impark.com*

LAZ 877.700.1123 *www.lazparking.com*

MPG 212.490.3460

MTP 888.277.7275

Park It Mgmt 212.929.9404

ProPark 888.776.7275 *www.propark.com*

Quik Park 212.832.2066

Standard 877.435.7634 *www.standardparking.com*

Ulltra 212.221.6111

If you want to make a complaint to the DCA:
Department of Consumer Affairs
42 Broadway
New York, NY 10004
212.487.4444

If you negotiate a rate directly with a valet and you encounter a problem, you will need to contact the DCA.

CROSS STREET FINDER

To find nearest cross street on an Avenue
1. Drop last digit of Avenue address
2. Divide by 2
3. Add/Subtract number below

Ave A, B, C, D	+3	Convent	+127
First, Second	+3	Lenox	+10
Third	+10	Lexington	+22
Fourth	+8	Madison	+27
Fifth		Park	+34
63 - 108	+11	Park Ave South	+8
109 - 200	+13	St. Nicholas	+110
201 - 400	+16	West End	+59
401 - 600	+18	York	+4
601 - 775	+20	Broadway	
776 - 1286	-18	1 - 754	
(don't divide by 2)		*(a named street*	
Ave of the Americas	-12	*below 8th)*	
Seventh		756 - 846	-29
1 - 1800	+12	847 - 953	-25
1800+	+20	953+	-31
Eight	+9	Central Park West	+60
Ninth	+13	*(don't divide by 2)*	
Tenth	+14	Riverside Drive	
Eleventh	+15	*(don't divide by 2)*	
Amsterdam	+59	Up to 567	+72
Columbus	+60	Above 568	+78

WEST SIDE HIGHWAY ENTRANCES AND EXITS

Southbound | Northbound

Southbound		Northbound
Dyckman St ⟷	**17**	→ Dyckman St/Henry Hudson Br
		⟷ Ft Tryon Pk/Cloisters
		← I-95 S/Crs Bronx Exp/181st St
	16	← 165th St/Riverside Dr
Riverside Dr/GW Br ⟷	**15**	→ Riverside Dr S
Cross Bronx Expwy W/I-95	**14**	→ I-95/GW Br/Cross Bronx Exp W/178th St
177th St →		
158th St ⟷	**13**	⟷ 158th St
125th St ⟷	**12**	⟷ 125th St
		→ NY 9A/Henry Hudson Pkwy S
95th–96th St ⟷		⟷ 95th–96th St
		→ Boat Basin
79th St/Boat Basin ⟷		⟷ 79th St
		← 72nd St/Riverside Dr
		← 57th St
56th St ←		

⟷	Enter and Exit
→	Enter Only
←	Exit Only

FDR DRIVE
ENTRANCES AND EXITS

Southbound		Northbound
Dyckman St ⇒		⇒ Dyckman St
I-95N/GW Bridge/179th St ⇒	24	⇒ I-95S/GW Bridge/179th St
		⇐ Harlem River Dr
W155th St/8th Ave ⇔	23	⇒ W 155th St/8 Ave
W142nd St/5th Ave ⇔	22	
		⇐ E 139th St
	21	⇒ Madison Ave Br/135th St
E 132nd St./Park Ave ⇔	20	
3rd Ave Br/E130th St/Lex Ave ⇒		
E 125th St/2nd Ave ⇐	19	⇒ E 125th St
	18	⇒ I-87/Willis Ave Br/Deegan Exp
Triboro Br ⇔	17	⇒ I-278/Triboro Br/Bruckner and
		Expwy/Grand Central Pkwy
E 125th St/2nd Ave ⇒		
E 116th St ⇔	16	
E 106th St ⇐	15	
E 102nd St ⇒		
E 96th St ⇔	14	⇒ E 96th St
E 92nd St ⇒		⇐ York Ave/E 92nd St
E 79th St ⇒		
E 73rd St ⇒		
E 71st St ⇐	13	
		⇐ E 62nd St
Queensboro Br/Rt25/E 63rd St ⇔	12	⇒ Queensboro Br/Rt25/E 61st St
E 53rd St ⇐	11	
E 49th St/UN Garage ⇔	10	
		⇐ E 48th St
E 42nd St ⇒	9	⇒ E 42nd St
E 41st St ⇒		
E 38th St ⇒		
E 36th St ⇒		
E 35th St ⇒		
Midtown Tnl/E 34th St ⇔	8	⇔ Midtown Tnl/E 34th St
E 30th St ⇒		
E 23rd St ⇔	7	⇔ E 20th–E 23rd Sts
E 15th St ⇐	6	
Houston St ⇔	5	⇔ Houston St
Grand St ⇔	4	
South St/Manhattan Br ⇐	3	
		⇐ Montgomery St
Bklyn Br-Civic Center (Pearl St) ⇒	2	⇔ Bklyn Br-Civic Center (Pearl St)
Old Slip ⇒		
Battery Park/South Ferry ⇐	1	⇔ South St
West St (Rt 9A) ⇐		⇐ West St (Rt 9A)
Bklyn Battery Tunnel ⇔		⇔ Bklyn Battery Tunnel

CUSTOM EDITIONS

Print your company logo, message, and contact information on the front cover.

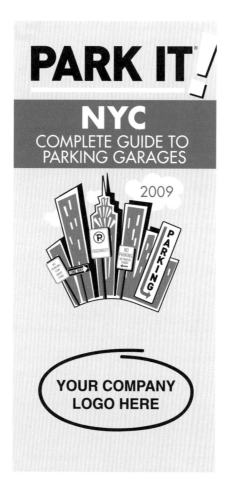

Custom Editions are great gifts for clients, visitors, business travelers, and newcomers to NYC. Present them as a holiday gift, promotional item, or thank you gift.

Your clients will think of you every time they save time and money on parking.

Contact sales@parkitguides.com for more information.

- **Help family and friends save time and money.**
- **Order them a copy of Park It! NYC!**

ORDER FORM

☐ YES, I want _____ copies of Park It! NYC: Complete Guide to Parking Garages at $13.95 each plus $3.50 per book for shipping and handling ($2 per additional book, New York State residents please add 8.375% sales tax). Allow 5 days for delivery.

☐ My check for $_____ is enclosed

☐ Please charge my ☐ Visa ☐ MasterCard

Name _____

Address _____

City _____ State ____ Zip _____

Phone (_____) _____

Email _____

Credit Card # _____

Exp. Date _____

Signature _____

Mail Order Form to: Park It! Guides
400 E 56th St, Suite 29F
New York, NY 10022

Fax Credit Card Order to   866.719.2807

Place Internet Orders at   www.parkitguides.com

ZIP CODE MAP

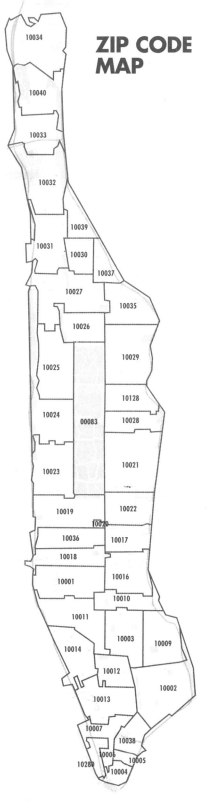